Music and Protest in 1968

Music was integral to the profound cultural, social and political changes that swept the globe in 1968. This collection of essays offers new perspectives on the role that music played in the events of that year, which included protests against the ongoing Vietnam War, the May riots in France and the assassination of Martin Luther King, Jr. From underground folk music in Japan to anti-authoritarian music in Scandinavia and Germany, *Music and Protest in 1968* explores music's key role as a means of socio-political dissent not just in the US and the UK but in Asia, North and South America, Europe and Africa. Contributors extend the understanding of musical protest far beyond a narrow view of 'protest song' to explore how politics and social protest played out in many genres, including experimental and avant-garde music, free jazz, rock, popular song and film and theatre music.

BEATE KUTSCHKE is Wissenschaftliche Mitarbeiterin at the Universität Leipzig. Her research focuses on music and protest around the year 1968 and she has published a monograph, a volume of collected papers and numerous articles on this topic. She is an internationally active researcher, who has presented papers around the world in German, English and French. She has taught in Europe, the United States (Harvard University) and Asia (University of Hong Kong). A recipient of various scholarships including a three-year research grant by the German Research Foundation, she is currently writing a third monograph. Her interests range from Baroque music and music after 1945 to music and aesthetics, music and politics, and music and ethics.

BARLEY NORTON is a senior lecturer in ethnomusicology at Goldsmiths, University of London. He has carried out extensive field research in Vietnam and other countries in Southeast Asia, and is the author of *Songs for the Spirits: Music and Mediums in Modern Vietnam* (2009). As part of a Getty-funded research project on experimental music performance in Vietnam, he made the ethnographic film *Hanoi Eclipse: The Music of Dai Lam Linh* (2010), which has been screened at numerous international film festivals.

Music Since 1900

GENERAL EDITOR Arnold Whittall

This series – formerly *Music in the Twentieth Century* – offers a wide perspective on music and musical life since the end of the nineteenth century. Books included range from historical and biographical studies concentrating particularly on the context and circumstances in which composers were writing, to analytical and critical studies concerned with the nature of musical language and questions of compositional process. The importance given to context will also be reflected in studies dealing with, for example, the patronage, publishing and promotion of new music, and in accounts of the musical life of particular countries.

Titles in the series

Jonathan Cross
The Stravinsky Legacy

Michael Nyman
Experimental Music: Cage and Beyond

Jennifer Doctor
The BBC and Ultra-Modern Music, 1922–1936

Robert Adlington
The Music of Harrison Birtwistle

Keith Potter
Four Musical Minimalists: La Monte Young, Terry Riley, Steve Reich, Philip Glass

Carlo Caballero
Fauré and French Musical Aesthetics

Peter Burt
The Music of Toru Takemitsu

David Clarke
The Music and Thought of Michael Tippett: Modern Times and Metaphysics

M. J. Grant
Serial Music, Serial Aesthetics: Compositional Theory in Post-War Europe

Philip Rupprecht
Britten's Musical Language

Mark Carroll
Music and Ideology in Cold War Europe

Adrian Thomas
Polish Music since Szymanowski

J. P. E. Harper-Scott
Edward Elgar, Modernist

Yayoi Uno Everett
The Music of Louis Andriessen

Ethan Haimo
Schoenberg's Transformation of Musical Language

Rachel Beckles Willson
Ligeti, Kurtág, and Hungarian Music during the Cold War

Michael Cherlin
Schoenberg's Musical Imagination

Joseph N. Straus
Twelve-Tone Music in America

David Metzer
Musical Modernism at the Turn of the Twenty-First Century

Edward Campbell
Boulez, Music and Philosophy

Jonathan Goldman
The Musical Language of Pierre Boulez: Writings and Compositions

Pieter C. van den Toorn and John McGinness
Stravinsky and the Russian Period: Sound and Legacy of a Musical Idiom

Heather Wiebe
Britten's Unquiet Pasts: Sound and Memory in Postwar Reconstruction

Beate Kutschke and Barley Norton
Music and Protest in 1968

Music and Protest in 1968

Edited by BEATE KUTSCHKE AND
BARLEY NORTON

Kutschke, Beate, and Barley Norton. Music and
Protest in 1968. Cambridge, United Kingdom:
Cambridge UP, 2015. Print.

CAMBRIDGE
UNIVERSITY PRESS

CAMBRIDGE
UNIVERSITY PRESS

University Printing House, Cambridge CB2 8BS, United Kingdom

Published in the United States of America by Cambridge University Press, New York

Cambridge University Press is part of the University of Cambridge.

It furthers the University's mission by disseminating knowledge in the pursuit of education, learning and research at the highest international levels of excellence.

www.cambridge.org
Information on this title: www.cambridge.org/9781107007321

© Cambridge University Press 2013

This publication is in copyright. Subject to statutory exception and to the provisions of relevant collective licensing agreements, no reproduction of any part may take place without the written permission of Cambridge University Press.

First published 2013

A catalogue record for this publication is available from the British Library

Library of Congress Cataloguing in Publication data
Music and protest in 1968 / edited by Beate Kutschke and Barley Norton.
    p. cm. – (Music since 1900)
Includes bibliographical references and index.
ISBN 978-1-107-00732-1
1. Popular music – Social aspects – History – 20th century. 2. Popular music – Political aspects – History – 20th century. 3. Popular music – 1961–1970 – History and criticism. 4. Protest songs – 20th century – History and criticism. 5. Nineteen sixty-eight, A.D. I. Kutschke, Beate. II. Norton, Barley.
ML3918.P67M82   2013
780.9 04–dc23
                                                                                        2012028037

ISBN 978-1-107-00732-1 Hardback

Cambridge University Press has no responsibility for the persistence or accuracy of URLs for external or third-party internet websites referred to in this publication, and does not guarantee that any content on such websites is, or will remain, accurate or appropriate.

Contents

List of figures [page ix]
Notes on contributors [x]
Acknowledgements [xiv]

In lieu of an introduction [1]
BEATE KUTSCHKE

1 Expressive revolutions: '1968' and music in the Netherlands [12]
ROBERT ADLINGTON

2 Music as plea for political action: the presence of musicians in Italian protest movements around 1968 [29]
GIANMARIO BORIO

3 "This Is My Country": American popular music and political engagement in '1968' [46]
SARAH HILL

4 Spontaneity and Black Consciousness: South Africans imagining musical and political freedom in 1960s Europe [64]
CAROL MULLER

5 Music and protest in Japan: the rise of underground folk song in '1968' [81]
TÔRU MITSUI

6 Vietnamese popular song in '1968': war, protest and sentimentalism [97]
BARLEY NORTON

7 "There Is No Revolution Without Song": 'new song' in Latin America [119]
JAN FAIRLEY

8 "The Power of Music": anti-authoritarian music movements in Scandinavia in '1968' [137]
ALF BJÖRNBERG

9 British rock: the short '1968', and the long   [154]
ALLAN F. MOORE

10 '1968' and the experimental revolution in Britain   [171]
VIRGINIA ANDERSON

11 Anti-authoritarian revolt by musical means on both sides of the Berlin Wall   [188]
BEATE KUTSCHKE

12 '1968' – the emergence of a protest culture in the popular music of the Eastern Bloc?   [205]
RÜDIGER RITTER

13 Gendering '1968': womanhood in model works of the People's Republic of China and movie musicals of Hong Kong   [222]
HON-LUN YANG

14 A revolution in sheep's wool stockings: early music and '1968'   [237]
KAILAN R. RUBINOFF

15 Music and May 1968 in France: practices, roles, representations   [255]
ERIC DROTT

Bibliography   [273]
Discography   [300]
Index   [304]

Figures

6.1 "We Go for Victory" by Trương Tuyết Mai, as printed in the newspaper *Tiền Phong* on 16 May 1968. [*page 102*]
6.2 Phạm Tuyên's original handwritten score for "Play Music for Our Dear American Friends". Photograph by Barley Norton, 2010. [105]
6.3 Trịnh Công Sơn's self-published score of "A Mother's Legacy" from the songbook *Songs of Golden Skin* (1967). [114]
9.1 King Crimson, introduction to "One More Red Nightmare". [163]
9.2 King Crimson, pentatonic arpeggios in "Discipline" (c. 2' ff.). [164]
9.3 Greenslade, rising tenths in "Drowning Man" (38"). [166]
11.1 Cornelius Cardew, "Bethanien Song" © reproduced by kind permission of Horace Cardew. [194]
11.2 Christfried Schmidt, *Kammermusik I. Von Menschen und Vögeln*, score, bars 40 and 41 of "Phönix" © reproduced by kind permission of Christfried Schmidt. [202]
13.1 Excerpt of the Beijing opera aria "Such is the Way to Lead a Life" from *The Red Lantern*. [227]
13.2 "Long Live the Factory Girls" from the movie musical *Her Tender Love*. [234]

Notes on contributors

ROBERT ADLINGTON is Associate Professor in Music at the University of Nottingham. He is author of *The Music of Harrison Birtwistle* (2000) and *Louis Andriessen: De Staat* (2004), and editor of the volume *Sound Commitments: Avant-garde Music and the Sixties* (2009). He has recently completed a book on avant-garde music in 1960s Amsterdam, and is editing a volume of essays on music and communism outside the communist bloc.

VIRGINIA ANDERSON studies, performs and sometimes records American and British experimental music and free improvisation. She has published articles on time perception in *Performance Research*, experimental organology in the *Galpin Society Journal* (2009) and the music of Cornelius Cardew in the *Journal of Musicological Research* (2006). Her more recent publications (2012–13) include chapters in books on musical minimalism, scores and notation and new approaches to experimental music research.

ALF BJÖRNBERG is Professor in Musicology at the Department of Cultural Sciences, University of Gothenburg, Sweden, where he received his PhD in 1987 for a dissertation analysing the songs in the Swedish preliminaries of the Eurovision Song Contest. His research interests include popular music, music and the media and music analysis. He has published on music video, the history of music broadcasting in Sweden, the cultural politics of the Eurovision Song Contest and the history of popular music in the Scandinavian area.

GIANMARIO BORIO, Professor of Musicology at the University of Pavia, has published on the compositional techniques of the twentieth century, music aesthetics, history of music theory and the audiovisual experience. In 1991–2, he was an Alexander von Humboldt Fellow at the University of Freiburg and in 1999 he was awarded the Dent Medal by the Royal Musical Association. In 2012 he was nominated Director of the Music Institute of the Giorgio Cini Foundation (Venice).

ERIC DROTT is Associate Professor of Music Theory at the University of Texas at Austin. His research focuses on cultural politics, contemporary French musical life, avant-garde movements in music and the sociology of music. He is author of *Music and the Elusive Revolution: Cultural Politics and Political Culture in France, 1968–1981* (2011), as well as articles that have appeared in such journals as *French Politics, Culture and Society*, the *Journal of the American Musicological Society, Journal of Music Theory* and *Perspectives of New Music*.

JAN FAIRLEY (†) was an independent writer and researcher and Fellow of the Institute of Popular Music, University of Liverpool. She worked as a music/arts journalist (NUJ), broadcaster (BBC), editor and researcher. Since 1988, she was a member of the editorial board of the journal *Popular Music* and worked as a lecturer at Liverpool University, Sheffield University and Queen's University, Belfast. In 1994, she was a Visiting Fundación Andes/British Council Professor in Popular Music and Musicology, Musicology Department, University of Chile, Santiago, Chile; and, from 1971 to 1973, Lecturer in British and American Literature and History, Catholic University, Temuco, Chile.

SARAH HILL is a lecturer in Music at Cardiff University. She is the author of *'Blerwytirhwng?' The Place of Welsh Pop Music* (2007), and co-editor of *Peter Gabriel, from Genesis to Growing Up* (2010). She has published articles on female vocality, Otis Redding and narrative structure in progressive rock, and is currently working on a cultural history of popular music in San Francisco, 1965–9.

BEATE KUTSCHKE is Wissenschaftliche Mitarbeiterin at Leipzig University. Her research focuses on music and protest around the year 1968 and she has published a monograph, a volume of collected papers and numerous articles on this topic. She is an internationally active researcher, who has presented papers around the world in German, English and French. She has taught in Europe, the US (Harvard University) and Asia (University of Hong Kong). A recipient of various scholarships including a three-year research grant by the German Research Foundation, she is currently writing a third monograph. Her interests range from Baroque music and music after 1945 to music and aesthetics, music and politics and music and ethics.

TÔRU MITSUI has been Professor Emeritus at Kanazawa University, Japan, since 2005, where he taught musicology and English. His academic interest in folk music and popular music began in the early 1960s and he has written numerous articles and books, including quite a few in English. He was Chair of the International Association for the Study of Popular Music (IASPM) in 1993–7 and Chair of the Japanese Association for the Study of Popular Music (JASPM) in 1990–3 and 2002–4.

ALLAN F. MOORE is Professor of Popular Music at the University of Surrey, UK. Author of more than 100 articles and books on popular music, he is on the editorial board of the journal *Popular Music*, co-founded the journal *twentieth-century music* and is series editor for Ashgate's Library of Essays on Popular Music. His hermeneutic methodology for popular song, *Song Means*, was recently published by Ashgate. He is currently engaged on preparing a third edition of his *Rock: the Primary Text* and has also begun working on a critical history of the English folksong tradition in the twentieth century.

CAROL MULLER is Professor of Music at the University of Pennsylvania and specialises in South African music and its diaspora. She has published numerous articles and several books, most recently with South African jazz singer Sathima Bea Benjamin, *Musical Echoes: South African Women Thinking in Jazz* (2011) with a website www.africanmusicalechoes.com. Muller is currently developing online classes with Coursera, at Penn, and is actively involved with the civic engagement and higher education movement. She is a gumboot dancer.

BARLEY NORTON is a senior lecturer in ethnomusicology at Goldsmiths, University of London. He has carried out extensive field research in Vietnam and other countries in Southeast Asia, and is the author of *Songs for the Spirits: Music and Mediums in Modern Vietnam* (2009). As part of a Getty-funded research project on experimental music performance in Vietnam, he made the ethnographic film *Hanoi Eclipse: The Music of Dai Lam Linh* (2010), which has been screened at numerous international film festivals.

RÜDIGER RITTER is a research fellow at the Research Centre for East European Studies (Forschungsstelle Osteuropa) at the University of Bremen in Germany. His main research interests relate to music and politics in Eastern Europe and the history of radio and jazz. He has published widely in both German and English, and his publications in English include the book chapter "The radio: a jazz instrument of its own" (2010) and the journal article "Between cultural alternative and protest: on the social function of jazz after 1945 in Central Europe (GDR, Poland, Hungary, CSSR)" (2011).

KAILAN R. RUBINOFF'S research on the historical performance movement in the Netherlands has been supported by grants from the Fulbright Programme and the Social Sciences and Humanities Research Council of Canada. She also writes about eighteenth-century improvisation, Baroque and Classical flute performance and 1960s experimental music. Recent publications have appeared in *twentieth-century music*, *Music and Politics* and *New Sound*. She is Assistant Professor of Musicology at the University of North Carolina at Greensboro.

HON-LUN YANG is Professor of Music at Hong Kong Baptist University. She has published on nineteenth-century America music, Russian émigré musical life in Shanghai, music and politics in contemporary China in journals such as *Twentieth-century China*, *International Review of the Aesthetics and Sociology of Music (IRASM)*, *Asian Music*, *Music and Politics*, *European Foundation for Chinese Music Research (CHIME Journal)* and *American Music*. She has also contributed chapters to the books *Music and Politics* (2012), *Liszt and his Legacy* (2012) and *Music and Censorship* (forthcoming), among others. She is currently writing a book on Chinese symphonic music and co-editing with Michael Saffle a volume entitled *East-West Musical Encounters*.

Acknowledgements

The editors would like to thank all the contributors to the volume for working with us so diligently. Special thanks are due to Allan F. Moore for his assistance: in the early stages of this book project he helped win various contributors for the volume in the fields of popular music studies and ethnomusicology. Thanks are also due to Miriam Wendling who translated Rüdiger Ritter's chapter, and Julia Martin and Philip Naylor who helped with proofreading and gave stylistic advice. We would also like to extend our deepest gratitude to Jan Fairley who, despite serious illness, worked tirelessly to complete her chapter. Jan's chapter in this volume was the last academic article she completed before she died on 9 June 2012. Our sincere thanks also go to Arnold Whittall, the Music Since 1900 series editor, to Vicki Cooper, senior commissioning editor at Cambridge University Press, and to Rebecca Taylor and Fleur Jones at Cambridge University Press for their painstaking work overseeing the volume through to publication.

In lieu of an introduction

BEATE KUTSCHKE

Paradigm shifts

Books are like musical artworks. As Adorno stated in his *Philosophy of New Music*, not all musical works "are possible at all times". The shape of a composition depends on the "tendency of the [musical] material" which changes over time.[1] Similarly, books – not always, but sometimes – emerge from research environments and zeitgeist. *Music and Protest in 1968* is such a book. It has become possible only now. What enabled it into existence are three paradigm shifts that have taken place most recently.

First, recent historical events, from the fall of the Berlin Wall in 1989 to Occupy Wall Street, the formation of flash mobs, the Arab Spring and the frequent protests during the G8 summits demonstrate that, like perhaps never before in human history, socio-political change has been effected largely through non-violent means. By the sheer quantity of its members and the use of *symbolic*, not physical 'weapons' – protest marches, discourse, posters, noise – protest movements enable peaceful revolutions and influence public opinion or government policy. Furthermore, what distinguishes them and their activities from other forms of social unrest and demands for socio-political change are their concerted actions without central

---

[1] What appears to be the tendency of the musical material, a kind of inherent law of development and change, is in fact the effect of the composer's individual experiences of his/her socio-political and cultural environment that manifest themselves in the musical material as "sedimented spirit". Adorno writes: "The meaning of musical material is not absorbed in the genesis of music, and yet this meaning cannot be separated from it. Music recognises no natural law; therefore, all psychology of music is questionable. Such psychology – in its efforts to establish an invariant 'understanding' of the music of all times – assumes a constancy of musical subject. Such an assumption is more closely related to the constancy of the material of nature than psychological differentiation might indicate. What this psychology inadequately and noncommittally describes is to be sought in the perception of the kinetic laws of matter. According to these laws, not all things are possible at all times [...] The demands made upon the subject by the [musical] material are conditioned [...] by the fact that the 'material' is itself [sedimented spirit] [...], an element socially predetermined through the consciousness of man. As a previous subjectivity – now forgetful of itself – such an [objective spirit] [...] has its own kinetic laws", i.e. laws of change and development over time (Adorno 1973 [1948], pp. 32–3).

organisation.² While the old workers' movement, the Old Left, for instance, was heavily based on a top-down organisation, the protest movements of the late twentieth and twenty-first centuries are marked by a reduction of organisation. Most recent protest forms such as flash mobs and critical masses pop up from nowhere – with an initiator, but no 'director'. Therefore, the agents of those movements that emerge from self-organisation are *conscientious* protesters in the emphatic sense; Kantian *autonomous* subjects.³

During recent years, protest movements have increasingly attracted the attention of social scientists, historians and linguists. The intensified focus on the movements and their specific self-dynamic action modes presents a kind of paradigm shift from the study of states, organisations and institutions to that of self-organising socio-political processes. In line with the increased attention on the mechanisms and nature of protest movements, one of the earliest protest movements of this 'modern' type – the student and protest movements of the 1960s and 1970s – has become the focal point, of both scholarly interest and the public alike. The fascination for the 'movements of 1968' or the New Left, as these student and protest movements have been dubbed, manifested itself in numerous publications and mass media events – particularly in 2008 when the "year that rocked the world" turned forty – and in the revival of the musical styles and fashions of the 1960s and 1970s.⁴

Why, however, should the protest movements around 1968 matter to musicologists *right now*, and why could a volume on 'music and protest in 1968' not appear earlier than *now*? The naissance of rock music, the revival of folk and the Woodstock Festival did not need to wait for the shift in social sciences to be investigated by musicologists. The developments and changes of these pop music genres have ever been an integral part of music history.⁵ So, what is the point of musicologists focusing on protest movements? Connected with the 'movement-oriented turn' in social sciences, history and linguistics in the 1990s and 2000s, there has also been a revaluation of

---

² Self-organisation and mass involvement in causes has been supported by new media – cell phones, internet and social networks.
³ In this light, Herfried Münkler's assertion that interstate wars – in which the states possess the monopoly on the use of force – have been replaced by new forms of conflict solution is certainly correct, but incomplete. The actors of the 'new wars' are not only warlords, modern mercenary soldier companies and guerrilla gangs (Münkler 2005 [2002]) but also protestors and grass roots movements.
⁴ *The Year That Rocked the World* is the title of Mark Kurlansky's monograph: Kurlansky 2004.
⁵ For popular music and counterculture, see Perone 2004 and Zimmerman 2008. For rock music: Grossman 1976; Hendler 1987; and Francese et al. 1995.

the student and protest movements. Scholars agree that the movements failed to attain their key objective: the abolition of the capitalist system. At the same time, however, the movements initiated a profound socio-cultural change. It is obvious that the new modes of living and behaviour which members had performatively realised in their personal life – sexual liberation, communal living, informal habits, in brief: a counterculture – have now filtered into the everyday life of many individuals who would not consider themselves typical '68ers. These are the external peculiarities. There is, however, also an internal, invisible side to it. A key factor that made the student and protest movements such a *fascinosum* is the specific spirit – the so-called 'spirit of the sixties' – or socio-cultural climate that is closely connected with '1968'. What a spirit or climate encompasses is generally difficult to define. The constituent elements are events, images, discourses and cultural products that contemporaries and later-born individuals assemble 'about' a time-period. These elements hint at the diverse attitudes, feelings and beliefs that shape mentalities. As for the 1960s and 1970s, the spirit of '1968' can be characterised as dissent, the rejection of heteronomy as well as intensified concern for and interest in the 'Other'.[6]

It is this spirit or climate of '1968' that constitutes the conceptual starting point of our volume. Socio-cultural climates, zeitgeist, have the ability to influence *every aspect* of socio-cultural life. This not only applies to modes of behaviour and styles of living, but also music. However, while music historiography related rock and folk – sometimes also (free) jazz – to the protests of '1968', it neglected the spirit's influence on the various other genres: classical, avant-garde and experimental music, and early music scenes. Thus, in music histories, the latter appeared to be entirely unaffected by '1968'. Only recently, various studies on avant-garde music, classical performance culture and historically informed performance (HIP) practice have revealed that 1968's impact on music is much wider than hitherto known. In recent monographs, journal articles and book chapters, various scholars such as Robert Adlington, David Bernstein, Gianmario Borio, Eric Drott, Kailan Rubinoff and myself have demonstrated that the avant-garde music in France, Italy, the Netherlands, North America and West Germany as well as the Dutch early music movement

---

[6] There is a peculiarity about zeitgeist or socio-cultural climate. On the one hand, they incorporate the essence of a historical phenomenon such as the student and protest movements of '1968'; on the other hand, they constitute the breeding ground, i.e. condition that brings the phenomenon into existence. To put it paradoxically: for the movements of '1968', the 'spirit of the sixties' or the 1968 socio-cultural climate is the effect *and* origin of the movements simultaneously.

and classical music were not only affected by the climate of '1968'; they were *in*fected and infiltrated by it.[7]

Investigating the impact of '1968' on music, however, also means a different approach to music history. Musicologists increasingly take a distance from determining music history by abstract decades ('the music of the 1960s and 1970s', for instance), but orient their temporal divisions on the contour of a socio-political and cultural era such as the student and protest movements of '1968' and its spirit. This methodological shift in music after 1945 also corresponds with the discussion on the 'nature' and 'essence' of the music of the Baroque era. Since there is no characteristic which can be found in all Baroque musical genres and styles between 1600 and 1750 and, thus, could serve as general criterion of Baroque music, the entries on this epoch in *Die Musik der Geschichte und Gegenwart* and *New Grove*, of 1994 and 2001 respectively, shift the focus from musical to cultural-historical and mental criteria ('mental' as referring to 'mentality' and the 'history of mentalities'). Silke Leopold suggests that what unifies (music) history between 1600 and 1750 are novel ways of presenting human beings through music,[8] and Claude V. Palisca discerns that striving for "the expression of affective states" is a shared characteristic of all Baroque music.[9] So, this is the second paradigm shift: the determinants of the borders of the period whose music is to be investigated are not the traditional criteria of music historical classification and division such as: styles, compositional techniques and genres; but socio-political and cultural situations, feelings, beliefs, attitudes and mentalities, ethical preferences etc.

Comparably with the music of the Baroque era, the music of '1968' is not marked by one single criterion or a pool of criteria that can be considered as typical for all the music of this time-period. As the chapters of this volume demonstrate, however, the variety of heterogeneous musical characteristics that define 'music and protest' in the 1960s and 1970s emerge from the same zeitgeist: the spirit of '1968'. As criteria such as feelings and attitudes, however, are vague and 'soft', the attempt to determine an exact date for the beginning and end of '1968', in music as well as in politics, is doomed to failure. This is reflected in our volume by the focus on a temporal centre – the year 1968 – that operates as cipher for

---

[7] Adlington 2007b and 2009b; Bernstein 2008, Borio 2007; Drott 2008 and 2011; Loy 2006; Rubinoff 2006 and 2011. See also the volumes of collected papers on music and '1968' by Jacobshagen and Leniger (eds.) 2007 and Kutschke (ed.) 2008. For a complete list of publications of Kutschke on this topic: see www.beatekutschke.de/Publikationen.htm.

[8] Leopold 1994.   [9] Palisca 2002.

a time-period, '1968' or the 'long 1968' (in single quotation marks) which roughly lasted from the end of the 1950s to the mid-1970s.

Transnationality and concernment

The third paradigm shift that enabled *Music and Protest in 1968* has taken place within scholarship on protest movements itself. In addition to self-organisation, another peculiarity of late-twentieth century protest movements such as the feminist movement and Occupy Wall Street is their 'independence' from state borders; their agents belong to a multitude of nations and their targets can be located in various global locations. This understanding of protest movements has also affected the view of the movements of the 1960s and 1970s. In the past, studies on '1968' tended to focus rather narrowly on Western Europe and North America because, until recently, '1968' was understood to have emerged only in the highly industrialised, consumer-culture countries of the Western world. Correspondingly, the above-mentioned studies on music and '1968' were limited to countries in Western Europe and North America. In contrast to this, the monographs of Christopher Dunn (2001) and Eric Zolov (1999) that study the 1960s and 1970s counterculture in Brazil and Mexico are two notably early exceptions.

It is clear today that, in focusing on Western Europe and North America, scholars neglected the much wider spread of the events of '1968'. During the past decade, however, historians and sociologists have not only assembled more and more countries and regions that were affected by '1968', but also investigated their cross-border activities and communication.[10] Today, there is agreement that the student and protest movements of '1968' were a transnational phenomenon. This is evidenced in the striking simultaneity of events in 1968 in Europe, Africa, both Americas and Asia. To mention just a few events: in February 1968, student protests escalated in the Roman university district. Two months later, in April, the attempted murder of the West German student leader Rudi Dutschke led to violent student riots against the right-wing Springer press in West Berlin. In the same month, the protests at Columbia University in New York climaxed. The Parisian student protests erupted in May 1968 and, in the same month, students rose up in Senegal, which developed into a fully fledged opposition against

---

[10] Davis *et al.* 2010; Gilcher-Holthey 2008; Harman 1988; Klimke 2010; Kurlansky 2004; Sievers 2004; and Wallerstein 1989.

the Senegalese regime.[11] In June, the student protests in Mexico started and culminated in the Tlatelolco massacre killing numerous students in early October.[12] In the Eastern Bloc, the Prague Spring, which started in January 1968, was finished off by the August invasion of Czechoslovakia by troops from the Warsaw Pact states. Throughout the whole year, Japanese students protested against a variety of grievances, first and foremost US-American imperialism and the Vietnam War.[13] The established convention of using '1968' as synonym or cipher for the student and protest movements of the 1960s and 1970s reflects this cluster of events.

Drawing on these recent developments in the general scholarship on movements, our volume proposes an entirely new picture of music and protest in '1968'. Reflecting the recent emphasis on the movements' transnational character, the book has been conceived from a global perspective, investigating music scenes not only in Western Europe and North America, but also in Eastern Europe, Asia, Latin America and South Africa. It sheds light on the fact that, like the socio-political movements, the music scenes that have been stirred up by the spirit of '1968' occurred globally and share the striking temporal coordination with those socio-political movements. In the late 1960s, major events expressing the spirit of '1968' cumulated. In this volume, the chapters of Robert Adlington, Eric Drott, Jan Fairley, Sarah Hill, Beate Kutschke, Tôru Mitsui, Allan Moore and Carol Muller refer to the Cuban *Encuentro de canción protesta* in 1967; the West German Waldeck festivals dedicated to singer-songwriter activities from 1965 to 1969; the rock oriented West German first International Essener Songtage in 1968 and the Woodstock Music and Art Festival in 1969; the Political-Demonstrative Experimental Concert in Amsterdam in May 1968, the Folk camps in Kyôto (in 1967 and 1968) as well as the Underground Concert held at two places, Osaka and Kobe, in March 1968. Musical-political activities were complemented by *anti*-musical, political interventions. In May and June 1968, opera houses, conservatoires and other art institutions in Paris, Lyon and other French cities were occupied; in December 1968 and January 1969, New Leftist students and pupils intervened in concerts in Hamburg and Frankfurt.[14]

This simultaneity without central planning is, no doubt, an effect of the self-dynamic character of the movements: the political and the 'musical' movements alike. However, both temporal coordination and

---

[11] Stafford 2012 (or earlier).
[12] The numbers of dead people comprised several hundreds (Poniatowska 1992 [1975], p. 207).
[13] Anonymous 2012a.   [14] Kutschke 2007a, p. 16.

self-organisation do not usually emerge without a strong motivational basis. The specific spirit of '1968', the synthesis of intensified concernment and interest for the 'Other', as I have defined above, seems to be a key factor in this context. The diverse responses to media reports of the Vietnam War operate as clear symptoms for what I dub the 'spirit of concernment and mutual interest'. Widely watched on television in the West,[15] the Vietnam War, especially the Tet Offensive, stimulated many to participate in anti-Vietnam demonstrations all over the world. Strikingly, it did so especially in New Leftist camps; the majority of viewers were not provoked to protest against the so-called 'television war' that was virtually happening in their living rooms. Other socio-political hotspots – the civil rights movement in the US, the cultural revolution in China, the guerilla war in Latin America and the crushing of the Prague Spring – received hardly less attention and sympathy by the New Leftists; they became part of reflections on how to change not only their own society but the world as a whole.[16]

In addition to protests, the specific concernment and interest of dissenters of '1968' manifested themselves in increased communication, exchange and, therefore, travelling.[17] New Leftist activists from different nations and continents met to confer about socio-political theories and techniques of protest.[18] Likewise, politicised musicians travelled widely to pass on their

---

[15] Not coincidentally, Marshal McLuhan coined his early-1960s metaphor of the world as "global village" in light of the contemporary advancements of information technology (McLuhan 1962, p. 36).

[16] In the 1980s and 1990s, neo-conservative critics pejoratively dubbed this New Leftist mentality as a "cult of concernment" (Stephan 1993).

[17] These international activities were prepared by a "world opening up" in the first postwar decades (Davis 2010). In other words, international exchange did not emerge from the open-mindedness of the New Leftist climate, but both slowly emerged and reinforced each other from the mid-1950s onwards culminating in what is recognisable from the present perspective as the spirit of '1968'. Being a globalised movement, the New Left was the *effect* and *agent* of globalisation at the same time. It was the *effect* of growing mobilisation and the worldwide media and information systems that brought glaring injustices happening in every part of the world to the politicised mind; it was the *agent* of cultural and intellectual transfer by shuttling socio-political theories and protest techniques between nations, continents and political systems divided by the Iron Curtain.

[18] They mutually emulated protest techniques such as sit-ins and teach-ins and the ironic, playful subversion of codes (Scharloth 2010). In late August 1968, representatives from West Germany, France, Finland, Spain, Switzerland, Canada and the US met at a conference in Ljubljana, Yugoslavia, to discuss the "anti-imperialist and anti-capitalist struggles and student revolts" and draft an international action programme. In September of the same year, Dietrich Wetzel visited a Latin American student conference in Merida, Venezuela, then acted as the delegate of the West German Socialist Student Association (SDS) at the "International Assembly of Revolutionary Student Movements" at Columbia University (Klimke 2010, pp. 100, 102–3). The lecture tour of Karl-Dietrich Wolff, leader of the West German SDS from 1967 to 1968, around the US in February/March 1969 has become famous.

music and learn about the practices and traditions of musicians from other cultures. This behaviour is certainly not new in musicians; they have always travelled and adopted styles from different cultures. The intensity of travel and exchange, however, seems to have significantly increased in the 1960s and 1970s. There is no chapter in *Music and Protest in 1968* in which transnational crosscurrents do not play a role at some point. According to our volume, the singer-songwriter scene was particularly vibrant: singer-songwriters from around the world met each other at regular events such as the East Berlin Festival des politischen Liedes (Political Song Festival),[19] the Fête de la Humanité (Humanity Festival) in Paris, the Italian Festa de l'Unità (Union Festival) and the Chilean Festival de la Canción Comprometida (Festival of Committed Song). It is important to note that, in the late 1960s, international music festivals were not only forums for *musical* exchange in the way that the 'classical' Cold War West German avant-garde festivals in Darmstadt and Donaueschingen had been – they also served as platforms for the development and reconfirmation of socio-political ideas and values;[20] and, sometimes, aesthetic questions were entirely overruled by socio-political concerns.[21]

The combination of the 'cult of concernment' and mutual interest, on one hand, with the anti-authoritarian, participatory-democratic impetus of the '68ers on the other, effected an unusually liberated, creative artistic atmosphere. Musical exchange was stimulated between not only different musical nations and cultures, but also styles and genres. In this volume, Virginia Anderson draws attention to the concerts of the free improvisation ensemble AMM who performed with the rock groups Pink Floyd and Soft Machine. Drones from Indian music were emulated in free improvisation and psychedelic music. Gianmario Borio points to folk singers who amalgamated vernacular labour songs with political songs in the rather modern style of Hanns Eisler. In her chapter, Kailan Rubinoff gives various examples for cross-genre activities of early and popular music performers. Judy Collins, the Rolling Stones and the Beatles integrated period instruments

---

[19] For lists of singer-songwriters from all over the world participating in these festivals, see: Anonymous 2012b (or earlier).

[20] One of the meetings that most overtly connected art with politics was the International Cultural Congress in Havana in January 1968. It is relatively well known that avant-gardists such as Luc Ferrari (France), Luigi Nono (Italy) and Peter Schat (Holland) as well as the folk, blues and jazz singer Barbara Dane (US) travelled to this conference. However, a comprehensive history on music and the cultural congress in Havana is still waiting to be written.

[21] The Internationale Ferienkurse für Neue Musik (International Summer Courses for New Music) in Darmstadt and the Donaueschinger Musiktage (Donaueschingen Festival) did not remain unaffected by the 1968 spirit of protest and dissent. See regarding Darmstadt: Iddon 2008.

into their work; avant gardists such as Wendy Carlos performed early music on electronic instruments like synthesisers; and Frans Brüggen performed New Music on the recorder and commissioned pieces for period instruments. Thus, what – from the perspective of the 1980s and 1990s – would appear to be postmodern plurality and 'anything goes', was in fact closely related to New Leftist concerns and open-mindedness.[22] Writers on postmodernity, however, have often overlooked the connection to the spirit of '1968' due to the emphasis on theorizing the dichotomy between modernity and postmodernity.[23]

In demonstrating that the impact of '1968' on music was epochal as well as global, the significance of our volume's subject matter 'music and protest in 1968' becomes visible. It defines a turning point: a period of music-aesthetical change that affected not only some, but, in fact, the majority of postwar musical genres and institutions.

The chapters

The outlined characteristics of music in the context of '1968' – self-organisation, concernment, transnational exchange and cross-genre productions – are crucial for the structure of this volume. The intensive international activity eradicates traditional distinctions between centre and periphery. There is no clear linear, one-directional propagation of the spirit of '1968' starting in one region and spreading like seismic waves from the epicentre over the whole world. Rather, dependent on the socio-political conditions, different regions or nations developed different kinds of '1968s', which Timothy Brown has dubbed 'small 1968s'.[24] This applies even more to the musical than to the socio-political '1968s'. In the 1960s and 1970s, various music scenes put out feelers to each other which resulted in a transnational and intercontinental network of interrelationships and influences. Similarly, musical activities – composition and performance – often defy easy classification as only 'avant garde' or 'chanson/political song' or 'rock'.

For this volume, the specific character of 'music and protest in 1968' means that conventional types of chapter order – according to places or temporality

---

[22] See Rubinoff (Chapter 14). For more information on the emergence of postmodernity from the spirit of '1968', see: Hentschel 2008; Iddon 2008; and Brown and Kutschke 2008.
[23] For further information, see: Luckscheiter 2007. He points out that, in France and the US, the '68ers (of the 1960s) are considered to be the first postmodern generation (Luckscheiter 2007, p. 152).
[24] Brown 2009.

or genres – are inappropriate. Likewise, the grouping of chapters into sections would have generated the impression that 'music and protest around 1968' can be broken down into a couple of themes or issues, repressing the fact that the 'phenomenology' of music and protest around 1968 is much too diverse to subsume all chapters under four or five subheadings.

Therefore, the order of chapters is based on rather loose connections. The first two chapters by Robert Adlington and Gianmario Borio reconstruct the relationship between music and protest in the Netherlands and Italy. Adlington's chapter on the Dutch Provo scenes addresses various lines of conflict typical for music and protest in '1968': especially capitalist commercialisation of popular protest music and the incomprehensibility of politically engaged avant-gardist protest music. Borio's chapter reconstructs musical 'workerism', that is how the New Leftist musicians' interest and concernment for the lower social classes filtered into Italian folk, film and avant-garde music. The third chapter by Sarah Hill sheds new light on popular music in the US and especially investigates how the civil rights movement and the murder of Martin Luther King affected various US-American music scenes. The fourth chapter by Carol Muller draws attention to another region of the world which was similarly shaken by racism and segregation: South Africa. Just as in the US, free jazz served to articulate the quest for freedom in South Africa. Unlike American free jazz musicians, however, South African musicians developed other, individual modes of expression. The fifth and sixth chapters by Tôru Mitsui and Barley Norton explore how music served to express the Asian protests against the Vietnam War. Whereas, in Japan, popular music amalgamated the protests against the Vietnam War with those against educational pressures in postwar Japanese achievement-oriented society, in Vietnam, 'paradoxical' protest songs emerged: North-Vietnamese *pro*-war songs that were adopted as 'protest songs' by the *anti*-war movement in the US and *sentimental* songs about lost love and human fate, that the South-Vietnamese singer-songwriter Trịnh Công Sơn wrote in order to express the suffering of the Vietnamese people and their yearning for peace.

In her chapter on music and protest in Latin America (Chapter 7), Jan Fairley presents another kind of paradoxical or improper protest song. Her subject matter is the *nueva trova* and *nueva canción* (both 'new song'), a musical genre whose musicians strongly rejected its classification as protest music. They did so because the term not only falsely suggested a close relationship to the US-American, oppositional 'protest song', but also was too limiting. In his chapter on music and protest in Sweden, Denmark and Norway (Chapter 8), Alf Björnberg points to a rather absurd situation: the spirit of

'1968' manifested itself in the musical culture *even though* the socio-political climate was by no means marked by extreme dissent or heavy protests.

The ninth and tenth chapters focus on music and protest in Great Britain. Allan Moore's contribution on progressive rock makes visible the relationship between musical means, on the one hand, and utopian and dystopic 'world views' that the lyrics of progressive songs articulate, on the other. Virginia Anderson points to a specific strand of avant-garde and experimental music, which can also be found in countries other than England. New Leftist, politicised composers of this strand articulate their socio-political dissent as refusal and ridicule. Their music is marked by a ludic attitude and the tendency towards nonsense.

Beate Kutschke (Chapter 11) investigates the diverse music scenes of East and West Germany in the context of what particularly characterised both German states in the 1960s and 1970s: the struggle against authoritarianism. The comparison between the different economic-political environments – capitalist vs. socialist-communist – reveals a decisive difference between music and protest in the West and East. Whereas in West Germany, anti-authoritarian protest succeeded in initiating the transformation of music as well as musical institutions, in East Germany, protest – as well as its potential for creativity – was stunted and ended in resignation. Rüdiger Ritter (Chapter 12) further explores the picture of '1968' in the Eastern Bloc. He shows that the popular music cultures, in each of the countries he focuses on – Hungary, Poland and the Czechoslovak Socialist Republic (ČSSR) – responded individually to the 'politicisation from above' that the socialist-communist cultural administrations of those countries imposed on music.

It is well known that the second feminist movement that developed throughout the 1970s was inspired by the youth upheaval and student protests of the 1960s. Hon-Lun Yang (Chapter 13) sheds light on how two popular music genres – Chinese model operas and Hong Kong movie musicals – reflected the transformation of gender relationships in the context of the 'small 1968s' in the People's Republic of China and Hong Kong.

Investigating the Early Music movement in the Netherlands and Great Britain in the 1960s (Chapter 14), Kailan Rubinoff analyses and explains an apparent paradox. Historically informed performance practice was, in essence, retrospective in terms of repertoire, but, as a result, became a 'revolutionary', reformist movement like the student and protest movements that had influenced it. The fifteenth and final chapter by Eric Drott explores the way French musicians – especially singer-songwriters and avant gardists – responded to and, thus, interpreted the events of May 1968 in France.

1 | Expressive revolutions: '1968' and music in the Netherlands

ROBERT ADLINGTON

"There never was a Dutch '1968'", historian Niek Pas has written.[1] This contention reflects two facts about the unfolding of events in the Netherlands during the later 1960s. First, unrest and subversion came early to the streets of Dutch cities, notably through the activities of the anarchist group Provo (1965–7) which stimulated a wave of playful protest and resistance against authorities and 'the establishment'. The activities of Provo combined with an intense industrial dispute among construction workers to make 1966 the Netherlands' 'crisis year',[2] in which street protests and violence profoundly unsettled a country hitherto regarded as Western Europe's placid backwater. These events served to vent frustrations that elsewhere only found comparable expression two years later, meaning that in 1968 itself, "literally almost nothing happened in the Netherlands".[3] Second, the Netherlands experienced what Hans Righart has described as a "moderate, cultural version of the sixties", in which exploration of new attitudes and modes of expression took precedence over the vigorous political-ideological activism developing in other countries.[4] Provo helped to establish this pattern through its emphasis upon creativity and imagination as primary weapons against "consumer enslavement". Militant student protest would not arise in the Netherlands until 1969, when a wave of university occupations swept the country. The authorities' forcible ending of a five-day occupation at the University of Amsterdam encouraged further radicalisation of some student groups, but rapid government legislation securing greater student involvement in the running of universities prevented this radicalisation from becoming anything more than a fringe phenomenon.[5]

That is not to disregard the significance of the Netherlands' "cultural version of the sixties". One of the primary distinguishing features of the international protest movements of the 1960s was the centrality accorded to the need for cultural change, as well as (or indeed instead of) revolution in a

---

[1] Pas 2008, p. 13. I am indebted to Eric Drott, Beate Kutschke, Jochem Valkenburg and Mattijs Warbroek for suggestions made during the writing of this chapter.
[2] Righart 2006, p. 211.   [3] Righart 2004, p. 96.   [4] Righart, cited in Pas 2009, p. 624.
[5] On student radicalization, see Verbij 2005. On the university legislation, see Righart 2004, p. 97.

more narrowly political sense. Events in the Netherlands exemplified this tendency. Nonetheless, chroniclers of the period continue to debate the respective significance of politics and culture for the '1968' phenomenon, reflecting debates that took place at the time between the 'politicos' on the one hand and the hippies on the other.[6] For some – especially those involved in the student movements of the time – the alternative lifestyles and countercultures of the period were but frivolous appendages to the struggles over capitalism waged by radical students and workers. For others, the new attitudes to behaviour, morality and expression emerging in the sixties achieved a more far-reaching alteration of peoples' lives "than political-revolutionaries and urban guerillas could ever have dreamed of".[7]

As elsewhere during the 1960s, 'dissenting voices' in the Netherlands were divided on the relative priority of inner transformation and outer revolution. What emerges most strongly from an examination of these diverse voices is that *all* parties set considerable store by the deployment of novel and imaginative means for expressing their ideas and aspirations. What Niek Pas has described as the "expressive politics" of Provo is thus an appropriate term for describing many facets of 1960s protest and dissent in the Netherlands, which in general demonstrated a particular attention to the stylistic aspects of communication – an expressive surplus, as it were, to the purely instrumental business of getting a message across.[8] This expressive quality was facilitated by the lack of pressing crises at a national level, which alleviated the pressure to focus upon essentials. It contributed too to a scene of great liveliness and creativity that attracted young visitors from around the world, and, in the long term, had a defining impact upon both the Netherlands' international reputation and its self-perception. But it also risked having the effect of shoring up the existing power bases against which dissent was directed: that of commerce, which found certain new expressive trends highly marketable; and that of government, which could claim to be 'progressive' by subsidising them.

This chapter assesses this 'expressive' aspect of protest in the Netherlands around 1968, as it manifested itself in the field of music. An initial assessment of the relationship of Provo to music provides the springboard for investigations of popular music and the avant-garde – elements of both of which Provo attempted to align in their manifestos for a new mass creativity. In the process, three contrasting (if partially overlapping) approaches to expressive politics may be discerned. Provo adopted the view of many 1960s radicals that politics and culture were inseparably

[6] Pas 2009, p. 628.   [7] Righart 2004, p. 17.   [8] Pas 2002.

intertwined and could not be considered independently; for them, creative innovation was a primary means to political revolution. This standpoint attracted the attention of a number of avant-garde musicians, who aligned themselves publicly with Provo. However, Provo's own commentaries upon music focused exclusively upon popular music, whose rebelliousness and proximity to commerce appealed and repelled in equal measure. An examination of the Dutch popular music scene, conducted in part through an exploration of the 'alternative' magazine *Hitweek*, confirms Provo's diagnosis of a culture strongly connotative of dissent yet largely uninterested in politics (narrowly conceived): here, the stylistic qualities of the music and associated codes of behaviour and appearance, in binding the young and alienating adults, formed a rich expressive means of rebellion that rendered political organisations, campaigns and manifesto-led activism irrelevant. Avant-garde musicians, on the other hand, became increasingly politically engaged towards the end of the decade, with striking consequences for the future musical life of the Netherlands. Their music's continuing adherence, during this period, to the imperative of progress had the appearance of being well matched to 'advanced' political views – by virtue of which musical works were ascribed with a certain expressive politics even when they were also intentionally wholly abstract in nature. As I will show, the tendency towards a conceptual complexity that was, strictly speaking, surplus to the requirements of the cause, continued even when some of these musicians partially renounced the avant-garde creed of aesthetic progress and placed their skills more fully at the service of the 'enslaved masses', as happened at the very start of the 1970s.

Provo and music

In May 1965 a leaflet was distributed around Amsterdam announcing a new "youth periodical", *Provo*, dedicated to "the renewal of anarchism".[9] The principal figures behind the journal, Roel van Duyn (22) and Rob Stolk (19), described themselves as "staatsgevaarlijke anarchisten" – literally, anarchists dangerous to the state.[10] The first issue of the journal declared that it was

> opposed to capitalism, communism, fascism, bureaucracy, militarism, snobbism, professionalism, dogmatism and authoritarianism [...] Provo calls for protest wherever possible [...] [and] considers anarchism the source of inspiration for this protest.[11]

[9] Cited in Pas 2003, p. 67. [10] Cited in Pas 2003, p. 133. [11] Anonymous 1965.

In Provo statements and publications a fundamental distinction was drawn between the "provotariaat", on the one hand – the "idle masses on the streets, students, and artists not involved in the employment process",[12] which were seen as Provo's principal constituency – and the "klootjesvolk" ("rabble" or "jerks") on the other. This latter group included not just the traditional Marxist enemy of the bourgeoisie, but also the majority of the working-class – the mass of "enslaved consumers and authority-worshippers", as *Provo* put it.[13] In this way, Provo's analysis of society symbolised a shift, typical of late 1960s protest, away from the class struggle dominating Marxist theory and towards critique of the cultural and expressive oppression of late capitalist society. Provo's principal strategy for resisting such oppression was the sustained discomfiture of both the authorities and the klootjesvolk, through a campaign of highly imaginative and well-publicised pronouncements and events.

    Provo's activities during the two years of its existence were largely defined by their playfulness and good humour. A central role was taken by weekly night-time 'happenings' on the Spui (a square in central Amsterdam) in which Provo teamed up with established 'happener' Robert Jasper Grootveld to mount provocative performances intended to attract large crowds and provoke the authorities into action. A series of 'white plans' – so called after Provo's early campaign for free white bicycles to tackle the city's traffic congestion – was also launched, which offered distinctive policy suggestions on a range of issues, from public transport to housing and family planning. The decisive event for Provo's national and international notoriety was the wedding on 10 March 1966 of heir-to-the-throne Princess Beatrix to the former Wehrmacht officer Claus von Amsberg. Plans for a 'day of anarchy' to coincide with the wedding were extensively trailed. The day itself became a famous event in Dutch history, with dozens of smokebombs thrown by Provos and others near the royal procession, a spectacle caught by television cameras from around the world. Three months later, on 13 and 14 June, full-scale riots – the most serious of the decade – gripped Amsterdam, leaving one fatality, over a hundred wounded and damage amounting to millions of guilders. These had originated in strike action by construction workers, but Provo was widely blamed for the escalation. In fact, leading Provos were taken by surprise by the disturbances, their attention having been focused instead upon the modest electoral success enjoyed by Provo candidates in the city council elections a couple of weeks previously.[14]

---

[12] Duyn 1967, p. 64.   [13] "Provootjes en vopootjes", in *Provo*, 2, cited in Van Duyn 1985, p. 89.
[14] Pas 2003, pp. 202–3.

The Provo campaign for the election, like many of Provo's other public activities, projected a strongly artistic character. Provo presented itself as "a kind of Gesamtkunstwerk", in which the standard communication media of party electoral machines were set aside in favour of vivid, hand-made billboards and posters, and by public spectacle of the kind already familiar from the weekly happenings.[15] This was entirely consistent with what Niek Pas has termed Provo's "expressive politics" in which style and image took precedence over rigid agendas and ideological dogmatism: "Provo was a different kind of politics: sensational, emotional, theatrical, expressive".[16] Provo took as a founding assumption the view that "the essence of human life lies in the expansion, the self-realisation, the development of one's own creativity".[17] This reflected the influence upon Provo's founders of Situationism, and in particular the Dutch artist Constant Nieuwenhuys, an early member of the Situationist International. Nieuwenhuys conceived a future in which mankind, freed by technological advance from utilitarian demands, would engage in endless creative play. Provo wished to accelerate the development of this "homo ludens", and argued for the value of "economically useless creation" in the here and now.[18]

Within this perspective both popular and experimental forms of creativity had a place. Both the creators of experimental art and the rebellious consumers of beat music were considered to belong to the provotariaat on account of their shared rejection of the world of work and their critical attitude to established society. Provo's dual interest in popular and experimental art also reflected the different personal interests of leading figures within the movement. For many Provos it was self-evident that, as Detlef Siegfried has recently put it, there existed a strong bond between "certain aspects of rock music, such as spontaneity, physicality, activism, violating the rules, and questioning authority" and the "formal aspects and content of the protest movements".[19] As teenagers a number of the Provos had had a keen interest in rock and roll, and the media frequently depicted the Provos in 'spontaneous' music-making.[20] Provo founder Roel van Duyn, on the other hand, had a background as a classical pianist and, in the words of Rob Stolk, "was certainly no fan of the Beatles".[21] Instead, he theorised extensively on Dada as the true "artistic pendant to anarchism", due to its "complete absence of laws".[22] In the happening – Provo's favoured means of propaganda and provocation – experimental and popular impulses were

---

[15] Pas 2002, p. 486. [16] Pas 2002, p. 487. [17] Van Duyn 1967, p. 108. [18] Van Duyn 1966, p. 25 [19] Siegfried 2008, p. 65. [20] Pas 2003, pp. 35, 39, 235, 312. [21] Van Tijen 1999. [22] Van Duyn 1967, pp. 107, 109.

productively brought together. For Provo, the happening typically presented an extreme or highly unusual theatrical situation in which, crucially, "everyone must be actively and creatively involved".[23]

If popular and experimental creativity in this way comprised crucial elements within Provo's cultural outlook, what emerges most clearly from Provo commentary on music are the shortcomings of each current as it manifested itself within capitalist society. Avant-garde music was in fact almost completely ignored, despite the fact that certain avant-garde musicians enjoyed close relations with Provo. The young composer Peter Schat, in particular, was friendly with Van Duyn and in summer 1966 offered the basement of his house as a base for Provo's printing operation.[24] Around the same time, avant-garde jazz saxophonist and composer Willem Breuker composed a *Litany for the 14th of June*, marking the violent street disturbances of that day, in which Provo had been implicated. But neither this work nor Peter Schat's *Labyrint* – the large-scale music-theatre piece which was premiered during Provo's tenancy in the composer's basement – received any attention in Provo publications or statements. Indeed the only reference made to Amsterdam's avant-garde musicians in publications by Provo appears in a spoof newspaper modelled on the right-wing daily *Telegraaf*, where a back-page column commented in mock-horror at the campaign of several young composers to modernise programming policy at the Concertgebouw Orchestra.[25] Rather than presenting direct advocacy of what the writer termed the "contemporary 'music' . . . [of this] gang of juvenile noise-makers", the column principally served to satirise the reactionary attitudes of the real-life *Telegraaf*, for Provo one of the most enduring symbols of the culturally conservative establishment.

By contrast, "beat music" received a good deal of attention in *Provo*, not least through a number of hit parade listings which presumably reflected the musical tastes of members of the editorial team, and in which Bob Dylan unsurprisingly had particular prominence.[26] In an interview with the pop music magazine *Hitweek* published shortly before Beatrix's wedding day, Roel van Duyn asserted that "Provo is beat" and "Hitweekers are Provos".[27] Yet this endorsement of "beat music" was in large part intended to foster youthful support for Provo's planned "Day of Anarchy". In the larger view, declarations of affinity with "beat" had to be reconciled with Provo's opposition to capitalism and consumerism, which had been loudly

[23] Van Duyn, in Constandse and Mulisch 1966, p. 22.   [24] Pas 2003, p. 208; see also p. 324.
[25] *De Teleraaf*, 2 (1967), p. 4.
[26] See *Provo*, 6 (January 1966); *Provo*, 7 (February 1966); *Provo*, 8 (April 1966).
[27] *Hitweek* (4 February 1966), p. 3.

declared from the very first issue of the periodical. The difficulty of achieving this reconciliation was clear from an article entitled "Biet(sers)", which appeared in issue 13 (January 1967). The title is a pun on the then-fashionable phonetic spelling of 'beat' and the Dutch word 'bietser', which means scrounger or bum. The authors explained that "we count as 'bietsers' beat groups which aim to give their performances purely for the sake of commerce, who are completely at the mercy of their normally gangster-like managers".[28] Singled out for particular contempt was the "filthily commercial" Dutch group The Golden Earrings, who in late 1966 had produced a hit promoting Coca-Cola – the most blatant imaginable submission to 'coca-kolonisatie' (as American neo-imperialism was often termed at the time).[29]

Partial exemption from this capitalist collusion was granted to Dylan and the Dutchman Boudewijn de Groot, both known for their protest songs. An article in issue 5 of *Provo* (December 1965) had already equated 'Provobiet' with 'protestsong'. Here, emphasis was placed upon Dylan's "sharp political commentary [...] social critique, [and] direct references to protest, rebellion and revolution". The difficulties of reconciling even Dylan's music with Provo ideology, however, is demonstrated by the author's valiant but implausible attempt to construct protest song as a form of 'happening' – the genre officially sanctioned by Roel van Duyn and other Provo theoreticians for expressing the subversive creativity of the provotariaat. This claim rested on the protest song's 'strong texts' (in contrast to the "below-par and even disgusting" lyrics of rock 'n' roll) which created a kind of subversive multimediality:

> The protestsong is a step on the path to integrated art, that is to say, the happening [...] The happening combines in ultimate form all sort of artistic expressions – literature and sound-effects (so-called music) and plastic forms – in mass creation. Similar art-feasts are currently the film (e.g. *The Knack*), spoken poetry and also protestsongs.[30]

In the event, the development for which Provo longed, namely the incorporation of the historical avant-garde's shattering of artificial generic boundaries and conventions within the sphere of popular music, only showed signs of becoming reality around the time of Provo's disbanding in May 1967. Jimi Hendrix's pyromaniac display at the Monterey Festival in June, for instance, would not have been out of place at one of the Provo happenings. It remained to be seen whether the immersive, multimedia experiments of

---

[28] Jaap/Anton [*sic*], "Biet(sers)", *Provo*, 13 (January 1967), p. 12. Many articles in *Provo* give only the first name(s) of their contributors.

[29] For more on coca-colonisation, see Kuisel 1991. [30] Martijn 1965, p. 24.

rock musicians that emerged in the course of that year, and which helped to sustain the Netherlands' vigorous youth counterculture, contained the 'staatsgevaarlijk' potential that Provo hoped.

Popular music and youth culture

The underlying reasons for Provo's frustration and fascination with 'beat music' have recently been laid out clearly by the pop music scholar Ger Tillekens.[31] His survey of the Dutch hit parades from the 1960s shows that many of the decade's most famous protest songs hardly registered with the general public, and the number of protest songs that did make the Top 40 listings barely made double figures. Despite the reputation of the decade's popular music as a primary vehicle for expression of the era's discontent, very few hit songs made explicit reference to political themes or even to sexual liberation. Most were preoccupied instead with issues of identity and relationships. Even when mainstream rock musicians began to address the upheavals of 1968, as happened most famously in songs such as the Beatles' "Revolution" and the Rolling Stones' "Street Fighting Man", the message was by no means an unconditional expression of support for the era's protesters and revolutionaries; indeed, each of these songs was harshly criticised by the leftist press in the Netherlands and elsewhere for this very reason.[32] Leading Dutch band Q'65 released their first, best-selling album *Revolution* in the immediate aftermath of the street unrest in the summer of 1966, but the title was a late change, and none of the songs referenced the year's events. Lead singer Wim Bieler was clear that

> we were not revolutionary in a political sense. We were just playing music [...] You were certainly aware that Provo was turning everything upside down, but that was in Amsterdam. Amsterdam was Provo and riots, The Hague [from which many of the best-known Dutch beat groups, including Q'65, originated] took care of the music.[33]

Tillekens' conclusion is that "in the sixties and the beginning of the seventies there was little penetration of sung social criticism amongst the broad public" in the Netherlands.[34]

---

[31] Tillekens 2008.
[32] Righart 2004, p. 60. For more on the reception of these two songs, see Platoff 2005 and Doggett 2007, pp. 194–203.
[33] Pols 1991.   [34] Tillekens 2008.

And yet despite this lack of political engagement, in the late 1960s pop music unmistakably felt like "an expression of opposition", both for those who were attracted to it and for those who were repulsed.[35] In part this was achieved purely musically: rock's arresting volume and strong beat invited complete physical involvement, but also (as Tillekens notes) presented a wall of sound that literally served to shut adults out. In part it was achieved precisely by cheerfully sardonic lyrics that exerted a strong aura of resistance to prevailing values and officially sanctioned codes of communication. In these ways, in Tillekens' words, "almost every pop song [of the period] can be understood as an indirect protest against the restriction of personal freedom and self-expression".[36] The tone of dissent was sustained as the psychedelic revolution took hold in 1967, and beat music's focus upon "having fun within the established system" was partly superseded by progressive rock's pursuit of escape or transcendence.[37] Popular music, mass-marketed not just nationally but globally, came to have a strongly unifying effect on an entire generation, strengthening the sense of a cohesive youth movement sharing common cause across national borders. For some commentators, as a consequence, the 'sixties', considered as a social and cultural phenomenon revolving around a youthful counterculture, could simply not have happened without pop.[38]

The magazine *Hitweek*, launched only a few months after Provo's inception, clearly reflected both the appeal of the emerging youth culture for politically engaged figures in the Netherlands, and the resistance of that youth culture to direct annexation by political causes. *Hitweek* strove for nothing less than the emancipation of 'twieners' – teenagers and early twenty-somethings – and it did so in the first place by giving extensive attention to rock and pop music. From the start it sought to take seriously the new wave of British and American bands and their domestic imitators, which were neglected by existing pop magazines such as *Muziek Parade* and *Muziek Expres*.[39] *Hitweek* faithfully mapped the rise and fall of emerging groups and trends throughout the four years of its existence (1965–9), with extensive articles in the very first issue on the Stones, the Beatles, Bob Dylan, the Who and the Kinks, and in subsequent issues attentive and critical coverage of the breakthrough moments of Hendrix, Zappa, Pink Floyd, psychedelic rock, Jim Morrison, Janis Joplin and many others. Detailed attention was also given to new home-grown groups whose number exploded in *Hitweek*'s first year. Equally central to the conception of

---

[35] Tillekens 2008. [36] Tillekens 2008. [37] Gary Burns, cited in Van Elteren 1994, p. 140.
[38] See for instance Righart 2004. [39] Mol 1985, p. 614.

Hitweek's founders was the policy of renouncing an authoritarian editorial voice, and instead offering maximum space for the views of the readers. "*Hitweek*", the first issue announced, "has no editorship, no chief editor, and all of that official status stuff is taboo". Readers were encouraged to "write, photograph, [and] make plans", with the intention that many of the magazine's pages should be filled by readers' contributions. The letters pages were especially important, offering a remarkable thermometer of trends and opinions among music-oriented youth, from every corner of the Netherlands. The magazine thereby gave considerable momentum to the country's youth movement, not least through what Hans Mol has termed its "radical alteration of the symbolic significance of pop music", from a divertissement provided by adults for the diversion of youth, to "the idiom par excellence in which youth expressed its identity".[40] For many, *Hitweek* would become a symbol of the decade.

Despite the renouncing of official editorship, a group of regular contributors gathered around the magazine, and helped to determine its tone and coverage. Among them were figures with established or emerging credentials of social engagement, who had high aspirations for the revolutionary potential of the nascent youth culture. André van der Louw came to *Hitweek* as an employee of the Vereeniging van Arbeiders Radio Amateurs (VARA), the broadcasting organisation historically associated with the workers' movement. He was an active member of the Labour Party (PvdA), and in 1966 shot to prominence by co-founding the splinter group Nieuw Links (New Left), which argued vigorously for a more radical course for the party, with a strong emphasis upon greater openness and accountability.[41] Van der Louw's VARA colleagues Wim Bloemendaal and Henk Bongaarts also became active collaborators on *Hitweek*, and shared his New Left perspective.[42] The beat poet, drugs guru and Provo publicist Simon Vinkenoog, meanwhile, acted as the magazine's regular 'house philosopher', providing a strong link to *Provo*, to which he also contributed.[43]

Unsurprisingly, given such contributors, *Hitweek*'s purview extended well beyond music. Regular attention was given to the activities of Provo, for instance, and to the authorities' sometimes repressive responses to Provo events. Sexual liberation was a further important theme, with a regular advice column for both male and female readers on sexual relations and contraception. Global events around 1968 received due attention: coverage was given to Vietnam, civil rights, the advent of hippies (both in California

---

[40] Mol 1985, p. 623. [41] Kennedy 1995a, pp. 196–7. [42] Heerma van Voss 1972, p. 31.
[43] Heerma van Voss 1972, p. 30.

and, during the summer of 1967, closer to home in Amsterdam), student protest (first Berlin, then Paris), the Soviet invasion of Czechoslovakia and Castro's Cuba. For *Hitweek*'s more ideologically committed contributors, high expectations were attached to the magazine's potent brew of pop and politics. Wim Bloemendaal, for instance, started out with the hope that

> pop music would become a sort of revolution [...] I often visited a beatclub in The Hague, and saw that everything and everyone went there. I thought that was wonderful: [...] you couldn't any longer tell which background someone came from! In the first days of pop, this music was such a tremendously binding element. And *Hitweek* was the banner on which it was all written.[44]

Yet despite such hopes, the pages of *Hitweek* attest equally clearly to the abidingly apolitical character of Dutch youth culture. Many of the magazine's young readers expressed scepticism over the "politically correct" views of the article and leader writers.[45] Readers' contributions criticised Provo's "negative manner" and condoning of violent confrontation, even branding them "a bunch of society-rapists".[46] Van Duyn's contention in the pages of *Hitweek* that "Provo is beat" touched a particularly raw nerve. One reader wrote:

> Don't let yourself be swindled by Roel van Duyn and his lot! With slogans like "provo is beat" they try to convince you that, if you love beat, you're a provo. It's not true! Of course we feel critical towards the existing order, but that's not to say that we're against everything. [...] Be for change in a positive-critical way (that is beat!), become a provo[cateur] of the provos, someone with a clear opinion, who's not swept along by empty slogans and semi-intellectual reasoning.[47]

Other readers sharply rejected the leftist viewpoint of some of the established contributors, warning of the looming threat of communism, for instance, and supporting the US war in Vietnam.[48]

Aside from readers holding views that (in Pieter Jan Mol's words) "would not embarrass the much reviled older generation",[49] there was a substantial part of the readership that simply had no interest in the political content. In 1969 a readers' questionnaire showed that articles about politics were among the least valued elements of the magazine, ranking some way below the strip cartoons, the sex-advice column and all of the categories of pop music coverage.[50] Consistent with this was an avoidance of political readings of rock music, beyond generalised remarks about its status as

---

[44] Bloemendaal, cited in Heerma van Voss 1972, p. 31.   [45] Righart 2006, p. 247.
[46] *Hitweek*, 29 October 1965, p. 5; and 5 November 1967, p. 4.   [47] *Hitweek*, 8 April 1966, p. 2.
[48] Mol 1985, p. 643.   [49] Mol 1985, p. 643.   [50] *Hitweek*, 28 March 1969, p. 7.

'protest'. For instance, a September 1968 article headed "Avant-Pop is Dangerous, *Hitweek* is Dangerous" celebrated the multimedia experiments of psychedelia, Zappa's *Freak Out* and the 'grande forme' of proto-progressive rock bands such as Captain Beefheart and the Bonzos. But the 'danger' of such music was identified in its capacity to bring on "an attack of hysteria" or to represent orgasm; no connection was made with the year's global turmoil.[51]

In the process the aspirations of *Hitweek*'s more politically oriented contributors went unrealised. André van der Louw later observed despondently how "it has not come out as the kind of revolution I hoped. I thought then that a mass creative movement must certainly have consequences for the emancipation of mankind. I no longer have that same optimistic feeling".[52] What Wim Bloemendaal termed pop's "tremendously binding element" created a sense of sharp generational differentiation that turned out to render any more politically radical experimentation superfluous. Moreover, the capitalist market proved more than happy to cater to the emerging needs of the young. Youth culture's challenge to established codes of morality and behaviour was expressed not just through music but also clothes, recreational drugs and other consumer goods. The belated admission of advertisements onto the pages of *Hitweek* was met by letters of delight from readers for whom youth marketing represented a natural extension of the magazine's raison d'être.[53] In this sense, as Mol notes, youth culture's gestures of protest, in as much as they were "limited to the level of *style*", proved "not only powerless in breaking the logic of the capitalist market, but in fact extremely functional for the operation of that market".[54]

Its complicity with capitalism notwithstanding, youth counterculture formed a crucial element of the Netherlands' distinctively 'expressive' 1968. The relative absence of politicisation indeed allowed room for greater attention to the expressive aspects of youth rebellion, with the result that by 1967 Amsterdam was internationally recognised as a 'magic centre' for young people seeking alternative experiences and ways of life. Aside from the Dutch capital's liberal attitude to soft drugs, Amsterdam offered regular hippie 'love-ins' at the Vondelpark, 'cosmic relaxation centres' such as Paradiso and Fantasio, and from the summer of 1968 an opportunity to sleep under the stars on the central Dam square.[55] Such essentially

---

[51] Domoy 1968. [52] Heerma van Voss 1972, p. 32. [53] Righart 2006, p. 243.
[54] Mol 1985, p. 638. Thomas Frank has observed that business culture experienced its own 'countercultural' revolution in the late 1960s, with a new generation of entrepreneurs sharing youth culture's rejection of a stultifying establishment; see Frank 1997, pp. 25–6.
[55] Kennedy 1995b, pp. 139–40.

hedonistic recreations retained threads of continuity with the earlier activism of Provo – notably in the focus upon the liberation of public space, and upon mass participation and creativity. As importantly, the counterculture provided lively and visible expression of the desire for social change, which could be instrumentalised by those – like Provo, Van der Louw and (from 1969) student activists[56] – with more explicitly political agendas. If youth counterculture was not to be the vehicle for political revolution, it nonetheless acted as a crucial stimulus for the developing activism of more overtly engaged figures.

The politicisation of avant-garde musicians

Dutch avant-garde musicians were much readier to identify openly with Provo than were popular musicians. The Provo-led protests surrounding the royal wedding in March 1966, for instance, provided the immediate context for the launching of a vigorous public campaign, spearheaded by five young composers (Louis Andriessen, Reinbert de Leeuw, Misha Mengelberg, Peter Schat and Jan van Vlijmen), against the unadventurous programming policies of the Concertgebouw Orchestra. In this way, the composers' case was made to seem part of a larger set of questions confronting the Dutch capital.[57] A fashion also emerged among progressive musicians for adopting 'anarchy' as a guiding aesthetic principle. "We are on the path to anarchy", Peter Schat proclaimed at the time of the premiere of *Labyrint*,[58] and this contention was reinforced by a lengthy article advocating an abandonment of both tonality and serialism in favour of "anarchy, a world of fragments and ad hoc solutions, chaos".[59] Schat's colleague Reinbert de Leeuw responded to Schat's arguments in two 1967 articles entitled "Formalisme en anarchie" and "Muzikale anarchie", the latter offering an admiring study of Charles Ives.[60] Andriessen too declared that "anarchy is the future", and his music in 1966 and 1967 conspicuously embodied the fashionable aversion to governing systems with works (such as *Souvenirs d'enfance* and *Anachronie I*) that delighted in promiscuous stylistic references and borrowings.[61] In a related development, 1967 saw Han Bennink, Willem Breuker and Misha Mengelberg found the Instant Composers Pool (ICP), a collective of improvising musicians

---

[56] On the role of the music of the Rolling Stones in the Netherlands' biggest student occupation, see Regtien 1988, pp. 205–6.
[57] See Andriessen et al., 1967, p. 32.   [58] See the interview in *De Volkskrant*, 27 June 1966.
[59] Schat 1966, p. 47.   [60] Both were reprinted in De Leeuw 1973.   [61] See Vermeulen 1968, p. 6.

whose musical practice embodied the creative individualism espoused by Provo.[62]

Yet the engagement of Dutch avant-garde musicians was by no means limited to this flirtation with Provo and anarchism. The slow unfolding of the Netherlands' '1968' – from its early start with the founding of Provo in 1965 to the delayed outbreak of student protests in 1969 and the rise of industrial militancy in 1970 – had a further consequence for engaged musicians, namely that they had the opportunity to explore a range of positions and responses to the era's diverse cultural-political manifestations.[63] In January 1968 a trip to the Cultural Congress in Havana converted Peter Schat to Cuban communism, and prompted a more explicit politicisation of his and his colleagues' musical activities – notably in an ad hoc "political-demonstrative experimental concert" (May 1968), which featured ardent political speeches between new musical works, and in the collectively composed music-theatre piece *Reconstructie* (1969), which offers a 'reconstruction' of the death of Che Guevara and casts US 'imperialists' as the rapists of Latin America. Student radicalism finally ignited in the Netherlands in 1969 with a wave of university occupations; in their ongoing campaign against the Concertgebouw Orchestra, Andriessen, Schat and their colleagues correspondingly adopted a strategy of direct action, including the disruption of one of the Orchestra's performances and an occupation of the Concertgebouw's offices. The wildcat industrial unrest of 1969 and 1970, fomented in part by Maoist student groups, in turn prompted a large number of the country's avant-garde musicians to join with the leader of one of the country's musicians' unions in the foundation of a movement – the "Beweging voor de vernieuwing van de muziekpraktijk" (Movement for the renewal of musical practice) – dedicated to the achievement for all musicians of the right of self-determination in the practice of their trade.

In the process of engaging with the ideological debates and political strategies of different currents of contemporary activism, avant-garde musicians were forced to reexamine core aspects of their own musical practice. Central among these was the standpoint of musical autonomy. At the time of the 1968 political concert, Schat and his colleagues adhered to the well-established mantra that "music is not able to express anything, let alone transmit political messages".[64] At the concert this view was reflected in musical works of apparently impregnable abstraction; the concert's

---

[62] On the anarchic individualism of ICP, see Whitehead 1999, pp. 46–53.
[63] For more detailed accounts of the activities described in summary here, see Adlington 2007a, 2008 and 2009a; and Rubinoff 2009.
[64] Schat 1968, p. 5.

'political-demonstrative' element was understood as lying solely in its novelties of presentation and in the political speeches. Within a year, however, the finishing touches were being put on *Reconstructie*, whose frank (sometimes crude) propagandising was underpinned by a play of musical idioms that, by associating the imperialists with pop music and the oppressed Latin Americans with serialism and free improvisation, signalled a clear recognition of the symbolic freight of musical material. *Reconstructie* thereby unwittingly laid bare another abiding motif of the avant-gardist outlook, namely the conception of popular music as irredeemably tainted. But this too was to be brought into question as the musicians' politicisation was touched by the workerist turn of radical student groups after 1969, which stressed the need for intellectuals to follow the masses, rather than lead.[65] This ethic, combined with the evident centrality of pop and rock music to youth protest, drew composers to reassess their former positions, so that by the early seventies new Dutch music was notable for its positive engagement with, rather than critical rejection of, vernacular forms – be it progressive rock (emulated in Schat's *Thema* [1970] and *To You* [1972]), jazz (Andriessen's *De Volharding* [1972]) or workers' songs (in works by Andriessen, Breuker and others). Similarly, sensitization to issues surrounding labour relations prompted composers to reevaluate their own function within musical production, a reevaluation that resulted in a blossoming of new, composer-founded ensembles (such as Het Leven, De Volharding and the Schoenberg Ensemble) intended to overcome the traditional managerial hierarchies (exacerbated in certain complex avant-garde music) of composer and performer. In cases like De Volharding, founded by Andriessen and Breuker in 1971, these new ensembles also carried an explicitly political remit, realised through regular contributions to rallies, protest marches and community events.

The Netherlands' prolonged '1968' thus brought about a revolution in Dutch musical life, giving rise to a scene recognised internationally for its stylistic diversity, distinctive infrastructure (especially in the form of the new 'ensemble culture') and the blurring of the traditional division of labour between composers, performers and administrators. Yet the profundity of these shifts notwithstanding, countervailing tendencies persisted within avant-garde musicians' activities which ensured that this revolution was sooner 'expressive' than (in line with Provo's founding aspiration) 'dangerous to the state'. No country during the late 1960s had established a firmer link between dissent and expressive adventurousness than the

---

[65] On Maosim in the Netherlands, see Verbij 2005, pp. 102–18.

Netherlands – Provo and youth culture had each played an important part in that – and musicians accustomed to conceiving themselves at the forefront of musical developments were not quickly going to abandon this tenet of their creative existence, for any reason. This remained the case even when the principle of aesthetic innovation came into evident tension with the purpose of service to a political cause or the role of propagandising to the greatest number.

Such tensions were evident to all at the 1968 political concert, when the works' abstruse negotiations with musical material left many among the large, expectant audience bewildered and restless, creating a rift between music and public which the composers sought to excuse with their insistence on music's unanswerability to worldly purpose. But they continued to be felt well after the insistence on autonomy had been abandoned and musicians had begun to place themselves and their music more fully at the service of the political cause. A case in point was an ambitious collaboration in 1973 between the composers Louis Andriessen, Gilius van Bergeijk and Victor Wentink, the writer Jacq Firmin Vogelaar and the communist-affiliated workers' choir Morgenrood Rotterdam. The intention was to create a new 'Lehrstück' (the didactic theatre form developed by Bertolt Brecht in the 1920s) dealing with the early development of the Dutch workers' movement up to the rail strike of 1902. But as Vogelaar recalled, the project stalled because of the gulf between the creative aspirations of the artists and the needs of the workers they sought to serve:

> [T]he music was not sufficiently Eislerian, the Rotterdam choir members couldn't get their voices round the dissonance, and the text also could not withstand the test of criticism, certainly not when every line was held against the light of the real workers' existence [...] It was a collision between two worlds. The choir members ultimately wanted nothing other than what they already knew.[66]

If Marx's 'subject of history' was less than impressed by the creative ambitions of the musicians who sought to advance their emancipation, the same cannot necessarily be said of the Dutch authorities, who increasingly during this period recognised the strategic value of the ideas of renewal and innovation.[67] By granting subsidies to art that was conspicuously advanced, the government projected itself as progressive without needing to undertake any more substantive reform or modernisation. Musicians' abiding preoccupation with aesthetic experiment thus carried the double danger of losing the interest of non-specialists while serving the agenda of

---

[66] Vogelaar 1993, p. 117.   [67] Kennedy 1995b, pp. 136, 148, 183, 195–7.

established power. A clear example was the production of *Reconstructie*, whose caustic attack on US imperialist adventures was (to the horror of right-leaning press commentators) generously bank-rolled by a government notable for its unwavering commitment to the North Atlantic Treaty Organisation (NATO). (The administration's long-serving foreign minister Joseph Luns was later to become NATO's secretary general.) Arts minister Marga Klompé defended the subsidy on account of the desirability of supporting art which promoted "not uniformity and thus conformity, but the transformation of the existing outlook" – an argument that could be made on the basis of the work's aesthetic experiments alone.[68] Engaged musicians realised that they thereby handed the state a publicity coup – they were quick to deploy Marcuse's concept of "repressive tolerance" as an accurate diagnosis of their own situation[69] – but on the increasingly regular occasions that government subsidy was offered for their activities, they found it difficult to bring themselves to turn it down.

"A social-cultural revolution, then, in place of a political one?" So asks Hans Righart in his study of the 'worldwide sixties'.[70] As Righart indicates, Provo's response to this question would have been to contend that the opposition was a false one. Without vigorously offering alternatives to existing behavioural and expressive norms, Provo argued, any political revolution would be hollow indeed. A similar faith in the transforming potential of new forms of expression united both the rebellious counterculture and engaged avant-gardists, although the relation they conceived between expressive innovation and social change was quite different in each case (and each differed again from the stance of Provo). Ultimately the 'expressive politics' of rock and avant-garde music did more to shore up than to undermine two central targets of 1968 radicalism: namely, capitalism and the state. This did not prevent them from bringing about revolutions of other kinds. In the course of the 1970s and beyond, the Netherlands – and Amsterdam in particular – cemented its reputation as a highly significant centre for contemporary composition, and as a hub for experimental youth from around the world, confirming a remarkable transformation from its postwar reputation as the epitome of 'calm and order'.[71] In establishing new roles for music and new possibilities for musical practice, 1968 altered the expressive landscape in the Netherlands for years to come.

---

[68] Klompé, cited in Vermeulen 1969, p. 124. For more detailed consideration of the stance of the government towards *Reconstructie*, see Adlington 2007a.

[69] The term cropped up in the libretto to *Reconstructie*, for instance, in a passage where the work's authors self-reflexively consider the act of accepting a commission from "the establishment"; see Adlington 2007a, p. 185.

[70] Righart 2004, p. 18.   [71] Pas 2003, p. 203.

2 | Music as plea for political action: the presence of musicians in Italian protest movements around 1968

GIANMARIO BORIO

In the decade leading up to 1968, class structure and cultural orientations in Italian society underwent major changes.[1] Phenomena that affected the Western world as a whole – the automation of production systems, the expansion of infrastructures and mobility, the boost to consumerism and the influence of the media in day-to-day life – had a significant correlative in Italy in the form of a mass migration from the land to the cities, above all to what was known as the 'industrial triangle' of Turin, Milan and Genoa. The new workforce in the metal, steel, chemical and electronic industries was confronted with the internal hierarchy of the factory, a different ecological reality and a metropolitan lifestyle. Inadequate urban planning helped to bring about a polarisation between the centre, where all the wealth, consumer benefits and cultural activities accumulated, and the periphery, comprising residential quarters that mushroomed not far from the factories. At the same time, however, the working class began to have access to social practices and commodities, which in the past had been the preserve of the upper classes or else had been looked down on. The sensation of freedom, which came with this sudden change in status, prompted aversion towards a society whose moral and civil values had remained unchanged since the end of the war, and indeed had not been entirely purged of the imprint of Fascism. The impact of these socio-economic changes was accentuated by the extension of compulsory schooling for all until the age of 14 (in 1962), and the lowering of university entrance requirements. Culture was beginning to play an increasingly important role in society, and the consequences could be seen in politics and in public discussion. Legislation on divorce, abortion, conscientious objection towards military service and the abolition of lunatic asylums – all introduced during these years following stormy debates both in and outside parliament – are examples of 'superstructural' reforms in the sense that they concerned spheres in which ethical and cultural issues played a pre-eminent role.[2]

---

[1] I wish to thank Serena Facci, Vincenzo Caporaletti and Veniero Rizzardi for reading early versions of this chapter and giving me precious advice on how to improve it.
[2] See Ginsborg 2003, pp. 298–347.

The convergence of these factors gave rise to a new type of intellectual who no longer identified with the categories of idealist philosophy and historicism that had predominated in the first part of the twentieth century. These intellectuals were more cosmopolitan, interdisciplinary and eclectic than their predecessors, and were conversant with the essays of Lukács, the Frankfurt School, the French existentialists, the structuralists and American sociology. While there were undoubtedly gifted leaders in the largest political party, the Democrazia Cristiana (DC), the hypocrisy and censoriousness that characterised its cultural policies oriented the new intellectuals towards the Partito Socialista Italiano (PSI) and the Partito Comunista Italiano (PCI). Following the death of its charismatic leader Palmiro Togliatti in 1964, the PCI was going through a process of transformation, which made it particularly receptive to the new trends. A polarisation took place in the strategy of the major parties: while those in government maintained strict control over the economy and the media, most original cultural and artistic initiatives looked to the PCI as their interlocutor. Dario Fo, Dacia Maraini, Alberto Moravia, Pier Paolo Pasolini, Edoardo Sanguineti and Leonardo Sciascia – to name only writers – are representative of this new figure in the public arena, constituting somewhat idiosyncratic versions of Gramsci's 'organic intellectual'. The personal histories of artists and intellectuals in the decade leading up to 1968 can largely be viewed in the dynamic of attraction towards, and repulsion from, the PCI.[3] The Vietnam War, the 'cultural revolution' in China, Afro-American movements opposing segregation, struggles for liberation in Africa and Latin America, the Soviet invasion of Czechoslovakia, the handling of workers' rights protests in the 'industrial triangle' and the reaction to youth unrest were the issues that coagulated dissent vis à vis the Party. New concepts of civil disobedience and strategies of counterculture were elaborated in reviews that claimed to be "to the left of the PCI": *Quaderni rossi* (which formulated the theory of union-independent workers' struggles), *Quaderni piacentini* (focusing on critiques of the establishment and liberation topics), *Quindici* (founded by Umberto Eco and Nanni Balestrini), *Re nudo* (speaking for the beatniks, Provos and Situationists) and *Ombre rosse* (reviewing cinema, drama and literature, related to Lotta Continua).

PCI's officials in charge of cultural affairs adopted an attitude of critical dialogue with the positions expressed by grass-roots movements, notably the student movement and the galaxy of the New Left. The cultural activities promoted by the Party – which included the local administrative sections,

---

[3] See Ajello 1997.

social centres, annual festivals of the Party newspaper *l'Unità*, residents' committees in urban districts, and also independent radio stations – served as repositories for demands and ideals. Conversely the new political subjects did not lose contact with the largest left-wing party, which at the high watermark of this process, in the elections of 1975 and 1976, accounted for one-third of all votes cast. In this context, with conflicts erupting and new identities being forged, music had a prime role to play. Its presence in politics was a transverse phenomenon relating to the sense of civil responsibility and ethical conviction shared by many musicians. The big event organised by the Federation of Italian Communist Youth (FGCI) at the Palazzo dello Sport, Rome in February 1975 to celebrate the thirtieth anniversary of the liberation from Fascism and the end of the War (which in Italy had also been a civil war) can be taken as representative of any number of similar initiatives. Some 15,000 people listened to the songwriters Ivan Della Mea, Paolo Pietrangeli and Giovanna Marini, the Chilean folk group Inti Illimani, the jazz bands of Giorgio Gaslini and Mario Schiano and excerpts of a composition by Luigi Nono. In such performances which reflected a wide range of technical and personal backgrounds, music brought activists together and was a soundboard for political messages, irrespective of genre and style. Indeed, the combination of different compositional and performance styles – in a context which was both ethically and emotionally highly charged – left its mark on all involved in this social process, making them more open to unconventional idioms and sensitive to the political implications of music making. As in the other arts, adherence to the issues raised by the Left led musicians to critically appraise modes of communication and to experiment with new forms of expression. The next sections will deal with three areas which seem to be particularly salient for these interconnections: (1) the attitude of socially aware composers towards workers' political struggles in the factories; (2) the understanding of folk music as an element of an antagonist culture; and (3) the connection between progressive rock and the identity of the new social movements.[4]

The composer in the factory

The phase known as 'the 1968', which was so crucial in the evolution of society and culture in the West, had two peculiar characteristics in Italy.

---

[4] For an in-depth analysis of a fourth aspect relating to free improvisation see Borio (forthcoming).

First, there was a confluence between the protests by students and the workers. Second, the PCI remained a point of reference for dissent even when the Left was at its most divided. In the sphere of music, Luigi Nono provides a striking illustration of this duality at work. Venetian by birth, Nono joined the PCI in 1952. In 1963 he stood for election as a member of parliament and in 1975 he was appointed to the central committee; throughout his career he maintained close contacts with all the most prominent leaders.[5] At the same time he was very aware of issues that remained on the fringes of, or even beyond the bounds of, official party policy: the spontaneous and at times violent outbreaks of workers' protests, guerilla warfare in third world countries, and the provocative activities of the student movement. His friendship with Massimo Cacciari is symptomatic of the interest and sympathy Nono nurtured for the heretic components of Eurocommunism. In 1968, Cacciari founded the review *Contropiano* together with Alberto Asor Rosa and Antonio Negri, who both belonged to the 'workerist' faction (*operaismo*). The way in which workers' unrest and union conflict are represented in Nono's *La fabbrica illuminata* (*The Enlightened Factory*) for woman's voice and tape (1964), owes much to the discussions that took place in *Quaderni rossi*, the theoretical organ of the Italian 'workerists'. Masterminded by Raniero Panzieri and Mario Tronti, this intellectual circle considered factory work as a permanent form of conflict and viewed union demands as a potential catalyst for revolution in the capitalist system as a whole. Original interpretations of some of Marx's writings (notably the *Grundrisse*)[6] combined with case studies, led to the representation of workers as brute manpower, as slaves to the ways of working dictated by machines. According to this perspective, workers were like faceless and unqualified operators employed to carry out standardised tasks; they were men and women who existed merely to provide for themselves and their families.[7]

In the social configuration that came to characterise the 'industrial triangle', the shopfloor was the focus for conflict, a simmering rebellion that could erupt at any moment in the form of insubordination, sabotage or wildcat strikes. Such ferments required the PCI and the unions to change

---

[5] Among his partners are included Enrico Berlinguer (national secretary of the PCI from 1972 to his death in 1984), Pietro Ingrao, Giorgio Napolitano (the current President of the Republic, between 1969 and 1975 responsible of the PCI's cultural section), Giancarlo Pajetta and Rossana Rossanda (from 1962 to 1967 in charge of the PCI's cultural section, she was expelled from the party in 1968 for criticising the invasion of Czechoslovakia, whereupon she helped set up *Il Manifesto*). See Trudu 2008.

[6] See Marx 1973 (1858); Negri 1991.   [7] See Wright 2002.

their approach to social analysis. A ground-breaking enquiry carried out by Giovanni Carocci at the Fiat works in 1957, involving some of the future adherents of 'workerism', pointed the way towards a critical, interventionist sociology, and Nono drew on this experience in composing *La fabbrica illuminata*. The tape used recordings of workers' voices and the sounds of machinery made by the composer himself at the Italsider steelworks in Genoa; it also featured electronic sounds, pieces for chorus and fragments of the solo part.[8] The text of the first two sections, written specifically by Giuliano Scabia and revised by Nono, deals with the workers' condition, while in the third section a poem by Cesare Pavese is set to music. Carocci's pioneering combination of investigating working conditions and political intervention gave rise to the so called 'con-ricerca' (collaborative research), a sort of ethnography of subversive situations based on the elimination of the gap between interviewer and interviewee, so that the intellectual and the worker could be of benefit to one another.[9] An enquiry based on these criteria brings out the 'workers' subjectivity', understood as the complex of experiences, frustrations, compulsions and linguistic utterances which define the individual worker in the physical context of production dynamics. This second dimension, which is complementary to the concept of the 'mass-worker', is manifested in various aspects of Nono's composition: in the dual role of the soloist, who performs live as well as being heard recorded on the tape, in the juxtaposition of soloist and massed chorus, and in the combination of public speeches and fragments of private life. Although there is no evidence in Nono's writings of any association with the 'workerists' circle or of any intentional link to the concept of 'con-ricerca', the historical contiguity is evident. Moreover, Nono combined his reaction to the Fiat enquiry with the idea of a diary in music elaborated some years previously in *Composizione per orchestra n. 2 – Diario polacco '58*. The diary form of the piece allows the discontinuity of experience to be observed and it enables the objective recording of events to coexist with their resonance in the diarist's conscience. With *La fabbrica illuminata*, rather than trying to mirror reality, the composer aimed to achieve a form of 'enlightenment' "by means of invention and construction".[10] In other words Nono sought to arouse awareness through the reorganisation of fragments of the experienced life.

Carocci's investigation and similar initiatives sparked off a wide-ranging discussion on factory work and the possibility of representing it using

---

[8] See Nono 2001 (Vol. 1), pp. 186–8, 206–9 and 446–9.
[9] See Carocci 1960 (1958) and Alquati 1975.   [10] Nono 2001 (Vol. 1), p. 448.

artistic means. The impulse for redefining the artist's social engagement came from a discussion of art and industrial landscape that took place in 1961 in an issue of *Menabò*, the review directed by Elio Vittorini and Italo Calvino.[11] In his introductory article Vittorini asked how literature could articulate, in its language and procedures, the increasingly apparent shift from the old world of agriculture and handicrafts to the new industrial order. A writer who rejected the psychological and picturesque approach that had characterised the nineteenth century did have several options, as can be seen in the 'factory novels' produced in these years, particularly *Gli anni del giudizio* by Giovanni Arpino, *Tempi stretti* by Ottiero Ottieri and *Memoriale* by Paolo Volponi. However, it is not easy to find a common denominator between a neutral attitude to the new reality, a documentary-style integration of the day-to-day idiom and an art form which takes sides with the proletariat and passes judgements while at the same time depicting situations. For example, Franco Fortini maintained that the 'social mandate' under which the Party had charged intellectuals with interpreting the needs of the working class had expired. He viewed the creative process of the artists as a tool of consciousness-raising and revolutionary anticipation: "industry is not just another topic, it is *the* manifestation of *the* topic, i.e. capitalism".[12] Umberto Eco also insisted on the importance of 'formation'. He praised works like Antonioni's *L'eclisse* for not taking situations of indigence and exploitation as their explicit subject matter, claiming that they provided deeper and more incisive examples of 'interventions on reality' than works that explicitly featured the shopfloor. Eco's position found a resonance in an article by Berio: he suspected political 'commitment' of being a cushy option resorting to ready-made solutions, and he argued that the creative act implied a confrontation with the social forms embedded in the musical forms. Composers, Berio suggests, had to become aware of the "semantics implicit in music's processes and rituals".[13]

---

[11] See issue 4 and 5 of *Il Menabò* (1964 and 1965). The essays by Fortini ("Astuti come colombe") and Eco ("Del modo di formare come impegno sulla realtà") are in Fortini 1965, pp. 68–89 and Eco 1976 (1962) pp. 235–90 (in English: "Form as social commitment" in Eco 1989, pp. 123–57). Some of Fortini's ideas were anticipated in Tronti 1962. On the debate on political commitment cf. Edoardo Sanguineti, "Avanguardia, società, impegno" (1966), in Sanguineti 2001, pp. 59–71; Berio 1964; and Pasolini 1999.

[12] Fortini, "Mandato degli scrittori e limiti dell'antifascismo", which appeared in three parts: I: *Giovane critica* 4 (1964); II: *Quaderni rossi* 3 (1963); III: *Quaderni piacentini* 17/18 (1964); the whole essay is in Fortini 1965, pp. 113–61. The quote comes from Fortini, "Astuti come colombe", in Fortini 1965, p. 75.

[13] Berio 1964, p. 130.

The film *Il deserto rosso* (*Red Desert*, 1965) by Michelangelo Antonioni can be considered a paradigm for an art form which is able to represent the unease in and around the factory, going beyond the didactic or documentary. A fundamental part in its success was due to the contribution of the composer, Vittorio Gelmetti: the electronic sounds highlight the crisis of the protagonist (Monica Vitti) and interact with factory noise recorded both inside and outside the chemical works. In a review of the first performance of *La fabbrica illuminata* Gelmetti pointed out a contradiction between the experimental approach, seen in the treatment of the tape, and a 'neo-expressionist trend' which emerged both in the formal layout (the opposition of soloist and 'orchestral tutti') and in the vocal lines (with their reference to sentiment and affectivity).[14] For Gelmetti, music – especially when it is associated with an image – has to take into account the acoustic plurality of modern society and he considered composition to be the art of manufacturing sound objects. Following his experience with Antonioni he collaborated in several films featuring life in the factory. First there were two shorts commissioned by leading industrial companies for promotional purposes: *La macchina del tempo* directed by Antonello Branca (Olivetti, 1968) and *Appunti per l'auto di domani* directed by Massimo Mida (Fiat, 1969). The most ground-breaking collaboration was with Ansano Giannarelli, a director who worked for Unitelefilm (a branch of the PCI's press and propaganda section) and who brought highly innovatory filming and narrative techniques to political subject matter. Together they worked on *Sierra maestra* (1969), a feature film based on the figure of Regis Debray, and also the short *Analisi del lavoro* (1971), which returned to the genre of enquiries into working conditions and featured film shot inside the SGS Thomson microchip works. Apart from a brief citation of Gramsci at the beginning talking about industrial machinery, the soundtrack consists entirely of a collage of compositions by Gelmetti (both electronic and instrumental) which sets up a multiplicity of relations with the images, highlighting the mechanics of precision mass production and their existential implications.[15]

In the context of film production associated with the PCI we can also mention *Apollon: una fabbrica occupata* by Ugo Gregoretti (1969), a short featuring the industrial action pursued by the employees of one of the

---

[14] Gelmetti 1964.
[15] *Analisi del lavoro* is available at http://aamod.archivioluce.com/archivioluce/jsp/schede/ videoPlayer.jsp?tipologia=&id=&physDoc=3232&db=partnerAAMOD&findIt=false&section= aamod.

foremost printers in Rome.[16] The film, a reconstruction of an occupation that lasted for over a year, was produced by the 'National centre for free newsreels', founded by Cesare Zavattini. The cast comprised the workers themselves and members of the PCI playing the management, with Gian Maria Volonté as narrator. *Apollon* set the seal on film as analysis of a real-life situation, a 'docufiction' revealing the economic and psychological strategies of the owner, the spontaneous rebellions of the workers, the differences of opinion among the strikers and the collective impulse for change. The music for the film was provided by a jazz trio headed by Mario Schiano, who improvised a sort of instant soundtrack that was recorded as the film was being projected. Although the role of the music was reduced in production, it remains a model for a piece of film music which engages physically, as it were, with the reality being narrated. In fact it stands as an alternative to the music, conceived in more traditional terms, which Ennio Morricone wrote for Elio Petri's *La classe operaia va in paradiso* (1971), in which Volonté played the leading role.

Folk music as an element of an antagonist culture

In *La fabbrica illuminata* Nono created an acoustic art form involving enquiry and denunciation which relied on a semantic reconfiguration of the noises of industrial machinery and workers' voices. In addition he took part in events promoted by the Party and the unions in which the work was performed and discussed by citizens who had received no musical education. Reactions varied from an increased awareness of the alienation characterising factory work, to specific interest in the technical aspects of the electroacoustic realisation, to rejection of the cryptic language of the art form, denounced as the product of bourgeois culture. There was in fact widespread diffidence towards the output of avant-garde composers among the militants engaged in the cultural scene, whether in the PCI itself or in the New Left. Militants felt that the function of music in the revolutionary process should not go beyond formulating messages on the exploitation of workers, on the constraints of established power and union struggles, and on the progress of social organisation in the future. Music was denied any validity in its own right and was only included because it was proving to be an increasingly powerful means for conveying political messages. This

---

[16] The film can be seen at http://aamod.archivioluce.com/archivioluce/jsp/schede/videoPlayer.jsp?tipologia=&id=&physDoc=3313&db=partnerAAMOD&findIt=false&section=aamod/#. See also Gregoretti's comment (Anonymous 2009). The whole recording is included as a compact disc (CD) in Faggiano 2003.

secondary function was made manifest in the ways in which television and the entertainment business conditioned the opinions and behaviour of the public; in this context too the strategy pursued by the Left was to take over the technical means and redirect them. To achieve this goal, politically engaged music had to be immediately comprehensible and feature texts relevant to the political agenda of the day. At the same time, however, it had to distance itself from mass culture, as represented by such hugely successful events as the Festival of Sanremo.

In 1958, musicians (Fausto Amodei, Sergio Liberovici, Emilio Jona, Michele Luciano Straniero and Margherita Galante Garrone) and literary figures (Italo Calvino, Franco Fortini, Gianni Rodari and Umberto Eco) formed the group Cantacronache in Turin. The purpose of this group was to collect, transcribe and perform the songs sung by Resistance fighters and political songs from the first half of the twentieth century. In addition, new songs were composed dealing with the existential condition of the lower classes in contemporary society, using both poetical and musical language which was sophisticated and at the same time immediately comprehensible. In 1962, following the breakup of this group, the Nuovo Canzoniere Italiano was founded in Milan, thanks above all to Roberto Leydi and Gianni Bosio. This new group focused on ethnographic research and produced songs reflecting current political issues.[17] The members of the Nuovo Canzoniere Italiano – in particular Ivan Della Mea, Giovanna Marini and Paolo Pietrangeli – were the authors of protest songs which, from 1968 onwards, were performed at street demonstrations, at the Festival dell'Unità, at regular meetings of the Left and during the occupation of factories and universities. Some of the new politically committed folk singers presented a broader repertoire ranging from songs of remembrance, struggle and mobilisation to more complex works embracing various traditions (labour songs and the narratives of Italian ballad singers but also political songs in the style of Brecht and Eisler, and Pete Seeger). Liberovici and Jona, for instance, concentrated on forms of musical theatre for children or featuring folk tales; Giovanna Marini gave concerts featuring an eclectic mix of blues, British folk, French chansons, Renaissance madrigals and elements from the Italian rural tradition. The publishing initiatives which grew up around the Nuovo Canzoniere Italiano were Edizioni del Gallo, the record label Dischi del Sole, a review bearing the same name and another called *La musica popolare* (created in 1975 by the student movement in Milan). The foundation of the Istituto Ernesto De Martino in 1966, honouring Italy's foremost anthropologist and dedicated to the study of popular and proletarian culture, represented

---

[17] See Bosio 1967; Boldini 1975; Dessì and Pintor 1976; Bermani 1997; Macchiarella 2005.

a decisive step forward in collecting and conserving the sources of popular music. Discussion of concepts of 'national-popular culture' and the 'subaltern class' as formulated by Gramsci was a fundamental aspect of the group's identity building.

The Nuovo Canzoniere Italiano made its debut at the Festival dei Due Mondi in Spoleto in 1964 with the show *Bella ciao*. In 1966 the group asked Dario Fo to direct a new production, *Ci ragiono e canto*, giving an important impulse to the performing style he was to perfect in *Mistero buffo*. In 1967, after parting ways with Fo, the collective staged *Sentite buona gente* at the Teatro Lirico, Milan, an anthology of songs and dances drawn from different regions of Italy. The production was based on a theatrical stylisation of manual labour and the representation of everyday situations, and was unique in putting on stage the true protagonists of 'subaltern cultures' without any attempt at 'interpreting', 'transcribing' or 'mediating'. In the first half of the 1970s the Nuovo Canzoniere Italiano gave a large number of performances, in collaboration with the cultural organisations of the PCI and the New Left; its two most successful productions were *Karlmarxstrasse* (1974) and *Fiaba grande*, performed at the Festival dell'Unità in Florence in 1976 in front of 30,000 spectators and televised by Radiotelevisione Italiana (RAI). Following the abduction of the DC-politician Aldo Moro and suspicions of ideological connivance with terrorist organisations, the group came in for criticism, not least from exponents of the PCI, and this, together with a certain waning of creativity, brought their activities to a close.

Cantacronache and Nuovo Canzoniere Italiano influenced the context we are considering in a variety of ways. First, the development of ethnomusicology in Italy is closely bound up with the above-mentioned experiences. The two pioneers in this discipline, Roberto Leydi and Diego Carpitella, carried out their fieldwork and elaborated their methodologies in contact with these two groups. At the instigation of the two ethnomusicologists, in the years leading up to 1968 the review *Marcatrè* published investigations and debates concerning 'class culture and contemporary folklore', pop music, cabaret and urban political songs. The experience of these groups prompted a reflection on what is meant by 'popular', in which Gramsci's elaborations were combined with the perspectives of sociology and anthropology. Music became the prime focus for studying popular culture – attracting the attention of scholars from other disciplines – because oral communication, participation in ritual events and the transmission of collective memory are all fundamental to music. At the same time, however, the extension of the repertory raised questions as to what is truly popular in 'musica populare'. With his concept of 'subalternity'

Gramsci paved the way for recognising a close link between popular culture and political struggle. The activity of collecting and classifying music from oral traditions in the regions of Italy – an extremely varied heritage in terms of both musical forms and types of vocality – had brought the agricultural world to the fore, giving it a new dignity and revealing the extent of its cultural and creative complexity. One by-product of this new attention to the rural world was the parochial, and indeed Catholic, identity exhibited in events like the Festival of Sanremo. In such events, the rural world was depicted as a reservoir of ancient, deeply rooted values which was a bulwark against the uncertainties of industrialisation and new lifestyles. Nonetheless, the output of the *Nuovo Canzoniere Italiano* acted as a watershed, shifting the focus onto specific contents and contexts. It also connected with the "dramatic moments of social dynamics and the emergence of protest situations that bridged the purely cultural sphere and that of class consciousness, tradition and revolution".[18] The goal was no longer (or not exclusively) the preservation of the disappearing musical heritage, but rather the constitution of a revolutionary culture in which music has a dynamic role to play. This favoured the recognition of a series of key factors in contemporary culture: the location of social conflict in urban and industrial zones, the subaltern classes as the greatest consumers of pop music, and lastly, the newly formed alliance between the proletariat and the sections of the middle classes that refused to allow their minds to be 'colonised'.

Second, socially aware singer-songwriters such as Luigi Tenco, Sergio Endrigo, Francesco De Gregori, Fabrizio de André and Francesco Guccini were strongly influenced by the rediscovery of the repertory of social songs, the folk revival and the composition of new songs of solidarity and struggle. One can clearly recognise the imprint of the Nuovo Canzoniere Italiano in Guccini's song "La locomotiva". But there is no doubt that this influence was much stronger in the groups devoted to reworking material from oral tradition with new and experimental instrumentation and arrangements ranging from a revival of 'early', medieval and baroque styles to jazz and rock. The Nuova Compagnia di Canto Popolare and Il Canzoniere del Lazio were two such groups. The former was founded in 1968 out of an interest in the blues and protest songs, and when the composer and musicologist Roberto De Simone joined them in 1970 the group developed a specific interest in the musical heritage of Naples and the region of Campania. The Nuova Compagnia di Canto Popolare revived traditional instruments, investigated the phonetics of the local dialect, and adopted various singing

---

[18] Casiccia and Straniero 1975, p. 7.

styles and gestures associated with everyday speech; all this gave rise to a peculiar music occupying a liminal zone between past and present, everyday life and theatre. In 1972 the group appeared at the Spoleto festival with a performance featuring villanelle, laudi and social songs that were no longer in circulation. Four years later, again in Spoleto, they presented the song "La gatta Cenerentola", hailed as their finest achievement. The Canzoniere del Lazio, based on a collaboration between a group of Roman musicians and the literature historian Alessandro Portelli, started out as militants presenting traditional protest material and went on to pursue more wide-ranging research which had much in common with contemporary experiments with rock and jazz.[19]

Third, the experiences represented by Cantacronache and Nuovo Canzoniere Italiano also influenced avant-garde composers. Berio collaborated on the first volume of *Canti sociali italiani* and in 1964 did fieldwork in the Liguria mountains with Roberto Leydi, a fellow pioneer at the electronics studio of the RAI in Milan. That same year he composed the song-cycle *Folk-songs* for voice and instruments featuring elaborations of eleven traditional songs from all over the world. Subsequently, he also composed *Questo vuol dire che...* for voices and tape (1969) with Sandra Mantovani, who had sung lullabies, work songs and Italian ballads with the Nuovo Canzoniere Italiano. Nono also had important contacts with the group. These date back to 1967, when the group decided to include avant-garde compositions in a series of concerts entitled *Altra Italia*, presenting works by Gaslini, Manzoni, Maderna and Nono at the Teatro del Popolo, Milan. The year before Giovanni Pirelli, rebellious son of a big industrialist and head of the Edizioni del Gallo, had collaborated in putting together the text for *A floresta é jovem e cheja de vida* (*The Forest is Young and Full of Life*), a composition dealing with the struggle for liberation that erupted in every part of the globe: in Vietnam, Latin America and Africa, and in the factories of Detroit and Turin, and at the University of California at Berkeley. Then in 1969, for the Edizioni del Gallo record label, Nono brought out the long playing record (LP) *Venezuela in questo momento di guerriglia*, including his *Musica-Manifesto n. 1* (1969). The second part of this work, "Non consumiamo Marx", used graffiti written on Paris walls during the May protests and militant documents produced at the Venice Biennale in

---

[19] Excerpts of the concert given by Nuova Compagnia di Canto Popolare at the Festival dell'Unità, Napoli in 1976 can be seen at www.youtube.com/watch?v=qY2inAEy41Y. A film of the Canzoniere del Lazio is available at www.youtube.com/watch?v=D_JdZQgJzdM.

1968 provided by Guartiero Bertelli, as well as live recordings of demonstrations from the collections of the Istituto De Martino. Nono took a keen interest in the research being carried out by the group and planned a collaboration with Giovanna Marini with the aim of "freeing myself from the traditional type of vocality".[20] In a conversation with Pirelli and two factory workers in Turin, Nono returned to a key question: how to create a sort of 'new folklore', a music linked to work on the shopfloor, the noises of the production line and the spontaneous gestures of mass demonstrations, a music which would replace the instruments of bourgeois culture with voices from real-life situations, loud speakers, metal scaffolding, tin sheets, hooters and other *objets trouvés*.[21] An early impulse for this search, which was to become crucial in Nono's works of the following decades, can be recognised in the exchanges with the multifaceted group of thinkers, writers and musicians gravitating around Il Nuovo Canzoniere Italiano.

Progressive rock and the dialectics of liberation

One particular feature of the Italian popular music scene was that it associated the innovative trends of rock with political issues. This emphasis on the social role of the musician, which, with the exception of a few bands like Matching Mole and Henry Cow, did not characterise the British scene, was fuelled by those responsible for music distribution and promotion. People involved in this sphere were either left wing themselves or, more cynically, saw in the protesting masses an attractive array of potential customers. The juxtaposition of political commitment with music-making, made tangible in the performances and reception of English groups on tour in Italy, emphasised the perception that progressive rock was a sort of *lingua franca* of opposition culture the world over. Unlike folk music, poised precariously between the nostalgic evocation of pristine origins and the formation of a new elite, the rock phenomenon was spontaneous, urban and international.[22] The originality and artistic quality of bands like Premiata Forneria Marconi, Orme, Banco del Mutuo Soccorso, Area, Stormy Six, Arti e Mestieri, Dedalus and Napoli Centrale were the outcome of several

---

[20] See Michele L. Straniero, "Colloquio con Luigi Nono su musica e impegno politico" (con la partecipazione di Gianni Bosio), in *La Musica Popolare* 3 (1976), pp. 7–25; republished in Nono 2001 (Vol. 2), pp. 47–75, quote on p. 65.

[21] See Nono, Pirelli and two workers from Turin 1975 (1971).

[22] See Pintor 1974; Mario Baroni, "La musica e i giovani", in Messinis and Scarnecchia 1977, pp. 146–56; Màdera 1978; and Fiori 1984.

different factors. First, many of the musicians had served an apprenticeship in the recording studios with accompanying pop stars, and some had been through music college. Second, they imported stylistic features and performing techniques from British rock, and had also spent periods in London or Paris, thus experiencing the underground at first hand. Third, they had acquired notions of free jazz and skill in improvisation and they were curious about the output of avant-garde composers, in particular concerning electronic music. Also, in some cases they had made a study of ethnic music from regions of the Mediterranean and the Balkans. These bands received various kinds of promotional support from: the *Festival dell'Avanguardia della Musica e Nuove Tendenze*; the radio programme *Per voi giovani*, which was broadcast each afternoon on the national network; articles in magazines with no political pretensions but wide circulation such as *Ciao 2001*; and journals devoted to experimentation in jazz and rock like *Muzak* and *Gong*. It was also the case that these rock bands were committed to left-wing initiatives: they performed during campaigns in favour of divorce, abortion, liberalising soft drugs, conscientious objection to military service, and at the festivals of l'Unità and New Left organisations, and at student demonstrations and university occupations.

When asked to define the various components of the anti-establishment protest movement, Andrea Valcarenghi coined the term 'youth proletariat'. There were at least three strands in this concept: the way in which Marxism was grafted onto the unrest and aspirations of the generation born in the decade following the Liberation (1945–55); the rise of a social formation which no longer recognised itself in terms of class or cultural level but rather in terms of the rejection of the establishment and consumer society; and a peculiar distillation of disparate trends in revolutionary thought (communism, anarchism, anti-colonialism, Situationism, libertarianism, grass-roots democracy).[23] From 1971 *Re nudo*, the magazine created and directed by Valcarenghi, organised a festival in collaboration with various other groups of the New Left called *Festa del proletariato giovanile*. Most of the progressive rock groups, jazz musicians and *cantautori* then active appeared in one or more of the six branches of this festival. As part of the magazine's activities Gianni Sassi, Sergio Albergoni and Gianni Emilio Simonetti founded a publishing house called Cramps (an acronym from Company Records Advertising Management Production Service). Cramps Records produced a vast repertory of experimental discs ranging from the rock of Area and Arti e Mestieri to the free improvisation of the group Nuova

---

[23] See Valcarenghi 2007 (1973).

Consonanza, to compositions by John Cage, Cornelius Cardew, Walter Marchetti, Paolo Castaldi, Robert Ashley, Alvin Lucier, Steve Lacy and the *Canzoniere del Lazio* as well as the work of the *cantautori* Eugenio Finardi and Alberto Camerini.

Sassi was a man of many facets: he collaborated in a cultural association based in a district of Milan, he founded an advertising company, he was the director of publishing ventures, he organised Fluxus events, he masterminded the image of Cramps and he contributed to the lyrics of songs sung by Area. Simonetti has always been more of an intellectual: his interest in the theory of art and culture was rooted in Fluxus and Situationism but extended to the theories of Adorno and the poststructuralists. In the preface to a book on the new trends in popular music he identified a return to the roots of music as a primordial form of human expression based on "collective cult and dance performance".[24] In this and subsequent passages we can recognise affinities with the essay on rock music Berio had published some years previously, which Simonetti failed to mention. The concept of collage played a key role: "Lastly some pieces (especially recorded works) go beyond the idea of 'song', developing a sort of aural dramaturgy comprising fragments of dialogue, different recordings superimposed on one another, and some electro-acoustic manipulations: in these cases we can talk of 'collage' form".[25] Referring to the same bands Berio cited (i.e. the Beatles, the Mothers of Invention, and the Grateful Dead), Simonetti relates these procedures to a characteristic feature of Dadaism, that is the creation of illusionary spaces. However, he gave a Marxist interpretation of the collage form referring to it as a "rejection of the whole of history, of all alienated reality".[26] The pop avant-garde was thus seen as working towards a deconstruction, which could reveal the mechanisms of the all-prevailing bad faith.

Area set out to jolt people out of their soporific lives by offering a shocking reconfiguration of reality. The cover of their first LP, *Arbeit macht frei* (1973), features a collage of symbols: on the front a row of individuals turned to stone and shut up in space suits, and on the back the entrance to a concentration camp, with Christian and communist symbols and the band members sitting on the ground, one wearing a keffiyeh. The first song, "Luglio, agosto, settembre (nero)", became one of their greatest hits. The title alludes to the terrorist group Black September (named after the massacre of Palestinians expelled from Jordanian territory in September 1970) who broke into the residence of Israeli athletes at the Munich Olympics in 1972 and claimed many victims. At first sight, one

---

[24] See Simonetti, 1973a, 1973b and 1975.   [25] Berio 1967, p. 132.   [26] Simonetti 1973a, p. 14.

might think that the musicians of Area were expressing solidarity with the terrorists, linking the Israelis with the atrocities the Jews themselves had suffered in the not too distant past. Yet one only has to read the texts, which are spoken and sung, to realise that there is much more at stake. The song begins with a woman reciting in Arabic a poem by Rafia Rashed extolling the renunciation of armed combat. The use of a language that was bound to be incomprehensible to most listeners, and the omission of a translation in the LP booklet, are calculated to maintain semantic ambiguity – a device which, from Dadaism onwards, has been a stock in trade to disorient and puzzle the receiver. At the same time, however, the tone of voice in which the poem is recited, recalling an invocation or prayer, may suggest that we are not confronted with a call to violence. In fact the last lines, sung by Demetrio Stratos – "It's not my fault if your reality makes me go to war with humanity" – spell out the true message: the force that has been used to date to destroy people and belongings should be channelled into demolishing the ideology that holds mankind hostage. The form of the piece displays a skilful montage of thirteen different sections, which employs various scales, rhythms and metres that are combined in different ways in each section.[27]

One of the distinctive features of Area is undoubtedly the voice of Stratos. From a background as a pop singer, he went on to experiment with more complex kinds of vocality, influenced by his study of oral traditions in the Mediterranean and the experimental works of avant-garde composers. The encounter with John Cage was particularly important, and he recorded an exemplary version of Cage's *Sixty-two Mesostics Re Merce Cunningham* for Cramps in 1976. The same year his solo album *Metrodora*, a compendium of his research into the potential of the human voice, established him as one of the leading innovators in this field, alongside Cathy Berberian and Michiko Hirayama. Even at this highly abstract level, Stratos never

---

[27] In brief, the thirteen sections of the song "Luglio, agosto, settembre (nero)" may be described as follows: (1) the recitation of the poem is followed by Stratos singing the first vocal theme (first verse) solo to a pentatonic scale; (2) instrumental presentation of a Balkan melody using the set 5-Z12 [0, 1, 3, 5, 6], a subset of the *maqam ajaz*, organised in two cycles of 4/4+2/4+3/8 and 7/4; Gibson Les Paul guitar with Bigsby vibrato tailpiece connected to a VCS3 synth; first cycle, guitar solo; (3) second cycle, tutti; second vocal theme (second verse) using aeolian scale; 2 cycles: 4/4+2/4 + 3/8; reprise of instrumental theme (2 cycles); (4) second vocal theme (third verse) as before; (5) reprise of instrumental theme; (6) second vocal theme (fourth verse) as before; (7) reprise of instrumental theme; (8) instrumental episode in 5/4 + 6/4, using hypodorian scale in a 'call and response' structure; (9) reprise of instrumental theme; 2 cycles with shortened note values; (10) improvisatory section in free metre; (11) re-elaboration of episode; 3+2+3+3+3 +3+3+3/4; accelerando; constructed on the 'call'; (12) reprise of episode: 2 cycles; (13) reprise of instrumental theme.

detached his subtle appraisal of vocal sonorities from a critique of institutions and liberation issues. The record cover bears the statement: "Western vocal hypertrophy has made singers today practically deaf to the different facets of vocality, leaving them walled up in a ghetto of preordained linguistic structures. It's incredibly difficult to go against this process of mummification and wean them off modes of expression which are enshrined in the institutions and culture of the ruling classes." The combination of aleatory performance and political engagement also characterised the concert Area gave in the Aula Magna of the Università Statale, Milan in 1976, in a period when occupiers were often clashing with police. The band performed a version of *Caos*, a piece based on controlled improvisations. The title of the piece refers both to the sound generated and to the revolutionary turmoil of the time. On stage in front of the students, three members of the group plus Steve Lacy and Paul Lytton improvised starting from five pieces of paper bearing the words "hypnosis", "sex", "irony", "silence" and "violence". The concert recording shows how the performance reflected the specific zeitgeist and drew on stimuli and provocations coming from the hall. With performances like these by Area, Italian progressive rock showed its capacity to adapt to highly charged situations of political conflict.

3 | "This Is My Country": American popular music and political engagement in '1968'

SARAH HILL

> To photograph people is to violate them, by seeing them as they never see themselves, by having knowledge of them that they can never have; it turns people into objects that can be symbolically possessed. Just as a camera is a sublimation of the gun, to photograph someone is a subliminal murder – a soft murder, appropriate to a sad, frightened time.[1]

There were many subliminal murders in the US of 1968, startling images of a victim nation shattered by events: Martin Luther King, Jr's body lying dead on a balcony of the Lorraine Motel in Memphis, his friends pointing in the direction from which the fatal bullet was fired; Ambassador Hotel busboy Juan Romero cradling the wounded Robert F. Kennedy in a modern-day *pietà*; the South Vietnamese Police Chief summarily executing a Viet Cong prisoner; and US athletes Tommie Smith and John Carlos giving the Black Power salute from the podium at the Mexico City Olympics. "Photographs depict a moment but they can *contain* years"[2] and there were many such moments, each one carrying the burden of history. There was also the soundtrack of the time: music reflecting the hope invested in two fallen American public figures, the condemnation of America's military engagement in Southeast Asia, the demand for an end to the oppression of the black communities at home. In this chapter I consider three elements of that soundtrack – folk, soul, rock; their different interpretations of 'protest', and their distinct legacies in the 'long 1968'.

Given the many political and social upheavals of 1968, it is perhaps surprising that remarkably little direct protest emerged from the US that year; rather there are gestures towards message, sonic signifiers of unrest and a foreshadowing of confrontations ahead. There were continued tensions arising from racial unrest, police aggression on peaceful (and non-peaceful) demonstrations against the war and the long final years of the Vietnam conflict. In some ways the obvious culmination of these moments was the Woodstock Festival in 1969. For three days the many

---

[1] Sontag 1979, pp. 14–15. [2] Dyer 2010, p. 9

counter-cultural and mainstream factions were united in fusions of musical style, sartorial statement and straightforward protest. Consider the following: Richie Havens bringing the sound of Greenwich Village folk clubs draped in a *dashiki*; Sly and the Family Stone fusing soul with San Francisco psychedelia; Jimi Hendrix bringing the noise of war to the waning Monday-morning crowd: three disparate, powerful and resonant performances, each carrying messages of politics, ideology and lifestyle from the 1960s into the unknown of the 1970s.

In terms of American political life, 1968 has almost mythical resonance. The year of a presidential election is always fraught with partisan tension and general public activism, but the path to this particular showdown bears some exploration. The events which unfolded during the early months of 1968 – the assassinations of Martin Luther King, Jr on 4 April and Senator Robert F. Kennedy on 5 June; the student protests at Columbia University in April and May – were manifestations of much larger social unrest. There were 486,000 American troops in Vietnam at the beginning of 1968. By the end of 1968 the total number of American combat deaths over the conflict's first seven years had exceeded 30,000. The impact of the war in Vietnam on nearly every facet of American cultural life was enormous: the presidential race, the draft, racial unrest, the image of America at home and abroad, were all coloured to some degree by the desire for an end to the conflict. Yet during the presidential campaign, the Republican and Democratic challengers' alternatives to President Lyndon Johnson's Vietnam strategy did little to address the need for domestic stability, and less to resolve the war.

Many Americans had faith in the rightness of American foreign policy, though by 1968 that was beginning to falter, and the more general anger felt towards the war in Vietnam was soon undeniable and vehement. The cost of the conflict, measured in dollars spent and in human lives sacrificed, increased as the 1960s turned into the 1970s – military and civilian deaths, prisoners of war, American soldiers missing in action – and by the end of 1968 half of the population personally knew an American casualty.[3] More vital to the public's shifting opinions of the Vietnam War was the fact that it was the first military conflict seen on American television.[4] Although at first

---

[3] Military records and casualty statistics are on the National Archives and Records Administration website (archives.gov/research/military/vietnam-war/casualty-statistics.html, accessed January 2012).

[4] There had been televised reporting of the Korean War (1950–3), but the percentage of the US population with televisions in their homes was significantly lower then than it was during the Vietnam conflict.

coverage focused primarily on the bravery of the American soldiers and presented a positive spin on the action, by 1968 the reporting became rather starker. While still broadcasting very little blood and gore, there were occasional glimpses of both that did little to improve the public's waning tolerance for war. In 1968, for example, viewers of NBC News saw the South Vietnamese National Police Chief, Nguyen Ngoc Loan, seemingly casually execute a Viet Cong prisoner, the still image of which earned photographer Eddie Adams the Pulitzer Prize.

The primary action of the Vietnam War in 1968 was the Tet Offensive. Despite a negotiated ceasefire for the period of the Vietnamese New Year (Tet) the Viet Cong launched a series of surprise attacks on towns and cities in South Vietnam.[5] The heavy fighting required of American military forces was such that the American people were confronted with a different truth. Reporting the Tet Offensive, CBS News anchorman Walter Cronkite, 'the most trusted man in America', was moved to declare in an editorial broadcast on 27 February 1968 that the US was "mired in stalemate" in Vietnam. Although merely a reflection of the general American sentiment, the uttering of such a view to a national audience forced President Johnson to realise that his reelection would be impossible. Indeed, the growing pressure on Johnson from within the Democratic Party led him to declare in a televised speech on 31 March:

I shall not seek, and I will not accept, the nomination of my party for another term as your president. But let men everywhere know, however, that a strong and a confident and a vigilant America stands ready tonight to seek an honorable peace, and stands ready tonight to defend an honored cause, whatever the price, whatever the burden, whatever the sacrifice that duty may require.[6]

The "honored cause" and "the sacrifice that duty may require" were perpetuated by Johnson's announcement in the same speech of a de-escalation of bombardment in North Vietnam, and his decision to send 13,000 more American troops to, and invest $2.5 billion more in, South Vietnam. Though Johnson was ostensibly continuing with his predecessor John F. Kennedy's policies, his popularity nonetheless suffered because of events in Southeast Asia. The series of challenges to Johnson's authority in the Democratic Party – the elevation of Eugene McCarthy and Robert F. Kennedy to potential nominees – no doubt precipitated Johnson's decision, but the clear and articulated shift in public perception of the rightness of

---

[5] For more on the Tet Offensive see Barley Norton's Chapter 6 in this volume.
[6] Quoted in Witcover 1997, p. 142.

American action led ultimately to the election of Richard M. Nixon in November 1968 and a further escalation of the conflict in Vietnam.

While before 1968 musical commentary on war – the second world war, Korea – was satirical, and occasionally brutal, by 1968 such commentary became starker, angrier and more direct. Yet despite the continued output by some of the stalwarts of the genre, by 1968 the very purpose of the 'protest song' was in dispute:

If there is anything definite that can be said about today's music, it is that the old-fashioned protest song has been junked, relegated to the god-forsaken past. There is a reason for that: protest songs, when they were bad, were preaching songs, instant pulpit [...] They refused to allow the listener to make any decisions; they took away his freedom by telling him that if he liked the song he was right, and if he didn't like it he was wrong. There isn't any way one can talk about 'digging' a protest song – first off, you had to *agree* with it. That style made 'content' obnoxious, and it still does.[7]

This can be seen in the distinctions between the 'folk' and 'rock' interpretations of, and engagement with, 'the protest song'. First there is the larger folk community, symbolised here by Pete Seeger, whose contribution to general 1960s anti-war sentiment was his song "Waist Deep in the Big Muddy", a cautionary tale in which misguided leadership on military manoeuvres in 1941 is evoked with reference to a non-specific contemporary military adventure.[8] This strand of folk protest was carried through the 1960s by singers such as Joan Baez and Phil Ochs, and was represented at the Woodstock Festival in 1969 by, among others, Richie Havens and Country Joe McDonald. These latter two musicians, though sharing a similar politics, and appearing at Woodstock in the singer-and-acoustic-guitar guise of the traditional protest singer, nonetheless offer distinctive approaches to the idea of a 'protest song'. Havens' performance of "Handsome Johnny" is somewhat more aligned with Seeger's "Waist Deep", and gives a similar sense of historical inevitability.[9] In the song, Handsome Johnny marches to the battlefields of Concord, Gettysburg, Dunkirk, Korea, Vietnam and Birmingham, with a varying array of weaponry. Yet after these invocations of historical battles at home and abroad,

---

[7] Marcus 1969, p. 90

[8] As a narrative, "Waist Deep in the Big Muddy" can be used to protest almost any military action which is perceived to be haphazard or poorly planned: "Now I'm not going to paint any moral / I'll leave that for yourself / [...] / But every time I read the papers, that old feeling comes on / We're waist deep in the Big Muddy and the big fool says to push on" (Seeger 1967).

[9] "Handsome Johnny" (Lou Gossett/Louis Gossett, Jr/Richie Havens) was released on Havens' *Mixed Bag* (Havens 1968).

the futility of the exercise and the inevitability of more war to come leads Havens to admonish: "What's the use of singing this song? Some of you are not even listening." The simplicity of the form and the message, and the directness of the address, are a contrast to Seeger's longer-winded narrative, but the intent is the same. By contrast, Country Joe McDonald's performance of "I-Feel-Like-I'm-Fixin'-To-Die Rag" brought to the Woodstock stage the specificities of the Vietnam conflict in a raucous, communal singalong.[10] The song's undeniable humour and musical style, more music hall than dustbowl ballad, distinguishes it from 'old-fashioned protest songs', enabling the late-1960s audience to 'dig' the message, in Greil Marcus' terms, as footage of the Woodstock Festival will attest.

If the point of a protest song was to get an audience to 'dig' it, then propounding political sentiment in the mainstream charts would be one method of attack. So in 1968 the 'rock' response to the war was represented by the Doors' "The Unknown Soldier" and Creedence Clearwater Revival's "Fortunate Son".[11] Again, there is a distinction of lyrical approach and musical intent. The Doors opt for lyrical allusion and direct sonic imagery – sounds of marching and gunfire interrupt a series of pithy, and somewhat banal, verses mourning another statistic in a faraway conflict. Creedence Clearwater Revival's "Fortunate Son", by contrast, exposes the inherent inequities in American society – wealthy sons 'born into' the presidency, dodging taxes, avoiding conscription yet demanding the ultimate sacrifice of those less privileged.[12]

---

[10] Originally written in 1965, "I-Feel-Like-I'm-Fixin'-to-Die Rag" (lyrics by Joe McDonald) was released on *I-Feel-Like-I'm-Fixin'-to-Die* (Country Joe and the Fish 1967).

[11] The Doors, "The Unknown Soldier" (lyrics by John Densmore, Robby Krieger, Ray Manzarek and Jim Morrison), in *Waiting for the Sun* (Doors 1968); Creedence Clearwater Revival, "Fortunate Son" (lyrics by John Fogerty), from *Willy and the Poor Boys* (Creedence Clearwater Revival 1969). Both of these songs charted on the US Top 40, "The Unknown Soldier" peaking at 39, "Fortunate Son" at 14.

[12] "Fortunate Son" has enjoyed a longer lifespan despite, and perhaps because of, its association with the Vietnam War. In US presidential elections since 1996 the candidates' military service has been a contentious, and central, topic: Bill Clinton was accused of dodging the Vietnam draft; Al Gore, a 'senator's son', enrolled in the Army and eventually served in Vietnam; George W. Bush, a congressman's son, in 1968 secured a six-year period of service in the Texas Air National Guard, which became an oft-debated issue during the 2004 presidential race, as his opponent was John Kerry, whose active duty from 1966 earned him the Silver Star, the Bronze Star, and three Purple Hearts; in the 2008 presidential election, Barack Obama, one of very few US presidents not to have served military duty, beat John McCain, a former prisoner of war in Vietnam. The degrees to which these candidates' military service has been invoked, either positively or negatively, has reflected the changing political climate in the US. Given the chronological distance from the Vietnam War, it is likely at the time of writing that the 2012 presidential election will be the first contest in nearly seventy years when neither candidate will be a veteran of the US armed forces.

To suggest that the 'protest song' was facing a crisis in 1968 is to forget that the symbolic space occupied by Pete Seeger and the 'traditional' folk music scene had of course been challenged earlier in the decade by Bob Dylan, when he 'went electric' at the Newport Folk Festival in 1965. It is Dylan's 'next step' that represents the first of three genres I wish to consider here.

'The old, weird America'[13]

The folk revival in the US was inseparable from leftist politics.[14] In the early 1960s the earnest participation of singers like Pete Seeger and Joan Baez in civil rights rallies was customary, the communal singing of "We Shall Overcome" inevitable, and the adoption by the movement of songs such as "Blowin' in the Wind" seemingly natural. The rhetoric of protest songs was clear, and the delivery unencumbered by technology: a 'protest song' in the early 1960s was often signified by the simple presence of a singer and his or her guitar.

But by mid-decade the impulse to 'protest' had fractured. The Civil Rights Act of 1964, while in no way complete or comprehensive, nonetheless caused a certain cessation of musical messages on behalf of the struggle. That is to say, the predominantly white protest singers who spoke for the voiceless in mainstream American culture were ultimately superseded by the end of the decade by those whose authority came from within the community. The direction that 'black' music took from that point onwards is perhaps the more enduring sound of the 1960s and will be explored further below.

Joan Baez and Phil Ochs, two singer-songwriters who remained entrenched in 'protest' throughout the 1960s, both released albums in 1968, but found the reception to their work in the new political and social climate somewhat muted. Baez released two records in 1968, *Baptism: A Journey through our Time* and *Any Day Now*.[15] The former was an anti-war concept album of sorts (praised as "a magnificent and impassioned out-cry against the ravages of war, violence and the insanity of spilled blood").[16]

---

[13] This is the term coined in Marcus 1997: "Once the poet Kenneth Rexroth was looking for a phrase to describe the country he thought lay behind Carl Sandburg's work [...] Rexroth came up with 'the old free America'." Marcus states that as he listened to Harry Smith's *Anthology of American Folk Music* he took the phrase "to name the territory that opens up out of the Anthology [...] The old, weird America is what one finds here – not Rexroth's rebuke to his readers, but an inheritance Smith's listeners might prefer to claim had reached them by mistake" (Marcus 1997, p. 89).

[14] See Denisoff 1973. [15] Baez 1968a and 1968b. [16] Grissim 1968, p 30.

The latter was a collection of Bob Dylan covers, both determinedly rooted in the political sentiments of the time. Phil Ochs ended a period of personal reflection and professional uncertainty in 1968 with *Tape from California*,[17] an attempt to prove himself more than just "an old protest-singer".[18] That label, 'protest singer', had by 1968 become a marker of regression.

Yet the very idea of 'protest' is a mutable one, and one which had been the topic of many commentators on popular music throughout the 1960s. As one example, Ralph J. Gleason was the long-standing jazz critic for the *San Francisco Chronicle*. He used his *Chronicle* columns throughout the 1960s to comment on the gulf between mainstream society and the 'underground' scenes he witnessed – jazz, political comedy, psychedelia – and served as a voice of reason in the often overwhelmingly conservative attempts to condemn them. In his column of 27 May 1968 Gleason attempted to demarcate genre boundaries:

> Jazz music was one of the first mass dissents from the patriarchal society we have devised in which everyone is treated like a child [...] After the jazzman, whose dissent was, in the main, an attitude and a stance rather than verbal (jazzmen in the past were notoriously a-political, for instance, though now that is changing) the New Youth of the rock generation came along and made the dissent quite verbal indeed. The rock dissent was much more effective than the jazz dissent because the Rock Generation turned on its elders and seized the market (and some of the means of production) and made popular music [...] into literature, communication and art as well as a tool of revolution.[19]

This excerpt is notable for its concise summation of the relationship between politics and music, and the differing tenses Gleason uses to discuss jazz (present: "now that is changing") and rock (past: "the rock generation [...] made the dissent quite verbal"). The problems inherent in any discussion of 'jazz dissent' are discussed below; what is important to qualify first here is that Gleason is writing about 'the rock generation' in the widest possible sense: the "New Youth of the rock generation" is, presumably, early-1960s-era Bob Dylan. When Gleason wrote this post, Dylan had just released *John Wesley Harding*,[20] a change in his musical direction following a period of self-imposed exile in Woodstock, New York. Whereas Bob Dylan's early songs had spoken to agents in the civil rights and anti-war movements, his 'turn' towards electric rock in albums such as *Highway 61 Revisited* and *Blonde on Blonde* had signalled his definitive disconnection with politics. *John Wesley Harding*, released at the height of psychedelia,

---

[17] Ochs 1968.   [18] See Anonymous 1968c, p 4.   [19] Gleason 1968.   [20] Dylan 1968.

bore no resemblance to the popular lysergic sound, and seemingly no overt political content, though naturally content was found where content was sought:[21]

"Drifter's Escape" [*John Wesley Harding*, track 6] is a weird Kafkaesque judgment. Dylan, as ever, catches the exact pulse of these days – just as with "The Times They Are A-Changing" and *Highway 61*. Here is the nation, as its own jury and judge, and the Trial has commenced. The Vietnam War, symbolised in the court and its process, has a personal and national level: "help me in my weakness" for "my time it isn't long". The choice is there [...] The choice is Black and White [...] Good and Evil exist only on Man's terms.[22]

Reading the lyrics to "Drifters' Escape" today, it is difficult to see where the Vietnam War fits into the narrative. Dylan seems rather to be paring down his lines, rhymes and phrases to something akin to the 'traditional' American folk song, or the long ballad tradition brought to Appalachia from the UK. Lyrically and musically, it is this shift towards 'Americana' – a stripped-down, unadorned production, a return to musical and lyrical roots – which was the more radical message, and which dictated another new direction in popular music even among psychedelic champions. The reference point for this is the series of recordings that Dylan made with The Band in Woodstock in late 1967, which circulated for many years as bootlegs before being released formally as *The Basement Tapes*.[23]

Cover versions of songs from *The Basement Tapes* bootlegs found their way onto the US and UK charts in 1968 – Manfred Mann's "The Mighty Quinn" and Julie Driscoll and Brian Auger's "This Wheel's On Fire" were Top 10 hits on both sides of the Atlantic – but the connection between Dylan's songs and earlier models is the important thing to note here. One of the primary sources to influence the 1950s folk music revival and the 1960s generation of rock musicians was Harry Smith's *Anthology of American Folk Music*.[24] For some in the 1960s, Smith's *Anthology* was a point of clarity in a period of uncertainty. According to Greil Marcus:

As a nation at war both at home and abroad, the U.S.A. was a faith and a riddle in 1967 [...] It took faith to solve the riddle: in the basement you could believe in the future only if you could believe in the past, and you could believe in the past only if you could touch it, mold it like the clay from which the past had molded you, change

---

[21] Indeed, one may argue that Dylan's silence following his motorcycle accident in 1966 mythologised his position as 'political spokesman' more than any recording. I am grateful to Lee Marshall for his insights into this period of Dylan's career.
[22] Mills 1968, p. 21.   [23] Dylan and The Band 1975.   [24] Smith 1952.

it. You could believe in the past only if you could reenact it. The present, the historical present, was meaningless.²⁵

There is a clear and direct lineage from Smith's *Anthology* to *The Basement Tapes*, yet situating *The Basement Tapes* in the continuum of American mythology invests in the collection a centrality surely unintended in the actual recording sessions themselves. But Marcus has argued persuasively that:

> So much of the basement tapes [sic] are the purest free speech: simple free speech, ordinary free speech, nonsensical free speech, not heroic free speech. Cryptic free speech, and thus what Raymond Chandler described as "the American voice": "flat, toneless, and tiresome" [...] a voice that can say almost anything while seeming to say almost nothing, in secret, with music that as it was made presumed no audience but its players and perhaps its ancestors, a secret public.²⁶

John Wesley Harding, *The Basement Tapes* and The Band's *Music from Big Pink*²⁷ captured the moment in popular music when musical style became the message. Though there was very little overtly political about any of this music, the suggestion of 'Americana' was significant in itself.²⁸ The instant familiarity of the musical form, and the potential for that form to transcend political moment and chronological time, create an almost instant nostalgia. Such nostalgia can be heard as evocative of a simpler age, but it can also be heard as a general sonic slate clearing. Psychedelia, as one 'sound of the 60s', was an expansion beyond musical reality, utilising in some instances the studio to affect an alternate consciousness, in some instances reflecting subjective consciousness through lyrics, or sonic experimentation. But to strip psychedelia of its embroidered effects would be to reveal an otherwise obvious structure – a blues standard, or a simple verse-chorus form: a return to simplicity, not terribly far removed from the Americana of Dylan and The Band – in a sense, a musical evocation of President Johnson's "strong, confident and vigilant America".

"Say It Loud..."

Johnson's "strong, confident and vigilant America" had its representations in other genres as well, to different effect. In 'black music' especially, 1968

---

²⁵ Marcus 1997, p. 70–1. ²⁶ Marcus 1997, p. 222. ²⁷ The Band 1968.
²⁸ And it is perhaps significant that of the primary progenitors of this Americana, four of those 'American voices' (Rick Danko, Garth Hudson, Richard Manuel and Robbie Robertson of The Band) were in fact Canadian.

provides a vital reference point. The musical expressions of shock rippling through the black community in the wake of the assassinations of Martin Luther King, Jr and Robert F. Kennedy – two central civil rights figures killed within two months of each other – provide a route map towards understanding, if not acceptance. Such music sought to unite the community at this testing moment, and continues to resonate today; indeed, the legacy of 1968 is audible in everything from funk to rap.

The assassination of Martin Luther King, Jr on 4 April 1968 further fractured an already splintering community. King's death had obvious and brutal repercussions in the wider culture, of course, and for the non-politically engaged audiences of rhythm and blues (R&B), jazz and other popular musics, the wave of riots and social unrest left nowhere to hide. Two musical moments reflect this: first, the concert given by James Brown at the Boston Garden on 5 April 1968; and second, the concert given by Nina Simone at the Westbury Music Fair on 7 April 1968, recorded and released as the album, 'Nuff Said.[29]

James Brown's concert the night following Martin Luther King's assassination was a complicated affair. In the immediate aftermath of the assassination riots broke out in over 100 US cities. The city officials perceived that the many thousands of people who were expected – largely from the black community in Roxbury – at the Boston Garden could either enjoy a night's entertainment, or create a riot of their own. Cancelling the concert would have resulted in other problems. If James Brown arrived in Boston only to find that his concert had been cancelled, he would have demanded compensation for lost earnings, and if the black community had heard that the (almost exclusively) white city fathers had cancelled the concert for fear of violence, violence would have ensued. The mayor's solution was to broadcast the concert live on local television station WGBH, thus effectively encouraging the black population of the greater Boston area to stay at home, and offering ticket holders refunds. James Brown arrived in Boston completely unaware of any of these arrangements, and was not immediately amenable to the suggestion that he donate his night's work to an empty house and a free television audience. The necessary financial agreements having been reached, the concert went ahead, thus averting the kind of destruction in Boston that had befallen other cities.[30]

---

[29] Simone 1968.
[30] It should also be noted that James Brown's concert was rebroadcast on two television stations and a radio station directly following the initial telecast.

Footage of the concert shows a certain level of tension, with Brown defusing potentially volatile situations with simple pleas for respect and understanding. Brown was never considered a politically engaged performer, or a proponent of non-violence, but in the wake of this concert, a certain weight of expectation fell on him. Despite his deepening engagement with the black communities of the US, some of his subsequent public appearances, such as those in support of the Democratic presidential candidate, Hubert Humphrey, caused a degree of friction between Brown and outspoken groups such as the Black Panthers. He responded by releasing "Say It Loud – I'm Black and I'm Proud",[31] one attempt at raising consciousness through music.

Recorded live in performance a mere three days after King's assassination, 'Nuff Said almost demands to be heard through the filter of loss. Nina Simone had sung of earlier tragedies – "Mississippi Goddam" being the most notable example[32] – but her plaintive "Why? (The King of Love Is Dead)" drove without anger to the centre of the community's enormous loss, posing a very simple question – "what will happen now that the King is dead" – about the fate of the black community.[33] Her performance of "Ain't Got No – I Got Life", two songs from the contemporary Broadway musical, Hair, carries a different significance.[34] The first mainstream 'rock' musical, Hair was ostensibly a cash-in of the hippie counterculture, celebrating the anti-war, draft-dodging, sexually liberated drop-out lifestyle of a 'tribe' of young people in New York. In her medley Simone strips the songs of any countercultural intent and instead provides a message of empowerment in a time of struggle.[35] "Ain't Got No" demarcates absence: "ain't got no home ... shoes ... money ... class ... mother ... culture ... god ..." – in its original context a laundry-list of the tangible goods rejected in the adoption of the hippie lifestyle. In Simone's performance,

---

[31] Brown 1968.

[32] "Mississippi Goddam" was written as a response to the racist murders of civil rights activist Medgar Evers in June 1963 and the bombing of the 16th Street Baptist Church in Birmingham, Alabama in September 1963. Simone performed the song at Carnegie Hall in 1964, declaring it to be "a show tune, but the show hasn't been written for it yet", bringing the audience subtly and ever deeper into the mire of racial politics in the US.

[33] For more on Nina Simone and cultural politics see Feldstein 2005 and Kernodle 2008.

[34] Hair (book and lyrics by James Rado and Gerome Ragni; music by Galt MacDermot), opened on Broadway in April 1968. It ran for 1,750 performances, and has enjoyed an astonishingly long afterlife in revivals, tours, and the 1979 film, directed by Milos Forman.

[35] It should be noted that Simone's performance of "Ain't Got No – I Got Life" was recorded in the studio; whether she performed the medley at the Westbury Music Fair is not certain, but the version released on 'Nuff Said is cross-faded with applause, suggesting that it should be heard as an integral part of the performance.

it becomes a statement of historical inequity. Then "I Got Life" becomes a rallying cry, a statement of pride: "Got my hair ... head ... brains ... heart ... soul ... sex". In its original context the closing refrain, "I've got life/I've got my freedom", is a clear statement of the 'hippie' ethos; in Simone's voice, a statement of defiance in the face of senseless violence.

Nina Simone was as aware as anyone of the more militant counterpart to Martin Luther King's non-violent protest, and *'Nuff Said*, in some regards, shows her own politics on the verge of a more radical direction. By 1968 the idea of 'Black Power' was very much in the public consciousness. Stokely Carmichael had coined the term in 1966 as a counter to King's peaceful non-violence. By opting instead for more direct confrontations Carmichael spoke for a new generation of activists, and influenced in no small way the 1966 formation of the Black Panther Party,[36] branded in 1968 by the US Federal Bureau of Investigation (FBI) Director J. Edgar Hoover as "the greatest threat to internal security of the United States".

But to suggest that Black Power emerged suddenly and unexpectedly is to suppose that the passage of civil rights legislation during the Johnson administration was sufficient to address the historical problems of race relations in the US. As Carmichael said in 1966, "Every civil rights bill in this country was passed for white people".[37] The supposition that popular music could or would be conciliatory when its surrounding culture was not, is therefore a misguided one. For in the immediate aftermath of Martin Luther King's assassination Carmichael told members of the press:

When white America killed Dr. King last night, she declared war on us. There will be no crying and there will be no funeral [...] The kind of man that killed Dr. King last night made it a whole lot easier for a whole lot of black people today. There no longer needs to be intellectual discussion. Black people know that they have to get guns. White America will live to cry since she killed Dr. King last night.[38]

Foregoing "intellectual discussion" does not preclude propounding ideology through popular music. It is therefore important to consider the direction that soul music took from this moment, virtually from the release of James Brown's "Say It Loud – I'm Black and I'm Proud", a song that can certainly be interpreted as carrying the message of Black Power.

---

[36] The Black Panthers equated the "racist war of genocide in Vietnam" with the "terror, brutality, murder, and repression of black people" in the US. See Bingham 2009, p. 62–5.

[37] Quoted in Lester 1969, p. 12.   [38] Quoted in Jaffe and Sherwood 1994, p. 74.

As with the divisions between 'black' and 'white' cultures in 1968, there were also divisions within black music. Motown, for example, continued to release singles aimed at the mainstream music charts,[39] while Stax Records was entering a difficult phase of administrative and financial difficulty.[40] Yet there are many examples of bands that recorded for either Motown or Stax, or neither, whose social conscience became a central focus of their music in the aftermath of 1968. The Chambers Brothers' 1968 release, "Time Has Come Today" is one such example.[41] A clear departure from their gospel and folk roots, "Time Has Come Today" established a fusion of soul and psychedelic rock, with a clear message – "my soul has been psychedelicised" – which was reflected in the aural trappings of West Coast 'hippie music', and which prefigured the kind of multiracial genre-crossing embodied by Sly and the Family Stone. The Staple Singers' 1968 release, *Soul Folk in Action*, is significant for the inclusion of songs such as "Long Walk to D.C." and "People, My People" which relay a very clear message to the black community; and their recording of The Band's "The Weight" returns that song's Americana to its gospel root.[42]

In this category of musicians must be included Curtis Mayfield and the Impressions, who gained mainstream recognition in 1968 with the album *This Is My Country*.[43] Its title track is a quiet plea in a time of upheaval, a sorrowful snapshot of inner city life. Mayfield's admonitions – "and I know you will give consideration/Shall we perish unjust or live equal as a nation/This is my country" – are in one sense an awkward attempt at provoking thought and mindful action. He is not capturing the contemporary vernacular of the streets in the way that James Brown did; Mayfield's gentle tenor does not carry the anger and urgency of Simone's alto. Rather, Mayfield and the Impressions are grasping at that mythical 'America' which was being excoriated in 'folk' music for its military aggression. This is an attempt at unifying the nation, much in the spirit of King's integrationist

---

[39] Marvin Gaye's "I Heard it Through the Grapevine" and Diana Ross and the Supremes' "Love Child" were both released in 1968.

[40] Isaac Hayes' late-60s recordings uncovered a musical seam which fused funk with Black Consciousness, and signalled a new direction in the Stax output.

[41] "Time Has Come Today" (music by Joe and Willie Chambers), from *The Time Has Come* (The Chambers Brothers 1967).

[42] Stevie Wonder, once the original Motown *wunderkind*, is perhaps the clearest example of soul music nurturing its activist roots in 'the long 1968'. His extraordinary output in the 1970s includes the albums *Talking Book* (Wonder 1972), *Innervisions* (Wonder 1973) and *Fulfillingness' First Finale* (Wonder 1974), each with their deeply insightful commentary on life in post-1968 black America. See in particular "Big Brother" from *Talking Book*, "Living for the City" from *Innervisions* and "You Haven't Done Nothing" from *Fulfillingness' First Finale*.

[43] The Impressions 1968.

approach, rather than via the Panthers' revolutionary activism.[44] But the all-embracing title, "This Is My Country" is not a statement of ownership as much as it is a recognition of the manifold difficulties of the past, present and future of American society.

If 'ownership' was ever an issue in general national discourse, it is surely embodied by the outward expressions of allegiance to the flag, and of patriotism. These ideas were challenged in 1968 by the supreme 'Black Power moment' of cultural memory: the bold gesture made by athletes Tommie Smith and John Carlos on the winners' podium at the Mexico City Olympics. The symbology of the moment – the raised fist, the defiant stance, the references to Africa – is deeply significant.[45] Its otherness, evoked in much contemporary black music, engendered the development of rap with its continued challenges to mainstream white society.[46]

To trace the idea of a musical 'challenge' back to an earlier moment, Nina Simone's placement in pop music history is fused not only with her political activism, but also with her connection to the broader history of black music, notably old-guard jazz. The history of jazz is inextricable from the history of race relations in the US; as such, its canon is riddled with difficulties. The evolution of avant-garde jazz, from the release of Ornette Coleman's *Free Jazz* (1960), through the fusion of jazz and ethnic musics later in the decade, coincided with many of the struggles of the civil rights movement.[47] But Ralph Gleason's suggestion above, that the new jazz provided its own soundscape of dissent, still raised the question of what the 'new jazz' actually represented:

[The] new jazz is being used as a forum for protest of the strongest kind – complete secession. In addition, avant-garde jazz is proving to be a fountainhead of

---

[44] The history and legacy of the Black Panther Party is deserving of much more than a mere footnote, but their ideology can be summarised by their ten-point plan, which demanded, in part: freedom, full employment, decent housing, decent education "that teaches our true history", free health care, "an immediate end to police brutality and murder of black people", an end to wars of aggression, freedom to all prisoners and "people's community control of modern technology". See Bingham 2009, p. 35.

[45] As a result of their Black Power salute the athletes were reprimanded by the International Olympic Committee, and expelled from the Games.

[46] It is important here to note the formation of The Last Poets in 1968. Along with Gil Scott-Heron, The Last Poets are often cited as the progenitors of rap. Certainly their alliance with the black nationalist movement of the 1960s informed much of their output, and even a cursory note of the song titles on their debut album, *The Last Poets* (1970), proves an engagement with the problems of the community which would later be continued in the 'message rap' of groups such as Public Enemy.

[47] Space limitations prevent a thorough discussion of the emergence and evolution of avant-garde jazz. For background and insight see Litweiler 1984 and Wilmer 1992.

secessionist jargon, a jargon which is the essence of the 'black power' concept [...] The musical sounds of protest by this new breed of [avant-garde jazz] musicians are many and varied [...] To what extent they represent and symbolise the feeling, thought, and mood of the new generation of American Negroes is still problematic. But the avant-garde jazz musician just may be the revolutionary intellectual communicating to all who have ears to hear.[48]

The same can be said of any of the 'protest musics' at issue here. Claiming to represent the 'feeling, thought and mood' of any community is a bold and contentious thing to do; the greater action is to support such claims with tangible work.

The founding of collectives such as the Association for the Advancement of Creative Musicians in Chicago in 1965 was a significant step in training young musicians in the community and encouraging local culture.[49] Similarly, the Black Artists Group, founded in St Louis in 1968 and funded by the National Endowment of the Arts, was another attempt at securing the furtherance of the music. The directions that some of the central figures of these organisations took in the 1970s provides a catalogue of innovations, but the tensions within this movement bear some discussion. If the jazz avant-garde is considered "an example of black cultural autonomy", it must be noted that it was nonetheless still embedded in the white-owned music industry; and, as Brian Ward has noted, even though "cultural nationalists drooled over Coltrane's *Africa/Brass* album as a sign of his return to roots,[50] few noted that he was at least as interested in and influenced by Indian music, and [...] modern classical experiments in serialism and atonality".[51]

These references to serialism and atonality are perhaps shorthand to some ears for 'noise' and 'inaccessibility'. But such shorthand is also a means of connecting jazz to the shifting sounds of mainstream rock music, for rock music at the end of the 1960s was nothing if not loud, and it is rock's trajectory out of 1968 which I now wish to follow.

"This Holocaust of the Decibels"

To consider the developments in rock music in 1968 it is necessary to return to another scene of protest. The Democratic National Convention, held on

---

[48] Miller and Skipper, Jr, 1972, pp. 34, 36.
[49] For a comprehensive history of the Association for the Advancement of Creative Musicians, see Lewis 2008.
[50] John Coltrane Quartet 1961. [51] Ward 1998, p. 410.

26–9 August, could have been a dull and predictable affair, were it not for the volatile combination of the Youth International Party (Yippies), the Chicago Police, the Illinois National Guard and Mayor Richard J. Daley.

The Yippies caused no end of controversy in the months preceding the Chicago convention, on both sides of the political divide.[52] From their inaugural press conference in May 1968 to the Chicago Seven trial in 1969 the Yippies engendered disbelief, scorn and support in almost equal measure. Their plans for the convention itself – a Festival of Life – were advertised with a host of famous names promised as entertainment. The tens of thousands of young persons that the Yippies predicted would descend upon Chicago for the Festival of Life never materialised, but those who did travel to Chicago were alternately denied permits to march or to demonstrate, and summarily beaten by law enforcement officials in full view of convention delegates and the news media. If the general public perception of America's engagement in Southeast Asia was beginning to falter, the scenes of carnage in Chicago which accompanied news from the Convention brought the war home to middle America.

The great chronicler of the event was Norman Mailer. As 'the reporter', he describes at length the sound of one of the many ad hoc protests which took place in Chicago that week:

[a] young white singer with a cherubic face was taking off on an interplanetary, then galactic, flight of song ... his sound an electric caterwauling of power come out of the wall ... screaming up to a climax of vibrations like one rocket blasting out of itself .... And the reporter, caught in the din ... knew this was some variety of true song for the Hippies and adolescents in the house, in this enclave of grass and open air ... these painted dirty under-twenties were monsters, and yet, still clinging to recognition in the experience, he knew they were a generation which lived in the sound of destruction of all order as he had known it...; there was the sound of mountains crashing in this holocaust of the decibels, hearts bursting ... discords vibrating, electric crescendo screaming ... and the reporter as affected by the sound ... as if he had heard it in a room at midnight with painted bodies and kaleidoscopic sights ...[53]

The assumption here is that Mailer stumbled upon a performance by Detroit's MC5, whose live performances represented the antithesis of the gentle hippie ethos of some contemporary folk music,[54] and an unexpected alignment with radical black ideology. Indeed, Mailer's near-psychedelic

---

[52] For an insight into contemporary Yippie ideology, see Rubin 1970.
[53] Mailer 1968, pp. 142–3.
[54] The MC5's debut album, *Kick Out the Jams* (MC5 1969) was recorded live in October 1968.

epiphany suggests another cultural tension of the time. The hippies, in the West Coast sense of the word, were not a politically minded culture. The general trend towards protest in the 1960s was certainly embraced by the student and radical communities of cities such as Berkeley, but the 'hippie music' of the kind Mailer evokes here – "painted bodies and kaleidoscopic sights" such as those in the storied Acid Tests of the middle of the decade – was decidedly on the wane by 1968.[55] The Yippies and the MC5, while advocating some of the tenets of the peaceful counterculture – LSD, free love – were more closely aligned with its radical fringe. The MC5's sonic assault on contemporary popular music, and their ideological ties to the Yippies and the Black Panthers, bears some investigation here.[56]

In early publicity campaigns, MC5 manager John Sinclair made bold statements about the band's programme, their "cultural revolution through a total assault on the culture":

I heard Stokely Carmichael in 1966 call for "20 million arrogant black men" as America's salvation, and there are a lot of arrogant black motherfuckers in the streets today [...] and for the first time in America there are a generation of visionary maniac white mother country dope fiend rock and roll freeks [sic] who are ready to get down and kick out the jams – ALL THE JAMS – break everything loose and free everybody from their very real and imaginary prisons [...] The MC5 is totally committed to the revolution.[57]

A 'commitment to the revolution' in the 'folk' or the 'soul' sense was perhaps more clear, and the directions those genres took beyond 1968 may yet maintain a sense of their historic impulse. In the case of this 'noise', the convergence of loud rock 'n' roll and political confrontation in its continued trajectory was one characteristic of the 1970s punk movement. The roots of this music can be found in seminal recordings such as *Kick Out the Jams*,[58] but also in the work of contemporary bands such as Blue Cheer and Iggy and the Stooges. This noise represents a turning point from the direct lyrical statements of the 'protest folk' movement to the general anger of punk. A sound and a sensibility, perhaps, wrapped in post-hippie garb.

---

[55] For more on the emergence of the LSD-fuelled music of the San Francisco Bay Area at mid-decade, see Wolfe 1968.

[56] Echoing the Black Panthers' ten-point plan, MC5 manager John Sinclair's "White Panther Statement" states their "full endorsement and support of Black Panther Party's 10-Point Program" along with "total assault on the culture by any means necessary"; "the end of money!"; "everything! free for everybody" and freedom to all schools, to all prisoners and to all soldiers. "All power to the people!" See Sinclair 1968, p. 13.

[57] Sinclair 1968. [58] The MC5 1969.

The music of the 1960s, in almost every sense, represented a new freedom for corporeal enjoyment and intellectual stimulation. But again, 'political' content provided a certain tension which has yet to resolve:

> Rock 'n' roll is not a means by which to 'learn about politics', nor a wavelength for a message as to what is to be done or who is to be fought. It is, at times (especially in such moments as August, 1968), a way to get a feeling for the political spaces we might happen to occupy at any particular time. Rock 'n' roll music and a rock 'n' roll song – a record – keeps those spaces open. That record holds back, for a moment, the tangible weight of enemies and outrages and violence, allowing us to move within a situation we create with a rock 'n' roll band, out of its response to our lives and our response to its song.[59]

These songs of 1968 had more than a "tangible weight" to hold back; they had the enormous weight of enemies, from presidential assassins to the Viet Cong; of outrages, from Mai Lai to Martin Luther King;[60] and of violence, "a nation at war both at home and abroad". Whether by humour, as in "I-Feel-Like-I'm-Fixin'-to-Die Rag", or with direct address, as in "Why? (The King of Love is Dead)", or in the power and energy of "Kick Out the Jams", these messages reflect the vitality of politically engaged popular music in 1968. But the Impressions' "This Is My Country" should really bear a question mark, implying as it does a disbelief at the rupturing of the country's 'united' state. The idea of a unified front in the United States in any sense – cultural, political, ideological – could never be made real in 1968. Those photographs cited earlier, those subliminal murders – Martin Luther King, Jr, Robert Kennedy, the Vietnam War, the Mexico City Olympics – are visual reminders of the lattice of fractures, present too in the diverging soundtracks – folk, soul, rock – which further challenge the myth of 'America'.

---

[59] Marcus 1969 pp. 103–4. He is writing broadly about the Stones' "Street Fighting Man", but the reference to politics and rock music resonates with the larger contemporary American 'rock' scene at issue here.

[60] The Mai Lai massacre took place on 16 March 1968, when American soldiers killed upwards of 500 unarmed South Vietnamese civilians. The event was not common knowledge in the US until the following year.

4 | Spontaneity and Black Consciousness: South Africans imagining musical and political freedom in 1960s Europe

CAROL MULLER

Introduction

Unlike in many other parts of the world, 1968 in South Africa was not a year marked by worker revolution or student rebellion because by the mid-1960s, the apartheid regime's legislative, military and national intelligence services had begun to crush all public displays of discontent. 1968 is, nevertheless, the year located midpoint between two political protests against the apartheid regime that were reported on around the world: the 1960 Sharpeville Massacre and the 1976 Soweto Uprising. While the global spread of revolutionary ideas and sit-ins, marches and uprisings in the 1960s had some impact on South African society and its musical practices, by 1968 many of its most prominent musicians had already left the country. In the wake of the Sharpeville Massacre South Africans began to depart in significant numbers and to protest the apartheid regime from beyond its borders. This was especially the case with members of the African National Congress (ANC), the Pan Africanist Congress (PAC) and the South African Communist Party (SACP) – after the apartheid regime banned their organisations.

Jazz and popular musicians were among those who left. At least half of those who travelled abroad in South African variety productions like *The Golden City Dixies* and later the musical *King Kong: An African Jazz Opera* decided not to return home when their tours ended. In 1959 Miriam Makeba left for Europe and the US, and under the watchful eye of Harry Belafonte testified before the United Nations Committee on Apartheid; Hugh Masekela joined her in 1960. While most of these musicians initially ventured out to pursue their art in places where they hoped they could survive as professionals, ultimately many found themselves engaged in some kind of political and cultural work for the anti-apartheid movement abroad over the next three decades. In 1962, Dollar Brand (Abdullah Ibrahim from 1968) and his jazz singing partner Bea Benjamin (Sathima Bea Benjamin from the 1970s) bid farewell to the Cape and Johannesburg jazz scenes. They travelled to Zurich, Switzerland, where South African bass player Makhaya Ntshoko and drummer Johnny Gertze later joined them. Their first international appearance was at the Antibes Jazz Festival in France in 1963. In 1964, jazz pianist, composer and bandleader Chris McGregor and his journalist partner Maxine travelled with their ensemble the Blue Notes to Antibes. Unable to make the hoped for musical connections there, they ended up with Brand and Benjamin in Zurich after the festival, living in the basement of an international student house until they all moved on to London and other parts of Europe and the US.

In retrospect, for South African jazz musicians living overseas, the 1960s was a decade of musical and political exploration of the possibilities and limits of freedom. It was clear when musicians left South Africa that they were seeking freedom from the growing repression of apartheid legislation and practice, but it was perhaps less obvious what such freedom would enable them to accomplish as South African musicians abroad. In this chapter I explore the quest for freedom as a specifically musical project that was increasingly tied to issues of political liberation and the imagining of the possibilities and contours of a new South African nation.

My narrative begins with a brief discussion of 1960s apartheid legislation and media control, and outlines a few places inside South Africa where the ideas and events of the 1960s had a local impact. Because of the apartheid regime's stringent repression of black resistance, it is largely in the realm of the non-material: ideas, consciousness, the spiritual and artistic, that protest was articulated.[1] I discuss several examples where small pockets of society questioned the social order through artistic, literary and musical means: Die Sestigers, an Afrikaans language literary movement; the writings on participatory democracy by political scientist Rick Turner; the Black Consciousness Movement led by Steve Biko; the 1968 student sit-in at the University of Cape Town; and South African Dave Marks' sound production at the Woodstock Festival in the US in 1969.

In the next part of the chapter, I examine the quest for freedom in the South African jazz community as it moved between Europe, the UK and the US in the 1960s. I begin with a brief description of South African jazz in the late 1950s in Johannesburg and Cape Town, and follow the travels to Europe of the Dollar Brand Trio and Chris McGregor and the Blue Notes in the 1960s. In South Africa, Brand and McGregor had modelled their music making on the works of Duke Ellington and bebop musicians like Charlie Parker and Dizzie Gillespie. As such their music forged ties with what is now often termed the 'old' African diaspora – African American

---

[1] Nasson 2008; Biko 2002 (1978); Plaut 2010; Turner 1978 (1972).

musicians with a history created from the transatlantic slave trade. After they left South Africa, the two groups began to expand their musical horizons into a more transnational realm as they met and occasionally performed with American and European 'free jazz' musicians in Europe, most notably at the Café Montmartre in Copenhagen. I briefly discuss three examples of jazz made by these South Africans in Europe in the 1960s: Bea Benjamin's recording session with Duke Ellington; a sample of Dollar Brand's recordings, and the 1968 recording by Chris McGregor and the Blue Notes to reflect on the qualities of 'freedom' articulated by each.

In the final part of the chapter I argue that the music these South Africans made in the 1960s embodied the freedoms articulated in the wider social and political revolutionary discourse of the decade and highlighted by the events of 1968: through theories of or desires for spontaneity, participatory democracy and Black Consciousness. In other words, I propose that South African jazz creatively improvised in the South African exodus constituted a parallel discourse of personal and collective freedom to the explicitly political agendas of 1960s political movements in Europe, the US and South Africa.

Implementing apartheid

The mid-late 1950s had already seen a series of protests by mostly black South Africans against apartheid laws and practices. Angered by the growing harassment of black men and women through the infamous pass laws – laws that controlled the movement of black South Africans between rural and urban areas – several thousand South Africans converged on the Sharpeville police station in Johannesburg. It was intended to be a peaceful demonstration but as the numbers of protesters grew the police panicked and opened fire. The 'Sharpeville Massacre' on 21 March 1960 left 69 dead and almost 200 wounded. News of the massacre spread around the world and the South African government was strongly condemned for its actions.

The regime responded by adding to its already substantial body of apartheid laws: increasingly repressive legislation that promoted the 'separate development' of its people by race, language and culture, likening this 'separate development' to the growing independence of African states from European colonial rule elsewhere on the continent. All urban areas were reserved for 'white' South Africans; everyone else was either moved to their own 'group area' or exiled in what the regime called 'independent homelands' or Bantustans. Black South Africans were only permitted in 'white' urban areas if they were employed full time. If they were not employed they could visit urban areas for no longer than 72 hours. A key part of the post-Sharpeville legislation was the 1963 Entertainment and Censorship law that created racial separation in all entertainment venues and heavy censorship of books, films and theatre performances, and this had a devastating impact on interracial jazz venues. Even more disturbing were the laws against 'terrorism'. The 1967 Terrorism Act No. 83 legalised indefinite detention without trial, without access to a lawyer or any person who was not a magistrate assigned to the prisoner. A 'terrorist' was basically anyone thought to have committed any kind of crime. A black person coming into town without the correct documentation could constitute such a crime. In the same period, the Treason Trials sent ANC leaders like Nelson Mandela, Govan Mbeki and Walter Sisulu to Robben Island prison with life sentences for attempting to overthrow the government, and the regime banned all liberation organisations including the ANC, the PAC and the SACP. In response, the ANC Youth League constituted Umkhonto we Sizwe, its armed wing, which ignited its first bomb in December 1961.

Increasingly, black South Africans who might in the past have acquired a permit to enter a South African university like the University of Cape Town or Witwatersrand were forbidden from registering at any university that was not assigned to their racial/cultural group. This period saw the growth of so called 'bush universities', i.e. universities in rural Bantustans. So the University of Transkei and Fort Hare University were campuses for Xhosa-speaking students only; the University of Zululand for Zulu-speaking students and so forth. This kind of action precluded most kinds of interracial student protest coming out of South African universities in the 1960s.[2]

White rebellion

While for black South Africans the 1960s was a period of significant daily oppression and struggle, for white (and to a lesser extent Cape Coloured) South Africans there were anomalies in the apartheid regime's control that allowed for pockets of resistance, international ties to a wider palette of revolutionary ideas and limited political and cultural mobilisation. The regime targeted some white individuals wishing to travel abroad, and began banning books and other documents containing 'radical' ideas with the 1963 Publications and Censorship bill; and yet there has long been active intercontinental movement by white South Africans between Europe, the

[2] The exception was the Black Consciousness movement led by Steven Biko.

UK, the US and South Africa. I provide here four examples of South African contact with the revolutionary ideas of the 1960s through the travel of people and ideas.

First, university study in France generated two significant political movements among white South Africans on their return to South Africa. In his early twenties, Afrikaans writer and poet Jan Rabie lived in Paris for seven years, returning to South Africa in 1955. Though he left South Africa certain of his commitment to Afrikaner nationalism, he returned from Europe with a strong belief that apartheid had to be eradicated. As such, he initiated through his writing what would consolidate in the 1960s into a literary movement known as Die Sestigers – or the sixties generation of Afrikaans writers. This group brought to the conservative and Calvinist Afrikaans community a new set of possibilities of what it means to be Afrikaans. They embraced the secular, the modern, racial tolerance and sexual freedom. Their members included Andre Brink, Breyten Breytenbach, Ingrid Jonker and Etienne LeRoux. Their goal was to liberate the language of Afrikaans from its cultural ties and oppressive links, and to thereby foster a revolution against apartheid.[3]

Second, political scientist Rick Turner had pursued his PhD on Jean-Paul Sartre at the Sorbonne in Paris and returned to South Africa in 1966. In 1970 Turner moved to the then University of Natal to teach, and became close friends with Black Consciousness leader Steve Biko who also read Sartre. Biko was a medical student at the University of Natal at the time, though he was expelled for his political activities in 1972, the same year that Turner published *The Eye of the Needle: Toward Participatory Democracy in South Africa*.[4] The intellectuals whose writing most shaped Biko's thinking were Martiniquan postcolonial writer Frantz Fanon and Algerian expatriate Aime Cesaire. As I discuss in the last part of this chapter, both Turner and Biko were key figures in the anti-apartheid struggle in terms of utopian thinking and racial self-consciousness, thinking that parallels ways in which musicians like McGregor and Brand articulated their music. Both Turner and Biko were assassinated by the regime in the late 1970s.

Third, in line with European and American counterparts, students at the University of Cape Town staged a sit-in in 1968 to protest the University's decision to rescind an offer of employment to black South African anthropology Ph.D. Archie Mafeje, after the regime threatened to cut funding if they hired a black man at a 'white' university.[5] Mafeje was never hired at the University of Cape Town but given an honorary degree posthumously for

---

[3] Anonymous 2011. [4] Turner 1978 (1972). [5] Plaut 2010.

his great intellectual contributions to African history. Such sit-ins were common in Europe and the US at the time.

Finally, white South African folk musician and popular songwriter David Marks, composer of the internationally popular song "Master Jack",[6] travelled to the Woodstock music festival in 1969 in the US. He was a sound engineer for the Woodstock weekend events and returned to South Africa to establish the Free Peoples' Concerts in South Africa in the 1970s. These concerts replicated the perhaps less politicised but equally powerful values and ideals of Woodstock in that they engaged less with racial politics and more with personal politics pertaining to ideas about sexual freedom and resistance to war as a political option.[7] While not explicitly anti-apartheid, there was a distinctive anti-establishment push from this series of musical events, and Dave Marks would go on to record, perform with and create an invaluable archive of several key black and white South African musicians active from the 1960s through the early 1990s.

Such modes of rebellious engagement were not available to black South Africans who rarely had the means or opportunity to travel abroad, except in white controlled groups of black performance. It is in this context that we might think about the evolving experimental jazz scene of the late 1950s and early 1960s in South Africa as an alternative space for working out ideas of political and personal freedom, for imagining a non-racial future for all of South Africa in the context of increasing legislation that divided and oppressed the majority of South Africans. This is certainly what jazz would become to those who used their musical skills and global connections to leave South Africa and find new outlets in Europe and the US from the early 1960s on.

South African jazz at home and abroad

The late 1950s and early 1960s were exciting years for the growth of an international and interracial community of progressive jazz musicians and audiences, initially in Johannesburg but increasingly in several venues in the city of Cape Town. While the University of Cape Town and the University of the Witwatersrand in Johannesburg hosted jazz performances on occasion, there were no formal music programmes for jazz studies until

---

[6] In 1968, the South African group Four Jacks and a Jill entered the American charts with the song "Master Jack", in the Billboard Hot 100 at no. 18 and reached no. 3 on the Adult Contemporary chart. The song also reached no. 5 on *Cashbox* and went to no. 1 in South Africa, Canada, Australia, New Zealand, Malaysia and Rhodesia (now Zimbabwe) (Anonymous 2012c).
[7] Hanley 2011.

the early 1980s. Chris McGregor, leader of the Blue Notes and later the Brotherhood of Breath, studied at the School of Music at the University of Cape Town in the early 1960s, though his training was in conventional European classical music, its history, performance and theory. For the majority of musicians, however, wartime entertainment corps experience, dance band performances, imported recordings and radio transmission from South Africa and neighbouring Mozambique comprised the main sources of knowledge transmission. South Africans were passionate listeners and very precise imitators.

Musicians listened closely to jazz recordings imported from the US, mostly in groups in public library jazz appreciation clubs, at each other's homes and in after-hours venues. Many of these musicians were also informed by avid reading of a wide range of literature by and about African Americans. Benjamin, for example, recalls the impact reading Billie Holiday's autobiography had on her as a woman of colour, and a singer.[8] On Sunday evenings in the early 1960s, jazz musicians and fans gathered at a place in Cape Town called The Ambassadors. The Ambassadors, a school for dance during the day, was transformed into a site of jazz experimentation on Sunday evenings. Pianist Dollar Brand/Abdullah Ibrahim was at the centre of the venue until, like every other racially mixed performance site, the challenge of keeping it open under the scrutiny of the apartheid regime proved too much.

After playing several farewell performances to raise the money for their air tickets, Dollar Brand and his musical partner, singer Bea Benjamin, left South Africa in February 1962 for Europe. Encouraged by Swiss graphic designer, jazz record collector and performance organiser Paul Meyer, who lived in Cape Town in the late 1950s and early 1960s, these two musicians travelled to Switzerland. Dollar Brand wrote of his reasons for leaving in 1966:

Night club owners were hostile and avoided me and my music like the plague. The feeling was mutual, though, because I had decided long before, they were not going to turn me into another juke-box [...] A black juke-box. The scene was a mess and after long hours of discussion with Bea Benjamin and close friends one fact emerged, we had to go.[9]

---

[8] See Muller and Benjamin 2011.
[9] The piece was written by Paul Trewhela. I found the reference in the Transcription Centre archive, London, but cannot be more specific in bibliographic information.

With Meyer's help they secured some work at the Club Africana, and in 1963 performed at the Antibes Festival and recorded with Duke Ellington and Billy Strayhorn in Paris.

The invitation to the Antibes Festival in 1964 also motivated Chris and Maxine McGregor and the Blue Notes to leave South Africa. They flew to Paris via Lourenço Marques (now Maputo), Mozambique. Maxine McGregor reflected on the impact on the musicians of arriving by train in Mozambique, finally beyond the clutches of the apartheid regime.

> For the first time in their lives the musicians were all free men. Even I [a white South African] who had not officially suffered from these things, felt strange. It felt, I imagine, how a prisoner must feel when released from prison – a strange freedom that you don't quite know what to do with...[10]

This was a freedom that the Blue Notes would most audibly articulate in their music in 1960s London.

The sense of freedom from apartheid bondage, however, was soon replaced by other kinds of alienation. Despite high hopes that they would make the necessary connections to the European or American jazz scene at that festival, the Blue Notes found themselves stranded on the beach at the end of the event. They called Abdullah and Sathima who arranged for the group to stay in the basement of their student house in Zurich. The Blue Notes arrived, did some playing together with the Brands and a few months later moved to London, with the Dollar Brand Trio and Sathima following soon after. While the McGregors made London their base for much of the decade, Brand and Benjamin were rarely in any place for longer than a few months – in the 1960s they travelled extensively around Europe, went to the Newport Jazz Festival in 1965 with Ellington, back to South Africa in 1968 and had returned to Europe and the US by 1970. For Sathima this incessant movement would ultimately mutate into an aesthetic of spontaneity in her approach to her life and music.

Three case studies

The 1963 recording with the Dollar Brand Trio, Bea Benjamin, Duke Ellington and Billy Strayhorn proved to be a pivotal moment in opening the doors of European and American jazz to Dollar Brand whose international career was clearly launched with the recording *Duke Ellington*

---

[10] McGregor 1995, pp. 68–9.

Presents the Dollar Brand Trio[11] (1964), which came out of that event. It was less immediately useful to Benjamin, whose tracks with the musicians were not released until the tapes were discovered in 1996.[12] And yet, as the story outlined below illustrates, Benjamin traces her aesthetic of musical spontaneity to that meeting with Ellington and Strayhorn, an aesthetic she passionately adheres to in all live and studio performances.

The experience of meeting and performing with Ellington and Strayhorn had a significant, but different impact on Brand as pianist, bandleader and composer, for it is in the path created by Ellington as a 'coloured' bandleader, a man who told the story of African Americans through musical means and in a sophisticated and modern way, that inspired Dollar Brand to experiment with, and reflect on, the African diasporic musical narrative. Brand took the liberty to extend Ellington's narrative to South Africa and to tell it from his own perspective. Now we can explore that journey in a representative sample of Brand's recordings from the 1960s.

Chris McGregor and the Brotherhood of Breath were not fortunate enough to be in the purview of Ellington and Strayhorn in February 1963, so the musical path they struck for themselves was different. Though McGregor made some solo recordings, mostly not commercially released, his primary passion was composing and arranging for big band – for the South African musicians he had helped bring to Europe. Largely unschooled, several of the band were not able to read music, but were brilliant, intense and emotionally driven improvisers. And so it was through the language of free jazz, largely absorbed and experimented with once they arrived in Europe, that we hear the Blue Notes pushing at the limits of musical and personal freedom embedded in a discourse of deep emotion and intense musical spontaneity.

Bea Benjamin's aesthetic of spontaneity

The Club Africana was important as a gateway to Europe for these South Africans and it was where Benjamin and Brand first played for Duke Ellington. The story has been told many times, and it runs something like this. One cold night early in February 1963, Benjamin heard that Duke Ellington was performing in the Club Africana neighbourhood. In short, she persuaded Ellington to come and listen to the Dollar Brand Trio, which he did, and working as an 'A and R man' for Frank Sinatra's Reprise Records, invited them to record in Paris. Ellington was to perform in Paris

---

[11] Brand 1997 (1964).   [12] Benjamin 1997.

on the Saturday evening, and on the Sunday morning he met Benjamin, Brand, Ntshoko and Gertze in Barclay Studio. Benjamin vividly remembered that day in the studio with Ellington and Billy Strayhorn as a day characterised by spontaneous interaction. Ellington arrived with a woman on one arm and Strayhorn at his side. He introduced Strayhorn: "This is Bea, this is Billy, and you should get to know each other, and we'll start with you, Bea." Benjamin recalled the moment years later:

I must say that the Ellington session was completely spontaneous. Completely from the get go, it was just, "Here's so and so, what are you gonna do?" Nothing was planned. At a certain point I started doing Ellington songs, and then he came out of the recording box and said, "Wait, those are my tunes, so I have to sit down at the piano". I couldn't believe that – he played for me [...] Even when Ellington ran out of the recording booth and said, "That's my song" and sat down and did it, Dollar Brand stunned him with what the key was. It was "I Got It Bad and That Ain't Good". Then he said, "Oh no, ok, you had better play this". And Dollar Brand took a backseat. He said, "No sir, it's your song". And you can hear, because we didn't do two takes, you hear that Duke is letting me sing first, and then, "Where is it? Ok, that is where she is going". When he got it, it was over.[13]

The sense of the spontaneous extended beyond the encounter with Ellington. Danish violinist Svend Asmussen – in town to record with Grappeli the day before – dropped by the studio. Benjamin remembers Duke saying, "Gee, just the person I am looking for. You sit in on this." German recording engineer Gerhard Lehner was working in the Barclay Studios on 23 February 1963. Lehner had fought in the Nazi army during the second world war until US forces captured him in Russia. Taken prisoner, he had been persuaded to work for the US Armed Services Radio in Munich. He was subsequently hired as the chief engineer at the Barclay Studios and had been involved with recording many of Ellington and Strayhorn's musical sessions. Each piece of that day is remembered as magical, ineffable and certainly unplanned.

Benjamin's recollections of performing with Ellington in Newport in 1965 reiterate her memory of the contingency of the moment, the spontaneity, the unexpected, but also the overwhelming sense of personal capacity Duke conveyed to her in that period. These have become qualities she privileges in all her performances, both live and in the studio. After singing an emotionally powerful rendition of "In My Solitude", the audience called for an encore. There had been no prior discussion about what song would fill the request. Benjamin continued,

---

[13] Muller and Benjamin 2011, p. 165.

I remember that because at Newport he said, "Do you know 'In a Mellotone?'" I vaguely knew it, even though I had never sung it in my life. I was positive of the melody, even though I didn't have all the words together. And he said, "Of course you know, let's go". And the band started playing, and I stood there. I repeated the words of the verse twice, and no one knew the difference. The band was playing behind me. There was Duke at the piano. I just had to sing, and this band – Cootie Williams, Cat Anderson – it was so beautiful, you just sang![14]

Spontaneity as aesthetic in music and life, is beautifully communicated by Benjamin in *Musical Echoes: South African Women Thinking in Jazz*. She sums up this aesthetic with the words: "I want my music to always feel spontaneous. Duke Ellington believed in one take. That means the dials are set, you call the tune, and you do it [. . .] Jazz music should be completely spontaneous."[15]

Dollar Brand/Abdullah Ibrahim's kind of freedom

Brand made several recordings from the late 1950s through the late 1960s. First, in South Africa there was recording with the Jazz Epistles, *Verse One* and *Jazz in Africa, Volume One* that incorporates American pianist John Mehegan and three additional South Africans.[16] Second, in Europe, there is *Duke Ellington Presents the Dollar Brand Trio, Round Midnight at the Café Montmartre, Anatomy of a South African Village* and *Reflections*, all by the Dollar Brand Trio.[17] Third, there is a duo recording with Brand and Argentinian saxophonist Gato Barbieri on the album *Confluences*.[18] Finally, there is *African Sketchbook*, a solo recording by Brand after his conversion to Islam.[19] I use these recordings to capture a comparative sense of how Brand and the Blue Notes embraced ideas of freedom in their 1960s musical output, transforming their engagement with the sound of American jazz in the political context of exile and the 1960s revolutionary spirit that pervaded the European and American public realm.

Brand's two early recordings with the Jazz Epistles before he left the country are clearly located in a bebop stylistic habitus, though the compositions are predominantly local.[20] Heard outside of South Africa, the music

---

[14] Muller and Benjamin 2011, p. 176. [15] Muller and Benjamin 2011, p. 236.
[16] Jazz Epistles, *Verse One* 1958; *Jazz in Africa, Volume One* 1992 (1959, reissued on CD in 1992).
[17] Brand 1997 (1964), 1992c, 1992b, 1992a. [18] Brand and Barbieri 1974. [19] Brand 1973.
[20] There are fourteen tracks in all, five have American attribution, and the rest are South African – three each by Moeketsi and Brand, one by Masekela, and two traditional African arrangements. Masekela's piece is titled "Dollar's Moods", and Dollar responds with "Blues for Hughie". Moeketsi's "Scullery Department" references the racist treatment of black musicians in 1950s South Africa – at intermission, after they had entertained the white clientele, they were sent to the kitchen or 'scullery' to eat. On one occasion Brand and

would probably have been identified as 'American'. This was before Brand travelled abroad and began to think in new ways about his South African musical pasts. With the 1963 in Paris with Ellington we already begin to see an opening up of acoustical possibilities: a hauntingly beautiful ballad pays tribute to South Africa's own Charlie Parker, Kippie Moeketsi; there are lively, upbeat performances in "Dollar's Dance", "The Stride" and "Jumping Rope" as well as a moderately paced interpretation of Monk's "Brilliant Corners".

Three recordings were produced out of a single evening in Copenhagen at the Café Montmartre. Recorded on 30 January 1965, *Round Midnight*, *Reflections* and *Anatomy of a South African Village* present a more complicated jazz identity. The three titles suggest a growing bifurcation in Brand's musical portfolio: *Round Midnight* and *Reflections* ostensibly pay tribute to the old African diaspora, while *Anatomy* references the contemporary [South] African experience. In terms of improvisation and compositional style, however, Brand is beginning to sound far more like an independent voice in jazz. While *Round Midnight* references the music of Thelonious Monk, who Brand admired and later met, there is also a Danish twist to the title. In the early 1960s performing in the 10pm slot was the honour accorded to American musicians; playing around midnight in Copenhagen's Montmartre was the lot of musicians considered less skilled – the non-American and Danish musicians. Dollar Brand had finally been elevated to the place regularly assigned to Americans, and so was scheduled to perform in the early slot on 30 January 1965. That was the case until American Ben Webster arrived in town unexpectedly. To his chagrin Brand was summarily moved to the later shift to give Webster the prestigious time slot. Brand began playing his session sometime around midnight.

Still performing with South Africans Gertze and Ntshoko, Brand's material on *Round Midnight* has become a distinct mix of diverse musical references. We hear in "The Stride" the piano as a percussive and rhythmic resource. Extensive use of repeating riffs in the right and left hands point to African traditional practices while the opening high register repeated motifs contrast in an almost sinister way with the low register riffs in the left hand. There is a relentless and restless urgency to the performance – one begins to imagine the danger of black South African township life through this music, by means of its dissonance, rhythmic displacement, and the gaps and tensions between upper and lower registers in his pianism. He is clearly taking liberties in presenting local experiences in his compositions and performances.

Moeketsi complained to the restaurant owner, who then organised a table for them in the main dining room to eat. This was an act in defiance of apartheid law.

In "Tintinyana", there are stronger gestures towards the sounds of gospel from the African Methodist Episcopal church of his youth – a church founded in Philadelphia by African Americans, who sent missionaries to Cape Town in the twentieth century. Brand's hallmark 'driving riff' is in the bass. The right-hand introduction is hymn-like: its repeating melodic motifs are memorable, underscored with the familiar sound of four-part harmonic progressions. In contrast, "Obluegato", a play on classical and blues worlds, is contrapuntal; the obligato sounds improvised, and it plays with the kinds of contradictions and tensions generated by words, music, and expectation that become characteristic of the Brand/Ibrahim style in later years.

According to a letter written by Brand to Dennis Duerden at London's Transcription Centre, *Anatomy of a South African Village* – the title of both the album and an extended piece on the recording – was soon banned by the apartheid regime.[21] It is a tone poem originally written for jazz orchestra in five parts, played on the recording by the Dollar Brand Trio. There are three other major pieces on this record: an extended and varied improvisation on Jerome Kern's "Smoke Gets in Your Eyes", a musical meditation on Brand's composition "Mama"[22] and then a rich collage of exploration and experimentation of a range of musical origins, bookended with his tune "Boulevard East", which evokes the endless bustle of a busy township boulevard. Inside "Boulevard East" Brand inserts his slow, reflective "Sunset in Blue" and the melodically and rhythmically exuberant "Easter Joy".

Brand published one recording in 1968 that speaks of a greater internationalism and inclusiveness in musical composition. *Hamba Kahle*[23]/ *Confluences*[24] is a joint recording with Barbieri on tenor sax and Brand on piano. Each musician presents two compositions, and they improvise on each other's material. The confluence or solidarity engendered between the two artists takes place in Europe but it is clearly a political and musical statement about jazz and the global South in a musical language of afromodernity from the North.

The definitive statement of 1960s Dollar Brand, however, is his 1969 recording, *African Sketchbook*, a project that sets the stage for a far greater focus on all things 'African' in the 1970s: one thinks, for example, of the recordings, *African Piano, Ancient Africa, African Space Program, African Marketplace* and so forth. Much like a visual artist, Brand creates a series of sketches of the pieces of South African music and culture that he

---

[21] The reasons for the ban are unclear. Perhaps it was considered as referencing Africa in a modernist discourse against the traditionalist bent of apartheid ideology.
[22] See Lucia 2002 for a detailed musical analysis of a 1970s rendition of "Mama".
[23] Zulu or Xhosa for Good bye, or Go Well. [24] Brand and Barbieri 1974.

remembers or wishes to bring to the attention of his listeners: from the "Air" on flute reminiscent of his great grandfather's Scottish heritage, to his Khoisan grandmother's lineage in "Krotoa",[25] "Slave Bell" and "Tariq", to the Xhosa and Chopi sounds in "Nkosi" and "Machopi", to the senses of place and home embodied in "Tokai", "Mamma", "The Dream", "The Aloe and the Wild Rose" and "African Sun", all framed by the three-language greeting, "Peace, Salaam, Hamba Kahle". In live performance as on CD these musical paraphrases interweave into a linear exposition of a range of experiences. This is the moment when Brand/Ibrahim begins what has become a core feature of his live renditions – an ongoing unfolding of personal and musical complexity, his incessant longing for home, and insistence on all of South Africa as a source for jazz performance that incorporates a range of music from across the proverbial colour bar. Freedom here is a refusal to be limited by the ethnic divisiveness and denial of black South African history by the apartheid regime. It insists rather on representing the totality of South African musical expression in the work of a single musician.

The challenge once Brand left South Africa was to develop a musical means to evoke the sounds of his early life without alienating his audiences; his was not just listening pleasure, but required listeners to labour over what they heard. In contact with the free musicians – Albert Ayler, Don Cherry, Gato Barbieri, Byard Lancaster, Elvin Jones and John Coltrane, he absorbed the idea of great black music. Out of that experience, Brand seemed to be striving to break out of the national mould that apartheid imposed: its lack of freedom of movement and association. Instead he played with ideas of national and transnational belonging imagined through a wide palette of musical possibility. In his music, Brand strives to transcend the limits of apartheid, by representing the full spectrum of sounds he remembers hearing, and those he was encountering on his travels. In other words, by the late 1960s Dollar Brand/Abdullah Ibrahim was defining himself as a musician of a particular moment in time: i.e. he had heard a wide span of jazz history on record in a variety of perhaps unexpected places, and his music began to reflect all of the richness of that past in addition to the wide ranging soundscape of his early life in Cape Town. He resisted the ideas of ethnic and racial separation, a belief reinforced by his conversion to Islam in 1968, which he has explained in many contexts as reflecting a desire for unity in the universe.

---

[25] Krotoa was a Khoisan woman who was an interpreter for Dutch settler Jan Van Riebeeck in the seventeenth century. Many Afrikaners claim her as an ancestor (see Engelbrecht 2009).

Chris McGregor and the Blue Notes: *Very Urgent*

"The emphasis on feeling – feeling as spontaneous excitement – is the predominant quality of Chris McGregor's music."[26] We capture something of the emotional intensity and in the moment spontaneity described by jazz critic, Simon Puxley on *Very Urgent*[27] (1968), one recording available with the all-South African Blue Notes in London in the period. It articulates the push to freedom that Moholo, Benjamin and the Paris uprising privilege: it erupts in four extended tracks of free jazz. For these Blue Notes freedom and spontaneity are the modus operandi. Allaboutjazz's Clifford Allen describes track three, "The Sounds Begin Again", as having a tenor/trumpet line that "erupts into shards, smears, squawks, as the rhythm section paints a canvas of pounding gesture and suspended time", and he describes Ronnie Beer's playing as "bent honks and heel-digging screams" along with Moholo's "continual bomb drops ringing like chimes".[28] The group did not stay together much beyond the recording, and when McGregor formed his new Big Band, The Brotherhood of Breath, the sound was more contained and the personnel more British. That said, it is clear from the recording that the South African political situation had indeed become "very urgent" and that extreme measure of the Blue Notes emotional outbursts of freedom were necessary steps in breaking the chains of the past to enable all South Africans to begin to imagine the possibilities of a more just social and political order.

Discourses of musical and political freedom

Our movement's strength is that it is based on an 'uncontrollable' spontaneity [...] The movement's only chance is the disorder that lets men speak freely, which can result in a form of self-organisation.[29]

In this final part of the chapter, we shift direction from the historical narrative to reflect on the subject of freedom: freedom *from* a set of restrictions placed on South African musicians that they hoped would not inhibit them once they left the country; and freedom *to* explore their full capacity initially just as artists, but increasingly as *South African* artists living abroad. Such freedoms were articulated in a set of interlocking ideas: improvisation, spontaneity and participatory democracy, all in the language

---

[26] Simon Puxley, quoted in McGregor 1995, p. 90. [27] Blue Notes 2008 (1968).
[28] Allen 2008. [29] Cohn-Bendit 2007, pp. 138–9.

of jazz in its conventional, experimental or 'free' forms. I will suggest that there is a clear resonance between the political ideas dispersed through the '1968' revolution internationally as the above quote by French student activist Daniel Cohn-Bendit suggests, and those used to talk about the music itself, even if these South Africans chose to examine ideas of freedom through musical and not explicitly political means.

The framing words on the subject of jazz and freedom – personal, musical and political – come from Benjamin:

> The reason I am doing jazz is it affords you a certain amount of freedom of thought, freedom to be different and unique. And it dares you: it lets you pull out whatever courage you have. You have to take risks. That's the whole thing. I could have inherited this courage, I think even things like that come through in the genes. My mother had to take risks. Just growing up in South Africa not being White, you learnt how to survive and take risks. My grandmother taught me to be careful and stay out of trouble, but eventually I rebelled against that, that whole rebellion thing led me to jazz, I saw that as *the* music of rebellion.[30]

In other words, for Benjamin, jazz constituted itself as a language of freedom to be her own person, to rebel, to find a voice for herself. The idea of the spontaneous is one in which the moment of performance shapes her sense of personal capacity, creativity and political possibility, as a woman and as a person of colour under a repressive regime. Spontaneity is an aesthetic that has also made sense for a woman constantly on the move – never fixed in a single place of abode, and constantly required to improvise. Living as the wife of a far more publicly recognised musician like Dollar Brand/Abdullah Ibrahim, Benjamin has also had to insist that she need not settle for less. In the absence of resources to rehearse for hours, she relies on the skill and listening capacity of male musicians to respond musically in the moment of performance or recording. For Benjamin this means she can demand of her musicians the absolute best that they can achieve in the limited time that they have.

For many in the 1960s, musical freedom was also articulated through the notion of spontaneity: an idea rarely invoked in jazz discourses any more. Interestingly, perhaps, in the political realm, spontaneity had become an idea integral to the power of the '1968' revolution in Europe. French student leader Daniel Cohn-Bendit argued that it was in spontaneous uprisings that protesters could begin to reflect on alternative ways of being – it is when there is an unexpected political happening that participants are able to ask themselves: "so what?"; "why does this matter?"; "how differently is it possible to

---

[30] Muller and Benjamin 2011, p. 300.

proceed?" In many ways, this idea parallels the writings of South African political scientist Rick Turner who argued in this period that for South Africans to move towards a new social order and political practice, they needed to stand back and create a 'theory' of new possibilities. And spontaneity was an approach to life necessary to survival as South Africans travelled from place to place in search of musical work and livelihood. Blue Notes drummer Louis Moholo talked about the notion of freedom with passion and eloquence, and it speaks to the kind of explosive spontaneity described in *Very Urgent*.

I was away from South Africa, away from the chains. I just wanted to be free, totally free, even in music. Free to shake away all the slavery, anything to do with slavery, being boxed into places – one, two, three, four – and being told you must come in after four [...] Free is it man, it's so beautiful. The word 'free' makes sense to me [...] Let my people go. Let my people go! And that's interlinking with politics: they embrace each other. It's a cry from the inside, no inhibitions.[31]

Finally, the self-confidence, self-sufficiency, some might add, self-importance, of Brand/Ibrahim as artist, historian and, increasingly, cultural worker in the medium of music, provides a powerful intersection with the ideals of South African Steven Biko's Black Consciousness movement, a movement that was assuming an important if less public presence on South African campuses in the late 1960s. It is hard to know how much Brand/Ibrahim engaged with Biko's ideas specifically, but it is clear that in many ways Ibrahim's sense of himself as artist, musician and composer embodied the principles of Black Consciousness espoused by Steven Biko. Freedom in this context was the capacity to recognise and reject an ideology of racial inferiority that characterised black South African life and a form of consciousness that was an outcome of colonial and apartheid ideas about White/European superiority to all things black or African. Freedom, in this moment, meant harnessing the right to rewrite history, to write his own version of history, through the borrowed language of jazz, a sophisticated interpretation of traditional music and African values. Freedom in this frame was the refusal to become a "black jukebox" even if it meant the daily struggle to survive abroad, accompanied by the lack of recognition of the richness of music at home among one's own communities. Freedom from racial oppression and towards integrated expression is what the music of Dollar Brand, his Trio, Bea Benjamin, Chris McGregor and the Blue Notes was all about.

---

[31] McGregor 1995, p. 216.

5 | Music and protest in Japan: the rise of underground folk song in '1968'

TÔRU MITSUI

In 1968, underground folk songs in Japan became popular on a national scale.[1] Emerging from student singer-songwriters in the Kansai region, these songs were influenced by currents of folk song in the US and were intimately connected to New Leftist student activism and protest. In this chapter, I chart the rise of the underground folk music movement through analysis of the most important songs in 1968 and highlight how these songs were a medium for student protest as part of campaigns that opposed the Vietnam War.

The emergence of the underground folk song movement was part of a broader range of musical change and experimentation in Japanese popular and art music in the late 1960s. In the field of contemporary art music, avant-garde composers were breaking new boundaries through collaboration with independent film producers and participation in the 'Shô Gekijô' or 'little theatre' movement in Tokyo,[2] which was analogous to the off-Broadway movement in New York. Liberation from conventional musical frameworks was also evident among jazz musicians who began to explore free jazz. Both avant-garde composition and free jazz, however, gained only a limited following and had a limited cultural impact. Free jazz "received overwhelming support from youth who aimed at reforming society",[3] but it "remained an extremely marginal pursuit [...] and its audience was very small".[4] In the field of popular music, young musicians who loved groups like the Beatles started to form bands that were referred to in English as 'group sounds' and quite a few songs from these bands were hits in the charts. Most of the hits, however, were composed by experienced songwriters who were already working in the music industry and who wrote songs that fused international popular styles with characteristics of mainstream Japanese popular songs, relying heavily on the minor key to convey sentimental lyrics about love.

---

[1] Throughout the chapter, Japanese personal names appear in the Westernised style with given names followed by surnames.
[2] Nihon Sengo Ongaku-shi Kenkyû-kai 2007, pp. 445–7.   [3] Soéjima 2002, p. 76.
[4] Molasky 2005, p. 158.

In tandem with developments in avant-garde art music, jazz and popular song, in 1968 the New Leftist student movement intensified causing campus strife at more than a hundred universities and colleges. Music was not central to student protest during campus demonstrations, but the song "The Internationale" – which was associated with revolts in Paris in the late nineteenth century and entered Japan in the 1920s via the Soviet Union[5] – was sung in unison by students at various gatherings as a kind of anthem of resistance.

At student peace rallies, however, protest songs, which were referred to as 'folk song' or 'folk' in English, were very important. These English terms were adopted from US folk song records that became popular in Japan in the early 1960s. Initially, 'pop-folk' music was popular among students, particularly those who lived in the Tokyo metropolitan area, and this led to a music scene known in English as 'college-folk'. This scene concentrated on the reproduction of American pop-folk songs by devotees who were typically the sons and daughters of well-to-do families. In contrast to the 'college-folk' scene in Tokyo, students in the Kansai region – which encompasses the three large cities of Kyoto, Osaka and Kobe – were more attracted to protest songs in folk song idioms by American singers.[6] They first sang them in the original English before singing them in translation and soon they started to compose their own songs based on American models.

The extent to which the Kansai folk song movement caught the imagination of the nation is evidenced through several songs entering the national charts in 1968. The first song to trigger a sensation at the very beginning of 1968 was a comical song with a topical theme called "Drunkard Returned from Heaven" ("Kaétté-kita Yopparai") and this was followed by other hits like "Examination-Hell Blues" ("Jukensei Blues"). Analysis of these songs in the next section is followed by discussion of how the underground folk song movement became closely intertwined with anti-war protest and the Peace for Vietnam Committee in Japan. Interestingly, one of the most popular anti-war songs, "Let's Join the Self Defence Forces" ("Jiéitai ni Hairô"), was at first mistakenly understood by the Japanese Defence Agency as a possible recruiting tool, rather than as a parody of the Self Defence Forces. As exemplified by "Let's Join the Self Defence

---

[5] See Morita 1984, p. 50.

[6] The Kansai region has a less rigid cultural hierarchy than in Tokyo, which became highly centralised after the government relocated from Kyoto to Tokyo in 1868. This is a possible contributing factor for the differences in the student music scenes in the Kansai region and in Tokyo in the 1960s.

Forces", Japanese songwriters also attempted to revive the tradition of *enka* songs from the early twentieth century to articulate social and political protests, alongside new protest music which was influenced by the songs performed by American musicians such as Pete Seeger and Joan Baez who toured Japan in the 1960s. The most strident forms of political activism and protest were initiated by young members of the Peace for Vietnam Committee, who called themselves 'Folk Guerilla' (in English). Anti-war demonstrations by the Folk Guerilla, which culminated in a series of rallies from February to July 1969, were vigorously suppressed by the police and ultimately extinguished. The last section of this chapter highlights how collective singing of anti-war songs, most of which became nationally popular in 1968, helped galvanise the Folk Guerilla's activities and how songs were an important medium for protest against the Vietnam War.

The Kansai folk song movement and 'un-gra' songs

Songs from the Kansai folk song movement that hit the charts in 1968 were labelled by the media as 'un-gra' songs, with 'un-gra' being an abbreviation of 'underground'. Before it was used in relation to music, the label 'un-gra' became popular in 1967 when experimental films produced by independent directors were dubbed as 'un-gra films'.[7] Following the enormous popularity of the song "Drunkard Returned from Heaven", which set the trend for later un-gra songs, record companies jumped on the bandwagon and fifteen singles were released as un-gra songs in February and March 1968.[8] "Drunkard Returned from Heaven" was composed, performed and recorded by the Folk Crusaders, a group of college students in Kyoto. It was released by Toshiba Music Industry on 25 December 1967 and in January 1968 the song topped the weekly single charts of *Original Confidence*, which was founded in the previous year as a smaller Japanese equivalent to *Billboard*. Eventually the single sold more than 2.3 million copies.[9]

The song's narrative is based on the story of a man who dies as a result of driving a car while intoxicated. After his death, he ascends the long stairs to heaven, which is described in the song refrain as a place where "wine tastes good and girls are pretty". The song is given a comic twist by the singer using a stereotyped dialect of a 'country bumpkin' and by the pitch of the vocal being raised, along with that of the instrumental accompaniment, by

---

[7] Nihon Kokugo Dai-jiten Henshû Iinkai 2000, p. 710.   [8] Mihashi 1979, p. 48.
[9] Original Confidence 1997, p. 286.

speeding up the reel-to-reel recording. God reproaches the man for his behaviour in the Kansai dialect,[10] but he continues to drink every day and finally God commands him to "Get out!". Banished from heaven, the man goes down the stairs leading up to heaven, but on the way he loses his footing and falls. When he regains consciousness after the fall, he finds himself lying in a field with his life restored. The narrative of the song tapped into great public concern at the time about traffic congestion and deaths on the road, which had increased dramatically due to rapid growth in the domestic car industry and the economy in general.

The musical style of the song is influenced by commercial American folk music of the mid-1960s. Performed in D major, the verse of the song follows an eight-bar chord progression using chords I and V (i.e. D/D/D/A/A/A/A/D). The chords are played minimally by an acoustic steel-stringed guitar following the rhythm of 2 crotchets followed by 4 quavers per bar, with the bass playing the root note of the chord on the first beat of each bar. The six-bar refrain is more upbeat with the last two bars being 'doo-wopped'. The humorous tone of the song is maintained not only by the surreal narrative that is delivered in a comical voice, but also by other musical effects that are inserted into the song. These include the sound of an ambulance siren and rhythms played on a wood block found in Buddhist temples.

Before being released by Toshiba at the end of 1967, "Drunkard Returned from Heaven" had already become popular in the Kansai region as it had been released by the Folk Crusaders themselves on their album *Harenchi* (*Unabashed*), when the idea of independent production was quite innovative. The band pressed just 300 copies of the album in October 1967 to commemorate the band members' college graduations and their disbanding. Despite the small print run of the album, the song became popular after being aired on 8 November by Radio Kansai's late-night show, Telephone Request. Late-night radio shows were promoted with the catch-phrase "a liberated area in the middle of the night" and they were very influential on students: "For young listeners, many of whom were students preparing for college-entrance examinations, radio helped ease their stress [...] Late night shows had little regulation, and DJs on these shows were keen to communicate and appeal to listeners in a different way compared with day-time shows."[11] The popularity of "Drunkard Returned from Heaven" on Telephone Request led to it "rising to second in the show's Top Ten

---

[10] The Kansai dialect has humorous associations for Japanese listeners mainly due to its widespread use among Osaka entertainers on radio and television.

[11] Maéda and Hirahara 1993, pp. 110–11.

within a week, and in the second week it gained the top spot where it remained for two consecutive weeks".[12] The young listeners who were enthralled by "Drunkard Returned from Heaven" also had a passion for another song on the album, called "Imjin River" ("Imjin Gawa"). Since the mid-1950s, the Imjin River has marked the divide between North and South Korea and it is described in the song as a river "across which water-fowls freely fly". The mild social protest of the song lyrics is combined with a sentimental melody in F major sung sweetly in unison by the members of the band. "Imjin River" was regularly played on local radio: Kinki Broadcasting (Kinki Hôsô) kept playing it for two months on their show, Songs of This Week.[13]

"Drunkard Returned from Heaven" and "Imjin River" were soon aired by radio DJs in Tokyo as well, and the popularity of these songs prompted the interest of major record companies. Toshiba Record Industry won the contract with the Folk Crusaders and "Imjin River" was planned to be released in February as a follow-up to the huge success of "Drunkard Returned from Heaven". However, in the end Toshiba decided to cancel its release, even though 130,000 copies of the single, recorded anew in their studio, had already been pressed. It was cancelled because the General Association of Korean Residents in Japan had insisted that it should be made clear that the song had originally been composed by two citizens of North Korea,[14] with the words written by Young-Saeng Pak and the music by Jong-Hwan Ko.[15] The Association also complained that the Japanese version, translated by Takéshi Matsuyama – a friend of Kazuhiko Katô, the lead guitarist and vocalist of the Folk Crusaders – did not closely follow the original,[16] which reflects the viewpoint of North Korea. Matsuyama and Katô had assumed that the song was a traditional Korean folk song.[17] Nonetheless, Tôshiba successfully released another lyrical song by the Folk Crusaders, "I'm Too Sad to Bear" ("Kanashikuté Yarikirenai"), with "Camel without Humps" ("Kobu-no-nai Rakuda") on the B-side. This single reached No. 6 in the charts and sold 259,000 copies.[18] After three more singles were released, the band finally disbanded in October 1968 as they had announced at the time of their signing to Tôshiba.

---

[12] Hirosé 1969, p. 215.   [13] Maéda and Hirahara 1993, p. 87.   [14] Kurosawa 1992, p. 71.
[15] Folk Camp 1969, p. 235.   [16] Maéda and Hirahara 1993, p. 112.
[17] Kokita 2002, p. 19. Matsuyama first heard the original sung at a Korean school in Kyoto as a junior-high school student around 1961 and Katô learnt it orally from Matsuyama about five years later.
[18] Original Confidence 1997, p. 286.

Apart from the Folk Crusaders' songs, the other most popular un-gra song in 1968 was "Examination-Hell Blues" as performed by Tomoya Taka'ishi. The words for the song were written in 1967 by Gorô Nakagawa, then a high school student, and they were originally set to the tune of Bob Dylan's "North Country Blues". Nakagawa stated in 1969 that he wrote the lyrics in order to "turn people's attention to the ordeal of students preparing for highly competitive exams" and that he set it to "North Country Blues" because Dylan's song (with lyrics translated into Japanese) was already popular through being "sung at folksong gatherings in Osaka".[19] Nakagawa's lyrics were published in August 1967 in a mimeographed magazine called *Kawaraban*, which was obviously modelled on *Broadside* in New York. The periodical was started in Kobe by Yuzuru Katagiri, a poet and a teacher of English who supported the Kansai folk song movement. In issues of *Kawaraban*, "lyrics in translation by Woody Guthrie, Pete Seeger, Bob Dylan, Tom Paxton, Malvina Reynolds, Phil Ox, etc. were published".[20]

According to Nakagawa, Taka'ishi wrote a new melody for his lyrics because the Dylan melody "sounded too gloomy for the song to spread".[21] It is highly likely that the more jovial melody for "Examination-Hell Blues" was influenced by the popularity of "Drunkard Returned from Heaven", especially because Taka'ishi composed it in January 1968 at the time when the Folk Crusaders' song became a massive hit. Taka'ishi quickly recorded "Examination-Hell Blues" and it was released in late February, by another major label, Japan Victor, to which Taka'ishi had already been signed in late 1966. The highest position of this single in the charts was No. 6, and it sold 113,000 copies.[22] Like the Folk Crusaders, Taka'ishi mingled in Kansai folk song circles and had moved to Ôsaka a couple of years before, although he was enrolled at a university in Tokyo.

The narrator/singer of "Examination-Hell Blues" ironically gripes about his dreary life as a high-school student preparing himself for entrance examinations for universities. Addressing the listeners, the lyrics include the lines:

Come here, everyone,
Listen to my tale.
I'm an unhappy examinee.
Listen to my tale,
It's insipid and dry as dust.

---

[19] Nakagawa 1969, pp. 185–6.   [20] Mihashi 1975, p. 233.   [21] Nakagawa 1969, p. 185.
[22] Original Confidence 1997, p. 188.

Taka'ishi sings the song in a light-hearted style with a tone of sarcasm. The medium-tempo, eight-bar tune in C major is cheerful and accompanied by chords I, IV and V. The band features a five-string banjo that plays arpeggios to a quaver rhythm throughout.

"Examination-Hell Blues" provided a medium for the expression of students' unhappiness at the societal pressures imposed upon them. Resistance to such pressures is also emphasised through a brief but direct reference to the influential protest song "We Shall Overcome". At the end of "Examination-Hell Blues" a chorus of voices sings "we shall overcome" in English with the lead voice also shouting "we shall overcome" over the top of the chorus as the record fades out. The song "We Shall Overcome" was known to many social-minded Japanese through performances by Pete Seeger, who toured Japan several times during the 1960s, and it became an anti-war anthem at demonstrations in Japan organised by "Beheiren" (the abbreviation of "Vietnam ni heiwa o" Shimin Rengô), whose official English name was the Peace for Vietnam Committee.

The Peace for Vietnam Committee and anti-war songs

The Peace for Vietnam Committee – the most prominent and active anti-war organisation in Japan – was formed in April 1965, two months after the United States Air Force began bombing North Vietnam. The Committee was made up of novelists, critics and academics, and they organised their first anti-war demonstration march to the American Embassy in Tokyo on 24 April 1965,[23] just a week after a ceasefire demonstration parade was held in Washington, DC. Japan was politically involved in the Vietnam War because its government consistently supported the American policy and many US military bases in Japan contributed to the war. Most notably, the main island of Okinawa was a key base for US fighter planes launching attacks in Vietnam.

Music was a prominent feature of most of the anti-war protests organised by the Peace for Vietnam Committee and some other groups. Pete Seeger's tour to Japan in late 1963, which included performances of the songs "Where Have All the Flowers Gone" and "We Shall Overcome", was an important inspiration for many Japanese musicians who wrote anti-war songs, and the influence of Seeger and other American folk singers like Joan Baez continued

---

[23] Peace for Vietnam Committee 1974, p. 6.

through the 1960s. In January 1967, for instance, Baez was invited to anti-war meetings held by student associations in Osaka and the Peace for Vietnam Committee in Tokyo. The participants, who numbered more than 2,000 in Osaka and 1,200 in Tokyo,[24] listened to Baez singing "We Shall Overcome" and "Blowin' in the Wind" with other guest performers.[25]

It was during 1967 and 1968 that the anti-war movement in Japan gained momentum, and Tomoya Taka'ishi, who became nationally known in 1968 through the success of "Examination-Hell Blues", was a key figure in the movement. He was instrumental in setting up the 'Taka'ishi Office' to help organise musical anti-war activities, and at numerous events he performed anti-war songs written by Japanese musicians, as well as Japanese versions of songs by American songwriters such as "The Times They Are A-Changin'", "What Did You Learn in School Today", "Blowin' in the Wind" and "Masters of War".[26] In late July 1967, the Taka'ishi Office organised the first Folk Camp, a two-day event consisting of song-writing sessions, panel discussions and an outdoor concert held in Kyoto. The participants in the Camp joined together for a group performance of Dylan's "Playboys and Playgirls" with new lyrics that satirised the special procurement measures that were in force due to the Vietnam War.[27] The second Folk Camp held in November 1967 and the 'Underground Concert' ('Underground Ongaku-kai') in March 1968 also featured many protest songs. The un-gra movement was now widely known due to the popularity of "Drunkard Returned from Heaven"[28] and the Taka'ishi Office adopted the word 'underground' in the title of the March concert, without having it abbreviated. The concert was "so to speak, a trade fair of un-gra songs with television directors and music writers from Tokyo being present among the audience".[29]

Around the same time, a concert called 'Folk School' was held in Kyoto in early 1968. At the second Folk School concert in Kyoto on 25 February 1968 a new student singer-songwriter in the Kansai folk song movement, Nobuyasu Okabayashi, caused quite a stir. He sang a song called "Go-to-Hell Song" ("Kuso Kuraé Bushi"),[30] the lyrics of which included harsh satire and included swear words. The song includes strong criticisms of the pillars of society, including a company executive, a politician and a Christian minister. He was a theology student at a university in Kyoto and his father was a Christian minister. The last verse is as follows:

---

[24] Peace for Vietnam Committee 1974, pp. 188 and 518. [25] Hirosé 1969, p. 212.
[26] Nakagawa 1969, p. 180; Hirosé 1969, p. 212. [27] Mihashi 1979, p. 34.
[28] Kurosawa 1992, p. 22; Hata 1993, p. 63. [29] Hirosé 1969, p. 219.
[30] Maéda and Hirahara 1993, p. 119.

One day a holy man of religion,
Preached a sermon to the congregation.
Keep restraining yourself in this world,
Then you are sure to go to Heaven.
Liar! I don't believe you!
You're a liar, you bastard.
Don't tell a plausible lie,
You holy servant of God.

"Go-to-Hell Song" was scheduled for release in May 1968 by Victor with "Doss-house Blues" ("San'ya Blues") on side B, but first they flinched at the original title and changed it, and then the lyrics were regarded as "ideologically prejudiced" by the phonograph ethical-code committee.[31] In the end, the "Go-to-Hell Song" was not released by Victor, and "Doss-house Blues"/"My Friends" ("Tomo-yo") became the single instead.[32] Both sides of this record became hits in early October. "My Friends", in which the singer addresses his comrades encouragingly in a bright voice to a tune in E major ("My friends, beyond this darkness, tomorrow is shining"), was perceived to be an anti-war and anti-establishment song, and was often chosen as a 'sing along' song at anti-war meetings on university campuses.

Of all the anti-war songs that were written in 1968, "Let's Join the Self-Defence Forces" became the most popular. It was published in the July 1968 issue of the magazine *Kawaraban*, although it was not recorded in the studio until August 1969. In the long run, it turned out to be the best-known anti-war song in Japan. The lyrics to "Let's Join the Self-Defence Forces" were written by Wataru Takada when he was a 19-year-old high school student from Tokyo. Takada's lyrics were set to the tune (by Malvina Reynolds) of Pete Seeger's "Andorra". Takada first performed the song in the third Folk Camp, which was held on 9–11 August 1968 at a large Buddhist temple in Kyoto. More than 250 people participated in the Camp, some of whom had come to see the popular group, Folk Crusaders, who were known not only through their records but also through their appearance on television.[33] This third Folk Camp was the first opportunity for Kansai and Tokyo singers to link up with each other, and this was Takada's first visit to the Kansai region. Takada's song and singing attracted a great deal of attention at the Camp.[34] Using polite language, Takada addressed the audience with lyrics such as:

---

[31] Okabayashi 1969, p. 111.   [32] Nagira 1995, p. 39.   [33] Mihashi 1979, p. 31.
[34] Taka'ishi 1969, p. 84.

Do you take an interest in guns, tanks and airplanes?
Welcome to the Self-Defence Forces!
We'll coach you with great care. (From verse 3)
To keep the peace in Japan, guns and rockets are needed.
With the assistance of Mr. America,
Let's beat the wicked Soviet Union and China. (From verse 4)

The chorus has the following lines sung to a cheerful sing-along melody in the key of A major:

Let's join, let's join, let's join!
This world is a paradise if you join.
Any man who is a real man,
Joins the Forces and falls like cherry blossom.

In a tongue-in-cheek manner, Takada mockingly invites the audience to enlist in the Self-Defence Forces. Established in July 1954, the Self-Defence Forces consist of ground, maritime and air forces, and today they have reached 240,000 strong. It is important to note that since their inception, the legal basis of the Self-Defence Forces has often been challenged because their existence seems to contravene the Japanese Constitution.[35] Takada's song was broadcast in August 1968 on TBS, a major television network, and it soon became the talk of the town. Once the song became well known, the Defence Agency baffled Takada when they asked him for permission to use the song to publicise their recruitment drive. Takada later reflected on this incident in a television interview: "I wanted to write a paradoxical song [...] Isn't it strange that, despite my intention, there were some who misunderstood the song by taking it seriously? People at the Defence Agency were among them."[36] Such different readings of the song's meanings highlight the ambiguity of songs as a form of protest and their susceptibility to different interpretations whatever the author's intent. In the end, however,

---

[35] Article 9 of the Constitution states that "the Japanese people forever renounce war as a sovereign right of the nation and the threat or use of force as means of settling international disputes" and in a later section notes that "land, sea, and air forces, as well as other war potential, will never be maintained [...] The right of belligerency of the state will not be recognised" (Department of Laws and Institutions 2010 (1946), Vol. 1, p. 4). Reflecting critically on Article 9 of the Constitution and the Self-Defense Forces, Charles Lummis, who was a member of the Peace for Vietnam Committee and taught political thought at a Japanese university, succinctly remarks that "the notion that the clear renunciation of the right of belligerency is not a renunciation of the right to establish a military for self-defense is absurd" (Lummis 1993, p. 168).

[36] Anonymous 1999.

the Defence Agency withdrew their proposal, acknowledging their failure to realise that the song was a parody. The official condemnation of the song was complete when the National Association of Commercial Broadcasters in Japan blacklisted the studio version of the song (which was released in 1969) in order to prevent it from being aired.[37]

Revitalising *enka*

The idiom in which Takada wrote "Let's Join the Self-Defence Forces" had its roots in *enka*, a type of song which was popular from the 1880s to the 1930s.[38] In fact, Takada also performed an *enka* song titled "Resignation Song" ("Akiramé-bushi") at the third Folk Camp held in August 1968, when he sang "Let's Join the Self-Defence Forces" for the first time in public. "Resignation Song" was written in the mid-1900s by Azenbô Soéda who was the most prolific writer of *enka*. The performance of this *enka* song was Takada's first public attempt to resuscitate Japanese protest songs from a different period. They were songs of social and political protest, which were quite different to songs now more widely known also as *enka*.[39] The first two stanzas of "Resignation Song" are as follows:

Wealthy landowners are selfish,
Civil servants are arrogant.
I was born to such a world,
I resign myself to fate.
What have you come here for?
To pay taxes and interests.
I was born to such a world,
I resign myself to fate.

The feeling of resignation in the song text is comical and satirical, and this is emphasised by Takada singing the words impassively to the second part of an American traditional dance-tune, "Black Mountain Rag". By setting old words to a new melody accessible to the young audience, Takada

---

[37] Mori 2003, p. 19.
[38] A history of the early form of *enka* songs by Tomomichi Soéda, who was the son of Azenbô Soéda, was published in 1963 as *Enka no Meiji-Taishô-shi* (*History of the Meiji and Taishô Periods in Enka*). It includes the texts of 157 songs, 45 of which are complete with melodies.
[39] The term *enka* reemerged with a new usage in the late 1960s, denoting a genre that is assumed to be typically Japanese in its musical and lyrical attributes, and in the early 1980s it became a mainstay of Japanese popular music (see Mitsui forthcoming).

recontextualised an old protest song for a new political context. Takada's interest in *enka* was encouraged by the music journalist Kazuo Mihashi, who he first met in the autumn of 1967. At the meeting, Mihashi showed Takada "a book about Azenbô's *enka*",[40] and in correspondence Takada discussed with Mihashi which of Azenbô's song texts could be sung to melodies by Woody Guthrie.[41]

Takada was not the only young singer-songwriter who showed an interest in *enka*. Hiroshi Iwai, a five-string banjo player and a singer-songwriter from Kyôto, recalled: "Sometime after the Folk Camp in Kyoto in the summer of 1968, I heard Wataru perform at Taka'ishi's concert at YMCA in Kyoto. He was singing the lyrics of an Azenbô *enka* to a Woody Guthrie tune. I was also having a similar try at that [. . .] That made me talk with him about Woody."[42] In September 1966, Taka'ishi had also performed a song by Azenbô, "Happy-Go-Lucky Song" ("Nonki-bushi", c. 1919), at his first public appearance. He recollected in 1969 that "*Enka no Meiji* published by Iwanami offered me very good guidance, and on other occasions I also sang three or four *enka* songs, including "I Don't Give a Damn" ("Doko-itoyasénu")".[43]

Two *enka* songs performed by Takada were included along with "Let's Join the Self-Defence Forces" on a side of the first LP released by Underground Record Club or URC, an independent record label established by the Taka'ishi Office in February 1969.[44] As major record companies in Japan were wary of releasing overt protest songs, URC was set up partly to avoid the self-censorship of the ethical-code committee, which had become customary practice within the mainstream music industry. In addition to the first LP, they released two singles, one of which consisted of original tracks by Trịnh Công Sơn, a distinguished Vietnamese singer-songwriter (see Norton, Chapter 6, this volume, for discussion of Trịnh Công Sơn's songs).[45] In April 1969 URC went on to release a controversial song by Okabayashi, "Go-to-Hell Song", which the major label Victor had refused to release, with "Song by a Skelton" ("Gaikotsu no Uta") on side B. "Song by a Skelton" was another fierce song, which Okabayashi first sang at the February 1968 Folk School concert. URC's subscription system to distribute these records was successful enough for the Club to be expanded into URC Records in July 1969. In parallel with this expansion, massive anti-war rallies were held in Tokyo and songs from the folk song movement in Kansai were sung at these rallies.

[40] Mihashi 1975, p. 64.   [41] Mihashi 1975, p. 65.   [42] Iwai 1992, p. 72.
[43] Taka'ishi 1969, p. 95.   [44] Kurosawa 1992, pp. 14–15.   [45] Kurosawa 1992, p. 91.

Folk Guerilla

In late February 1969, the Tokyo Peace for Vietnam Committee and their supporters marched from their office to Shinjuku Station, one of the most important transportation centres in Tokyo. On the way, they sang to the accompaniment of a couple of guitars, and held a singing demonstration in an open area called the Chika Hiroba (Underground Square) at the west entrance to the station. This action was motivated by young members of the Osaka Peace for Vietnam Committee, who participated in an indoor meeting, titled "1969 Anti-war Folk and Debate", held by the Tokyo Peace for Vietnam Committee on 11 January.[46] The members had travelled to Tokyo several times since late 1968 and on their trips to Tokyo they held a series of singing demonstrations, which they called 'Folk Caravan', in the large cities of Nagoya and Yokohama.[47] These young volunteers had started off by assembling in the underground shopping complex under Osaka Station to hold regular, small anti-war demonstrations, which included singing songs together. Yoshiyuki Tsurumi, one of the representatives of the Peace for Vietnam Committee, wrote in June 1969: "Since February some of the young members of the Committee, who now call themselves Tokyo Folk Guerilla, appeared every Saturday and held a meeting to sing anti-war songs together."[48] In the April issue of a periodical published by the Peace for Vietnam Committee, a female student member of the Folk Guerilla remarked:

What I had in mind when singing folk songs was that the songs are a rage against, and a satire on, those who made war as if nothing were the matter. They expressed anger at those who withdraw into their shells, doing nothing while knowing that a war has broken out, and they gave us a sense of solidarity.[49]

In the June issue of the periodical, another female student, who was one of the Folk Guerilla organisers, reported on one of their demonstrations:

Around six o'clock [...] suddenly two guitars began to be strummed [...] Just at that moment, a large number of people quickly drew near [...] The two guitar players were grabbed by the arm by the policemen [...] They kept playing "We Shall

---

[46] Muro 1969, p. 22.   [47] Muro 1969, pp. 22 and 24.
[48] From Yoshiyuki Tsurumi, "Hansen folk ni kaigenrei", in *Asahai Journal*, June 1969, cited in Tsurumi 2002, p. 312.
[49] From Kazuko Ebata, "Naze folksong o utau-noka", in *Beheiren News*, April 1969, cited in Muro 1969, p. 26.

Overcome" and "My Friends" [...] We continued to sing those songs, over and over again and again – they had never sounded so beautiful before. I felt my heart tightening with deep emotion [...] We moved around, singing, and arrived at the east entrance [...] While singing there for a while, we were informed that singing had been resumed at the west entrance. And this time three guitar players headed there.[50]

It was a demonstration on 17 May at the Underground Square in Shinjuku Station held after three months of 'guerilla' activity that the Tokyo Folk Guerilla reached the headlines. A reporter of a major newspaper who must have arrived there around the time when the guitar players headed to the west entrance gave the following description of the demonstration:

Suddenly three young men took out guitars, and were at once surrounded by a large circle of people [...] Fifty policemen in uniform were on patrol, and the very moment the three young men began to play the guitars they were held by thirty policemen and taken away. Protesting against this use of force, about a hundred members of the Peace for Vietnam Committee, being joined by passers-by, yelled out at the policemen in chorus, "get back, get back!" It was followed by mass singing of "My Friends", and thereupon a hundred riot policemen, who had waited in readiness in the car park, were ordered out to prevent their singing.[51]

It was estimated that the crowd of protestors and spectators at the Underground Square numbered about 2,000. At later demonstrations in May the crowd swelled to around 5,000 people and this escalated further during demonstrations in June and July. Several days after a larger demonstration on 12 July, when some 7,000 people gathered, the Metropolitan Police Department changed the sign 'Underground Square' to 'Underground Walkway'. This redesignation meant that holding a meeting there was a violation of the Road Traffic Act. On the day of the next demonstration on 19 July 2000, riot policemen were sent out to prohibit it. A large number of people were arrested and this finally put an end to the regular Folk Guerilla rallies at the Station.[52]

In the insider observations and the agitated press coverage that reported the 'guerilla' activities, occasionally specific songs were referred to, but no importance was attached to the songs' origins. The writers in Tokyo seemed to be unaware that the songs performed at Folk Guerilla rallies drew on the Kansai folk song movement. However, as shown by reports by student

---

[50] From Miyo Takano, "Nishiguchi Hiroba wa daré no mono?", in *Beheiren News*, June 1969, cited in Muro 1969, pp. 14–15.
[51] From a report in *Yomiuri*, 18 May 1969, cited in Muro 1969, p. 12.   [52] Tsurumi 2002, p. 313.

activists and the press, the songs performed by the Folk Guerilla included the very songs discussed in this chapter. Moreover, in addition to songs such as "We Shall Overcome", "The Internationale", "My Friends", "Imjin River" and "Let's Join the Self-Defence Forces", the Folk Guerilla also adapted some songs, making them directly relevant to the demonstrations they were involved in. For example, "Let's Join the Self-Defence Forces" was modified to become "Let's Join the Riot Police". The new lyrics for this song were as follows:

Do you dislike demonstrations?
You're welcome to join the Riot Police!
With truncheons, tear bombs and a water truck,
Let's obstruct the demos.

Another song performed at the demonstrations, "Riot Police Blues", was a new version of "Examination-Hell Blues" with the narrator becoming a riot policeman:

Come here, everyone,
Listen to my tale,
I'm an unhappy riot policeman,
Listen to my tale,
It's insipid and dry as dust.
[. . .]
Alas! At noon we go to the park,
It was packed with demonstrators.
As I'm unpopular with girls,
I threw a stone in despair.

Conclusion

Protest songs in Japan around the year 1968 were strongly influenced by songs from America, and the songs suitable for singing in unison at anti-war rallies were mainly the product of student singer-songwriters who were part of the Kansai underground folk song movement. '1968' in Japan was therefore marked by an outpouring of youthful musical creativity and protest in the Kansai region. One of the main motivations for those young musicians in the underground movement was the desire to compose protest songs that commented on both domestic and international events. Many of these songs drew on models provided by American singers such as Pete Seeger,

Bob Dylan and Woody Guthrie and some became popular hits across Japan. As well as incorporating Western influences, however, the Kansai folk movement also looked for historical models of protest within Japanese music and recontextualised *enka* songs of protest from the early twentieth century. Young Japanese singer-songwriters, then, looked for both new and old musical forms for inspiration in their attempts to form a musical culture of protest in 1968.

6 | Vietnamese popular song in '1968': war, protest and sentimentalism

BARLEY NORTON

Vietnam holds the paradoxical position of being both central and marginal to the worldwide phenomena of 1968. Central because the Tet Offensive – the series of coordinated attacks launched on 30 January 1968 by forces of the northern Democratic Republic of Vietnam (DRV) and the National Liberation Front (NLF) against numerous sites in the American-backed southern Republic of Vietnam (RVN) – was a tipping point in the war, which led to a wave of anti-war demonstrations across the world. The tragedy of war in Vietnam fuelled widespread political and social unrest, helped galvanise diverse protest movements around a potent symbol of struggle and was a catalyst for artistic protest around the world.[1] Despite the significant impact of the war internationally, both Vietnams – the DRV and the RVN – were also marginal in the sense that they were quite isolated from the other crises and countercultural movements in different parts of the world around 1968. The preoccupation with the escalating war meant that the impact on both Vietnams of the 'spirit of 1968' was mainly restricted to events abroad that were directly related to the conflict, most notably anti-war protests in the US.

Given that the Tet Offensive dominated the year 1968 in Vietnam, this chapter examines how the experience of war influenced musical expression and how musical protest was configured in relation to the fractious politics of war. Although much musical activity in both Vietnams around 1968 was connected in some way to the conflict, this chapter is restricted to an examination of Vietnamese popular song, known as ca khúc. A key reason for concentrating on ca khúc is that it was one of the most influential mediums for protest and for the expression of sentiments about war.[2] This chapter therefore explores issues relating to both 'music and protest' and 'music and war'[3] during Vietnam's 'long 1968'. As the tragic events of

---

[1] Research on the cultural impact of the 'Vietnam War' has primarily focused on popular music in the US (e.g. James 1989). For an account of "Vietnam protest theatre" in the US and Europe see Alter 1996.
[2] This is not to say that other types of Vietnamese music did not address issues relating to war and protest, and a longer study would benefit from a discussion of other music genres including 'folk song' (dân ca) and the music theatre forms, cải lương, chèo and tuồng.
[3] See Pettan 1998 and O'Connell and Castelo-Branco 2010 for other research on music and war.

1968 were part of a longer war, Vietnam's 'long 1968' can be understood as spanning the length of the second Indochina war, the so-called 'Vietnam War', from the late 1950s to 1975.

Musicians who composed ca khúc in the 1960s drew on a Western-influenced songwriting tradition that gradually emerged towards the end of the French colonial era in the late 1930s and 1940s. After experimenting with adding Vietnamese lyrics to fashionable popular songs from Europe and the US – a trend known as 'our lyrics to Western melodies' (lời ta điệu tây) – some musicians began to compose their own songs in a 'reformed' (cải cách) or 'modern' (tân) style indebted to Western models.[4] Many early ca khúc had sentimental, romantic themes. Around the start of the Franco-Vietnamese War in 1945, nationalist and communist leaders saw a need for patriotic, revolutionary songs. Strongly promoted by the Vietnamese Communist Party, the overtly political lyrics of 'revolutionary song' (ca khúc cách mạng) voiced support for the 'war of resistance' against the French. In contrast to revolutionary songs, song with sentimental themes was referred to as 'pre-war music' (nhạc tiền chiến). This label consigns musical sentimentalism to the past, to a time before war. In practice, however, the label was ideological rather than temporal: even though communist cadres deemed 'pre-war music' to be inappropriate for revolutionary times, such music continued to be written during the Franco-Vietnamese War. The opposition between revolutionary and sentimental song remained important in a divided Vietnam after the end of the Franco-Vietnamese War in 1954. Once the DRV was established under a communist leadership, only revolutionary ca khúc whose lyrics accorded with socialist rhetoric were permitted, and sentimental song was pejoratively referred to as 'yellow music' (nhạc vàng). In the RVN, however, the tradition of writing sentimental ca khúc blossomed, especially among student populations in urban areas.

This chapter addresses the development of revolutionary and sentimental ca khúc during the Vietnam War. I discuss the role revolutionary ca khúc played in the war by outlining how the "Song Drowns Out the Sound of Bombs" movement in North Vietnam and the Liberation Music Groups of the NLF used music to incite and sustain the war effort. While these songs aimed to bolster support for the war among the Vietnamese population, they also became connected to international protest movements through being adopted by anti-war protest singers like Pete Seeger and Barbara Dane in the US. My account of revolutionary ca khúc considers such international musical exchanges and documents some of the responses by Vietnamese

---

[4] For an account of the early development of ca khúc see Gibbs 2004. See also Tú Ngọc *et al.* 2000.

songwriters to anti-war protests in the US. In the final section of the chapter, I turn to the most famous singer-songwriter in the RVN, Trịnh Công Sơn, who spoke out against war with daring sentimental songs, which captured the hearts of Vietnamese like no other musician living in the late 1960s. Extending the tradition of pre-war songs far beyond its beginnings in the 1940s and 1950s, Trịnh Công Sơn challenged the headlong pursuit of war with songs about love and peace. Fuelled by war and politics, Vietnam's 'long 1968' was marked by intense creative activity in the field of songwriting and the legacy of this period has continued to exert influence on Vietnamese popular song to this day.

A brief introduction to war in Vietnam

Vietnam was divided into North and South along the 17th parallel as a result of the Geneva accords, which were negotiated in May 1954 after the decisive defeat of French forces by Vietnamese troops at Dien Bien Phu a month earlier. The battle of Dien Bien Phu marked the end of the nine-year Franco-Vietnamese War, and in the North a communist government was established under the leadership of President Hồ Chí Minh. According to the Geneva accords, the separation of Vietnam into North and South was meant to be a provisional measure leading to nationwide elections and a final political settlement. The American-backed regime that emerged in South Vietnam under President Ngô Đình Diệm, however, refused to participate in nationwide elections and the country remained divided.[5]

After some initial moves by North Vietnam to start an insurgency against the regime in the South in the late 1950s, leaders in the North established the National Liberation Front on 20 December 1960. President John F. Kennedy increased American military presence in Vietnam during the early 1960s in support of the RVN regime. But Ngô Đình Diệm, a staunch Catholic, was increasingly unpopular, and a Buddhist demonstration in the central city of Hue in May 1963 against religious discrimination was harshly suppressed by RVN troops.[6] In protest against such violent suppression, on 11 June 1963 the Buddhist monk Quảng Đức self-immolated in central Saigon in full view of the international press, and images of the monk in flames shocked the world. Ngô Đình Diệm was murdered in a coup in November 1963, but Buddhist activism and protest against the RVN regime and the presence of the American military continued. After Quảng Đức's sacrifice, self-immolations

[5] Karnow 1984, p. 678. [6] Karnow 1984, p. 279.

by more Buddhist monks and nuns followed and major Buddhist demonstrations were held in Hue and other cities in South Vietnam in 1966. As American troop strength in Vietnam continued to rise during the mid-1960s, protests in the US against the war increased and some US citizens also self-immolated, including Norman Morrison in 1965.

It was the Tet Offensive, however, which decisively 'changed the face' of the war. As part of the Offensive, the old imperial city of Hue, which was part of the RVN, was stormed and held for nearly a month by North Vietnamese troops before RVN and American troops finally retook it. In the fierce fighting in Hue, thousands of civilians, as well as troops, were massacred and the city itself was reduced to ruins. Footage of the carnage in Hue and other cities was broadcast on primetime television across the world and large anti-war demonstrations in the US, Europe and Japan followed. Although the Tet Offensive ended in military defeat for the combined forces of the DRV and the NLF, they had struck a major blow in terms of international perceptions of the war.

When Richard Nixon was elected as President in the US in November 1968, he attempted to force the North Vietnamese government to accept a permanently divided Vietnam through relentless bombing and covert diplomacy. Ultimately, however, he failed in his aim. The American troops withdrew, leaving the RVN army to fend for themselves, and the final victory for the North Vietnamese came when they captured Saigon on 30 April 1975. With official reunification in 1976, the country was renamed the Socialist Republic of Vietnam under the leadership of the Vietnamese Communist Party.

Songs of war in Vietnam, songs of protest in the US

The Vietnamese Communist Party sought to use music and the other arts as a form of mass propaganda. Following Marxist teachings on the didactic role of arts in society, Vietnamese cultural cadres saw music as an 'ideological weapon' to strengthen people's commitment to the war and the new communist society. Edifying song lyrics with a clear, unambiguous meaning were favoured to convey messages about the inevitability of victory over the American 'imperialists', and about love for the nation and the Party. Importantly, music was not just something to be listened to: the Party encouraged mass participation in musical activities to foster comradeship between troops, and between troops and the rest of the populace. As part of this strategy of musical participation, a "Youth

Song Movement" (Phong Trào Thanh Niên Ca Hát) was established in 1966. The Movement's key aim was to propagate new, youth-oriented songs that would strengthen resolve for the armed struggle and encourage people to join the front. It was conceived as a grass-roots movement, with songs to be sung at impromptu performances throughout the country.

Articles in the newspaper *Tiền Phong* on 16 May 1968 provide information about the first phase of the Youth Song Movement from July 1966 to March 1968. Over 300 songs by professional and amateur musicians were written during the first phase and 37 of these were selected by the Central Committee of the Youth Song Movement for wide circulation.[7] Songs on the list include "We are on the Road" ("Có Chúng Tôi Trên Mặt Đường") by Phạm Tuyên, and "We Go For Victory" ("Thừa Thắng Ta Đi") by Trương Tuyết Mai.

The score of "We Go For Victory" appears alongside the song list in the *Tiền Phong* newspaper, and it is typical of many other songs that were published in later issues.

As Figure 6.1 illustrates, "We Go For Victory" is written using Western staff notation. The vocal melody in the key of G major is in the form ABBA. The A section is marked "marching rhythm, grandiose, proud" (nhịp đi, hùng tráng, tự hào) and features dotted rhythms and an emphatic melody that revolves around the tonic and dominant triads. The B section is marked "cantabile" and has a more expansive melody with a descending melodic shape. The lyrics of the song are a call to arms and include the following lines:

The drums urge us to go on the road,
The drums call us to unite and enlist in the army.
Today we leave our native villages and go on the road.
There is a storm in the South,
Destroy the American invaders.[8]

Published scores of ca khúc usually consist of just the vocal melody and lyrics, with no instrumental accompaniment or chord symbols, and "We Go For Victory" follows this convention. The Youth Song Movement encouraged *a cappella* performances by groups of young people as they mobilised for war. When instrumentalists were available, they devised their own harmonic accompaniments on instruments like the guitar, mandolin and accordion.

---

[7] Central Committee of the Youth Song Movement 1968.
[8] All translations from Vietnamese in this chapter are my own.

Figure 6.1 "We Go for Victory" by Trương Tuyết Mai, as printed in the newspaper *Tiền Phong* on 16 May 1968.

The slogan "Song Drowns Out the Sound of Bombs" (Tiếng Hát Át Tiếng Bom) became a popular synonym for the Youth Song Movement. It was coined in response to US air raids against North Vietnam, which began in 1965 with the "Flaming Dart" and "Rolling Thunder" campaigns. In addition to inflicting casualties and destroying supply lines and infrastructure, the overwhelming scale of these bombing raids was a form of psychological warfare, which sought to break the spirit of the people. The "Song Drowns Out the Sound of Bombs" movement aimed to combat this military offensive by bolstering unity and morale, and by directly inciting soldiers to shoot down US planes.

A book published in 1968 titled *Song Drowns Out the Sound of Bombs* vividly describes how the movement operated within the army. It consists of anecdotes about, and reflections upon, the cultural activities of the anti-aircraft military unit, Company 21. When under attack from the US planes, the book notes that some soldiers "lacked courage" and were so "frightened of death" that instead of manning the anti-aircraft guns they dived for cover under the fortifications.[9] In order to overcome their fear, troops underwent training in 'revolutionary ideology', which included being taught songs such as Tô Hải's song "Ready, Fire!" ("Sẵn Sàng, Bắn!") to sing while under attack. Such examples demonstrate the important role music played in inciting combat.[10] Music and dance performances, plays and poetry readings were also regularly organised to celebrate military success. The book documents, for instance, how Company 21 held a celebratory party with songs accompanied by a mandolin, a Vietnamese two-stringed fiddle, and a small drum after shooting down an F4 plane and two F105 planes.[11]

As US raids continued to be unleashed over North Vietnam through the early 1970s, the "Song Drowns Out the Sound of Bombs" movement continued. In December 1972, Phạm Tuyên – who participated in the first phase of the movement from 1966–8 – wrote two well-known songs about Hanoi under fire: "Hanoi Dien Bien Phu" ("Hà Nội Điên Biên Phủ") and "Sleepless Nights in Hanoi" ("Hà Nội Những Đêm Không Ngủ"). At that time,

---

[9] People's Army Publishing House 1968, p. 26.
[10] Based on research on the war in Croatia during the 1990s, Svanibor Pettan 1998, p. 13, suggests that there are three main functions of music in war: "encouragement – of those fighting on the front lines and those hiding in shelters and alike; provocation and sometimes humiliation directed towards those seen as enemies; and call for the involvement of those not directly endangered". Much of the pro-war music during the Vietnam War might be thought of as 'encouragement'. However, 'encouragement' encapsulates quite a broad range of possibilities in the context of war and it has connotations that are arguably more appropriate for musical cajoling, persuasion and morale-boosting, rather than direct forms of incitement and aggravation to fight to the death.
[11] People's Army Publishing House 1968, p. 25.

B52 bombers were relentlessly bombing Hanoi in an operation nicknamed the Christmas bombings. Most people had been evacuated from Hanoi into the countryside, but Phạm Tuyên remained in Hanoi as head of the music service at the Voice of Vietnam Radio. In an interview I conducted with him in Hanoi in 2008, Phạm Tuyên explained how he wrote the songs while living in an air-raid bunker at 58 Quán Sứ street in central Hanoi.[12] The bombing, he said, was so ferocious that he did not expect to live to hear the songs performed. On the evening of 29 December, however, Phạm Tuyên performed "Hanoi Dien Bien Phu" live on the radio: he accompanied the song on the piano and sang it in unison with two other singers.

Like many revolutionary songs, "Hanoi Dien Bien Phu" is a 'march' (hành khúc) in two parts. Written in the key of F major, the first part is written in 2/4 time and has strong military-style dotted rhythms; the second switches to 4/4 time, has more expansive phrases and briefly modulates to the relative minor before the final climax in the tonic major. Army leaders referred to the Hanoi bombing raids as a 'Dien Bien Phu battle in the air', and the lyrics recall the famous victory against the French at Dien Bien Phu in 1954. The lyrics of the first verse are as follows:

When a B52 is shattered and on fire, it lights up the sky.
The spirit of Thang Long shines brightly.
[...]
A Dien Bien Phu battle will bury the enemy's dreams of invasion.
Oh Hanoi, here is Thang Long, here is Dong Do, here is Hanoi, our Hanoi![13]
The new Dien Bien Phu battle shines a halo of victory.
Oh Hanoi, although it is heart breaking that the enemy has destroyed the
    streets, we will stamp on the heads of the enemy.
We are so proud of Vietnam.

The lyrics of the second verse include the rhetorical question, "Do the American imperialists hear our Hanoi's answer?" It turned out that 29 December was the last day of the twelve-day phase of bombing and at our meeting Phạm Tuyên remarked on this unlikely coincidence: "Everybody said that they [the Americans] must have heard the song so they didn't bomb any more."

---

[12] Alongside Phạm Tuyên in the bunker was another composer called Phan Nhân who also composed a song in response to the bombing campaign in the capital, "Hanoi – Belief and Hope" ("Hà Nội – Niềm Tin và Hy Vọng"). For a score of this song see Nguyen 2007, pp. 148–9.
[13] Thang Long and Dong Do are old names for Hanoi. This line quotes the lyrics, but not the music, of Nguyễn Đình Thi's famous 1946 song "People of Hanoi" ("Người Hà Nội").

Figure 6.2 Phạm Tuyên's original handwritten score for "Play Music for Our Dear American Friends". Photograph by Barley Norton, 2010.

Three years before "Hanoi Dien Bien Phu" was written, Phạm Tuyên saw a short video tape about the huge 1969 demonstration, "Moratorium to End the War", in Washington DC. At the demonstration, Pete Seeger led a rendition of "Give Peace a Chance" with the massive crowd. Touched by what he saw, Phạm Tuyên wrote a song called "Play Music for Our Dear American Friends" ("Gảy Đàn Lên Hỡi Người Bạn Mỹ"), which he dedicated to Pete Seeger (Figure 6.2). The song lyrics include the following lines:

Tonight, Washington is alight with the fire of resistance,
Song resounds everywhere, the truth spreads a dazzling light.
The Potomac River at night reflects a beautiful image of you,
Holding a guitar and singing, to save lives.
Play my friend!
[…]
Follow the sound of guns in South Vietnam.
Rise up American people, together we will break the chains on our hands.
Fight together for peace, to destroy the invading army.
Let's enthusiastically sing together the song of struggle!

Phạm Tuyên had never met Pete Seeger when he wrote the song, but along with other musicians from the Vietnamese Musicians' Association, he went to greet Seeger when he visited Hanoi in 1972. Recounting this meeting to me, Phạm Tuyên said: "I was very moved when I went to Gia Lam airport in Hanoi to meet Pete Seeger and his Japanese wife. When they stepped off the plane, Seeger said 'Where is the musician who wrote that song?' I said it was me, and he immediately strummed his guitar and sang "Play Music for Our Dear American Friends". He sang it without words, to 'la'." Moved by Seeger's impromptu performance of his song, Phạm Tuyên clearly felt that the feelings of solidarity that he had expressed for Pete Seeger and the anti-war movement in the US had been reciprocated.

Vietnamese songs that reflected on the anti-war protests in the US were relatively rare during the war. Apart from the "Moratorium to End the War" demonstrations, however, Norman Morrison's self-immolation in Washington DC was another protest that captured the imagination of songwriters and poets in Vietnam. The songwriter An Chung's 1965 song "Morrison, the Human Torch" ("Ngọc Đuốc Mo-ri-xơn"), with words by Tân Huyền, was one of several songs composed by North Vietnamese songwriters in response to Morrison's self-immolation.[14] The lyrics glorify Morrison's sacrifice, as illustrated in the four lines of the chorus:

Morrison, the human torch, is so brave,
The fire that cremated him raises a cry of hatred.
That fire is like a brilliant halo,
It burns in the hearts of so many people.

Within the DRV, then, there were some musical responses to the anti-war movement in the US, but most songs were oriented towards events in Vietnam. This was also the case with NLF songs, most of which were concerned with inciting a mass uprising against the 'American enemy'.

Musical activities within the NLF were coordinated by Liberation Music Groups (Đoàn Văn Công Giải Phóng). These ad hoc groups were formed under the extreme conditions of guerrilla warfare and their members included soldiers with limited musical training. The organisation of the Liberation Music Groups was modelled on similar groups that were established during the war against the French. Musicians such as Lưu Hữu Phước and Xuân Hồng, who were veterans of the Franco-Vietnamese war, were central to their formation and many of the ca khúc they initially taught to NLF soldiers dated from the 1940s and 1950s.[15] One example is Lưu

---

[14] Other songs and poems about Morrison's self-immolation include Vĩnh Cát's song "Sáng Mãi Ngọn Đuốc Mo-ri-xơn" ("Morrison's Torch Shines Forever") and Tố Hữu's poem "Emily" ("Emily Con Ơi"), dedicated to Norman Morrison's youngest child Emily.

[15] Xuân Hồng 1993, p. 648.

Hữu Phước's song "On the Road" ("Lên Đàng"), a 1944 song that had become a popular song of resistance during the Franco-Vietnamese War. Lưu Hữu Phước also composed the melody for the song "Liberate the South" ("Giải Phóng Miền Nam"), which became the official anthem for the NLF.[16] The chorus of the song includes the lines:

Rise up, heroic people of the South!
Rise up, and face the storm.
Pledge to save our country.
Pledge to fight to the death.
Advance with guns and swords in hand!

"Liberate the South", like many of Lưu Hữu Phước's songs, was in the style of a march, but some ca khúc written by NLF musicians also incorporated folk influences. The melody of Xuân Hồng's "Song for Sewing Clothes" ("Bài Ca May Áo"), for instance, features pentatonic phrases that loosely imitate Vietnamese folk song. According to the composer the rhythm and melody of the song, which was written in 1961, was influenced by 'hò' folk songs that he learnt from his mother as a child.[17]

Some NLF songs came to the attention of US musicians active in the anti-war movement like Pete Seeger and Barbara Dane, who famously sang together at the Washington demonstration in 1969. The scores for "Liberate the South" and "Song for Sewing Clothes", as well as four other songs by NLF songwriters, were published in a book titled *The Vietnam Songbook*, which was compiled and edited by Barbara Dane and Irwin Silber in 1969. The front cover of the book has the caption "More than 100 songs from the American and International Protest Movements – and Fighting Songs of the Vietnamese People". In the introduction, the editors add that the protest songs in the book range from those that "are of a simple pacifist, humanitarian nature", to those that "expose the hypocrisies of American jingoism", to those that express "support for the struggle of the Vietnamese people".[18]

The adoption of NLF 'pro-war' songs by anti-war activists in the US underlines that contextual nature of musical protest. Whether or not a song is considered to be a 'protest song' is dependent on the asymmetrical power

---

[16] "Liberate the South" was written jointly by Lưu Hữu Phước, Mai Văn Bộ and Huỳnh Văn Tiểng under the pen name Huỳnh Minh Siêng (see Mai Văn Bộ 1993). See Gibbs (2007) for further historical details about "Liberate the South".

[17] Xuân Hồng 1989, p. 195. A rare recording of "Song for Sewing Clothes" and other songs performed by the Liberation Music Groups operating in the jungle in 1965 can be found on the record *Chants des Maquis du Vietnam*, released on the label Le Chant du Monde.

[18] Dane and Silber 1969, p. 7.

relations in which it is embedded. Typically, a song is understood to be a 'protest song', when it opposes a hegemonic orthodoxy. In *The Vietnam Songbook*, therefore, all songs whose lyrics opposed the US government's foreign policy and the presence of the American military in Vietnam are framed as a form of protest.

The sentimental songs of Trịnh Công Sơn

Like many of the DRV and NLF musicians mentioned above, the identity of the singer-songwriter Trịnh Công Sơn (1939–2001) was formed in the crucible of war. Yet his reaction to the conflict could not be more different. Rather than fighting, he went to great lengths to avoid the draft.[19] Rather than writing revolutionary songs about vanquishing the 'American enemy', he wrote songs about lost love and human fate, about nature and beauty, about the pain and suffering of war and about the desire for peace. The sentimental ethos of Trịnh Công Sơn's songs is starkly opposed to the militarism of revolutionary music.

This opposition is vividly represented in the film *The Land of Sorrow* (*Đất Khổ*), directed by Hà Thúc Cần, which was filmed in South Vietnam in 1971 and 1972.[20] In the film, Trịnh Công Sơn plays 'himself', that is he plays the role of a singer-songwriter, whose character is strongly autobiographical. The story line of the film refers to key events in the war, including the Buddhist protests in Hue in 1965 and the Tet Offensive in 1968, and it includes real footage of civilians fleeing the so-called 'summer of fire' in 1972. Trịnh Công Sơn performs three of his songs in the film. The performance of one of these songs, "Rebuild People, Rebuild Homes" ("Dựng Lại Người Dựng Lại Nhà"), takes place in what looks like a dumping ground for disused military equipment. Perched on a rusty armoured vehicle, Trịnh Công Sơn strums his guitar and sings the song in unison with a group of five young singers to an attentive, youthful audience who are scattered among the old military vehicles. The lyrics of the first verse are:

Together, let's go on the road,
To rebuild Vietnam.
Let's walk swiftly, deep into high forests,

---

[19] When Trịnh Công Sơn received his first draft notice in 1967, he went to elaborate lengths to avoid it. He even drank large quantities of diamox to make him ill so he would fail the army medical exam (see Trịnh Công Sơn 1989).
[20] Hà Thúc Cần 1974.

And carry back timber,
To build new homes.
Rebuild villages so our people can return,
Rebuild new houses for our homeland.

Many revolutionary songs – like Trương Tuyết Mai's song "We Go For Victory" discussed earlier – urge people to 'go on the road' (lên đường), to leave their villages and join the armed struggle. In contrast, the first line of "Rebuild People, Rebuild Homes" urges people to 'lên đường' for the quite different purpose of rebuilding Vietnam. The melody of "Rebuild People, Rebuild Homes" is somewhat reminiscent of the revolutionary marches so beloved by the Youth Song Movement: it is written in 2/4, it uses a 'major' hexatonic scale, and it has strong, regular rhythms that emphasise each beat of the bar. But Trịnh Công Sơn combines a rousing melody with lyrics that urge people to mobilise in order to rebuild rather than to destroy. In this way, Trịnh Công Sơn destabilises the conventions of revolutionary ca khúc.

Straight after the performance of "Rebuild People, Rebuild Homes" in the film, a group of men move in front of the crowd. One of them announces that he would like to sing a song called "Determined to Win" ("Quyết Thắng"). The man then explains his choice of song: "As I see it, if we want peace, we must fight first . . . don't you think so?" The audience, however, reacts badly to this intervention: they do not want to hear "Determined to Win" and a fight breaks out, preventing the man from singing it. In the chaos of the scuffle, a guitar gets smashed and Trịnh Công Sơn is quickly ushered away by his group of singers.

It is not clear whether this scene from the film is based on a real event, but it nonetheless illustrates how music was a forum of intense ideological struggle between those who wished to use music to incite armed combat and songwriters who were against the war.[21] The lyrics of many of Trịnh Công Sơn's songs from the war period speak of the human suffering caused by war, of the yearning for peace and of a new dawn of reconciliation and reconstruction after the end of the war. But, unlike revolutionary ca khúc, Trịnh Công Sơn's songs do not justify war as a necessary step on the path towards peace.

---

[21] It is important to note that Trịnh Công Sơn was by no means the only songwriter in South Vietnam to compose songs which, in quite different ways, have been referred to as 'anti-war'. Others included Tôn Thất Lập and Trần Long Ẩn, who were the most prominent members of a student music movement called "Sing for Our Compatriots to Hear" ("Hát Cho Đồng Bào Tôi Nghe"), and Nguyễn Đức Quang, who was associated with a movement known as "Sweet Vietnamese Song" ("Du Ca Việt Nam"). The famous composer Phạm Duy also wrote anti-war songs (see Schafer 2007a, pp. 614–16). Unfortunately, there is insufficient space in this chapter to discuss these different strains of anti-war protest in South Vietnamese popular song.

Many of the songs that Trịnh Công Sơn wrote from 1965 to the end of the war in 1975 have been dubbed 'anti-war' (phản chiến), because of their humanist and pacifist stance.[22] It is difficult, however, to separate his anti-war songs from others, and Trịnh Công Sơn characterises all his songs in positive rather than negative terms, as songs articulating the desire for peace and love for his homeland.[23] In his writings about his music, Trịnh Công Sơn emphasises that all his songs are fundamentally about love, even those that were prompted by witnessing the human tragedy and suffering of war. "Love", he writes, "enables song to be born. Pain and joy are transformed and give birth to music. Music like that is love, it is the interior of a person's human life that is full of mixed emotions of sorrow and joy."[24] Trịnh Công Sơn's commitment to song as a medium for expressing the full range of human sentiment, from grief to love, is a recurrent theme in his writings. By emphasising the interdependence of music and life's flow of emotions, he argues for a musical aesthetics of love that implicitly rejects the formulaic socialist realism of revolutionary song.

By the time *The Land of Sorrow* was made, Trịnh Công Sơn's songs had become so popular that he was referred to as a 'phenomenon'. As John Schafer has outlined, it was Trịnh Công Sơn's anti-war songs written in the late 1960s – particularly those collected in the songbooks *Songs of Golden Skin (Ca Khúc Da Vàng)* (1966–7) and *Prayer for Vietnam (Kinh Việt Nam)* (1968) – which created the "Trịnh Công Sơn phenomenon".[25] Trịnh Công Sơn's fame grew following his first major public performance with the female singer Khánh Ly on a makeshift stage in front of the faculty of arts in 1965.[26] Over the next few years, Trịnh Công Sơn and Khánh Ly performed together across South Vietnam, including regular performances at the Quán Văn club in Saigon. The format of their performances was reminiscent of the 1950s and 1960s folk song revival in the US: they both sang to a rhythmic strummed guitar accompaniment played by the songwriter himself.[27] Through her performances and recordings, Khánh Ly became 'the voice' of Trịnh Công Sơn. Cassette tapes of Khánh Ly's studio recordings of his songs were very popular and the printing of songbooks enabled others to learn them. Even after the RVN government

---

[22] See Bửu Chỉ 2005 (2001) and Schafer 2007a.
[23] See Trịnh Công Sơn 1989, p. 460, and Schafer 2007a, p. 610.
[24] Trịnh Công Sơn 2005 (1996), p. 170.
[25] Schafer 2007a.   [26] Trịnh Công Sơn 1989, pp. 459–61.
[27] Recordings of performances by Trịnh Công Sơn and Khánh Ly at the Quán Văn club can be heard at www.tcs-home.org (accessed August 2011). This website is an extensive repository on Trịnh Công Sơn in both Vietnamese and English. It includes recordings and scores of the songs discussed in this chapter and some English translations of song lyrics.

issued a decree banning his songs in early 1969, Trịnh Công Sơn moved from one printing press to another to ensure that he could still self-publish his songbooks.[28]

In the rest of this section, I discuss some of the musical characteristics of Trịnh Công Sơn's 'anti-war' songs from the late 1960s and early 1970s. In a section of writing in which Trịnh Công Sơn reflects on why he chose popular song as his artistic medium, he refers to ca khúc as "a marvellous marriage between lyrics and music", as a musical form that is capable of expressing "the inner feelings of every human life".[29] Taking the lead from such comments, I consider the expressivity of Trịnh Công Sơn's songs as a form of protest through an examination of the relationship between words and melodic contour.

Following Trịnh Công Sơn's death in 2001, numerous publications about him have been published.[30] Most of the Vietnamese authors of these publications are intellectuals, artists, poets and musicians, who were in his circle of friends and acquaintances. Drawing on these sources, John Schafer's articles on Trịnh Công Sơn provide fascinating insights into the cultural significance of the songwriter and his 'soft philosophy', which was influenced by Buddhist ideas and European existentialism.[31] Schafer is attentive to Trịnh Công Sơn's music, but his analysis focuses primarily on song lyrics. Vietnamese authors have also tended to focus on Trịnh Công Sơn's poetic mastery, analysing the meanings of his lyrics as if they were poetry on the printed page. Some even argue that he is a poet, rather than a musician, and that his lyrics can effectively be read aloud, rather than sung.[32] Such a standpoint ignores the simple but important point that "lyrics aren't poetry", to quote Simon Frith.[33] The meaning of songs cannot be reduced to the semantic meaning of lyrics divorced from their musical setting because how the words of a song are heard and understood depends on how they are musically performed.

The view that Trịnh Công Sơn's music is subordinate to his lyrics also ignores the fact that it was musical performance that created the Trịnh Công Sơn phenomenon, not the spoken word. His songs have often been

---

[28] Trịnh Công Sơn 1989, p. 462.
[29] Trịnh Công Sơn 1989, p. 469.
[30] These include, among many others, Nguyễn Trọng Tạo and Nguyễn Thụy Kha 2001, and Trịnh Cung and Nguyễn Quốc Thái 2005 (2001).
[31] See Schafer 2007a and 2007b.
[32] Hoàng Tá Thích 2007, p. 73, for instance, gives two examples of Trịnh Công Sơn's lyrics that "do not need to be sung". In a similar vein, Vũ Thư Hiên (2001) states that "Trịnh Công Sơn is a poet. A great poet. Music is just a vehicle that he assembled to carry his poems to us."
[33] Frith 1996, p. 159.

described as 'simple' (đơn giản), an assessment that implies that his music and musicianship is worthy of little further analysis or comment.[34] The ability to compose captivating 'simple' melodies is a hallmark of successful songwriters, but analysing why songs are memorable and emotionally affecting is a difficult and elusive task. Remarking on the 'simplicity' of Trịnh Công Sơn's melodies the musician Phạm Duy writes:

> In terms of music, all of Trịnh Công Sơn's songs are not sophisticated or complicated because they are set to simple melodies in a way appropriate for the 'sound of sighing' of that time. His songs only need a guitar for accompaniment; if the harmonic accompaniment is too florid it would not be in keeping with songs that are arranged as 'ballads'.[35]

Phạm Duy's comments are highly suggestive: in what ways are Trịnh Công Sơn's 'simple melodies' suitable for the 'sound of sighing' of the time? How do they express the 'sighing' of the Vietnamese people? Phạm Duy acknowledges the appeal of Trịnh Công Sơn's songs, but he does not discuss the 'simple' melodies any further. The Vietnamese literature on Trịnh Công Sơn often notes how his songs "enter people's guts" (thấm vào lòng người),[36] a phrase that encapsulates how deeply his songs touch listeners. But how do his songs achieve such emotional impact? In the following brief discussion, I take some preliminary steps towards addressing this question.

Trịnh Công Sơn was fond of composing melodies with an arch-shaped contour, an ascent followed by a descent in pitch. This is a balanced musical shape, based on the symmetry of departure and return. Trịnh Công Sơn's use of arch-shaped melodies is not remarkable in itself, as it is commonly found in popular songs in Vietnam and the West.[37] But what I think is worthy of comment is the way he creates different musical effects through combining arch-shaped melodies with different tunings and lyrical content.

Songs such as "Singing on the Corpses" and "A Lullaby of Canons for the Night" have arch-shaped melodies using the 'minor' hexatonic scale: C, D, E♭, F, G, B♭. Lyrically, these songs are known as being strongly 'anti-war'. "Singing on the Corpses", for example, was written in direct response to the horrific loss of life Trịnh Công Sơn witnessed himself, while in Hue during the Tet Offensive. The lyrics describe corpses strewn

---

[34] See Đặng Tiến 2005 (2001).
[35] Phạm Duy 2001, p. 62. [36] Văn Cao 2001 (1995), p. 10.
[37] See Middleton 1990, p. 205, for an analysis of a song with an arch-shaped melody from the Tin Pan Alley repertory.

around after the battle and the confused reaction of bereaved women. The final lines are as follows:

Afternoon by the mulberry groves,
Singing on the corpses.
I have seen, I have seen,
Trenches filled with corpses.

A mother claps to welcome war,
A sister cheers for peace.
Some people clap for more hatred,
Some clap to repent.

In contrast to the dark lyrics about death, the vocal melody has a dreamy, folk-like quality. In Khánh Ly's recording of the song, her voice seems to soar at a distance above the death and confusion depicted in the lyrics.[38] On the ascent of phrases she employs her characteristic full tone, only softening her vocal timbre slightly on the resolution after each melodic descent. The momentum of the song is maintained by an insistent rhythmic accompaniment of two quavers followed by a crotchet per bar, which continues throughout, underpinning Khánh Ly's sustained vocal delivery.

In "Singing on the Corpses" there is a tension between the meaning of the lyrics and the expressivity of the music. The unsettling, dark lyrics contrast with the reassuring repetition of the arch-shaped vocal phrases, which make the song sound like a melancholic lullaby. The melodic departure and inevitable return of the arch contours, the insistent rhythm and the minor hexatonic scale, all contribute to the construction of a consoling, sentimental musical world that provides space for reflection on the human suffering and chaos of the Tet Offensive.

In other songs, Trịnh Công Sơn exploits a disjuncture between words and music for different ends. Apart from the minor hexatonic scale of "Singing on the Corpses", another popular tuning he used for his vocal melodies was the 'major' hexatonic scale C, D, E, F, G, A.[39] Many of the songs that use

---

[38] Khánh Ly's pre-1975 recording of "Singing on the Corpses" is included on the 4-CD box set *Khánh Ly: Ca Khúc Da Vàng* produced in California by Hương Xưa Productions. Khánh Ly's recordings are not circulated in Vietnam, but CDs of her pre-1975 recordings are popular amongst the Vietnamese diaspora and can be heard on numerous websites.

[39] These 'major' and 'minor' hexatonic scales are used for melodies of seventeen out of the thirty-seven songs published in three songbooks published from 1967–9, i.e. *Songs of Golden Skin*, *Prayer for Vietnam* and *We Must See the Sun* (*Ta Phải Thấy Mặt Trời*). Most of the other songs also use different hexatonic scales. Only one song, "Marching Song" ("Hành Ca"), from these songbooks uses a pentatonic scale and only a few use all seven notes of the diatonic scale.

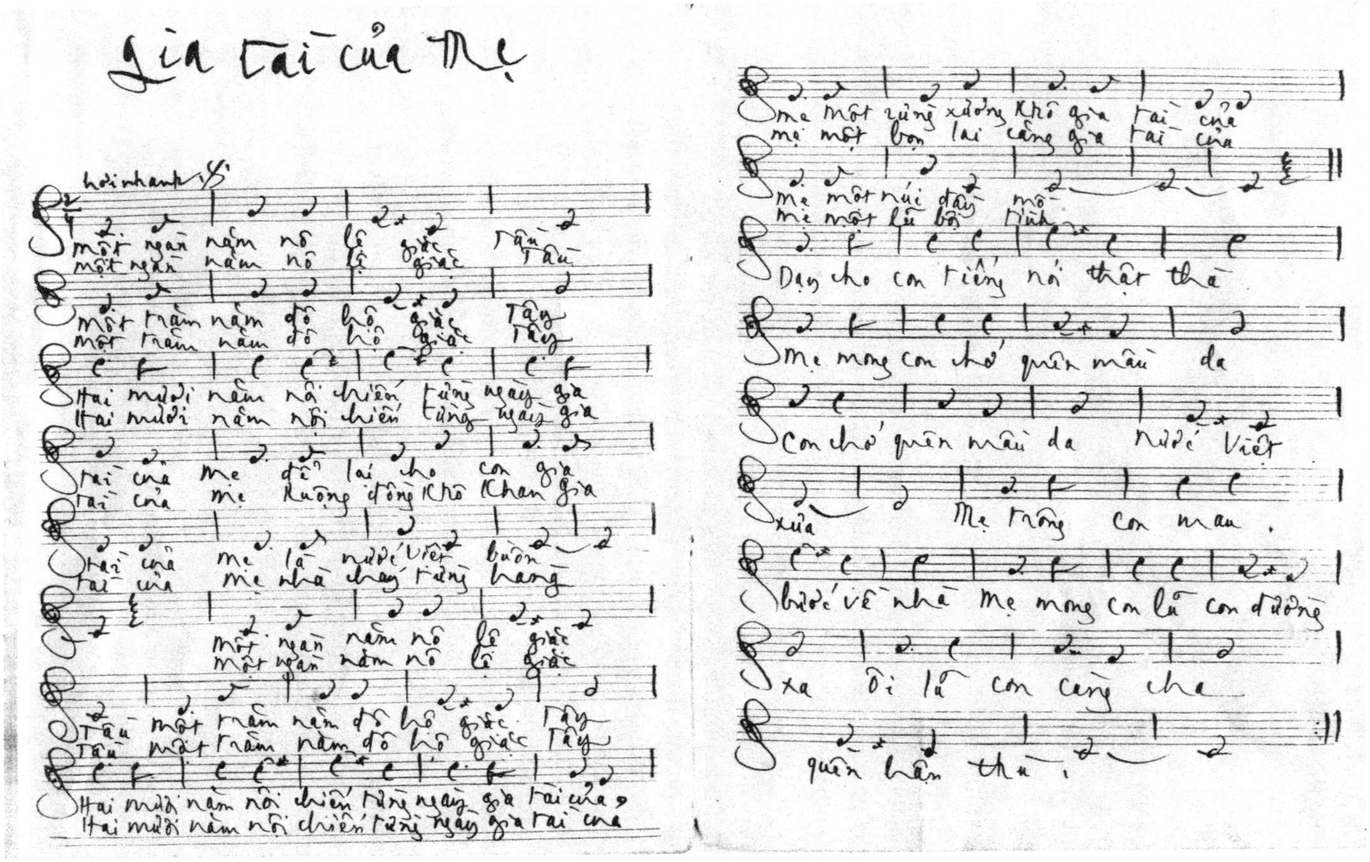

Figure 6.3 Trịnh Công Sơn's self-published score of "A Mother's Legacy" from the songbook *Songs of Golden Skin* (1967).

this scale – such as "Rebuild People, Rebuild Houses", "I Shall Revisit" ("Tôi Sẽ Đi Thăm") and "Hue Saigon Hanoi" ("Huế Sài Gòn Hà Nội") – have an upbeat message of reconciliation after war. But the lyrics of some other songs, like "A Mother's Legacy" ("Gia Tài Của Mẹ"), undercut the jovial melodies creating a quite different sentiment. The words of the highly controversial song "A Mother's Legacy" offer a damning indictment of the legacy of foreign occupation and war (Figure 6.3). The first two verses are as follows:

A thousand years enslaved by the Chinese,
A hundred years ruled by the French,
Twenty years of civil war,
A mother's legacy for her children,
A mother's legacy is a sad Vietnam.
[...]
A mother's legacy, a jungle of dried bones.
A mother's legacy, a mountain covered with graves.

As can be seen in the score, the lyrics are set to a sprightly, 'major' melody written in 2/4 time. The accompaniment on Khánh Ly's recording of the song has a strong 'oom-pah' rhythm throughout, with the strong accent on the second beat of the bar driving the melody along. Like "Singing on the Corpses", the melody of "A Mother's Legacy" features arch-shaped phrases. But the ascending-descending phrases of the song are bright and catchy, in a way that is reminiscent of a nursery rhyme, rather than a melancholic lullaby. Combined with such music, the lyrics become darkly ironic, taking on a quite different meaning than if they were just words alone. The seriousness and gravity of the lyrics is satirised by the cheerfulness of the music, and the result borders on the tragic-comic. In "A Mother's Legacy" – as well as others like "Vietnamese Girl" ("Người Con Gái Việt Nam") and "Love Song of a Mad Person" ("Tình Ca Của Người Mất Trí"), which uses all seven notes of the major scale – it is the disjuncture between music and words that serves to highlight the absurdity and tragedy of Vietnamese killing Vietnamese and the madness of 'civil war'.

Through combining lyrics and melody in novel ways, Trịnh Công Sơn marks out a compassionate musical space for sharing feelings of love and loss, suffering and sadness. Songs like "A Mother's Legacy" might be productively thought of in terms of Michael Herzfeld's notion of cultural intimacy, understood as the "recognition of those aspects of a cultural identity that are considered a source of external embarrassment but that nevertheless provide insiders with their assurance of common sociality".[40] Vietnam's history of domination by foreign powers referred to in "A Mother's Legacy" is a potent source of external embarrassment and "rueful self-recognition",[41] while at the same time it serves to bind all Vietnamese together around their shared plight. The cultural intimacy and 'weak' sentimentalism of Trịnh Công Sơn's songs offer a quite different basis for common sociality and national unity than the official rhetoric of sacrifice and patriotism found in revolutionary song.

Just before the end of the war in April 1975, Trịnh Công Sơn accepted an invitation to perform his song "Circle of Unity" ("Nối Vòng Tay Lớn") on the radio in Saigon. Sung to an urgent melody featuring march-like rhythms, the lyrics of the first verse call for all Vietnamese to join hands together and unite:

From mountain jungles to the distant sea,
We form a circle to unite our country.
From far and wide, we now return.
Our happy reunion is like a sandstorm,
Whirling under the open sky.
We join our hands together,
To form a circle of unity around Vietnam.

Despite Trịnh Công Sơn's attempt to foster a climate of peaceful reconciliation through song, reunification was not a cause for celebration for many in the South. Facing recrimination from the new communist government, there was a mass exodus from the country. Nevertheless, the hopeful message of unity projected by the lyrics of "Circle of Unity" is consistent with Trịnh Công Sơn's efforts to sing for peace, whatever the odds.

---

[40] Herzfeld 1997, p. 3. My brief examination of sentimentalism in Trịnh Công Sơn's songs is influenced by Martin Stokes' study of popular music in Turkey. Drawing on Herzfeld and others, Stokes (2010) discusses songs by prominent Turkish musicians in terms of a public discourse of love and shows how sentimentalism in popular song has sustained lively debates about citizenship, civility and national virtue in the public sphere. A much longer chapter would be required to thoroughly discuss Trịnh Công Sơn's music and life as a public figure in relation to theoretical ideas of cultural intimacy. Nonetheless, it is worth noting that the ways in which Trịnh Công Sơn conveys an affectionate sense of national belonging, which is quite different to the models of national citizenship offered by official state discourse, has some striking parallels with the Turkish musicians discussed by Stokes.

[41] Herzfeld 1997, p. 6.

On the musical legacy of Vietnam's 'long 1968'

The countercultural movements that erupted in the West in '1968' have been understood as a profound social and cultural transformation.[42] The 'Vietnam War' was implicated in this process of transformation through being a catalyst for widespread anti-war protests, but the events of Vietnam's 'long 1968' were far removed from the rise of anti-authoritarian youth cultures in the West. In North Vietnam, the government's tight control over cultural expression precluded overt forms of musical protest against the war. But as I have outlined in this chapter, some pro-war songs by DRV and NLF composers became protest songs in the context of anti-war activism in the US. A few songs with lyrics about anti-war protests in the US were also written by North Vietnamese composers for propaganda purposes. The situation in the RVN was different; music was also used for military purposes, but some anti-war demonstrations were held and Trịnh Công Sơn – as well as some other musicians like Phạm Duy, Tôn Thất Lập and Trần Long Ẩn – wrote songs that, in different ways, voiced opposition to the war. Due to space constraints this chapter has focused on Trịnh Công Sơn's anti-war songs, but there was a wide range of protest music in the RVN around 1968. Tôn Thất Lập's song "Sing for Our People to Hear" ("Hát Cho Dân Tôi Nghe"), for instance, was one of the anthems of the student-led anti-war movement called "Sing for Our Compatriots to Hear" ("Hát Cho Đồng Bào Tôi Nghe"), which organised street demonstrations, public debates and performance events in Saigon and other cities in South Vietnam in the late 1960s and early 1970s (see Norton, forthcoming).

When the war ended, marking the end of Vietnam's long 1968, the government of the unified Socialist Republic of Vietnam cracked down on all forms of musical activity that were perceived to threaten the development of the new communist society. Trịnh Công Sơn was the most prominent of a group of South Vietnamese songwriters whose music was condemned and banned as 'yellow music' (nhạc vàng). As Philip Taylor has pointed out, after 1975, "the commodity market and the lush offerings of popular music [in the South] were systematically discredited as signifiers of 'civilisation', the 'modern' or historical progression of society".[43] Communist leaders viewed the expressive, melancholic themes of yellow music as "neo-colonial poison",[44] which had polluted the musical traditions of the South. In the late 1970s and 1980s the style and lyrical content of ca khúc was tightly controlled

---

[42] See, for example, Klimke and Scharloth 2008.   [43] Taylor 2001, p. 54.   [44] Taylor 2001, p. 32.

by the communist leadership and 'red music' (nhạc đỏ) that followed in the tradition of wartime revolutionary ca khúc was promoted by the state.

In the wake of the economic and cultural reforms, known as 'renovation' or 'đổi mới', which were initiated in the late 1980s, sentimental popular songs have undergone a resurgence and Trịnh Công Sơn's popularity has reached new heights, underlining the government's failure to eradicate 'yellow music' from Vietnamese cultural life. Although many of Trịnh Công Sơn's pre-1975 songs are still not allowed to be circulated,[45] some have received government approval, and since the 1990s public concerts and recordings by young singers have popularised these songs for a new postwar generation. Revolutionary music has not disappeared entirely in the renovation period: it is still broadcast on the state-controlled media and performed at commemorative events and state functions. But in a Vietnam that has abandoned the pursuit of a communist society based on a command economy, revolutionary music no longer makes sense the way it did during war and it lacks a broad base of popular support.

As the forces of globalisation have increasingly influenced Vietnamese culture, popular music has diversified enormously. Since the late 1990s, an emergent youth culture has embraced genres such as rock, rap and electronic dance music. In the midst of such diversity, the opposition between revolutionary and sentimental ca khúc, discussed in this chapter, no longer dominates Vietnamese popular music as it once did. Nonetheless, the fact that Trịnh Công Sơn's songs, and sentimental song in general, still hold a central place in mainstream popular music in Vietnam highlights the significance of the musical legacy of Vietnam's 'long 1968'.

---

[45] Schafer 2007a, p. 630, estimates that around 250 songs by Trịnh Công Sơn were legally circulating in Vietnam in 2003, which is less than half the total number that he composed.

7 | "There Is No Revolution Without Song": 'new song' in Latin America

JAN FAIRLEY

He who has a song will have torment [...]
He who follows the good path will court danger,
chairs that invite him to stop,
But it is worth it to have good song that torments.[1]

In this chapter I focus on specific aspects of the independent, creative network of musicians who in the late 1960s and early 1970s bonded together as the *nueva canción* or 'new song' movement across the Latin American continent, the Caribbean and Spain. I trace *nueva canción* through various key phases.[2] *Nueva canción* describes a music enmeshed within historical circumstances which included: the forging of revolutionary culture in Cuba; the coming together of political parties to form a coalition to elect the first ever socialist president through the ballot box in Chile in 1970; resistance to brutal Latin American dictatorships, which were established mainly in the 1960s and 1970s, and the so-called 'dark years' under the rule of these dictatorships,[3] followed by the struggle for 'new' democracies. For *nueva canción* musicians, the 'long 1968' was a period that stretched back to 1959, when the Cuban Revolution first demonstrated to the Latin American continent that social, political and economic change was possible, and extended forward to 1979, when the Sandinista rebels successfully overturned the Somoza dictatorship in Nicaragua.

Nueva canción brought together a generation of musicians born in the 1940s and 1950s who supported social and political change in their respective countries. Gradually, they became aware of each other, meeting at festivals and international events. This loose network of musicians became known as a movement, which was in many cases based on personal

---

[1] Silvio Rodríguez, "Historia de las Sillas" ("Story of the Chairs"); composed 7 October 1969. Rodríguez 1996, p. 225.

[2] This chapter draws on interviews and ethnographic work with the musicians discussed and many other cultural activists and commentators over the period between 1970 and 2011 in Chile, Cuba, Argentina, Uruguay, Peru, Bolivia, Venezuela, Mexico and Spain. For a complete list see www.janfairley.co.uk.

[3] The 'dark years' of dictatorship began in: Brazil in 1964; Chile in 1973; Uruguay in 1973; and Argentina in 1976.

friendship. Their music was often referred to by different names in different countries. It was known as: *nuevo cancionero* (new song book) in Argentina; *nueva canción* (new song) in Chile and Peru; *nueva trova* (new song) in Cuba; and *volcanto* (volcanic song) in Nicaragua. Across Latin America, however, *nueva canción* was used as an umbrella term.

This chapter differs from the work of other scholars who have written about *nueva canción* in that it problematises the term, focusing on the fact that *nueva canción* musicians never saw their music as 'protest song'.[4] *Nueva canción* was regarded as a social force in itself and a key resource for helping bond "individual subjectivities into collective expression".[5] Musicians who composed and performed *nueva canción* were committed to positive, progressive social change through music. I suggest that 'new song' in its various forms was an emblematic music of the 1960s, 1970s and 1980s. Functioning as both a national and international music, *nueva canción* has become part of the active memory of this period. Its potent legacy can be seen in the fact that many high-profile commercial singers today continue to be influenced by it: *nueva canción* continues to be perceived as a legitimate, unifying and active force for peaceful change.

'1968' in Mexico

In Mexico on 2 October 1968, ten days before the Olympics were scheduled to take place in the country, more than 300 students, who were peacefully demonstrating in La Plaza de las Tres Culturas in Mexico City, were mown down by a hail of military bullets.[6] This act was immortalised in the following days by singer Judith Reyes in her ballad "La tragedía de la Plaza de las Tres Culturas" ("The tragedy of the Plaza of the Three Cultures").[7] The tragedy of the student deaths was underlined in Reyes' ballad by her use of the traditional *corrido* form, which was originally a nineteenth-century song form that was closely associated with the Mexican Revolution.[8] *Corrido* was originally sung and sold in

---

[4] For example see Moore 2006; Marsh 2010.   [5] Turino 2008, p. 234.
[6] See Poniatowska 1971.
[7] A recording of this song can be heard on Judith Reyes' album *Cronica Mexicana* (Reyes n.d. [early 1970s]).
[8] Unlike the nascent Mexican rock movement (Zolov 1999), musicians in the 'new song' movement did not see rock as countercultural. Rather they considered it as a commercial transnational form that was the opposite of and different to their search for something

sheet form at markets and on street corners, and historically it functioned as a chronicle for people who had little access to education. With roots that can be traced back to the fifteenth-century Spanish romance, *corrido* draws on a stock set of catchy melodies to directly report an event or story in a dramatic, declamatory style, and it has a swinging, waltz-polka like rhythmic form. By drawing on *corrido* in "La tragedía de la Plaza de las Tres Culturas", Reyes asserted that *corrido* was still pertinent, and had sufficient flexibility and popularity to maintain its position as an important Mexican and South American musical genre.

The exclusively Mexican focus for Reyes' work, particularly in the late 1960s and 1970s,[9] meant that she never became known as a 'new song' singer, even though her songs were widely admired and respected. However, this was not the case for her fellow Mexican musicians in the band Los Folkloristas. Founded in 1966, Los Folkloristas were a pioneering urban folk group, who also used traditional forms such as the *corrido*, but they reworked traditions through new musical arrangements, which gave them a contemporary aesthetic. By embracing a Mexican and continental repertoire, Los Folkloristas assumed an international outlook. The most notable example of this was Los Folkloristas' version – sung by the Mexican female singer Amparo Ochoa – of Gabino Palomares' ground-breaking song "La Maldición de Malinche" ("Malinche's Curse"). This song set a benchmark for a new approach to songwriting and performance, which was associated with activism across the continent among students and others struggling for legitimate social and political change. Its significance came from the fact that it mapped the arrival of the Spanish *conquistadores*, and the lyrics argued that "foreigners with blond hair" continue to receive a better welcome than indigenous Mexican people, who are described as "humiliated strangers in their own land".[10] The song also captured the political attitudes of many in the late 1960s in the way it told a story of Spanish colonialism being replaced by North American neo-colonialism.

The Folkloristas' musical arrangement attracted attention and broke new ground because of the way that it used instruments from the different historical periods evoked by the verse of each song. The arrangement moves from the early conch shells, trumpets and shakers of the pre-Hispanic period, to indigenous flutes and drums, to the guitars and strings

---

original rooted in tradition that expressed the aspirations and sentiments of their generation. This oppositional attitude to rock was not monolithic, viz. the work of Victor Jara with Los Blops; and later in the 1980s of Mercedes Sosa with Argentine *rock nacional* artists.

[9] See Marsh 2010.   [10] Ochoa 2012; see also Los Folkloritas 1975.

of the conquest. Through the instrumentation, the song therefore symbolically maps the historical trajectory of Mexico from pre-Hispanic to modern times. Los Folkloristas released the song on a disc called *El Cancionero Popular* (*The Popular Songbook*) with the small independent label Discos Puebla.[11] Such discs circulated outside commercial networks: they were sold among activists, at music events, in small music kiosks and local shops, through political parties, student unions, trade unions and at *peña* nightclubs. Although the discs themselves received limited distribution, they were also copied on cassette and exchanged among influential friendship networks. Such distribution was uncannily effective and transcontinental. The inside of the Los Folkloristas cardboard disc cover included the texts of all twelve songs on the disc, illustrated by graphic lino-cuts following *corrido* street tradition. Such packaging indicated that lyrics mattered. At the same time, the music on the disc showed that Los Folkloristas, like Judith Reyes, were following in the footsteps of a long tradition that stretched back at least a century.

These songs on disc and cassette did what Vanessa Knights called "cultural work being done by associated popular musics",[12] in that they became part of the struggle as well as symbolic of it. To know the songs, to hear them, to personally distribute them by sending cassettes to others, to enthuse about them to friends, became a way of participating in the struggle for social change itself. Even though this might happen at a distance, it was an act of solidarity. In time, such independent recordings became an integral part of an axis of cultural and economic solidarity between South America and Europe.[13] Judith Reyes' work, for example, came to European notice when the Paris-based Solidarity Committee with the Struggle of the Mexican People (CSLRPM) brought out a disc of her work in the 1980s,

---

[11] Los Folkloritas 1975. The label Discos Puebla was an initiative of a member of Los Folkloristas. Many small independent record companies emerging in South America during this period were run and financed by musicians, trade unions, political parties or other interested parties. Another key example was Chile's DICAP label, originally funded by the Communist Party to help the student music group Quilapayún gather funds to travel to a European youth festival. This group took copies of their album *Por Vietnam* as a greeting to those they met there (Quilapayún 1973).

[12] Knights 2007.

[13] The transcontinental and international focus of the 'new song' movement involved exchange between musicians through events such as: Das Festival des Politischen Liedes (The Political Song Festival), held in East Berlin's Oktoberklub from 1970 onwards; the Fête de la Humanité in Paris; and other cultural events mostly organised by the youth sections of socialist and communist parties in different countries during the 1960s, 1970s and 1980s. European Youth Festivals organised by socialist countries celebrating cultural exchange have played a key part in bridging South America to Europe, offering the opportunity for musicians from both continents to meet.

relicensing pre-existing Mexican material.[14] This distribution of recordings via such European solidarity committees was characteristic of the 1970s and 1980s, when the music integral to social struggle in Latin America became available in Europe.

In Reyes' case it saw her hitherto 'national' work reframed within an international, ideological discourse that was simultaneously both Marxist and integral to the language of a perceived Cold War anti-imperialist struggle. In the sleeve notes to LPs distributed in Europe, Reyes was described as an 'artist and militant', as part of 'the political Latin American song', part of the democratic struggle against 'international imperialism'.[15] This and other discs spoke of the role of such music as forming part of a 'revolutionary vanguard', its role to demystify the 'lying images of a demagogic government', the music, in 'solidarity with the peoples who struggle against oppression and imperialist exploitation'. In the view of those distributing the music of these musicians, cultural imperialism was not merely to do with the foreign ownership by US companies of national resources or US training and support of the national military forces, which was an attempt to avoid another Cuban revolution or socialist governments elsewhere on the continent. Rather cultural imperialism was also manifested in the US domination of the international media and music business.

As mentioned above, the songs of Mexico's Los Folkloristas and contemporaries across the continent often became identified with the movement known as *nueva canción*. As Alegre and Camacho (2006) have argued, *nueva canción* brought people together, told them what was going on and emotionally empowered them. It also articulated the social and symbolic universes of different movements, making activism a pivotal affective experience. However, there was nothing monolithic about this creativity, nor was there any blueprint or model that characterised the music that the individual singer-songwriters and groups involved were making. There was no common repertoire or sound. On the contrary, musicians composed their own music and forged their own distinctive styles and repertoires. Although the sounds of *nueva canción* were diverse, what linked them was the shared belief that music would naturally express their desires, realities, truths and world-view, and resist the compromises perceived as inherent in commercialism. The Cuban singer-songwriter Silvio Rodríguez summed up the work of *nueva canción* musicians as "capturing the subtle shades and distinctions of life, everything there is between black and white. If you can write a text as poetry, there is always a brave human message comes

---

[14] See sleeve notes by Reyes n.d. [early 1970s].   [15] Reyes n.d. [early 1970s].

through, it's your life that is there".[16] While some musicians were militants in political parties, many were not members of any particular party at all: at the time the so-called 'left' embraced a broad spectrum of political parties from communist, socialist, Christian Democrat and various other independent parties with nuanced positions. Music-making was itself perceived as participative social action. Perhaps this is one of the reasons why the rubric *nueva canción* was preferred to terms such as 'protest song' and 'political song'. How much the appropriateness of terms mattered became evident during the 1967 Cuban Encuentro de Canción Protesta or Protest Song Meeting.

Cuba in 1967: *'nueva canción'* not *'canción protesta'*

Held between 29 July and 10 August 1967, the Cuban Encuentro de Canción Protesta (hereafter referenced as the Encuentro) was the key event that crystallised the debate concerning nomenclature. The meeting involved fifty participants from eighteen countries and five continents.[17] This was not an isolated international event: the Encuentro was part of a much larger Cuban initiative involving various high-profile meetings grouped together as part of the Organization of Latin American Solidarity (OLAS), which were hosted by Cuba's intellectual cultural centre, the Casa de las Americas. The meetings held in Cuba in 1967 and 1968, which brought experienced professionals and experts from different parts of the world together, were designed to 'make waves' (in Spanish the acronym *olas* means waves) during the Cold War period. In the 1960s, Cuba had become isolated due to the impact of the official US embargo and international meetings were designed to lesson this isolation.[18]

Cuban writer José Ossorio, who wrote the report on Encuentro based on verbatim notes for the journal of the Casa de las Americas, argued that the Encuentro gave "artists, activists and artist-activists, of many

---

[16] Fairley 2006, p. 15.
[17] Musicians came from South America: Chile, Argentina, Uruguay, Mexico and Brazil, as well as from the UK, the US, Italy, Portugal and Spain: Cataluña.
[18] Following the 1962 Cuban Missile Crisis, which saw confrontation between the Soviet Union and the US almost bring the world to the brink of war, the island of Cuba found itself caught in the middle, unable to determine its own destiny outside this sphere of influence. Following the crisis, Cuba was effectively quarantined by the US, formalising an economic blockade which isolated Cuba from the rest of the Americas and Europe until the mid-1990s (and the blockade still formally operates today).

nations unprecedented opportunity to exchange ideas, compare techniques and formulate strategies which could almost immediately be tested in practice".[19] The event helped break down the isolation many singers felt in their own countries. What they had in common was their creativity experienced as activism through music-making. For many, participation had a profound effect. As Uruguayan singer Daniel Viglietti remarked,

> my life has a 'before Cuba' and an 'after Cuba'. In my youth I lived on another planet. I became politicized little by little... The decisive moment was the Bay of Pigs [the 1961 attempted invasion of Cuba by US backed mercenaries] which spurred me to express myself politically in my songs. The Encuentro de la Canción Protesta enabled me to know the Cuban revolution. You saw there just what could be done, and you felt you wanted that for your own country and one had to achieve it.[20]

Cuba's use of the term 'protesta' was both ambiguous and shrewd: the Encuentro title reclaimed the word 'protest', which at the time had been used predominantly by the US media and the Johnson government to ghettoise and diminish both the 'freedom songs' of the civil rights movement and the music associated with the anti-Vietnam War effort. The Encuentro aimed to challenge the appropriation of 'protest' by Cuba's hostile neighbour, the US. Musicians attending the meeting, however, rejected the term *protesta*, arguing that their songs were far from protest, even when they had social and political themes. All music they felt was political in one way or another. In a sense they saw both US and by inference the Cuban use of 'protest' as a language heist, whereby 'protest' obfuscated what was intended because it offered a narrow meaning of songs before they were ever heard and led to false presumptions about hortatory or dogmatic content.

Although many of those who came together in 1967 agreed that rubrics such as political song, social song, revolutionary song, committed song and revolutionary political song were valid, they favoured the term *nueva canción*. For example, the Catalan musician Raímon – who was a member of the seminal Catalan cultural group Els Setze Jutges (The Seven Judges), which campaigned against the censorship of Catalan language, songs and concerts and other forms of oppression by the Franco dictatorship – remarked,

> I am completely against that term 'protest song', it seems to me narrow and limited for what we are each doing in different parts of the world. In Italy and Cataluña we

---

[19] The following account is based on Ossorio's 1967 report for Casa de las Americas, from which all quotes (my translation) come, see pp. 138–56.
[20] Anonymous 1970a; see also Benedetti 1974.

say 'new song' *(nova cançó)* [...] which suggests the appearance of a sociological phenomenon in the world. It's a definition which defines so much.[21]

This was an important point for Raímon, not least because he was banned from singing his most popular song "Al Vent". Written in 1960, "Al Vent" merely told of the freedom of the wind to move about freely, and at Raímon's concerts, audiences often sang it for him, to outwit censorship.

Strong arguments against the term 'protest song' were also voiced by Irwin Silber, the US musician and editor of the influential US magazine *Sing Out!*, who attended the Encuentro with the American blues singer and activist Barbara Dane. Silber spoke of the cooption of 'protest song' by the Johnson presidency. It was, he said, a term negated by commercialisation which resulted in the "diluting [of] its message" so that it was "being used against the people rather than for them".[22] He cited Johnson's demagogic use of civil rights freedom anthem "We Shall Overcome" which had turned the phrase into a government slogan. The proper term for the songs of the civil rights movement, he argued, was 'freedom songs'.

The idea of song having an explicit message, however, also elicited hard debate. Discussion of what might be meant by 'message' was framed by the Cuban struggle against colonialism and US imperialism. Participants at the Encuentro agreed that song could communicate with large numbers of people and argued that song should be at the service of that objective rather than being an object of consumption used by capitalism to alienate. Those participating considered that they had a responsibility to "enrich their work searching for artistic quality and thereby find revolutionary attitude, taking a position defined by their people and the problems they faced within the societies in which they lived".[23]

1969–70: Cuban *nueva trova* emerges during the repressive 'grey period'

Paradoxically at the very moment of the Encuentro, two young Cuban musicians, Silvio Rodríguez and Pablo Milanés, were having a difficult time. Proto-Stalinist cultural ideas were being applied in heavy-handed fashion by a number of bureaucrats as the 1959 revolution was becoming more defined and institutionalised as a result of moving closer to the USSR for economic support. Cultural bureaucrats such as Luis Pavón

---

[21] Ossorio 1967, pp. 139–40. [22] Ossorio 1967, pp. 142–3. [23] Ossorio 1967, p. 144.

Tamayo, who directed the Council on National Culture (today the Ministry of Culture); Jorge Serguera, who presided over the Cuban Institute of Radio and Television (ICRT) and was linked to the 'revolutionary trials' against those opposing the state; and Armando Quesada, who took charge of theatre in the country, took what were regarded as retrograde acts against artistic freedom. In Cuba it was the beginning of the tense build-up to the period now retrospectively and officially called the 'quinquemio gris' (the 'grey five-year period'). Despite the fact that by the early 1970s Rodríguez and Milanés were to become core members of Cuba's nascent *nueva trova* (new song) movement, and in the late 1970s and 1980s outside Cuba became leading 'new song' musicians popular across the continent and Spain with a huge international reputation, in 1968 they were both coming under unwelcome scrutiny and were perceived as potentially subversive.

Officially in the Cuban media there was a search for an acceptable youth music, which had an unequivocal didactic tone to it. The music of Milanés, Rodríguez and others was experimental; they wrote guitar-based songs with local and transnational influences coupled to poetic, metaphorical lyrics, which often expressed self-doubt and vulnerability. Their music perplexed those, such as the aforementioned Serguera, who made decisions about which cultural forms should be permitted media access, and it challenged bureaucratic precepts of what revolutionary culture should be. With Soviet socialist-realist, hymn-like, dogmatic models in mind, the often existential songs by Milanés and Rodríguez did not conform to the conventional idea of revolutionary song. These young musicians' original compositions expressed the perceptions of young people growing up in the Revolution with lyrics that broke all stereotypes. Their music was inspired by multiple sources – from classic Cuban *trova* (troubadour) songs by musicians like Sindo Garay to Brazilian styles, to the Beatles and other rock and Western pop music – and this eclecticism disconcerted some 'official' listeners. Anything linked to the US, even its countercultures and the 'protest songs' by US singer-songwriters like Bob Dylan and Joan Baez, was thought to have no place in revolutionary Cuba because in Cuba there could be nothing to critique or 'protest' about.

Bureaucrats were puzzled by songs like Rodríguez' "Playa Girón", which in three succinct verses questions the nature of creativity, and what constitutes truth and sacrifice. Addressing poets, musicians and historians in turn, the song asks how anyone who has not had a certain experience – such as being a fisherman on the ship *Playa Girón* which was named after the Bay of Pigs invasion – can write a song about it. The melody of "Playa

Girón" coupled with its questioning tone did not fit with the aims and objectives of the revolution. At the same time its poetry made tribute to the fishermen and those who by inference fought for Cuba at the Bay of Pigs.

In 1967, just prior to this repressive grey period, neither Rodríguez nor Milanés were formally invited to the Encuentro (although Rodríguez attended a peripheral event). Cuba's official Encuentro delegate was traditional singer Carlos Puebla. His lively swinging *guajira* (country music) songs whose lyrics serenaded the revolution, Fidel Castro and Ché Guevara were based on the affinity of an older generation who had been part of the revolution and who fully embraced the rhetoric of revolutionary achievements and principles.[24] Pueblo's songs were embedded in his own experience of being part of the revolutionary struggle in the 1950s, when he regularly carried out clandestine performances for other revolutionaries.

While the Encuentro took place, 24-year-old Pablo Milanés was incarcerated in a Military Production Unit (UMAP) prison camp for 'bohemian behaviour'. At the time, the existence of the UMAP camp was challenged by various Cuban artists and intellectuals. In the camp Milanés had a guitar and composed songs – at least four in 1966 and six in 1967 – including the seminal "Pobre del Cantor" (Pity the Singer). His song, which became emblematic of both the *nueva trova* and *nueva canción* movement, includes the refrain,

Poor singer of these days,
who does not risk his strings,
so as not to risk his life.
Pity the poor singer who never knew,
that we were the seed,
and now we are this life.[25]

Following his release shortly after the Encuentro, Milanés accepted an invitation to visit Haydée Santamaría, the founder and director of the Casa de las Americas, Cuba's main cultural centre and the intellectual base for poets, writers and musicians. At the Casa de las Americas, Haydée Santamaria was a key actor in the establishment of what were in effect 'oppositional spaces' for some of the artists who the bureaucratic authorities found challenging. Another important figure for a more visionary mode of culture in Cuba was Alfredo Guevara, the founder

---

[24] See Puebla 1972 and 1976.
[25] My translation. For the original Spanish lyrics see Díaz 1994, pp. 49–50. See also Moore 2006.

and president of the Cuban Cinematographic Institute (ICAIC).[26] Both Santamaria and Guevara were directly linked to Fidel Castro and the guerilla struggle in the Sierra Maestra, so were privy to powerful networks.

At the end of 1969, with the support of Santamaría and Guevara, Rodríguez and Milanés were invited to sing at Casa de las Americas and join the newly formed Experimental Sound Group (GESI), which was part of the ICAIC.[27] The creation of GESI and the performance opportunities at the Casa de las Americas provided protected spaces, both prior to and during the 'grey five years', for a collective of creative musicians who might otherwise have found it difficult to gain permission to work legitimately. At ICAIC the collective's work involved composing for film and television while also supporting each other in creating their own individual songs during the difficult 'crisis' period in revolutionary culture.[28]

In this artistic quasi-institutional framework, Milanés and Rodríguez and their cohorts were taught musical skills such as harmony and composition from top musicians, and composed songs and soundtracks geared to the content of new ICAIC films of which many were shown in regular television news slots.[29] Meanwhile, while fostering the work of Rodríguez, Milanés and other musicians and their links with counterparts in other countries (such as Uruguay's Daniel Viglietti and Chile's Isabel and Angel Parra), Casa de las Americas dropped the 'protest song' tag they had used for the Encuentro in favour of the term *nueva trova*.[30]

In the 1970s, official Cuban cultural policy meant space and status had to be fought for within state structures. Rodríguez and Milanés as well as colleagues like Noel Nicola and Sara González could make music for films as the GESI collective, but they had no formal public space to perform in. To have access to such space they had to move from their marginal position and become legitimated by the state. For young GESI musicians to be able to perform their work to a general public they needed formal, state recognition outside creating music for the ICAIC. This recognition came through the mediation of the Young Communist (JJCC) movement, notably via members of the group Moncada who had emerged at universities and were active

---

[26] ICAIC stands for Instituto Cubano de Arte e Industria Cinematográficos.
[27] GESI stands for Grupo de Experimentacitón Sonora.
[28] See, for example, songs of the *Grupo de Experimentación del ICAIC* (1973, 1974, 1975, 1976).
[29] For example, Grupo de Experimentación Sonora 1984.
[30] For example, Various artists 1974 and Viglietti 1973. The defining image of the Encuentro, known as the 'rose with the crying thorn', was used transnationally and transcontinentally and for record sleeves, labels and books. For example it was used in Chile for the Parra's record label within DICAP recording company, and in Uruguay and Italy as part of the design for music book covers.

within the JJCC .[31] In November 1972 in the city of Manzanillo, the First Meeting of Young Troubadours was held, formally recognising what became known as the *nueva trova* movement, and this became institutionalised in Cuba's cultural system through an island-wide youth movement. This was an unprecedented move on behalf of creating cultural centres for young musicians. Formal recognition[32] saw musicians associated with the movement recognised as salaried, cultural workers by the Ministry of Culture, a position that meant they had to rehearse and go on tours in order to perform for a cross-section of Cuban society. As cultural workers, musicians also gained access to the state recording facilities and were able to release their own recording projects. Little by little *nueva trova* songs gained a mass audience, so much so that Cuban cultural commentator Pedro Sarduy ironically joked that they "went from being banned to being obligatory".[33]

Chilean and Cuban musical exchange

While *nueva trova* was fighting its corner in Cuba, *nueva canción* on the continent was developing an ever-stronger presence. It found its strongest home in Chile due to the renaissance in cultural activity and creative energy that were integral to the years leading up to the 1970 election of the Popular Unity government led by President Salvador Allende, which brought together a vibrant coalition of parties on the left and centre. The first ever festival of *nueva canción* held on the Latin American continent was the First Festival of Chilean New Song held in July 1969. The Festival came about due to the joint efforts of the Vice-Rector of Communications of Santiago's Catholic University and renowned radio disc-jockey Ricardo García, and it was followed by two more *nueva canción* festivals.

The First Festival was clearly designed to pay tribute to tradition while drawing a clear line between *nueva canción* and folk songs allied with the establishment and the landowning rich who had previously governed the country.[34] To underline this division, in 1969 the first prize was jointly awarded to singer-songwriter (also leading theatre director and composer)

---

[31] JJCC stands for Juventudes Comunistas de Chile.
[32] The Movimiento la Nueva Trova linked to the Brigada 'Hemanos Saíz' de Música, an organisation promoting culture among young people in Cuba which has provided one of Cuba's main twentieth and twenty-first century cultural infrastructures. See also the LP *La Canción, una Arma de la Revolución* (Various artists 1974).
[33] Sarduy, personal communication, May 2009. See also Moore 2006.   [34] See Carrasco 2003.

Víctor Jara and folk singer Ricardo Rojas. Jara's song "Plegaría a un Labrador" ("Prayer to a Labourer") was a secular reworking of the Lord's Prayer addressed to workers rather than God. Because of its radical text and striking music it became a paradigm for the Chilean *nueva canción* movement, which relied upon the vital creativity of a host of young groups and musicians, many of them involved in student activism for educational reform.[35] They performed in the many peña nightclubs that mushroomed throughout the country during these key years (from the early/mid-1960s until 1973), as well as in factories, schools, universities, shanty towns, markets and meetings of all sorts. As Rodrigo Torres Alvarado (2002) has argued, Jara and colleagues built on the tradition of alternative musicianship established by folklorist Violeta Parra, creating work that spoke clearly to the times yet was rooted in rural tradition, forging a new style of performance and communication and changing the relationship between art and reality. In the words of Violeta Parra's 1960 song "Yo Canto la Diferencia" ("I Sing the Difference"), they did not pick up the guitar for applause, but to sing for the people about "the difference between what is true and false".[36]

The cultural renaissance in Chile during the Allende period was clearly connected to cultural policies and programmes that aimed for social and political change. Musicians canvassed on behalf of Popular Unity party, as did artists, writers and poets such as Nobel prize winner Pablo Neruda. Following the elections in 1970, President Salvador Allende appeared on a stage in the centre of the Chilean capital Santiago surrounded by musicians under a banner which declared "There's No Revolution Without Song".[37]

Chile and Cuba developed strong dynamic links through the music of *nueva canción* and *nueva trova*. First links were forged between the two countries through Isabel and Angel Parra's participation in the 1967 Encuentro. Then the achievements of the Popular Unity party and the Allende government received the support of the Cuban government. Castro himself made a famous visit in 1971, a visit that was meant to last a week but which stretched to a month. The success of Chilean *nueva canción*, its vivacity and energy and the closeness of its relationship with its audience, gave it an immediate reputation across the continent and beyond. As the first ever country to elect a socialist president through the ballot box, the eyes of the world were on Chile during this key period, with visitors coming from far and wide, both formally and informally.

In 1971, the influential Chilean *nueva canción* group Quilapayún were invited to Cuba and, while visiting, they unexpectedly had an opportunity to

---

[35] See Carrasco 2003. [36] Torres Alvarado 2002, p. 39. [37] See Fairley 1985.

discuss the role of song and culture with Fidel Castro in person. As a result of this discussion a group of young, disparate Cuban musicians were brought together for a project that saw them travel to Chile. There they worked for several months building their own repertoire through getting to know the broader South American repertoire the Chileans were famous for. For example, they worked with Víctor Jara, Angel and Isabel Parra and the groups Quilapayún, Inti Illimani and others. In Chile, this young Cuban musical collective took the name Manguaré, and on return to Cuba became part of the *nueva trova* movement. Manguaré brought Andean and other international sounds to young people through the chain of *nueva trova* centres across the island.

Similarly, in 1972 Rodríguez and Milanés travelled to Chile, which was their first ever trip out of Cuba to a South American country. They were invited by the Young Communist Party on the initiative of Isabel Parra who following the 1967 Encuentro had returned to Cuba in 1970, 1971 and 1972 to perform with GESI musicians. In Chile, Rodríguez and Milanés sang with Víctor Jara, Isabel and Angel Parra and others in a major event in Chile's National Stadium. They gave many concerts and hung out "each night at the Peña de los Parra".[38] They participated in the Fourth Festival of Committed Song or Canción Comprometida. Soon after, the Cubans met up again with the Chileans at the 1972 Latin American Music Meeting (Encuentro de Música Latinoamericana) in Havana which Victor Jara and Isabel Parra attended. Performing links and personal friendships between all these musicians have continued right up to the present day.

Dictatorship: the solidarity years

In the 1970s, the struggle for social and political change in South America was abruptly cut short by the spate of military dictatorships, which brutally overthrew democratic governments, and many of the supporters of these governments were imprisoned, killed or exiled. Apart from Cuba and Mexico, *nueva canción* was driven into exile, in the main to Europe, but also to Canada. There it found large audiences among the labour, socialist and communist parties in Italy, France, Scandinavia, the Netherlands and the UK. It was also heard in Portugal following the 1974 'Carnation' Revolution; in Spain in 1975 after the end of the Franco dictatorship; and in parts of Eastern Europe, especially East Germany and Hungary.

---

[38] Sanz 1994, p. 161.

Following the 1973 coup d'état in Chile, the *nueva canción* movement was silenced and until the 1990s Chilean *nueva canción* could only be heard abroad. Books and records associated with the Popular Unity government, its publishing house Quimantú and the recording company Discoteca del Cantar Popular (DICAP) were burnt in the streets, and people were arrested for having such material in their homes. For those who survived torture, imprisonment or 'disappearance', there was no choice: those released from prison were exiled according to a military decree which banished them abroad for twice as many years as their prison sentence. Canada and most European countries formally participated in refugee schemes.

Víctor Jara was brutally tortured in the basketball stadium known as the Estadio Chile and was then summarily shot against a cemetery wall. Angel Parra and members of Los Curacas (the group who accompanied him at the Peña de los Parra nightclub) were imprisoned in Chacabuco, a disused nitrate mine that had been converted into a concentration camp. In 1975, just before Parra and Curacas members were released and went into exile, a camp concert was recorded for posterity on a recorder provided by one of the camp guards. The concert included performances of songs Parra had written in the camp, popular tangos and hymns, as well as a group performance by all the inmates of Beethoven's "Ode to Joy".[39]

Travelling to Europe as Popular Unity cultural ambassadors, the musicians in the groups Inti Illimani and Quilpayún were given homes by the local government in Rome and Paris respectively, beginning a long exile that lasted until the late 1980s.[40] After taking refuge in foreign embassies, Isabel Parra, the *nueva canción* singer-songwriter Patricio Manns and the composer Sergio Ortega were exiled in Paris. The exiled musicians continued to tour; they became the 'heart and soul' of a sustained solidarity movement and brought *nueva canción* into mainstream European political culture.

In Uruguay, in the intervening period in 1972, Daniel Viglietti was arrested because of his music. His most famous songs from a series called *Songs For My America* were "Dale Tu Mano al Indio" ("Give Your Hand to the Indian") and "A Desalambrar" ("Tear Down the Fences"), which asserts that the land belongs to ordinary people not the rich. With the help of French intellectual Jean-Paul Sartre, Viglietti was released and exiled in Paris. In Argentina, the 1976 military dictatorship saw many artists forced to adopt a very low profile or go 'underground'. Singer Mercedes Sosa, one of the founders in 1963 of Argentina's *nuevo cancionero* (new song book)

---

[39] The recording of this concert was released on the disc *Chacabuco* (Various artists 1975).
[40] See Fairley 1985, 2002.

movement in Mendoza province – a precedent which also sowed the seeds for *nueva canción* on the continent as a whole – managed to continue performing in Argentina for three years after the military dictatorship came to power.[41] She was eventually forced to move to Madrid in 1979, after being arrested at a concert with many of her audience. In 1982, Sosa returned to Argentina to a great welcome from fans and musicians alike. She began to champion and sing 'national rock' (*rock nacional*), a musical movement that had sustained young people during the dark years of 'disappearance' and the 1982 Falklands/Malvinas War.[42] By fusing *nueva canción*, 'national rock' and Argentine folk songs into her repertoire, the charismatic Sosa received great acclaim for unifying different genres of music that appealed across generations over the whole continent.

In Cuba, Rodríguez and Milanés and other members of the *nueva trova* movement consolidated their position. Due to its massive popularity at home and abroad, their music gradually overcame institutional opposition in Cuba and it became the most popular music on the island and all over the Spanish-speaking world. While they became effectively the 'music of the revolution' they maintained their independence while supporting musical and cultural infrastructures on the island. Singing to everyone from Cuban workers to Bolivian miners, their songs became iconic over the continent during the 'dark years of dictatorship'.

Following the end of the Malvinas/Falklands War, which brought about the downfall of the Argentine military dictatorship, Cuba's Ródriguez and Milanés were invited to give the concert *En Vivo en Argentina* (*Live in Argentina*) at the Buenos Aires stadium, Estadio Obras, in April 1984. They performed songs with their own backing trio and in a group with 'guest' Argentine artists, which included Léon Gieco, Piero, Víctor Heredía, Cesar Isella, Cuarteto Zupay and Antonio Tarrago Ros. The lyrics served to map the history, trials, tribulations and deep grief of the period. The performance ended with everyone involved singing an anthemic version of "Canción Con Todos" ("Song With Everyone"), which presents a vision of everyone in the Americas being united together.[43] At the time the concert title *Live in Argentina* had two essential meanings: it referred both to the 'liveness' of the music and to being 'alive' in Argentina. The concert was significant because it marked the fact that Argentina had lost the war and the subsequent downfall of the military dictatorship.[44] The pervasive

---

[41] See García 2009. [42] See Vila 1987.
[43] A recording of the concert was released on CD: Rodríguez and Milanés 1984.
[44] See Vila 1987.

strength of *nueva trova* and the invitation to Rodríguez and Milanés is notable as this was their first major concert in Argentina. In 1990, Rodríguez was also invited, after the end of the Pinochet dictatorship, to return to Chile for the first time since 1972 to give the first major stadium concert in honour of his friend, the murdered singer Víctor Jara.[45]

From the 1983 'Nicaraguan Peace' concert to the 2009 'Cuban Peace Without Borders' concert

Between the mid-1960s and the early 1970s the *nueva canción* movement went from activism through music to a situation where some protagonists found their music mattered so much they were banned, imprisoned, killed or driven into exile. Recordings of live concerts held in Cuba, Argentina, Nicaragua and other places during these and subsequent years act as indexes of the power of music to unite, remember and fortify. The dark years of the 1970s eventually gave way to 'new democracies' in Nicaragua (1979), Argentina (1983) and Chile (1988). Although *nueva canción* musicians endeavoured to organise themselves officially from an office in Mexico, attempts largely floundered for logistical reasons. Nevertheless, a number of key festivals under the rubric *nueva canción*, as well as other national festivals featuring *nueva canción*, were held. The power of *nueva canción* music in this period was witnessed at such events, some of which were captured in historic recordings. These include the recording of the 1983 *April in Managua Central American Peace Concert* (1984), released on the Varagram label, which was supported by the effective if small finances of European solidarity campaigns.

The positive legacy of *nueva canción* as a forum for promoting progressive attitudes through music continues today, albeit with the commercial/non-commercial axis blurred due to post-Cold War shifts and the rise of issue politics in neo-liberal times. The trope is still peace, as witnessed at the 2009 Paz Sin Fronteras II (Peace Without Borders) concert held in Havana, Cuba, on Sunday, 20 September 2009, organised by Juanes, the seventeen-times Latin Grammy award-winning Colombian superstar and social activist. Juanes is a huge fan of Silvio Rodríguez and he knew many of Rodríguez' songs by heart when he was only 8 years old.[46] Although it was declared that the concert had 'nothing to do with politics or ideology', its aim to further encourage a thaw in US–Cuban relations echoed the first Paz Sin Fronteras

---

[45] Rodríguez 1991. [46] Fairley 2008, pp. 34–5.

concert organised by Juanes on 16 March 2008. This first concert was organised on the border between Colombia and Venezuela at a time of border crisis between the two countries, and its transcontinental and transnational rosta included veteran Rodríguez and Spain's Luís Eduardo Aute.[47]

The pervasive influence and longevity of *nueva canción* in its various guises owes much to the fact that it was never created in 'protest' at all. Rather it was an integral expression of the complex life experience of a generation of different individuals who networked together. The words of Silvio Rodríguez, the international popularity of whose songs has exceeded that of any other 'new song' singer, sum this up:

> My generation became adults during the revolution's infancy when it was tackling urgent social problems. I was only 14 when with about 6,000 others I was involved in the literacy campaign teaching volunteer militia men defending the island on beaches to read and write. We were privileged to be struggling for ideals in everyday life which was an amazing way to acquire a revolutionary conscience. We saw contradictions and discrepancies and we said so, assuming the revolution in all its complexity and expressing it in our songs. That's been our luck.[48]

To conclude, the musicians who formed the *nueva canción* movement were the first Latin American musical generation that had a continental and international vision to forge dynamic links with minimal resources, completely outside the commercial music industry. They proved the value of 'activism' through music. Their music was pervasive during the 1960s, 1970s and 1980s, due to the strength of its ideological beliefs, the political context and the experiences exchanged during performances at meetings and festivals. *Nueva canción* musicians more often than not through poetic metaphor captured the zeitgeist: for this reason their music has continued to have a seminal influence on subsequent generations to this day.

---

[47] See Fairley 2009.   [48] Fairley 2006, p. 15.

8 | "The Power of Music": anti-authoritarian music movements in Scandinavia in '1968'

ALF BJÖRNBERG

Introduction

In Scandinavia, as in numerous other areas around the globe, the spirit of protest and reform of '1968' manifested itself in a number of ways. This included a vigorous anti-war movement, student protests and the forming of new left-wing political parties and women's movements. While music to some extent served as a tool for struggle in all these contexts, the most prominent musical consequence of '1968' in the Scandinavian countries was the rise of politically radical *music movements* that focused on the cultural politics of musical life and the role of music in the larger perspective of socio-political struggle, and these musical movements continued to be active throughout much of the 1970s. The Scandinavian area is historically marked by cultural parallels across its three constituent nations, namely Sweden, Denmark and Norway. The cultural climate in Scandinavia was to a large extent characterised by social-democrat governments, which aimed to achieve a 'democratisation of culture' from the early 1960s onwards. Despite such common tendencies across Scandinavia, scholars have suggested that progressive musical movements were most pronounced in Sweden. For example, Eyerman and Jamison state that:

The Swedish progressive or non-commercial music movement, a network of companies, organizations, musicians and activists which flourished in the 1970s, was fairly unique in its strength and longevity, and in its long-term impact on popular culture, compared to similar phenomena elsewhere.[1]

Although the cultural developments in Scandinavia in this period have been quite thoroughly researched,[2] previous accounts tend to obscure

---

[1] Eyerman and Jamison 1998, p. 142; also cf. Gravem 2004, p. 39; Arvidsson 2008, p. 9.
[2] The existing literature on the Scandinavian progressive music movements comprises both contemporary accounts (e.g. Eriksson 1975; Fornäs 1979; Piil 1981; Wallis and Malm 1984) and a growing body of more recent research on the period in question (e.g. Arvidsson 2008; Eyerman and Jamison 1998; Gravem 2004; Thyrén 2009). In addition, more recent research has been done which, although not focusing on the music movements, provides wider perspectives on the cultural-political climate of this period (e.g. Björnberg 1998; Lindelof 2004, 2007; Smith-Sivertsen 2007).

the musical and cultural continuities in the 1960s and 1970s. This chapter highlights how the events during this period indicate that progressive music movements and public cultural policy-makers formed a community of interests. Underlying this community of interests, however, were divergent outlooks and aims, and this resulted in the formation of alliances between activist movements and public institutions that were uneasy and unstable.

The main argument proposed in this chapter is that '1968' in Scandinavia was characterised, in a rather unique way, by movements formed around music that focused on musical politics, rather than music being perceived as an auxiliary aspect of movements centred around socio-political causes. It may even be argued that in the Scandinavian nations, the political mobilisation characteristic of the times was significant mainly in cultural-political, rather than socio-political, terms. Furthermore, a comprehensive analysis of the 'musical 1968' in Scandinavia requires that it be understood as a sustained process rather than as a number of independent, sudden events. Finally, it will be argued that one important reason for the relative success of grass-roots, activist music movements was that the aims of these movements were aligned with long-term continuities in public cultural policies.

The cultural and political situation in Scandinavia in the early 1960s

At the beginning of the 1960s, the political situation in the Scandinavian countries can be characterised as one of relative stability, with large social-democrat parties playing a prominent political role. In tandem with an economic policy that supported the continued development of the modern welfare state, matters of cultural politics received increasing attention. Radical liberals joined forces with social democrats in order to strive for reform, cultural democratisation and secularisation.[3]

In contrast to this relative political stability, however, the musical sphere was undergoing rapid change. The US-inspired wave of rock music in the late 1950s heralded changes in the Scandinavian popular music scene that led to it being increasingly divided along generational lines, and 'rock' became the generic term used for youth-oriented popular music. In Sweden, however, the term 'rock' was replaced in the early 1960s by 'pop',

---

[3] See Arvidsson 2008, p. 30.

which lacked the problematic connotations of working-class rebellion associated with the older term.[4] The same rationale appears to have been operative in the terminology used in Denmark and Norway, although in these countries youth-oriented music in the 1960s was referred to as 'beat', while 'pop' (at least in Denmark) had connotations of lowbrow, poor quality popular music, which was not generation specific. In parallel with these terminological changes, jazz, which previously had held a central position in the Scandinavian countries as popular dance music, rapidly changed its status and function. Jazz increasingly became a music for listening rather than for dancing, it moved into new performance venues suitable for listening only, and it was subject to new broadcasting practices (e.g. jazz was mainly broadcast in late-night, off-peak slots on the radio and was presented in a 'highbrow' manner). The perceived opposition between jazz and the pop/beat styles was most clearly evident in Denmark, where "jazz was especially emphasised by cultural radicals, who used it to 'hit pop music over the head with'".[5] Similarly, within the field of art music, there was a growing opposition between the stylistically conservative 'traditionalists' and the postwar generation of avant-garde modernists, an opposition that was most pronounced in Sweden.[6]

In a musical and cultural situation characterised by rapid change and growing antagonisms between the advocates of different musical genres, governments perceived a growing need for active measures within the publicly subsidised music sectors to renew the processes of production and distribution under the catchphrase 'democratisation of music culture'. Originally, this democratisation aimed to provide new groups of listeners access to 'serious music', but in the process the high-culture concept of serious music also gradually widened to include jazz, and later 'folk' or 'traditional' music and (aesthetically) 'progressive' pop/rock. One important tool for the implementation of public music policy was the use of extensive sociomusicological surveys to provide statistical data, which formed the basis of arguments about the reforms required to remedy inequalities in musical opportunity. In Sweden, the first widely publicised survey was published in 1967,[7] and its results clearly indicated differences in patterns of music

---

[4] See Björnberg 1998, p. 163.
[5] Piil 1981, p. 57; translations from non-English sources are the author's. 'Cultural radicalism' has been a significant position in the Danish public sphere since the 1920s; 'cultural radicals', while taking up a modernist position in some cultural matters, have tended to share with cultural conservatives a critical view of mass culture (see Lindelof 2007, p. 34).
[6] Arvidsson 2008, p. 49.   [7] Nylöf 1967.

listening and music consumption, which could be related to the unequal distribution of musical resources in society.[8] The survey results were used to justify increases in publicly subsidised cultural activities, including adult education 'music study circles', municipal music schools and municipal youth centres, which provided young aspiring musicians with instruments and rehearsal facilities. Nylöf's survey was published in an appendix to the final report of the government Concert Agency Committee, a report that led to the formation in 1968 of a new state-run institution for music distribution, the Rikskonserter or National Concert Agency.

Music in the broadcasting media

Public service broadcasting organisations played a vital role in the development of Scandinavian music in the 1960s and 1970s. Well into the 1980s, the Danish, Norwegian and Swedish airwaves were dominated by the national public-service broadcasting monopolies, Danmarks Radio (DR), Norsk Rikskringskastning (NRK) and Sveriges Radio (SR) respectively. In the 1950s, these corporations were characterised by a cautious expansion policy: a second national radio channel was started in 1951 in Denmark (DR P2) and in 1955 in Sweden (SR P2). Throughout this decade, programming policies attempted to maintain a delicate balance between erudition and entertainment in radio programming. In the early 1960s, however, a major reorientation of the programming policies of SR and DR took place as a direct result of the influence of commercial pirate radio activities in the Scandinavian mediascape. Competition from pirate radio, whose formats predominantly featured 24-hour-a-day programming of mostly popular music, led to the establishment in 1962 of a third SR radio channel, SR P3, which focused on popular music, and the DR followed suit with the launch of DR P3 in 1963. In comparison, broadcasting developments were much slower in Norway, which was not affected by pirate radio; NRK P2 started as late as 1984 and NRK P3 in 1993. The pirates thus prompted a major breakthrough for the easy-listening radio format in what was previously a conservative Scandinavian public-service mediascape. Public debate at the time characterised this breakthrough as an unexpected and rapid 'democratisation' of music broadcasting policies, in the sense that the public-service monopolies

---

[8] Previous socio-musicological surveys in Sweden had mainly been performed by the public-service broadcaster, including a remarkable project as early as 1928 (see Björnberg 1998, pp. 34ff.).

had finally been forced by external competition to comply with the tastes and wishes of large sections of the radio audience.

Another result of pirate competition was the SR's launching in the early 1960s of two chart-based popular-music radio shows, Tio i Topp (The Top Ten), dominated by Anglophone songs, and Svensktoppen (The Swedish Top), which was restricted to songs with lyrics in Swedish. This resulted in the establishment of a genre classification system based on the language of song lyrics, a system which existed throughout the 1960s: popular songs with lyrics in foreign languages – primarily English – were classified as 'pop', while songs with Swedish lyrics were categorised as *svensktopp*. This genre system, and the way it was reflected in broadcasting programming, proved highly favourable to the Swedish mainstream-pop music industry in the 1960s. Svensktoppen was followed by the Danish and Norwegian counterparts, Dansktoppen in 1968 and Norsktoppen in 1973, but the timelag allowed the Swedish music industry to acquire a leading role in Scandinavian mainstream pop production, a situation which was to have consequences for subsequent developments in the 1970s.[9]

Despite the similarities between the Danish and the Swedish broadcasting media situation in the 1960s, and a somewhat defensive channel expansion and changes in programming practices – both in response to pirate radio – there were also important differences. In Denmark, for instance, an academically influenced cultural-political ideology, espousing traditional values of 'musical quality', was more effective within the broadcasting media, resulting in a more restrictive policy towards mainstream pop in comparison to the more pragmatic (or, as some would say, opportunistic) attitude prevailing in Sweden.[10] To some extent, these differences were also reflected in the way the respective broadcasting organisations responded to the developing music movements of the 1970s, as will be discussed further below.

The development of '1968' in Scandinavia

In the Scandinavian context, the question 'when was the start of '1968'?' can be answered unequivocally: it began in 1963. This was the year when new trends in the folk song or ballad scene became evident in all three

---

[9] A detailed account of Danish–Swedish relations in 1960s mainstream pop production is provided by Smith-Sivertsen 2007, pp. 76ff.
[10] See Smith-Sivertsen 2007, Lindelof 2007.

Scandinavian countries. These new trends were influenced by recent US folk song, which gradually changed the styles of the national ballad traditions known as *visa* (in Sweden) and *vise* (in Denmark and Norway). In general, *visa/vise* are characterised by informal performance practices and strophic songs, ranging from traditional folk song to recently composed songs that often had literary pretensions. In Denmark, Norway and Sweden, new venues appeared featuring artists performing traditional as well as newly written material that was strongly influenced by the 1960s US folk scene.[11] Cornelis Vreeswijk, an important Swedish *visa* artist, has been characterised as bringing "something of the spirit of the sixties – of revolt and alienation – into what by then had primarily become a conservative and rather marginal musical genre".[12] By 1965, the 'protest singer', epitomising the dawning politicisation of popular music, appears as a well-established performer identity in Sweden.[13]

In all three countries, the influence of US folk song and, from the mid-1960s onwards, US and British rock music on domestic folk song or ballad traditions was a significant contributing factor in Swedish, Danish and Norwegian becoming acceptable languages for rock lyrics. In Denmark, folk singer Povl Dissing was a pioneer in this respect.[14] In 1967, his style shifted from acoustic performances of mainly traditional Danish material to a US-influenced folk-rock style. According to Smith-Sivertsen, this shift was epitomised in the Danish-language version of Shel Silverstein's song "Lemmebesomethin'", which was accompanied by the blues-rock group Beefeaters.[15] The first signs of Swedish rock bands using Swedish instead of English for their lyrics were noticeable in 1968 and, by the turn of the 1970s, rock music with lyrics in the languages of all three Scandinavian countries had become the norm. This change was an important prerequisite for the increasing politicisation of rock/pop music, as 'politicisation' was mainly interpreted in terms of song lyrics with an explicitly political content. As Arvidsson notes, "writing in Swedish was a distinguishing action: the new pop music was in Swedish, if one had something to say to one's audience it should not be hidden in a language which everybody may not have understood".[16]

The period from 1968 to 1972 has been characterised as one of a 'commercial vacuum' in Swedish pop/rock music, in the sense that the Swedish music industry quite suddenly seemed to lose interest in recording

---

[11] Arvidsson 2008, pp. 128f.; Gravem 2004, pp. 41f.; Smith-Sivertsen 2007, pp. 131f.
[12] Eyerman and Jamison 1998, p. 150.   [13] Arvidsson 2008, pp. 12, 130.   [14] Piil 1981, p. 58.
[15] Smith-Sivertsen 2007, pp. 129ff.   [16] Arvidsson 2008, p. 256.

and marketing domestic rock music.[17] In view of the fact that the Swedish music industry held a leading role in Scandinavia at the time,[18] this may seem somewhat paradoxical. However, the emphasis at this time was on mainstream pop and Swedish-language cover versions of foreign material, rather than the domestic production of experimental pop/rock that drew on popular music from the stylistic centres in the US and the UK. As a consequence, in 1967 and 1968 record production figures of Swedish pop/rock declined, and several venues for live rock music were closed down or converted into discotheques. The result of this was that Swedish pop/rock "during a formative period [...] came to be supported by people outside the established record companies with clear left-wing sympathies".[19] In Norway, the situation was similar.[20] In Denmark there appears to have been less of a commercial vacuum, as the late 1960s witnessed the formation of Danish rock 'super groups', such as Burnin' Red Ivanhoe, Young Flowers and Savage Rose. These groups, however, stood out as progressive in an aesthetic rather than a political sense.[21]

By contrast, in Sweden in the 1970s, 'progressive music' was conceived of in squarely political terms. The earliest seeds of the so-called 'progressive music movement' consisted in actions such as the protests against a commercial 'Teenage Fair' held in Stockholm in the autumn of 1968; however, the definite moment of its birth is usually considered to be the first open-air music festival arranged at Gärdet in Stockholm in 1970. This festival featured several of the new, politicised groups and artists who were against the commercial music industry.[22] The movement developed during the first half of the 1970s in a variety of organisations and activities such as local 'music forums' (which cooperated with the national Contact Network [Kontaktnätet] organisation), independent record companies owned by musicians or music activists (e.g. MusikNätet Waxholm [MNW], Silence and Nacksving), record distribution organisations (e.g. SAM-Distribution, The Disc Pushers [Plattlangarna]) and the journal *The Power of Music* (*Musikens Makt*), which was published from 1973 to 1980.

As already hinted above, the parallel Norwegian music movement was to a large extent modelled on the Swedish example: it featured the musicians' organisation Ensemble (Samspill), which started in Oslo in 1972, the record company Mai (set up in 1973) and the (rather short-lived) journal *Our*

---

[17] Bjurström 1983. Note that in contemporary Swedish parlance, the generic term for 'youth music', regardless of its perceived degree of rebelliousness, was still 'pop'; its replacement by 'rock' started some years into the 1970s.
[18] See Smith-Sivertsen 2007.   [19] Arvidsson 2008, p. 186.   [20] Gravem 2004, pp. 56f.
[21] Piil 1981, p. 95.   [22] See Eyerman and Jamison 1998, p. 147.

Music (*Vår Musikk*), which was published during 1973.[23] In general, however, the Norwegian music movement was less organised than its Swedish predecessor.[24] According to Piil, the Danish music movement was "a movement whose explicit political aim was that musicians themselves should be in control of all stages in the production and distribution of music".[25] But this statement is only justified from around 1973/1974 onwards. In Denmark, anti-authoritarian movements coalesced in particular locations, such as the 'alternative environment' of Christiana in Copenhagen, and around political groups who campaigned against nuclear power and the European Economic Community (EEC) and groups that aimed to 'politicise private life'. These movements were culturally productive in several ways: alternative environments provided enclaves for musicians to live, work and perform at alternative music venues, and the work of anti-authoritarian movements also inspired other musicians.[26]

As in Norway, the Danish music movement featured a less integrated organisational structure compared to its Swedish counterpart. Arvidsson suggests that the main reason for the particular 'strength and longevity' of the Swedish music movement lies in the unique conditions provided by "the combination of non-governmental organisations [NGOs] within the framework of the Swedish Welfare State, cultural politics and a broadcasting monopoly".[27] A comparison with the neighbouring Scandinavian countries indicates that the first of these factors played the most decisive role. The Swedish music movement adopted its organisational forms and practices from previously existing organisations, such as the temperance movement, the trade-union movement and the tenants' association movement; these had originated in the form of grass-roots NGOs but had, in the course of the long-term social-democrat predominance in Swedish politics, gradually assumed something of a semi-governmental character as they became institutionalised and drawn into state networks of power.

One enemy in common: commercialism

By the 1970s, the Swedish government's ambition to facilitate a 'democratisation of culture' had developed into a broader agenda of radical change in government cultural policies. In public cultural-political discourse, voices were heard urging for a wider, more 'anthropological' conception of culture,

---

[23] Gravem 2004, p. 10. [24] Gravem 2004, p. 12. [25] Piil 1981, p. 112.
[26] Piil 1981, pp. 22f. [27] Arvidsson 2008, p. 16.

in contrast to the traditional view that equated culture with the highbrow 'fine arts'. These demands filtered into the musical field, stimulating experiment and reforms in higher music education, particularly music-teacher training. The aim of these reforms was to integrate into the curricula previously 'neglected genres', which in practice meant all genres except Western art music. Jazz, for instance, played an increasingly prominent part in higher music education from 1970 onwards. As a technically complex music with a growing theoretical superstructure of its own, jazz proved relatively easy to integrate into existing educational structures. New macrogenres in music education were defined under designations such as 'the Afro-American tradition' (in Sweden) or 'rhythmic improvised music' (in Denmark and Norway).[28]

Although such an inclusive, anthropological concept of culture proved to be incompatible with existing cultural institutions that focused on the fine arts, the progressive music movements and government policy-makers throughout most of the 1970s united around the issue of 'commercialism'. In 1974, the Swedish parliament passed a Bill on cultural policy that aimed to "counteract the negative effects of commercialism in the area of culture".[29] Among the alleged potential negative effects of commercial cultural activity mentioned in the Bill was the inability to "guarantee a diversity in supply", the inability to guarantee "an even distribution across the nation of valuable products" and the inability to enable "cultural workers to earn a living". The Bill also stated that, "it is especially important for society to offer alternatives to the private cultural supply which is pursued with an aim of pure speculation".[30] The notion expressed in this statement – that some forms of cultural production are motivated exclusively by purely commercial interests – may be compared with similar views expressed in music-movement rhetoric, such as "the commercialization of music starts when profit becomes the guideline for quantity, form and content".[31]

One remarkable fact about the Bill was that it was passed unanimously by the parliament, thereby creating the impression that the entire Swedish political spectrum, from left to right, stood united in the struggle against commercialism. One possible reason for this unanimity may have been that the formulations in the Bill were vague enough to allow for both culturally conservative interpretations (commercial culture as 'low-quality culture') and more radical ones (commercial culture as a pacifying force preventing social change). Although the Swedish Bill was unique as regards its extensive

---

[28] See Björnberg 1993. [29] Sveriges Riksdag 1974, p. 295.
[30] Sveriges Riksdag 1974, p. 297f. [31] Piil 1981, p. 83.

cultural-political scope, a parallel piece of legislation was the Danish Music Bill passed in 1976, which aimed at a comprehensive regulation of the non-commercial sections of musical life.

Anti-commercialism also formed the focus of the Alternative Festival (Alternativfestivalen), which was the most conspicuous manifestation of cultural-political unity between the Swedish progressive music movement and the authorities in the 1970s. The festival was arranged in 1975 in protest against the public-service broadcaster SR's hosting of the Eurovision Song Contest (ESC) finals on 22 March that year, which was a consequence of pop group Abba's victory in the 1974 ESC with the song "Waterloo". Abba's combination of a 'rootless' cosmopolitan pop style,[32] sophisticated recording-studio production, glamorous on-stage visual image and their manager Stig 'Stikkan' Anderson's blatant concern for economic profit, resulted in Abba – and by extension, the entire ESC, as the epitome of bland and commercial mainstream pop music – becoming emblematic of 'commercial music' in the polarised cultural-political climate in Sweden during the mid-1970s.

At the Alternative Festival virtually all of the publicly subsidised musical organisations in Sweden joined forces with the music movement in the struggle against 'commercialism'. In addition to the music-movement organisations noted above, the participating organisations included groups that supported musicians, such as the national choir organisation Körsam, the Society of Swedish Jazz Musicians, the National Society for Jazz Organisers, the Swedish Choir Association, the Swedish National Fiddler's Society, the Society of Professional Troubadours, the Swedish Association of Musical Artists and the Stockholm Blues Society. Supporting organisations also included several left-wing and centre political parties, the public institution Rikskonserter and even groups representing sections of the public-service institution that organised the ESC finals: the Sveriges Radio Freelance Group, the Sveriges Radio Producers' Association and the Radio Choir. The Alternative Festival not only attracted considerable public attention and stimulated intense public discussion on culture and politics, it also stimulated SR representatives to declare that after the 1975 finals, the broadcaster would withdraw from further participation in the ESC 'for good' – an abstention which in practice lasted one year.[33] Inspired by the Swedish event, in 1976 a Norwegian Alternative Festival against the ESC was arranged, but it had relatively little support outside of the political music movement.[34]

---

[32] See Frith 1989.   [33] See Björnberg (forthcoming).   [34] Gravem 2004, pp. 120ff.

Even if the Alternative Festival is characterised as a one-off practical manifestation of agreement between activists and the authorities, public policy-makers in the mid-1970s were quite outspoken in their critique of commercialism. This can be seen, for instance, in a 1975 collection of essays published as a result of an initiative by the government Committee for the Organisation of Higher Music Education (OMUS),[35] which explicitly aimed to stimulate public debate about music policies.[36] The book contains sixteen essays that map out the contemporary Swedish musical sphere, and most of the authors identify the activities of the commercial music industry as a central problem. As Gravem points out, although the OMUS investigators did not directly represent the view of the government, if this publication was viewed in connection with other facts about Swedish cultural policy, it was obvious that Swedish authorities not only shared, but also in practice supported the non-commercial ideology of the music movement.[37] Another example is a book written by Per-Anders Hellqvist (published in 1977),[38] in which he formulates an acerbic critique of the transnational (US-based) music industry, the standardisation of music, studio production techniques and 'background music'. At the time Hellqvist was a recording executive at Rikskonserter, so his views could easily be perceived as an expression of public policy. Such anti-commercial sentiment was also evident to some extent in Norway.[39]

Politically progressive or aesthetically progressive?

In Swedish cultural-political discourse of the 1970s, the antithesis to the 'commercial' was the 'progressive'. However, the notion of the 'progressive' had an implicit tension between different interpretations: 'progressive music' could be defined politically if the music promoted left-wing political causes, or aesthetically if the music was technically advanced, innovative and experimental. As suggested above, in the Swedish context, the political interpretation was the default interpretation.[40] The Swedish use of the term 'progressive' therefore contrasts with the Anglophone usage in expressions such as 'progressive rock'. Of course, this terminological discrepancy was known to Swedish music-movement activists, and throughout the decade, the tension between political and aesthetic progressiveness was played out

---

[35] Organisationskommittén för Högre Musikutbildning.   [36] Nordström *et al.* 1975.
[37] Gravem 2004, p. 39.   [38] Hellqvist 1977.   [39] Gravem 2004, p. 62.
[40] See Arvidsson 2008, p. 256.

within different genres – rock, jazz and art music – as well as across genre boundaries. The question of whether it was possible for instrumental music to have political content was a recurrent theme in the pages of the journal *The Power of Music* (*Musikens Makt*), and in the mid-1970s a conflict was prevalent within the SR over whether 'progressive' programming policies could include improvised instrumental music or British progressive rock, which was not overtly political.[41] In this respect, jazz was perceived to be particularly problematic. Arvidsson provides an account of strategies used by jazz musicians to legitimise their music as progressive, which included the use of song titles carrying overt political references, collective forms of ensemble playing, and the incorporation of musical elements from US free jazz, non-Western music and Swedish folk music.[42] Still, critiques were launched against jazz for "perpetuating the bourgeois artist myth".[43]

This problem was also felt within art-music genres such as classical concert music and electro-acoustic music. Due to the high degree of institutionalisation in regard to the transmission, production, distribution and performance of these genres, adaptation to the changing cultural climate proved difficult. Nonetheless, intense discussions concerning the political responsibility of contemporary art music were played out during the second half of the 1960s and the early 1970s, not least within the Stockholm Conservatory of Music.[44] Establishing how contemporary art music could convey political content was a key issue. In this respect, the avant-garde genre of 'text-sound composition' – a genre flourishing in Sweden in the 1960s, consisting of electro-acoustic works featuring electronically processed spoken texts as one element – was something of an exception: thanks to its verbal content, it could function as a suitable form for politicised art, and several overtly political pieces in the genre were produced in the late 1960s. In general, Sweden held an advanced position in electro-acoustic music in the 1960s thanks to support from the government and the SR, but in the early 1970s electro-acoustic as well as conventional modernist composers were increasingly marginalised due to a perception of elitism that was difficult to erase. Instead, within the field of art music, the political currents of the time were expressed primarily through attempts at the realisation of postwar ideas concerning the democratisation of musical life through institutions such as Rikskonserter, Music Radio and music schools.[45] For a period of time in the early 1970s, the text-sound concept

---

[41] See Björnberg 1998, pp. 253f.   [42] Arvidsson 2008, pp. 173ff.
[43] Music critic Bengt Eriksson in journal *Tonfallet* 1974, 13, quoted in Arvidsson 2008, p. 175.
[44] Arvidsson 2008, pp. 134ff.   [45] Arvidsson 2008, p. 387.

crossed over into the 'youth music' channel SR P3 in the shape of sound collages with overt political content. One prominent example was the 1971 production "Pentagon", a half-hour long piece consisting of spoken poetry expressing an anti-militarist world-view over a montage of music, which was partly electronically processed.[46] In comparison with the expanding music movement, however, this still functioned as a rather esoteric minority concern.

The situation in Denmark appears rather different compared to Sweden (and, to my knowledge, Norway). In Danish cultural-political discourse, political and aesthetic progressiveness were not perceived as the poles of a dichotomy as they were in Sweden. Instead, the rise of the Danish music movement was contemporaneous with the legitimisation of rock music as a form of 'high-culture', as aesthetically valuable concert music for concentrated listening, designated by the aesthetically conceived umbrella term, 'improvised rhythmic music'. This can be seen, for instance, in the way DR television in the 1970s adapted the conventions of the high-culture concert to the presentation of rock music, with the result that the "values and ideals from the music discourse of bourgeois music culture were transferred to rock music and emphasized".[47] Thus, the notion that music could be politically progressive by virtue of its advanced aesthetic qualities was more acceptable in a Danish context. By extension, the fact that the Danish music movement was less strictly organised than the Swedish one appears to reflect a situation in which overtly politicised organisational structures were not regarded as a necessary condition for the critical orientation of rock music: by the end of the 1970s, it had become the norm for Danish beat groups to "express a critical view of society".[48]

Transnational music and 'the people's music'

Despite the undeniably "international character of the '1968 movement'",[49] determining unambiguously the 'transnational' or 'national' character of different individual movements or musical genres remains a more complicated matter. In the case of Scandinavia, it is significant that the music movements originated from a political climate in which the question of national independence was a central issue. As the protests against US warfare in Vietnam, steadily increasing on a global scale from the mid-1960s

---

[46] See Björnberg 1998, p. 249. [47] Lindelof 2004, pp. 3f. [48] Piil 1981, p. 110.
[49] Arvidsson 2008, p. 9.

onwards, developed into sustained activist movements with a committed cultural and political agenda, these movements promoted action against US 'cultural imperialism'. In Denmark and Norway, particular circumstances affected the question of national independence: in both countries, referenda were held in 1972 on the question of membership in the EEC (the predecessor of the European Union). According to established historiography, the origin of the Norwegian music movement was closely connected to the popular campaign against Norwegian membership in the EEC in the lead up to the referendum, but this is characterised by Gravem as a "creation myth" created in response to the need within the movement for a well-defined moment of origin.[50] As for Denmark, Piil argues that "the popular movement against the EEC was the first big national event in which the youth-rebellion 'generation' took part" and suggests that the Danish referendum functioned as "a politicizing catalyst for some Danish beat groups, as the resistance against the EEC contributed to enlarging the awareness of the value of beat music as a means of agitation in a political struggle".[51]

With the issue of national autonomy placed firmly on the political agenda, unsurprisingly the respective domestic folk music traditions constituted an important element in the cultural projects of the Scandinavian music movements. In all three countries, but particularly in Norway and Sweden, the notion of long-term 'authentic' folk music traditions was well established in public consciousness as well as in music scholarship. In Norway, this idea may be related to a specifically Norwegian tradition of 'conservative counterculture', centred on the opposition between centre and periphery, that is, between the centralised power of city culture and local or rural culture.[52] This emphasis on local cultural specificity may provide part of the explanation for the different outcome of the EEC referenda: Denmark joined the Community but Norway did not. Although the question of EEC membership was not an issue at the time in Sweden, the ascription of a particular cultural value to folk music was justified by other arguments as well. For instance, it was argued that the folk music of the lower classes was an important aspect of national history.[53] In this way, the national folk music tradition was therefore defined as politically progressive. The discrepancy between this ideological positioning of national folk music and the rather modest popular interest it engendered (in comparison with more recent popular styles that were often explicitly transnational in origin), led to national folk music being referred to by value-laden neologism, 'the

---

[50] Gravem 2004, pp. 49f.   [51] Piil 1981, pp. 39, 109.   [52] Gravem 2004, p. 14.
[53] Arvidsson 2008, p. 324.

people's music'. This term invoked contentious debates about the role of music in creating a sense of national unity.[54]

Due to the geographical, historical, cultural and linguistic proximity of the Scandinavian countries, it might be expected that musical and cultural exchange between them was extensive. Indeed, each country copied organisational models from their neighbours and in 1974 the joint Nordic Association of Non-commercial Phonogram Producers (NIFF)[55] was formed. Several music-movement artists also performed in the neighbouring countries. However, the impact across the borders was quite limited in some respects, for instance, record sales across the three countries were rather insignificant. A plausible explanation for this fact was that the neighbouring countries were perceived as too close culturally to appear very remarkable. It could be argued that another contributing factor was that the Swedish cultural and political debates of the 1970s were rather narrowly national and the focus on independent Swedish music production resulted in isolationist tendencies.[56] Such tendencies were partly due to the fact that 'national culture' was primarily defined in opposition to the increasingly international outlook of (particularly Swedish) mainstream pop music in the 1970s.

Conclusion: when did '1968' end and why?

By the turn of the 1980s, the Scandinavian music movements were rapidly losing much of their previous cultural and political impact. One important reason for this was the tension that developed between an activist ethos and the increasing professionalisation of the most successful music-movement artists.[57] As the music movements became more professionalised, the practices of 'alternative' labels such as MNW, Silence and Mai became similar to those of the commercial music industry, to such an extent that in 1980 the Norwegian Eurovision Song Contest entry was composed and performed by Sverre Kjelsberg, who was associated with the Mai label.[58] This turn of events, which indicated a marked change in the relationship between the leftist music movement and 'commercialism', resulted in an

---

[54] See, for instance, Eriksson 1975, pp. 19, 140, 198; cf. Gravem 2004, p. 15; Arvidsson 2008, pp. 104ff.; Thyrén 2009, p. 195.
[55] Nordiska Icke-kommersiella Fonogramproducenters Förening.
[56] Arvidsson 2008, pp. 350, 381.
[57] Eyerman and Jamison 1998, pp. 145, 155; cf. Arvidsson 2008, p. 314.
[58] See Gravem 2004, p. 158.

intense debate about what the appropriate politics should be for progressive activists in a commercial environment.[59] Meanwhile, the increasing professionalisation and success of the commercial sector of the Swedish music industry gradually led to what by the 1990s was described as the Swedish 'music-export miracle'.[60]

A second reason for the decline of the Scandinavian leftist music movements relates to a generational shift. The music movements were mainly sustained by the postwar generation of baby-boomers, and as this generation grew older during the course of the 1970s, they gradually became less inclined to devote large amounts of time to activist work.[61] The next generation of music activists were the punk rockers, who started appearing in the Scandinavian countries in 1977, but they differed in important respects from the previous 'progressive' generation. The punks were 'working-class' but were not politically progressive in terms of the organised left-wing party-politics model espoused by the music movements, so they proved an ideological problem to the progressives. The basis of the music movements was middle-class student groups, even though they claimed to represent the 'working class' in their political rhetoric.[62] In some respects, the punk rockers continued the activist ethos and practices of the music movements, but without the organisational superstructure, which was increasingly perceived as bureaucratic and stagnant. In contrast to the well-organised record companies of the music movements, record production in 1970s punk was focused on 'indie labels', which were low-budget outfits that prioritised releasing singles. Smith-Sivertsen provides an account of a rather curious parallel phenomenon in Denmark, where the hegemony of aesthetically 'legitimate' rock music in the national media forced Danish-language mainstream pop into the 'underground'. During the 1980s, live performances of mainstream Danish pop only took place in venues outside the capital and dissemination was primarily through low-price cassettes sold at petrol stations and the like.[63] Danish mainstream pop only resurfaced again in the 1990s with the reinstitution of Dansktoppen.[64]

A third reason for the decline relates to changes in the broadcasting networks. From the early 1980s onwards, the hegemonic status of national public-service broadcasting media in Scandinavia was in decline, as the existing public-service monopolies were exposed to increasing competition from video recorders and cable and satellite television. By the turn of the

---

[59] Gravem 2004, pp. 147ff. [60] On this 'miracle', see Björnberg (forthcoming).
[61] See Gravem 2004, p. 122. [62] Arvidsson 2008, pp. 381, 379.
[63] Smith-Sivertsen 2007, pp. 101ff. [64] Smith-Sivertsen 2007, pp. 101ff.

1990s, there was further far-reaching broadcasting deregulation that opened the airwaves to commercial competitors. Parallel to this, the public consensus that previously existed on the benefits of public-service monopolies dissipated. To the extent that the Scandinavian music movements of the 1960s and 1970s were concerned with agendas of national autonomy and national culture, their anti-authoritarian projects were also to a significant degree symbiotically linked to the authoritative voices of national public-service broadcasters.

9 | British rock: the short '1968', and the long

ALLAN F. MOORE

The impact on British popular music of the 'events of 1968' took essentially two forms. The first was immediate, but seems in retrospect as desperately superficial as the attitude to these events of most of the British public. I outline the results of this impact in the first section below, with particular reference to the contemporary British music press, for whom the events of '1968' got in the way of proper entertainment. The second had repercussions which continue to resound today. For the first time, some musicians working within British popular music developed a visionary attitude towards society.

The larger legacy of '1968', then, was the conviction it gave some musicians that popular music need not remain ephemeral in its concerns. Jon Anderson and Yes saw, and promoted through the 1970s, a utopian social vision. Peter Sinfield's lyrics for King Crimson described a dystopic near future, which the band's music matched. Almost the entire progressive rock movement from Genesis to Gentle Giant, from Emerson, Lake and Palmer to Van der Graaf Generator, explored these twin themes with a passion matched only by the refusal of any vision at all in the ensuing punk rock movement; in developing progressive rock, musicians went beyond mere entertainment. My claim in this chapter is that their visionary impulse can be found inscribed in some of the music they produced.

The immediate impact

In *New Musical Express* (*NME*) at the beginning of May 1968, as street fighting erupted in Paris, music journalist Richard Green bemoaned the negative effects psychedelia was having on pop music, which resulted in a "lack of professionalism" in the attitude of musicians.[1] Three months later, Chris Welch wrote in the rival periodical, *Melody Maker* (*MM*), of the same dramatic changes to pop music seen in recent months. Writing particularly of the musicians involved in the bands Cream, Traffic and Family, he told

---
[1] Green 1968a, p. 16.

his readers that "What seems to have happened is that the musicians from the rhythm and blues, jazz and folk scenes, have finally broken through [to the mainstream] with music taken from all these sources using the pop group concept as the stepping stone to success and recognition".[2] Green's context and motive was a hoped-for revival of 'rock' (what we would now recognise as rock 'n' roll), centred on Birmingham band the Move. Welch argued that the change he observed was developmental rather than revolutionary, insisting that these "far out musicians" had great respect for the technically expert performances, if syntactically unsophisticated songs, of commercial musicians. He cited Marmalade and the Herd as exemplars.[3] Within the month, the Beatles released "Revolution".[4] Contemporary listeners to John Lennon's diatribe may have heard it as catching the mood of the times with its apparent address to those on the barricades, although in its equivocation[5] "the political left felt betrayed by Lennon's refusal to either condone the violence [in Vietnam, against Martin Luther King and against the New Leftist protesters] or to offer a solution".[6]

A month or so earlier than "Revolution", the Rolling Stones had recorded Mick Jagger's equivalent, "Street Fightin' Man".[7] While less obviously equivocal, it is open to interpretation: as regret that "London town" was too "sleepy" to be involved in contemporary events; as the Stones distancing themselves from the action; and as marking the distance between talk (the song) and action (they did not undertake). Jagger's view of it may perhaps be gleaned from his sending the lyrics to the revolutionary Marxist paper *Black Dwarf*.[8] Although released at the time in the US, the single was held back in the UK until 1970. On 26 June 1968, iconoclastic keyboard player Keith Emerson had set fire to the US flag during a performance by his band The Nice at the Albert Hall, as part of an upmarket anti-apartheid event attended by many US dignitaries.[9] In *MM* on 6 July, he was reported as defending the incident, saying that The Nice's version of "America"[10] was inspired by both the "brutality" of America (represented by the music of Leonard Bernstein) and the "pure" motives of American youth (represented by, of all things, Dvorak's *New World* symphony, which the paper has

---

[2] Welch 1968, p. 12. [3] Welch 1968, p. 13. [4] Beatles 1968b.
[5] On the *White Album* version of "Revolution 1" (Beatles 1968a), recorded over three weeks in May–June 1968, Lennon sings "When you talk about destruction,/Don't you know that you can count me out . . . in". On the faster single version, "Revolution" (Beatles 1968b), recorded early in July 1968, the ". . . in" is omitted. MacDonald regards this subtle change as resulting from a hardening of Lennon's hitherto unfocused apoliticism (MacDonald 1995, pp. 223–9, 237–8).
[6] Roessner 2006, p. 149. [7] Rolling Stones 1968. [8] Chambers 1985, p. 102.
[9] Macan 2006, pp. 23–4. [10] Nice 1968.

Emerson attributing to Debussy).[11] The following week, Pink Floyd's second album *A Saucerful of Secrets*[12] hit the charts. Although generally exploratory of a psychedelic space, the achievements described by Corporal Clegg (on his eponymous track),[13] i.e. the gaining of his wooden leg and his medals, are clearly the result of his deceitful actions. Yet in those lyrics, newspaper reporters treat his mother with disinterest while apparently lauding Clegg. Then, amid warlike samples towards the end of the track, a kazoo's ironic rendition of what sounds like a familiar tune[14] makes clear the musicians' attitude. And then, a further week later, on 20 July, *MM* reported with a studied, uncommitted voice, rare political moves by a few musicians. The paper simply noted Scott Walker's refusal to travel to South Africa to perform because of the apartheid regime, and Gram Parsons' departure from the Byrds over the same issue, noting that the British Musicians' Union were trying to organise a ban on overseas musicians who had performed in South Africa.

This recital of events in which British, or UK-domiciled, musicians were involved might suggest a keen interest in the events of 1968, their violence and militaristic contexts, whether in the US (political assassinations and the Chicago riots, anti-Vietnam protests), France (student protests), South Africa (entrenched apartheid) or Czechoslovakia (the Soviet invasion). This is, however, almost the sum total of what was reported or even, perhaps, worth reporting in the music press. While there were some journalistic differences over interpretation, as represented by Richard Green and Chris Welch, socio-political 'events' were treated as pretty irrelevant to musical activities. In this regard, a young John Peel was outspoken. Although he already had a reputation as a supporter of 'far out' pop music, he declared in *NME* later in July that "the Underground" were identifiable by the superficiality of their social attitudes. He argues that they should live an "alternative", but that there isn't one available.[15] This expression of nihilism was unusual in this era. The superficiality of which Peel complains is nicely

---

[11] I assume this is an error on the paper's part. Green 1968b, p. 14.   [12] Pink Floyd 1968.
[13] Pink Floyd 1968.
[14] The tune is the same as that of the chorus to Dave Richards' evangelical song "For I'm Building a People of Power". This, however, was not copyrighted until 1977. Pink Floyd may conceivably be referencing a pre-copyright earlier version I have been unable to track down (although I find this unlikely), or be using a tune that was just generally in circulation (it has a rather childlike simplicity).
[15] Peel 1968. Exactly who he meant by the 'Underground' is unclear – as a term it normally meant musicians from outside the mainstream who had developed a cult following, particularly those who had been initially active in blues and folk clubs (but who often had no recording contract, or maybe a contract with a small, underfunded, enterprise). It also included those, like Jimi Hendrix or Cream, who were forging the genre conventions of what would become simply 'rock'.

characterised by a report from the end of August, this time in *MM*, focusing on the troubles the (very minor) band Fluff were having in Prague. The paper carried a photo of tanks rolling in, and a brief report on the disappointment of promoter Roy Guest and the band at the situation they found themselves in. It seems they just wanted the chance to play their music. This distance between the attitudes of British musicians and those in revolt is also apparent in a report from the Burg Waldeck International Festival of Folksong and Chansonniers in West Germany, a festival which was interrupted from the audience with calls for active protest rather than just musicians singing about protest. British singers Colin Wilkie and Shirley Hart are reported as leading a 'singers' strike' before reluctantly coming on stage. When they asked the audience whether they wanted songs, the positive response led them to tell "troublemakers" in the audience to "shut up and listen", which they almost uniformly did.[16] Producer Joe Boyd later put a positive slant on this sort of response:

The British are good at subtlety. There may have been no violent revolution, but homosexuality was legalised, the lord chamberlain's office abolished,[17] Radio One initiated, the concepts of civil, human and women's rights, protection of the environment and relaxation of the futile war on drugs all marched forward.[18]

The lack of overt support for the revolutionary movement among musicians is here suggested, by someone in the thick of contemporary musical activities, to be a normative British response. The implication of Boyd's comment, though, is that 'bigger things' nonetheless happen.

Aiming for bigger things

In early 1969, EMI launched their Harvest label, intended to market (progressive, or heavy) product to the growing college audience, a move that resulted in vast increases in album sales.[19] But the majors were not to have things entirely their own way. 'Folkie' Roy Harper had sat in with Pink Floyd and Marc Bolan's Tyrannosaurus Rex at the first Hyde Park free festival on 29 June 1968, and was planning subsequent events. Although he had only one

---

[16] Winter 1968. What is key here is not whether this was an accurate report of events (there is some evidence to suggest the dispute was more over the political content of songs sung), but that the British music press uniformly adopted a 'non-politicisation of music' stance.
[17] The Lord Chamberlain was charged with censorship of the media.   [18] Boyd 2008.
[19] Decca had launched Deram in 1966; Philips followed with Vertigo in 1969. Other majors followed suit.

album behind him, he was already concerned to gain control of his recorded output (a thing unheard of for a mere musician), threatening CBS that he would not deliver the second album without this control.[20] During 1969, *MM* began regular coverage of what was becoming progressive rock, arguing that it was popular (because it had a wide audience) and that it would be long-lasting, which meant that it had permanent value.[21] This attribution was, in part, founded on the references to 'classical' music that progressive musicians were starting to incorporate in their pieces. The consequence of these references was not simply musical: Richard Williams argued that the use of Holst's "Mars" in "The Devil's Triangle" on King Crimson's *In the Wake of Poseidon*[22] exemplified the legitimisation of a popular avant garde,[23] while Mark Plummer suggested that albums like this avoided the trivialities of pop by retaining remnants of the communality of the counterculture.[24] As early as 1970, then, we see the desire to assert the foundation of the 'seriousness' of progressive rock on those countercultural roots, on the memory of those events of 1968. Harper's desire for control over his output, a control he eventually fully exercised, as did Robert Fripp with King Crimson's work, was not readily reflected in the subject matter of his songs, and is perhaps only apparent in his penchant for length.[25] This is a feature which many other musicians would develop over the early 1970s: it is one of the distinguishing characteristics of what would become progressive rock and is one of the features that links this broad movement with the 'underground' that Peel felt to be so disappointing.

The events of 1968 had neither single cause nor single aim, and yet at the forefront of many who participated was the desire for fundamental change.[26] Such a desire was, however indecipherably, at the root both of the hippie movement and the activities of rioting students. It is this which leads Bill Martin, perhaps the most philosophically minded critic on the rock music of the ensuing decade, to argue for a continuity between these aims and what resulted in progressive rock: "As the late sixties gave way to the seventies, many people were prepared by their social experience to be open to experimental, visionary, and utopian music that was brilliantly crafted and performed".[27] He is fond of these terms: "progressive rock was the carrier of a utopian, visionary, and critical *trace* of the sixties".[28]

---

[20] Wilson 1968, p. 14.   [21] Dawbarn 1969.   [22] King Crimson 1970.   [23] Williams 1970.
[24] Plummer 1970.
[25] Both personal autonomy and a desire to escape being subjected to the corporate machine were key to the countercultural vision. See Moore 2004, pp. 78 and 85.
[26] See Moore 2004, pp. 77–8 for a survey of writings on the countercultural 'new consciousness'.
[27] Martin 1998, p. 2.   [28] Martin 1998, p. 59.

Edward Macan takes a similar line: "progressive bands [...] drew on sixties idealism to launch themselves forward [...] concerns solidly grounded in the sixties counterculture were to inform the progressive rock movement throughout the 1970s".[29] It is this commitment to vision which distinguishes progressive rock from other popular musics, and it is the vision of a better society which links progressive rock to those movements of '1968'. But there is a problem with Martin's equation of 'visionary' and 'utopian', for elsewhere he distinguishes between them:

> Even in the science-fiction elements of progressive rock we see this romanticism and pastoralism, either in the form of communitarian utopias or in the dystopias of America-style industrialism and 'pop culture' run wild. Indeed, progressive rock's inaugural album, *In the Court of the Crimson King*, goes down all of these paths.[30]

Indeed, Martin provides yet other pairings of terms to try to understand this visionary split. He distinguishes 'radical affirmation' (which in the hands of bands like Renaissance tends towards escapism, i.e. the avoidance of critical engagement) from 'radical negation' (in bands like Henry Cow, and which can tend towards cynicism).[31] He also distinguishes the 'apocalyptic' (Van der Graaf Generator) from the 'millennial' (Yes).[32] In all this parade of opposites, we are left to take Martin's word, for as with so many critics, the meaning of the music appears to equate to the meaning of the lyrics. Some years before, Iain Chambers had made similar points, but rather than praising the search for the visionary, he decried it. Chambers argued that rock took over from pop at the point where "musical basics" were mastered, equating 'authenticity' with artistic autonomy.[33]

> The counter-culture's project had once provided an extensive claim for both this [equation] and the rest of rock's claims on the future. But as that vision contracted, the music tended to seek residence in the abstract refuge of the artist intent on separating his [...] artistry from 'vulgar commerce'.[34]

I have real sympathy with Martin's assertions of vision at the expense of cynicism, but I depart from him in seeing this vision as primarily utopian. In this respect, Chambers' jaundiced and European (rather than US) perspective is perhaps more accurate. While Martin is right to argue a utopian vision in the output of Yes, in the larger repertory the dystopic drive seems dominant, certainly in the British visionary music of the period. A review in

---

[29] Macan 2006, pp. 107–8. [30] Martin 1998, p. 105. [31] Martin 1998, p. 116.
[32] Martin 1998, p. 198.
[33] See Moore 2002 for a discussion on the various ways authenticity has been argued in rock.
[34] Chambers 1985, p. 111.

Record Collector, of 2002, divided the prog world into four: music for simpletons; music for wimps; music for professors; and music which kicked butt, by means of which the reviewer identified, respectively Pink Floyd, Yes, Gentle Giant and then both King Crimson and Van der Graaf Generator.[35] The dystopic vision can be seen across three of these four categories, the exception being Yes. Note that for much of their output, Bill Bruford drummed for both Yes and King Crimson: perhaps these divisions are not fundamentally musical. Edward Macan also departs from Martin: "Even when it projects grim dystopias [...] prog remains idealistic and visionary; the style is never cynical, and its warnings of disaster seldom come without an implied pathway of deliverance".[36] After a brief introduction to the nature and range of these dystopias, I pursue this argument with respect to harmony, for I believe it is only by discussing the music that we can determine how the music might mean. There are two particular formations which are pertinent: *anti-diatonic* progressions and *parallel tenth* progressions.

A variety of visions

So, I begin with the dystopic visions. Their essential characteristic is that in society things can go wrong, and probably will. A clear starting-point must be the movement's initiatory album, King Crimson's *In the Court of the Crimson King*. The opening track simply asserts the world experience of the "21st-Century Schizoid Man",[37] a prediction we may have to take seriously for at least a moment. The album was strange in the context of 1969, which partly accounts for its dominance: it was not remotely about personal relationships, and it was 'heavy' in terms both of style (using baritone sax, mellotron pads, generally deep, thick, textures) and tone (the hippie who takes things 'too seriously'). The track "Epitaph"[38] momentously pits the lone acoustic guitar against the massed sound of the band, an early manifestation of this textural trope. Its lyrics now appear, perhaps, rather juvenile, but the sense of ringing phrases such as "knowledge is a deadly friend when no-one knows the rules" still has the power to move, particularly when combined with Greg Lake's deadpan, distanced delivery (as if he is receding from a comfortable spatial relation with his listeners) and its lack of movement in any textural strand. Earlier warnings of coming

[35] Anonymous 2002.   [36] Macan 2006, p. 256.   [37] King Crimson 1969.
[38] King Crimson 1969.

doom (Paul Simon's "The Sound of Silence"[39] or Bob Dylan's "Masters of War")[40] had clear geographical locations (respectively "narrow streets, subway walls, tenement halls" and desks miles from actual conflict, i.e. the Pentagon and similar locations). In "Epitaph", the sense is all-pervasive – we are all involved.[41] Gregory Karl argues that such dystopias are endemic to early King Crimson.[42]

The range of visions is wide. Genesis' "Watcher of the Skies"[43] views a far future when humanity is dying out. The 'watcher' expresses a certain resignation, but a stronger sense of indifference. Van der Graaf Generator's "Lemmings"[44] considers a future where even death brings no respite. With the final verse's "what course is there left but to live?", writer and singer Peter Hamill's desperate nihilism far exceeds in eloquence and sheer power anything punk ever produced. Jethro Tull's *A Passion Play*[45] takes a not dissimilar line in finding, with heavy doses of irony, inadequacy in the afterlife such that there is no alternative but to return. Gentle Giant's "Knots"[46] is similarly personal, although here the hell is the sheer impossibility of interhuman communication: it needs no fantastical setting to make the point. The same is true of String Driven Thing's "It's a Game",[47] although here the meaninglessness of existence is embraced with dripping irony – such a glitteringly rich texture and sparkling vocals. The Strawbs' "New World"[48] brings us back to the world of "Epitaph", both in its analysis and its acoustic-guitar-against-the-band texture, although here resignation is replaced by anger at the apparently inevitable course of destruction on which society is set. Emerson, Lake and Palmer's "Karn Evil 9",[49] and even "Tarkus",[50] imagine similar scenarios in fantastical settings, but our complicity in our own downfall is no less implied here. This complicity, perhaps, is the root of the dystopic visions progressive rock presents to us. In Gryphon's "Major Disaster",[51] dystopia is brought close to home, perhaps trivialised, but even here in one of the brightest (texturally and harmonically speaking) outputs of the prog era, this tone resonates. It is only Yes who succeeded in escaping it entirely.

---

[39] Simon & Garfunkel 1965.   [40] Dylan 1963.

[41] For me, the whole apocalyptic tone of heavy metal originates in the gothic doom found here and in Van der Graaf Generator, moving via Hawkwind to Led Zeppelin and Black Sabbath and thence beyond the UK.

[42] Karl 2002, p. 129.

[43] Genesis 1972. The borrowing, for the title, of a phrase from Keats' "On first looking into Chapman's Homer" typifies the self-conscious artistry with which some of these visions were couched.

[44] Van der Graaf Generator 1971.   [45] JethroTull 1973.   [46] Gentle Giant 1972.

[47] String Driven Thing 1973.   [48] Strawbs 1972.   [49] Emerson, Lake and Palmer 1973.

[50] Emerson, Lake and Palmer 1971.   [51] Gryphon 1977.

Anti-diatonic progressions

So much for the subject matter. It is of course the music which makes this subject *matter*, and the music takes a number of different courses. Here I concentrate on two seemingly contradictory harmonic practices that underpin some expressions of this dystopic vision. By *anti-diatonic* progressions I refer to pitch-class collections which partition the aggregate equally; the key feature of diatony, of course, is its asymmetrical (7:5) partitioning.[52] Thus, within the aesthetic of vernacular and popular song, equi-partitioning of the aggregate is aberrant, unnatural. I address three forms of such partitioning: that of the diminished triad; that of the whole-tone scale; and what effectively acts as the conjunction of the two, the octatonic scale. All are familiar from earlier European tonal harmony and in its time, each mounted a challenge to then contemporary diatonic normality, whether that challenge was uttered by Bach, by Debussy, or by Stravinsky.

As the basis of a harmonic progression, the diminished triad could be argued to have developed from the blues, but a more likely source is the simple movement of chord shapes in the guitarists' left hand up the fretboard. The Surfaris' early track "Scatter Shield"[53] exemplifies this (at 20") where the riff, which outlines a minor third, is itself transposed up a minor third.Transpositions of a motif up a series of minor thirds has clear negative connotations in the Strawbs' "Sheep",[54] from 1971 where (from 46") such a series of transpositions depicts the anguish of sheep entering the slaughterhouse, from the viewpoint of a young farmer's son who becomes vegetarian as a result. Three minor-third transpositions lead to use of the full octatonic scale at the track's climax. The opening to "Hell"[55] (from about 55"), on the first album by Gracious, is depicted particularly through arpeggiated diminished triads, transposed through a chromatic scale, in a deep register on the Hammond organ replete with fuzz, degenerating into an Emersonian cacophony.

Aspects of the whole-tone scale often appear as either arpeggiations of an augmented triad or a prevalence of bass movement by tritone. There are a number of examples from both Italian and French progressive rock, while the central section of Van der Graaf Generator's "Lemmings"[56] is based on successive augmented triads. It is however only King Crimson, and Robert Fripp in particular, who explore this whole harmonic area with

---

[52] The diatonic scale uses seven of the available twelve pitches in an octave, omitting the remaining five. Symmetrical partitions (6:6, 4:8, 3:9) all challenge the identity of any tonal centre.
[53] Surfaris 1964.   [54] Strawbs 1971.   [55] Gracious 1970.   [56] Van der Graaf Generator 1971.

Figure 9.1 King Crimson, introduction to "One More Red Nightmare".

any consistency. In "Fracture" from 1974,[57] from 45 seconds, 026/046[58] trichords in the guitar combine with a whole-tone scale in the bass. The introduction to the same year's "One More Red Nightmare",[59] uses 026/046 trichords as surrogate triads in a quasi-12-bar pattern, but (towards the end) doubled at the tenth (see Figure 9.1).

The lyrics clarify the emotionally negative nature of the song. More recent examples justify an interpretation of these formulations as an intrinsic feature of the King Crimson idiolect, even where the meaning of the lyrics is less clear. There is even a touch of this approach in the otherwise stylistically distant phase-two Crimson (active in the early 1980s), where, two minutes into "Discipline",[60] the pentatonic arpeggios are effectively transposed through two minor thirds (see Figure 9.2).

---

[57] King Crimson 1974a.
[58] This notation counts semitones from a starting-pitch, thus 026 becomes C-D-F# (for example) and its transpositions. 046 = C-E-F#, etc. The similarity to minor or major triads (e.g. B-D-F# or C-E-G), with one note altered by only a semitone, probably accounts for their acceptability.
[59] King Crimson 1974b.   [60] King Crimson 1981.

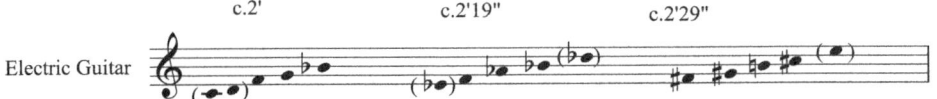

Figure 9.2 King Crimson, pentatonic arpeggios in "Discipline" (c. 2' ff.).

Phase-three Crimson (reformed in the 1990s and still active) returns to the 12-bar/whole-tone combination in the ironic "ProzaKc Blues"[61] (at 27"). "FraKctured",[62] from the same album, returns to the free quasi-whole-tone patterns of the earlier "Fracture", while "The Slaughter of the Innocents"[63] is based on bare tritones. "VROOOM VROOOM"[64] returns to the texture of "Red"[65] (around 22"), but now places arpeggiated augmented triads beneath 014/034 arpeggios;[66] the opening to "Level Five"[67] suggests a variation on this approach.In "Coda: I Have a Dream",[68] an altogether utopian vision recalling Martin Luther King's famous speech is placed in an aural (edgy, dense, compressed) context we are used to hearing as highly dystopic, as the never-ending sequence effectively drops by a tone at a time.[69] In its avoidance of familiar pop harmonies, and its substitution by a language which challenges the naïve ear, this approach suggests a perspective in which the uneasy dominates.

Parallel tenths

Where the period gets particularly interesting is that these same visions are often clothed in a harmonic language which is anything but insecure, a strong aspect of the recourse to Anglican hymnody which Edward Macan considers a key stylistic marker of progressive rock.[70] In many cases, negative emotional content is set to parallel tenths. Because the source of this musical topic (parallel tenths) is the Anglican hymnody Macan identifies (and, further back, precursors such as Mendelssohn and Sebastian Bach), and because the tone of such hymnody is of Protestant striving and resolution (towards the positive), this topic implies that same quality in offshoot traditions.

[61] King Crimson 2000.   [62] King Crimson 2000.   [63] King Crimson 1996.
[64] King Crimson 1995.   [65] King Crimson 1974b.
[66] For example, C-C#-E or C-D#-E and their transpositions.   [67] King Crimson 2003.
[68] King Crimson 2000.
[69] Since Robert Fripp's exploration of equi-partitioned aggregates is extensive, it would repay much more careful study than I have given it here.
[70] Macan 1997.

Two examples will demonstrate the pre-progressive, 'normative' positive connotation. The Beatles' "Penny Lane"[71] opens brightly with a series of slightly disguised parallel tenths between Paul McCartney's voice and his bass. The lugubrious verse of Procol Harum's "A Whiter Shade of Pale"[72] uses the same motion. Even some early King Crimson tracks use hooks based on parallel tenths: "Court of the Crimson King"[73] itself (the opening, between voices and bass), the sax melody (and bass) of "Pictures of a City"[74] (around 1'33") and John Wetton's voice and bass in "Easy Money"[75] (around 1'25"). In the first two of these, the connotation is one of momentousness; in "Easy Money" the lyric is full of disdain. An early track using such parallel tenths to a somewhat negative end is Thunderclap Newman's "Accidents",[76] from 1969 (the opening progression between voice and bass), but it is in the next few years that this negative connotation becomes more prevalent.

Genesis' "Watcher of the Skies"[77] (at 2'18") is very clear in this regard. I have already identified its dystopian vision, which unfolds in the chorus as Peter Gabriel's melody moves in descending tenths with the upper part of Tony Banks' keyboard texture. After the tumultuous opening of Gnidrolog's "Long Live Man Dead",[78] the guitar settles into an accompanimental pattern for the recorder solo, based on an ornamented sequence of parallel tenths circling round the tonic. Part of the affective power of Gentle Giant's "Think of Me with Kindness"[79] comes from the downward parallel tenths (56") which underpin the refrain, and which are then replaced by rising lines at the beginning of the ensuing verse; their subsequent "Way of Life"[80] is riddled with tenths, but more on the surface of instrumental passages. In contrast to "Think of Me with Kindness", the power of Greenslade's "Drowning Man"[81] comes partly from the ascending organ tenths (around 38"), but note that the upper pedal rises at the end of the sequence, producing consecutive fifths with the bass (marked by arrows in Figure 9.3). No matter how subtle this tiny moment, it is tremendously telling. These musicians have understood the surface of the Anglican hymnodic style in creating a quasi-version endemic to the progressive period, but the consecutives proclaim it a flawed understanding. What is even more startling in relation to "Drowning Man" is that the lyric is so

---

[71] Beatles 1967.   [72] Procol Harum 1967.   [73] King Crimson 1969.
[74] King Crimson 1970.   [75] King Crimson 1973.
[76] Thunderclap Newman 1969. The lyric bemoans the protagonist's inability to explain the troubling disappearance of children, or to understand his own response.
[77] Genesis 1972.
[78] Gnidrolog 1972. The opening lyrics typify the song's negative outlook: "The white skull lifted hand/[...]Wrote in blood poisoned red/Long live man dead". The entire song explores this tone.
[79] Gentle Giant 1972.   [80] Gentle Giant 1973.   [81] Greenslade 1973.

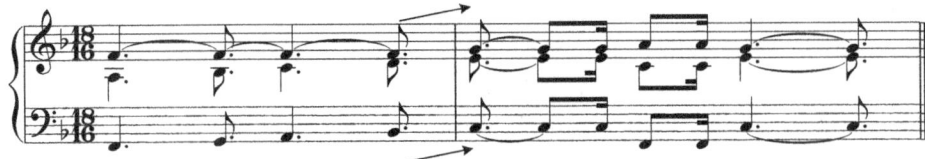

Figure 9.3 Greenslade, rising tenths in "Drowning Man" (38").

negative: "Forgive us all our trespasses, as we do not forgive", within a narrative ruminating imprecisely on a post-battle scenario.

This combination of negative emotional content with the positive connotation of parallel tenths is particularly persuasive, and nowhere more so than in a number of contexts in the work of Van der Graaf Generator: the tracks "Refugees",[82] "Pilgrims" and "Childlike Faith in Childhood's End"[83] are particularly clear. "Refugees" takes a regretful stance, but the intense desire for an unreachable utopia is beautifully captured in both the texture and the returning lyric "West is Mike and Suzy". The track was originally written some time between late 1968 and the autumn of 1969.[84] In it, a utopia is already inhabited by, and totally identified with ("West is"), friendly, playful (i.e. "Suzy"[85] rather than the more formal 'Susan') approachable friends. But, since the lyric posits that "we" are "refugees", such a utopia is beyond us, hence false. As for texture, it is founded on parallel tenths operating between flute and 'cello. In their "Pilgrims",[86] the same musical topic underpins the proud chorus (at 2'18", for instance), bookending it. Finally, "Childlike Faith in Childhood's End" envisions the end of ordinary humanity in the 'real' beginning of the race's supersessors. Less the Übermensch of Nietzsche via David Bowie, this is more the simple world-weariness of sci-fi; while the plot is related to that of Genesis' "Watcher of the Skies" (i.e. the migration of 'humanity' for distant worlds), the track borrows its plot from the end of Arthur C. Clarke's novel with a similar name.[87]

This reminder of the prevalence of the dystopic in progressive rock finds it expressed in two very different harmonic formulations – one which, in a realist reading, conforms to the sentiment, and one which might be held to run counter to it. This is not to say that these harmonic formulations by any means dominate (although, since progressive rock is not a style, it cannot be said to have *a* harmonic language), but they do point to a more

---

[82] Van der Graaf Generator 1970. [83] Van der Graaf Generator 1976.
[84] Christophoulos and Smart 2005, p. 57. It is, thus, an earlier employment of this topic than most of those I have already identified.
[85] Peter Hammill apparently had in mind the actress Susan Penhaligon.
[86] Van der Graaf Generator 1976. [87] Clarke 1956.

comprehensive approach to the way the movement's dystopias are presented musically.

Possible utopias

What of the opposite pole? Despite its ubiquity, I suspect the unmodified 'utopia' is not the most useful here, for rather than presenting visions of an ideal perfect society, what progressive rock can be found to offer is something more amorphous: the possibility of achieving a better society, perhaps, or even just an escape from the negatives, from alienation. The band Yes are by far the best source for relevant examples. Some years ago I published an essay in which I argued that elements of Yes' music could be regarded as signifying a rather unfocused spirituality ("a rather unspecific ecological pantheism with touches of universal siblinghood"),[88] an expression which fits well into this context. The means by which such an expression is achieved are rather diverse; there is nothing equivalent to the specific harmonic procedures identified above. Thus, at 8 minutes 20 seconds into "I Get Up I Get Down",[89] Jon Anderson's extremely high vocal register becomes supported by equally high parallel vocal backing and by a pair of high, repeated church organ chords with flute stops for what, in terms of lyrics, comes across as a lament for the earth mother. The complete absence of the bass end of the texture here, unusual as this is, marks out this passage as notable. While the lyrics give a strong clue as to how to read the track, the texture amplifies this. Most rock relies on dominant bass frequencies. These have sometimes been read negatively in social terms (connoting the licentiousness associated with the urge to sexual cavortings on the dance floor in the music of Elvis Presley and other rock 'n' rollers, for instance). Semiotically, this texture of Yes' must be marked out as different and, ecologically, bass-empty textures can easily be read as an escape from erotic materiality towards a more 'refined' plain. The passage comes to a resolution as Anderson's voice rises by step to close on the fifth degree of the scale, the line's apex, having asked "will we ever learn?". At this point (12'11"), the full organ cuts in, marking the point as one of intermediate closure. The implication of this closure seems to be 'yes we can'.

A similar soundworld underpins the beginning of Yes' fifteen-minute track "Awaken".[90] It opens with a sparse, treble-dominated texture which accompanies lyrics which invoke being rather than becoming, even going so far as to

---

[88] Moore 1996, p. 32.   [89] Yes 1972.   [90] Yes 1977.

call on the sun to stand still. The ensuing rich texture is dominated by Anderson singing barely related streams of words ("awaken gentle mass touch", for instance) from opposite sides of the soundbox, effectively cocooning the listener within this richness, since the track's meaning is not one to be discerned semantically, i.e. from the outside. This omission of the conventional (harmonic) use of the bass end of a standard texture had previously been employed by Pink Floyd to signify travelling in space, whether outer or inner (in tracks like "Interstellar Overdrive",[91] for instance), and this is also a common conceit for Yes: the early "Astral Traveller",[92] for instance, or the later "Arriving UFO".[93] That such encounters are always viewed positively, and with the potential for spiritual development, by singer Jon Anderson, again positions these as harbingers of a potential utopia.

Progressive rock does contain other exemplars, beyond the music of Yes, but none are thoroughgoing. I give a few varied examples. Genesis' "Supper's Ready"[94] has a rather muddled and not altogether consistent narrative, but across its more than twenty minutes and seven distinct sections it contains aspects of a portrayal of an apocalyptic battle between good and evil. This begins in the most homely way possible, as Gabriel's persona recalls a disturbing late night experience in which he sees his wife's face almost melt, and ends with the magnificence of the building of the New Jerusalem. Both opening and ending use the same stretch of music, at first intimate, subsequently majestic and even pompous. The denouement of an apocalypse in this revelation clearly marks the narrative as one in which a utopia is achieved. But note that this track appears on the same album as "Watcher of the Skies",[95] which I have already described as presenting a dystopic vision. "Watcher" opens the album, "Supper" closes it. Perhaps this observation implies a reading of the entire album as resulting in one final utopia (although other tracks on the album, particularly "Get 'em Out by Friday"[96] present alternative dystopias).

It is also possible to find Emerson, Lake and Palmer presenting possible utopias. I think this is the way to understand the close to their version of *Pictures at an Exhibition* (1972). In the context of Mussorgsky's original piano cycle, the final movement, "Great Gates of Kiev", essays a triumphalism which is texturally bare but forceful, and harmonically plain and uncluttered. Emerson, Lake and Palmer retain both the expression and much of the material, although the triumphalism is underscored both by Carl Palmer's drumming and also by Greg Lake's lyrics and their delivery.

[91] Pink Floyd 1967. [92] Yes 1970. [93] Yes 1979. [94] Genesis 1972. [95] Genesis 1972.
[96] Genesis 1972.

Lake's final declaration, "there's no end to my life, no beginning to my death, death is life" is suitably portentous and, in its denial of death as final closure, perhaps to be read positively.[97] As I have already said, though, the tone of "Tarkus" or of "Karn Evil 9" is very much darker.

Beyond these isolated instances, it is hard to find visions which might be described as utopian. The lyrics to Camel's "Song Within a Song"[98] equate the "song" to a "dream" in which we can drift "forever". In this sense it is escapist, while the laid-back harmonies and the clean timbres suggest such dreaming is a positive experience. With other examples, there is less a sense of there being a positive future for all, than that the present can be made bearable. In Caravan's "In the Land of Grey and Pink"[99] which is, again, escapist, the unchanging and untroubled harmonic sequence could perhaps be read as an achieved security beneath the matter-of-fact voice.[100] The Moody Blues' *To our Children's Children's Children*[101] was intended as a concept album about space travel, in which the far future is seen as a positive outcome. One final example sums up for me much of what passes for positivity of expression in this repertory, and that is the Strawbs' almost throwaway "Journey's End",[102] which appears on the same album as the dystopic "New World".[103] Over what is, entirely fortuitously, the same harmonic sequence that underpins Genesis' "Watcher of the Skies", the Strawbs' Dave Cousins describes a world-weary traveller who, at journey's (i.e. life's) end "no longer needs a friend". The heavily reverberant piano, which is his only accompaniment, seems to symbolise the only friend who has remained, and without whom he can finally do (as the piano finally fades into his distance). In that this represents a final resolution of life's narrative, it is a purely personal resolution and this, it seems to me, distinguishes all these potential 'utopias' from the earlier dystopias – the dystopias are generally social, the utopias tend towards the individual. Again, I think only Yes stand fully aside from this analysis.

More than any other musician of the time, it might seem that Bill Bruford was most heavily implicated in this complex of visions – drumming, as I mentioned earlier, for the vast majority of the output of King Crimson on the one hand, and for periods with Yes on the other. As such, his

---

[97] It is not unequivocal: the penultimate line "no beginning to my death" might cause one to wonder.
[98] Camel 1976.   [99] Caravan 1971.
[100] As with Emerson, Lake and Palmer, there is no consistency. Caravan elsewhere invoke H. P. Lovecraft's horrific inter-war Cthulhu mythos (Lovecraft 1951).
[101] Moody Blues 1969.   [102] Strawbs 1972.   [103] Strawbs 1972.

(minimal) comments on musicianly intention at the time carry weight. He recalls the end of psychedelia and the heady early days of the progressive era:

> The scene was in perpetual change and permanently fluid. After The Beatles, everything was up for grabs. The only rule I could find was that we shouldn't sound like the other guys. My personal agenda was, and remains, to do with trying to make a contribution on my instrument – drums – in the wider sense. My interest in the Summer of Love, psychedelia, student riots and lysergic acid was therefore marginal, at best.[104]

I rather suspect that this was a dominant attitude among British musicians. While the events of 1968 did have an immediate, politicising effect on some of the UK's leading popular musicians, that effect diminished within months, and in this the hold of those events was no greater on musicians than it was on contemporary UK students and others at least marginally associated with the counterculture. But the very idea that popular music need not be mere entertainment, and could involve the entertaining of potential societies, seems to have begun gestating at that time. The political effects of 1968 may have been ephemeral, but the cultural effects were anything but. The possibility that one might ask questions of the meaning of popular music, questions which impacted on the sorts of society one might create, arose because of the way musicians' world-views were moulded by the events of 1968.

---

[104] Lindblad 2008.

10 | '1968' and the experimental revolution in Britain

VIRGINIA ANDERSON

Britain is exceptional as one of the few European countries to have escaped occupation or drastic governmental change in the years around the second world war.[1] And unlike America's expansion into Southeast Asia, Britain's empire was in decline.[2] Consequently, the British '1968' experience was unique – conservative, isolated and politically untouched. As Mick Jagger noted in his song, a "sleepy London town" culture prevented "street fighting" men like Tariq Ali from organising protests of the order of the May riots in France and Germany. Instead, Britain's counterculture dwelt in an 'underground' scene distinct from the mainstream popular and artistic culture of 'swinging' London. This underground culture – its drugs, alternative lifestyles, blues and soul-based rock, happenings (freeform multimedia events more commonly called 'raves') and even its eventual protest – followed American countercultural scenes, especially those of New York and San Francisco. The Underground was, using concepts originated by the British cultural theorist Raymond Williams, both *oppositional*, seeking "a different way to live and [...] to change the society in its light" and *alternative*, finding "a different way to live and [wishing] to be left alone with it".[3]

So-called 'high-art' movements were a part of the British Underground, including Beat poetry, American abstract expressionism and the multi-art movement Fluxus (including composers such as La Monte Young and Philip Corner); the American experimental indeterminacy of John Cage, Christian Wolff, Morton Feldman and Earle Brown was also an active element of this subculture. In fact, up to 1967, Beat poets, such as Alan Ginsberg and Michael Horowitz, and experimental composers, such as Cage and Cornelius Cardew, not only influenced the Underground, but were among its primary artistic figures. After 1967, though, there was, as the underground cartoonist, jazz musician and publisher Jeff Nuttall noted, "a shift [...] from poetry and art and jazz and anti-nuclear politics to just sex and drugs, legalise pot";[4] moreover, popular music became sophisticated

---

[1] The Atlee government (1945–51) brought in socialised medicine.
[2] The Northern Ireland "Troubles" only gained the sobriquet of "England's Vietnam" after the "Bloody Sunday" armed suppression of civil rights protesters on 30 January 1972.
[3] Williams 2005 (1980), pp. 41–2.   [4] Green 1988, p. 223.

enough to be central to underground music. No longer celebrated by the counterculture, British experimentalists like Cardew and members of the multi-arts group the Scratch Orchestra nevertheless paralleled its course; first, as an *alternative*, through a quasi-hippie arts culture based on Confucian thought, and then as an *oppositional* force, based on Maoism and revolutionary politics.

This chapter examines, first, the background to the 'experimental revolution' in British Old Left activity and the rise of the New Left, and second, the British version of Cagean experimentalism – in opposition to the Western European avant garde,[5] in its relationship with the Beat aesthetic, and finally, as expressed via Fluxus, the first British experimental movement. It also assesses the central role of the London underground newspaper, *The International Times* (more commonly, *IT*) in its coverage of experimental music and, conversely, the ways in which experimentalists (often working in the Underground themselves) actively promoted their work through *The International Times*, until the commercialisation of the counterculture marginalised 'high-art' scenes. The chapter concludes with a case study of the Scratch Orchestra, first comparing its *alternative*, 'hippie-ish' traits with those highlighted in contemporary and present-day hippie studies, and then taking into account the *oppositional* Scratch Orchestra, engendered by anarchistic, Situationist and artistic divisions, which led to a crisis of leadership and ideology, and ultimately to a Maoist, Stalinist aesthetic.

British music in the Old and New Left

Just as many creative artists in the US were attracted to communism in the interwar years, a fair number of British composers were drawn to the Old Left Communist Party of Great Britain (CPGB). Among the better-known British composers, Alan Bush and Bernard Stevens were the most constant and loyal Party members, but many others took part in Party activities in the years before 1956. Michael Tippett briefly joined the CPGB in the 1930s, hoping to convert its membership from the Socialist Realism of Stalinism to the artistic freedom of Trotskyism.[6] Benjamin Britten wrote for Worker's Music Association (WMA) choirs in the 1930s,[7] and Elisabeth Lutyens and Humphrey Searle

---

[5] Following Nyman 1999 (1974), 'avant garde' here refers exclusively to the Western European postwar Schoenbergian tradition (such as Darmstadt); 'experimental' refers to Cagean indeterminacy and early minimalism.
[6] Hanlon and Waite 1998, p. 71. See Bullivant 2009, p. 451.
[7] Although nominally separate, the WMA was closely linked with the CPGB.

were WMA members.[8] Bush never left the party; possibly stung by charges of formalism, he restricted his postwar style to a simplified nationalism.[9] Stevens broke Stalinist strictures by using limited twelve-tone and chance organisation. Although a life-long communist, Stevens left the CPGB over its support for the Soviet suppression of the Hungarian revolution in 1956.

So, too, did the historian Edward Palmer Thompson, who in 1957 formulated 'socialist humanism' (a domestic Marxism, partly informed by William Morris),[10] in the *New Reasoner* and *Universities & Left Review*, which merged in 1960 to become the *New Left Review* (*NLR*). Although it would become the training ground for counterculture journalism, in its 'first New Left' phase (1960–2), *NLR* arts coverage focused on theatre and cinema, publishing only two music articles. One of these featured Bruce Turner, a bandleader and Marxist, who dismissed African-American modern jazz as a "gimmick",[11] describing it as an "absolutely conscious, brazen attempt to become Hindemith's and Stravinsky's [sic] by people who just are not equipped".[12] A subsequent letter to the editor called this patently racist view "untenable".[13] In the 'second New Left' phase (lasting into the 1970s), Perry Anderson assumed *NLR* editorship, focusing on "theoretical exposition and construction aimed at the creation of a Marxist culture in Britain".[14] Anderson was part of the 'bomb culture' generation, a concept formulated by Nuttall as describing "people who had not yet reached puberty at the time of the [Hiroshima] bomb [and who] were incapable of conceiving life *with* a future".[15] The second *NLR* was, nominally, Trotskyist, favouring Continental New Left thinking and emphasising popular culture – yet embracing many of the same arts as the subsequent 1960s counterculture. Alan Beckett, who would help to found the countercultural *International Times*, reviewed free jazz and Chicago blues, an obsession of late 1960s rock groups.[16]

The musical revolution was not yet experimental, however. During its 'second New Left' phase, the *NLR* favoured European modernism over American experimentalism. Michael Parsons, for example, accused John Cage of laziness in the very first *NLR* music article of the second New Left.

All his careful planning of the right conditions for pure chance does not amount to real *work*, since there is no exercise of intelligence or judgement in what he does. And after all music is concerned with intelligence and intention, and this is what

---

[8] Hanlon and Waite 1998, pp. 71–2. [9] Schafer 1963, p. 58. See also Bullivant 2009, p. 432.
[10] Davis 2008, p. 48. [11] Whahnel and Lovell 1961, p. 45.
[12] Whahnel and Lovell 1961, p. 48. [13] Keen 1961, p. 52. [14] Davis 2006, p. 337.
[15] Nuttall 1968, p. 22. [16] Including Taylor, Monk, Dolphy, Coltrane and John Lee Hooker.

relates it to other human activities and to society, and gives it validity in terms of human effort. To back out of this is really a gesture of despair, of throwing up one's hands and saying "nothing matters".[17]

Although by 1968 Parsons would co-found the experimental Scratch Orchestra, at this time he knew Cage's music only through Luigi Nono, who had written, "Chance is [...] attractive only to the composer who is unable to make decisions",[18] contending instead that "the revolutionary [should destroy] existing forms in order to replace them with new ones which are in the process of development".[19]

Nono's view of chance reflects not only the musical conservatism of the European avant garde at the time, but the remnants of Old Left thinking. In 1962, the Communist Party Music Group denounced Cornelius Cardew for his Cagean "modern trends in composition", asserting that "the latest fashion – indeterminism – in particular is a policy of despair, an admission that life has become too much for us, and that we are incapable of controlling it, something no communist can agree to".[20] While the Communist Party Music Group censured musical indeterminacy for its metaphor of social despair, Nono's personal dismissal of Cage – "We need not wait for history to judge because fraud is immediately obvious"[21] – presumes a Marxian historical progress. The American experimentalists' alternative tradition was oppositional, both to this linear, progressive history and to compositional rigour; moreover, they also opposed the European avant garde in their works and aesthetic. It was this American alternative tradition, paired with ideas derived from Beat poetry, which ultimately laid the groundwork for the interaction between British experimentalists and the Underground.

Experimental alternative tradition

British composers of the 'bomb culture' generation (who were born between 1932 and 1940) include the Manchester Group (Harrison Birtwistle, Peter Maxwell Davies and Alexander Goehr), as well as Cardew, Richard Rodney Bennett, David Bedford, Michael Parsons and John White. These composers found British musical life too conservative, stuck in an almost nineteenth-century aesthetic. Composer Dave Smith recalls that in 1967 Elisabeth Lutyens (the first British composer to adopt serialism) told an audience at Selwyn College, Cambridge, "Britain hasn't

---

[17] Parsons 1964, p. 86.   [18] Nono 1960, p. 45.   [19] Nono 1960, p. 41.
[20] Hanlon and Waite 1998, p. 82.   [21] Nono 1960, p. 45.

had an avant-garde composer since Dunstable."[22] Except for Parsons and White, these composers studied in Europe or the US after music college; for instance, Cardew studied with Stockhausen. However, the relationship of the Continental avant garde to the Second Viennese tradition was internal and familial, a cultural extension rather than a counterculture. Alexander Goehr accepted the avant garde; writing that in leading the Manchester School, "I was trying to state what was and what was not real modern music."[23] As a consequence of their ties to this tradition, these composers played a negligible part in the 1968 revolution. If anything, they formed a tangential association with 'swinging' London, an establishment culture that took in mainstream pop, Bond films and the Playboy Club, as well as couture, design, publishing and government-supported high arts.[24] Maxwell Davies' *Eight Songs for a Mad King* (1969) was discussed in 'swinging' London society, as was David Fanshawe's more accessible *African Sanctus* of that same year.

The experimentalist attitude towards the Second Viennese tradition and its progeny in Darmstadt, however, was external and oppositional, leading directly to a musical style that became a part of the counterculture up to 1968. Cardew rebelled against Stockhausen's editorial control of *Carré* and his method of working.[25] According to John Tilbury, after meeting Cage, Cardew dismissed "what he regarded now as the pretentious and numbing dogma which pervaded at Darmstadt, mocking its supreme irrelevance, and even pitying its sagging, yet still earnest protagonists".[26] The American experimental attitude towards the philosophy of the Darmstadt School provided an important ideological model for the British experimental revolution. Cage regretted the Darmstadt "vogue for profundity", which resulted in masterpieces separate from "life".[27] Christian Wolff described how David Tudor, after hearing Adorno give a complex explication of Cage's *Cartridge Music*, said, "you haven't understood a thing".[28] In 1966, Morton Feldman claimed that New York School artists and composers were alternative, if not actively oppositional, creating "art without all this dialectical justification".[29] Using a Biblical metaphor and a culinary

---

[22] Smith 2010. See also Bullivant 2009, pp. 434ff. [23] Cross 2001.
[24] 'Swinging London' culture was characterised in *Blow Up* (1966, dir. Michelangelo Antonioni) and satirised in *Austin Powers: International Man of Mystery* (1997, dir. Jay Roach), and its sequels.
[25] See Tilbury 2008; also Cardew 1961. [26] Tilbury 2008, p. 80. [27] Cage 1961, p. 130.
[28] Wolff 1998, p. 380. [29] Beckett 1966, p. 7.

pun, Feldman contrasted the New Yorkers with a tradition that was grounded in the Second Viennese School (*Zweite Wiener Schule*).

I think I realised that I was thrown out of Eden [...] I think Boulez and Stockhausen think they're in Paradise. Because evidently, the great idea, the great system, is analogous to Paradise, an intellectual Utopia. I know I was thrown out because I ate the apple – Stockhausen's just eating *Wienerschnitzel*. I don't know what Boulez eats.[30]

Cardew taunted the avant garde just as the American experimentalists did, calling Boulez, "that funny little man gabbling away in front of a blackboard with arrows and words like 'Morphology' [sic] 'Syntaxe' 'Statique' 'Dynamique' 'Critères sélectifs'".[31] Cardew's last tie to the European avant garde occurred while studying with Petrassi in Rome in 1964, where he first tried experimental free improvisation. Years later, he acknowledged, "I stopped writing like Stockhausen around 1964."[32] He described Stockhausen's *Klavierstück IX* (1962) as "a weak, aesthetic version"[33] of Young's *Arabic Numeral (Any Integer) for HF* (1960); he satirised Stockhausen's *Plus-Minus* (1963) in his own *Solo with Accompaniment* (1964) and attempted to leave what he called "Stockhausen country"[34] in performances of *Plus-Minus* with Frederic Rzewski.

Cardew's rejection of the European avant garde and his interest in indeterminacy and graphic notation alienated him from his British contemporaries. In 1960, Richard Rodney Bennett attacked Cardew's *Generation Music I* concert:

Der Cornelius gave a concert of really stunning boredom at the Conway Hall with another demented youth [Tilbury]: Feldman, Cage, Cage [sic], Cardew, Feldman. An audience of 70 sat transfixed with gloom while they produced, very slowly and laboriously, a series of small tired noises [...]; the whole effect as soporific as an evening spent listening to the complete Methodist Hymnal.[35]

Like the American experimentalists, Cardew interacted more with writers and visual artists than with other composers. His schoolmate David Sladen introduced Cardew to Wittgenstein's *Tractatus* (inspiring Cardew's *Treatise* [1963–7]). Through Sladen, Cardew became music reviewer for the journal *New Departures*, founded by Michael Horowitz in Oxford, and played piano for their occasional festival *Live New Departures*.

---

[30] Beckett 1966, p. 7. [31] Tilbury 2008, p. 80. [32] Amirkhanian 1975.
[33] Cardew 1966, p. 959. [34] Cardew 1967. [35] Tilbury 2008, p. 82.

Experimentalism, Beat culture and the dawn of the Underground

New Departures writers identified with the Beat movement, which became an important influence for the 1960s Underground. The Beat/experimental association stems from the first 'happening' at Black Mountain College in 1952, when Robert Creeley and Charles Olson, the 'Black Mountain' poets, performed with Cage, Cunningham, Tudor and Rauschenberg. 'Happenings' engendered underground raves, but in the popular imagination the opposite occurred. For instance, at the Uncommon Market, a rave and auction to benefit the *International Times*, at the Roundhouse, Camden Town (a former railway shed that presented many underground events) on 29 January 1967, Mike Lesser used rolls of white paper, paint and Biddy Peppin's 56-gallon jelly dessert to "[bask] naked in [...] a jelly and paint composition on newsprint". Profiling this event in the article "London isn't swinging any more, it's raving mad", Michael Vestey claimed that the Underground had led both popular music icons and modern 'high' artists astray:

Personalities for whom there is much admiration, include writer William Burroughs, author of *The Naked Lunch*, now living in London, Paul McCartney, who attends their raves, [rock] groups like the Move, the Cream, the Pink Floyd and [the experimental free improvisation group] AMM, Negro comedian Dick Gregory, writer Norman Mailer, and poet Alan Ginsberg. Composers John Cage and Cornelius Cardew are lit brightly in the *avant garde*. This is a collection of tremendous talent which is squandered in the interests of experimentation and exploration.[36]

Although underground groups produced their own take on the 'happening' to produce raves (Peppin's enormous jellies were a regular feature of Pink Floyd's early concerts), Beat writers, experimental composers and other artists and art movements led the Underground astray by their example. Lesser performed his Uncommon Market event assisted by writers from *The Insect Trust*,[37] a journal devoted to William Burroughs. The Fluxus 'intermedia' group, too, was influential. In the Fluxian Festival of Misfits at the Institute of Contemporary Arts, London, from 28 October to 8 November 1962,[38] Robin Page, an English Fluxus artist, performed his *Guitar Piece* by kicking a guitar through the audience, outside, into and along, Dover Street.[39] A Fluxian interest in the destruction of high-art

[36] Vestey 1967, pp. 15–16. [37] Vestey 1967, p. 14. [38] Higgins 2002, p. 135.
[39] Home 1991, p. 53.

culture flourished in London. Ralph Ortiz and Paul Pierrot demolished a piano at the Destruction in Art Symposium (DIAS), which occurred in London, 9–11 September 1966.[40] Pianos, symbolic of concert music, were used and abused throughout the era by, for example Annea (then Anna) Lockwood (who wrote *Piano Burning* [1968] in London) and Michael Chant (his Scratch Orchestra Improvisation Rite MC10 [1969],[41] in which seventeen people play loudly and simultaneously on one piano).

The International Poetry Incarnation at the Albert Hall on 11 June 1965, featuring American Beats, *New Departures* poets, Fluxians and Situationists, launched the London underground scene and gave it its artistic direction for the next two years. This event proved wildly popular, its attendance equalling Bob Dylan's sold-out concerts there a month previously.[42] Nominally a poetry reading, the Incarnation was, according to Nuttall, a happening:

> an atmosphere of pot, impromptu solo acid dances, of incredible barbaric colour, of face and body painting, of flowers and flowers and flowers, of a common dreaminess in which all was permissive and benign.[43]

Poetry became popular; experimental music, too, was 'hip', an integral part of underground performance, as can be seen from its coverage in the *International Times*.

Experimental music in the Underground

The *International Times* (*IT*) embodied "the internationalism of the 1965 poetry reading, cultural, post-Beat, off-beat, and art-oriented".[44] *IT* outlasted its rivals *Oz*, *Black Dwarf* and *Friendz* (or *Friends*) and was the sole counterculture listings guide until *Time Out* launched in August 1968. *IT*'s founders included Barry Miles (known as 'Miles'), a music writer who founded the Indica Bookshop and Gallery, John 'Hoppy' Hopkins, a photographer and journalist who began the UFO Club and the London Free School, and Jim Haynes, an American who started the Traverse Theatre and the Arts Laboratory. *IT* became a forum for Beat writers, *New Departures* poets, the burgeoning psychedelic pop scene, plus other aspects of alternative culture, including experimental music. *IT* was

---

[40] Home 1991, p. 63. This event included Yoko Ono's action score, *Cut Piece*.
[41] Cardew 1969b.   [42] Estimated at 7,000 (Moller 2006, p. 152).   [43] Nuttall 1968, p. 192.
[44] Fountain 1988, p. 31.

launched on 15 October 1966 with a rave at the Roundhouse, which featured not only the bands Pink Floyd and the Soft Machine, but also the Fluxus artist Yoko Ono and AMM.

AMM (the meaning of the acronym is secret) is a free experimental improvisation ensemble whose original members were former jazz musicians Keith Rowe, Eddie Prévost, Lou Gare and Lawrence Sheaff. Cardew joined in January 1966; Christopher Hobbs joined in April 1968, replacing Sheaff.[45] AMM music – non-tonal, primarily drone-based and punctuated by silences – inspired the acid drones of English psychedelia. 'Hoppy' co-produced *AMMMusic* (1966); AMM performed with Pink Floyd and the Soft Machine at the Marquee Club, London (in the Spontaneous Underground series).[46] In early 1967, Pink Floyd and AMM performed at the "untypically well-lit UFO" Club,[47] as Granada Television filmed Pink Floyd for the documentary *Underground: Scene Special*.[48]

AMM thus continued the Beat trend for 'art' to inspire pop, and for pop, in turn, to promote 'art'. Miles described the New York band The Group Image as "a mixture of the Soft Machine and A.M.M. [sic] – heavily experimental, heavily amplified",[49] and the Beatles' "Revolution No. 9" as, "the same as [Cage's] *Fontana Mix* [...], only the Beatles record will reach an entirely new audience".[50] In 1966, Miles and Paul McCartney, an early supporter of *IT*, attended one of AMM's weekly sessions at the Royal College of Art. McCartney "contributed [to the performance] by running a penny along the coils of the old-fashioned steam radiator that he was sitting next to on the floor".[51] Miles believes that "John Cage had the most influence" on McCartney, particularly his anecdotal reading piece *Indeterminacy* (1959).[52] McCartney told Miles that Cage and Stockhausen had supplanted Elvis: "the idols now, the people that I can appreciate now are all much more hidden away in little back corners, [...] performing for themselves".[53]

IT advertised regular Friday concerts by AMM at Kingly Street, and Sunday experimental concerts and workshops at the Arts Lab. This latter series, focusing on John White's Machine pieces and later the Promenade Theatre Orchestra, were the earliest performances of British minimalist music. *IT* also documented countercultural education not only as alternative seats of learning but also as venues for both psychedelic bands and experimental groups. Nuttall praised "the students with Corny Cardew at

---

[45] Tilbury 2008, pp. 285 and 304.   [46] Miles 1968a, p. 3.   [47] Chapman 2010, p. 131.
[48] Povey 2007, p. 51.   [49] Miles 1967b, p. 7.   [50] Miles 1968b, p. 10.   [51] Miles 1997, p. 237.
[52] Miles 1997, p. 236.   [53] Miles 1967a, p. 9.

Watford [College of Art]".[54] The Anti-University opened in 1968, with Cardew and Lockwood among its inaugural staff.[55] Cardew's experimental music class at Morley College, a Victorian institute for workers' self-improvement, lasted until 1973.

All aspects of artistic life existed in the counterculture, including promotion. Tony Cox and Harvey Matusow promoted their partners Ono and Lockwood in *IT*. Victor Schonfield, a former associate of the *New Departures* poets in Oxford, created Music Now to promote AMM, Cardew and the Scratch Orchestra, as well as visits by Musica Elettronica Viva (MEV), Christian Wolff, and others. *IT*'s 'high-art' music was almost aggressively experimental. Of four pages in the 1968 *IT* New Music Supplement, two focused on Cardew, Tilbury and Bedford, and one on Hugh Davies' electronic studio. Here Schonfield reviewed the Arts Lab Festival of New Music, 13–14 January 1968, as presenting "nearly all the main composers of the last fifteen years' European music",[56] all of whom were American and British experimentalists. Schonfield subsequently objected to the inclusion of short biographical sections on Stockhausen, Boulez, Messiaen and Berio in the supplement. He accused the editors of "a shallow acceptance that the names most gossiped about in the straight music establishment (with its standards unchanged since about 1900) were the ones you should cover – regardless of whether they used new forms or produced content of any worth".[57] Conversely, the normally high-art Macnaghten Concert series bought their only quarter-page advert in *IT* for the London premiere of Paragraph 1 of Cardew's experimental piece *The Great Digest* (later *The Great Learning* [1968–71]) that October.[58]

The British Underground was both cognisant of worldwide protests in 1968 and aware of its own non-involvement. A Surrealist Group manifesto, "We Need You, Dany Cohn-Bendit", appealed to the Paris May Day leader because "WE HAVE NO PASSION."[59] An *IT* translator of a German interview with Rudi Dutschke changed the term 'anti-authoritarian' to 'underground', "as this seemed to be the only way to have the interview make any sense outside of Germany".[60] John Hopkins (for once not 'Hoppy') accused Tariq Ali of leading protestors at the anti-Vietnam march on the American Embassy in Grosvenor Square on 17 March 1968 into the fray unprepared, suggesting that he study other protests and revolutionary literature.[61]

---

[54] Nuttall 1968, p. 214. [55] Norse *et al.* 1968, p. 6. [56] Langston *et al.* 1968, p. 10.
[57] Schonfield 1968, p. 2. [58] Anonymous 1968b, p. 18. [59] Anonymous 1968a, p. 2.
[60] Bensen 1968, p. 6; Gross 1968, p. 2. [61] Hopkins 1968, p. 11.

By 1968, for Nuttall, "the arrival of capitalism" commercialised the counterculture,[62] as *Hair*, a musical that presented a sanitised view of hippies, opened in London. The alternative press increasingly ignored so-called 'high' arts. By 1971, a review of The Plastic Ono Band, *Fly*, began, "I'll tell you something, the avant-garde scene really pisses me off. Completely."[63] Although marginalised, experimental music increasingly paralleled underground culture, especially in the alternative, 'hippie-ish' Scratch Orchestra.

Alternative British experimental culture: the Scratch Orchestra

The Scratch Orchestra (hereafter 'Scratch'), founded in 1969 by Cardew, Howard Skempton and Michael Parsons, escapes a firm 'hippie' definition. Most hippie culture studies focus on communal private life,[64] but the Scratch, as an ensemble, was a workplace culture. Some members had middle-class homes and jobs; many were students, others 'Bohemian' or working-class. Most hippie studies focus on American groups,[65] and British hippies had different models and motivations. Yet aspects of hippie culture parallel the Scratch culture. Just as Kenneth Westhues described hippies through their social behaviour,[66] we too can describe the Scratch as 'hippie-ish' in its governance, tenets, emphasis on pleasure and travel and politics.

Organisation and ideology

The Scratch Draft Constitution,[67] published in June 1969, is nominally antinomian, calling for a total 'rebooting' of the rules of music: no previously existing musical rules apply by right. As the Parisian May Day slogan "It is forbidden to forbid" defined freedom,[68] so the Draft Constitution declared that music is "flexible and depends entirely on the members of the Scratch Orchestra".[69] However, just as Westhues considered hippie communities to be only briefly disorganised,[70] the Scratch was 'free' by legislation. The Draft Constitution divided music into composition, free improvisation, Improvisation Rites (text instructions that indicated a musical situation),[71] activities and an education project (Scratch Music). Members controlled concerts in order of reverse seniority (Hobbs, then aged 19, presented the

---

[62] Green 1988, p. 223.   [63] "Bo" 1971.   [64] Issitt 2009, pp. 13–23.
[65] Including Issitt 2009; Westhues 1972; and Allen 2005.   [66] Westhues 1972.
[67] Cardew 1969a, pp. 617 and 619.   [68] Hobsbawm 1994, p. 332.   [69] Cardew 1969a, p. 617.
[70] Westhues 1972, p. 85.   [71] Cardew 1969a.

first concert), a rule enacted to counter any 'establishment' hierarchy. There were no auditions.[72] Of suggested notations – "musical, verbal, graphic, collage"[73] – 'verbal' notation (text instructions) predominated, as many members could not read traditional notation.

Just as Westhues included the *I Ching* among hippie ideologies, the Scratch composers used the *I Ching* as a compositional device.[74] The text of Cardew's *The Great Learning* (1968–71), the introduction to the Confucian book *Dà Xué*, was also an Eastern ideology. However, not every member accepted the ideology of *The Great Learning*. Some members, including Cardew, learned Chinese to read the original, but other members rejected the governmental model of *The Great Learning* as anti-egalitarian. If anything, the Scratch 'religion' is experimentalism, its opposition the avant garde. They advertised such adverse comments as Stockhausen's assessment that "they can't possibly improve"[75] in a way that indicated that they could not improve because they were perfect. Stockhausen obviously meant here that the Scratch was too incompetent to improve. The Scratch, by presenting his criticism as praise, implied that Stockhausen (a 'square') could not understand them.

Sex and drugs, travel, community

Although common to hippie life and to performance art, the Scratch rarely displayed nudity.[76] Pictures of Lesser, covered in paint and jelly, sliding on his stomach along a twenty-foot piece of paper at the Uncommon Market, and Judith Euren, sliding along a lawn in an Scratch event, look strikingly similar.[77] Lesser is totally nude; Euren, however, is demurely clothed. Birgit Burckhardt explained, "in the Scratch Orchestra the sense of Erotic is diffused into a more general 'pleasure-principle'".[78] References to relationships are anecdotal and tangential, like workplace gossip.[79] There is little evidence of drug use in the Scratch. The common use of loose tobacco and rolling papers in Britain makes the determination of hashish or marijuana use from filmed evidence unfeasible. Hobbs claimed that the membership used "fags and alcohol" and visited pubs after Scratch events.[80] It is impossible to think that the Scratch was drug free, but drugs were not central to their work.[81]

[72] Ascough 1999. [73] Cardew 1969a, p. 617. [74] Tilbury 2008, p. 420.
[75] Scratch Orchestra 1971. [76] See Schneemann 1997 (1979).
[77] Vestey 1967, p. 12; Fowler 2006. [78] Tilbury 2008, p. 432.
[79] Tilbury 2008, pp. 430 and 683. [80] Hobbs 2010.
[81] Tilbury 2008, p. 423, mentions "exotic vegetation".

The Scratch embraced another hippie trait, pleasure. Members enjoyed double meaning, word play and whimsy. They appropriated *Alice in Wonderland*, Beckett's *Watt* and other literature using 'logical illogic'. For Westhues, many communes lived happily, "by using what the upper-middle class throws away".[82] The Scratch instrumentation included found objects such as Psi (*née* Peter) Ellison's wind-up gramophones. Many Scratch activities facilitate comfort; Michael Parsons' *Night Rite* (his Scratch Orchestra Improvisation Rite, codenamed MPNR21) provides mattresses for performers to rest.[83]

Allen wrote, "the hippie counterculture, unlike the New Left, was imbued with a near-Jeffersonian vision of an agrarian republic";[84] the Scratch, too, favoured rural life. Cardew proposed that the orchestra buy or rent land to camp on during their north-east England tour.[85] Scratch newsletters, offering housing, goods and concert information, resembled a village notice board. For the Art Spectrum Exhibition at the Alexandra Palace in August 1971,[86] the Scratch built a rustic cottage. When touring, the Scratch performed in town and village halls from a central base campsite. In Hanne Boenisch's film *Journey to the North Pole*, Stefan Szczelkun's van and Cardew's Volkswagen bus (typical hippie transport) negotiate a rural road accompanied by the percussive, almost tribal, Paragraph 2 of Cardew's *The Great Learning*.[87] Campsites were multigenerational. The Scratch performed and created art installations (e.g. stone pillars and cairns on rocks in a nearby stream) as part of their campsite 'home life'.

Individual Scratch presentations explored travel, both real and imagined. Tim Mitchell's *Tube Train Rite* (codenamed TMTTR38),[88] a set of lines with the instruction, "Mark out a journey (inwardly/outwardly/spatially). Make it," is one of many psychogeographical and 'pataphysical Scratch pieces involving real or imagined travel. When the Welsh-language HTV news programme interviewed the Scratch on their 1970 Village Concerts tour, the crew told Bryn Harris that the Scratch was following the routes of troubadours.[89] The show's archive notes, marked 'funnies', reveals a more common view of the 'hippie' Scratch Orchestra: "people play their instruments all together & do strange dance moves!"[90]

---

[82] Westhues 1972, p. 86. [83] Cardew 1969b. [84] Allen 2005, p. 279.
[85] Anonymous 1971. [86] Tilbury 2008, pp. 534–5. [87] Boenisch 1971–2.
[88] Cardew 1969b. [89] Harris 1983. [90] Owen 2009.

Politics

Westhues called the Yippie protests at the 1968 Chicago Democratic Convention "the last attempt of the movement to become political".[91] The Scratch performed at a benefit for the Chicago defendants on 26 January 1970 at the Roundhouse, to "relive the barbarities of US Justice with theatre, films, lights groups and unlimited freak outs".[92] In his *IT* review, Arthur A. Pitt claimed that drinks at this event were spiked with acid, resulting in a "constant tin tray, iron pipe, bent cymbal, anything-you-can-find-to-hit percussive debacle that persisted most of the evening, bore no relation to the music of the performers and ruined Mighty Baby's set".[93] Although it is not clear that this "percussive debacle" was the Scratch, it describes their performances, albeit negatively. Hugh Shrapnel and Michael Chant remember playing in the Roundhouse gallery, perhaps in protest.[94] Chant noted in his diary that, "Cornelius was beaten at the Round House; all planned but he gave up", and believes now that the Scratch had been disinvited, but played anyway.[95] This was, however, one of the few political acts for the apolitical, 'hippie-ish', Scratch. Real political action came only from internal factions, which led to the demise of the Orchestra.

Scratch Orchestra opposition and Maoism

It is mistakenly thought that the Scratch was always Maoist,[96] but it was not. Some Scratch Orchestra factions (called 'sub-groups') were musical: the Promenade Theatre Orchestra and CPE (named for its performers Chris May, Phil Gebbett and Ed Fulton) were trained, reading, musicians; Comet was a pop band; Private Company worked in mixed media. The only 'political' group, the Slippery Merchants, were anarchistic and near-Situationist. They invaded school playgrounds dressed in 'wig-out' costumes, in activities called 'School Raids'.[97] These invasions resemble a 1968 incident when twenty-five members of King Mob (a Situationist offshoot) invaded Selfridges department store dressed as Santa Claus to give away the store's merchandise to children.[98] The Slippery Merchants also interrupted the Queen Elizabeth Hall concert by the Scratch on 23 November 1970, performing "101 Activities" as a protest against Cardew's

---

[91] Westhues 1972, p. 87.   [92] Anonymous 1970b.   [93] Pitt 1970, p. 11.
[94] Shrapnel 2010; Chant 2010.   [95] Chant 2010.   [96] For instance, Taruskin 2009.
[97] Harris 1983.   [98] Savage 2002 (1991), p. 58.

position as leader of this nominally leaderless group.[99] The tolerant Scratch credited their disruption in the programme, and in establishing their name, the Slippery Merchants felt that they had become organised. As organisation was antithetical to their beliefs, they disbanded.

As the sub-groups pulled in different directions, a near-Marxian conjunctural crisis grew imminent, and a Marxian solution offered. In Hanna Boenisch's film of a tour of north-east England in June 1971,[100] Keith Rowe read out the first documented Marxist declaration in Scratch history: "'In the world today, all culture, all literature and art belong to definite classes and are geared to definite political lines. This is a fact'. And that's a statement from Mao Zhedong."[101] Other members disagreed: John White said, "Society is too large a concept for me", while Cardew, speaking in German, stated that the Scratch had "another vision for music" than politics. Later in the film, Rowe suggested a Scratch version of "The Internationale". Tilbury countered that *The Great Learning* was perfect, except for its text, "but we can always adapt that without the composer's knowledge".[102] Ironically, the Scratch was to adapt *The Great Learning* with Maoist texts for the 1972 Promenade concert, with the composer's cooperation.

Cardew convened 'discontents' meetings, where the direction of the Scratch was debated. Tilbury was the most effective Marxist speaker, and a new dominant ideology, Maoism, emerged. An ideological study group (known as the Id Group) was established almost immediately, but Cardew did not join it until weeks later, when he made his "big switch" to a Marxist–Leninist aesthetic.[103] For another year or so, the orchestra remained partly, and awkwardly, experimental. The International Carnival of Experimental Sound (ICES '72), devised by Harvey Matusow and held at the Roundhouse and The Place in August 1972, was the final British experimental festival associated with the counterculture. ICES '72 featured nearly 300 experimental composers and performers, including Cage, Charlotte Moorman, Gavin Bryars and the Portsmouth Sinfonia. White and Hobbs played as a duo, as the Promenade Theatre Orchestra had dissolved on political lines. The Scratch did not play at ICES '72; AMM also played as a duo, as Rowe and Cardew had by this time left AMM on political grounds (Hobbs had left earlier). Rowe did not return to AMM until the late 1970s; Cardew and Hobbs never returned. Other concerts by the transitional Scratch included Wolff's *Burdocks* on Munich radio that month, where the controversy was

---

[99] Published as "1001 Activities" in Cardew 1972.
[100] On this tour, Cardew was censured in the tabloid press for a performance in which he drew nudes and four-letter words on toilet paper (Tilbury 2008, p. 522).
[101] Boenisch 1971–2. [102] Boenisch 1971–2. [103] Potter 1995, p. 152.

experimental, as Carole Finer interpreted a number '7' in the score by playing seven folk songs on her banjo. Cage, Feldman and Tudor condemned the Scratch because they ignored Wolff's intentions, but Wolff, who did not attend, said, "given the nature of [the Scratch . . .] it would have been very beautiful".[104]

The BBC Promenade concert of Paragraphs 1 and 2 of *The Great Learning* on 24 August 1972 is perhaps the most dramatic political protest by the Scratch. The Id Group wrote a new Maoist text to replace the Confucianism, and proposed banners carrying slogans such as "Revolution is the Great Learning of the Present". Although Cardew tried to mediate between the doctrinaire Id Group and the differently doctrinaire BBC, the BBC banned the slogans and questioned the new text.[105] Despite Cardew's assessment of its failure,[106] the performance might have been electrifying had the BBC not intervened.

The political Scratch lasted until 1974, when Cardew joined People's Liberation Music (PLM), a political pop group founded by Tilbury, Laurie Baker, Vicky Silva, and John Marcangelo. "Mr Media Man" (1973), by Baker (music) and Tilbury (lyrics), is a satire on media 'spin'. The slick lead (Marcangelo), feline backing singers and 'funky' electronic accompaniment reflect Baker's experience as a bass player throughout *Hair*'s run. In concert music, the old communist Alan Bush wrote movingly about Cardew's piano piece *Thälmann Variations* (1974) and contributed to a fund after Cardew was arrested.[107] A clear programme was necessary to deliver the protest message. *Thälmann Variations* and other works of this time exhibit this clarity, but they lack the "'anarchy' of contemporary aesthetics".[108] Cardew's revolution became, for the rest of his life (he died in 1981 in a hit-and-run accident), entirely political: he became a leader of the Communist Party of England (Marxist–Leninist), succeeded by the Revolutionary Communist Party of Britain (Marxist–Leninist). Although he performed in some experimental concerts and employed some limited indeterminacy, by embracing revolutionary politics Cardew effectively left the experimental revolution.

The experimental legacy and counterculture

In 1974, Michael Nyman distanced experimental music "from the music of such avant-garde composers as Boulez, Kagel, Xenakis, Birtwistle, Berio, Stockhausen, Bussotti, which is conceived and executed along the

---

[104] Wolff 1998, p. 256. [105] Tilbury 2008, pp. 592–6. [106] Cardew 1974.
[107] Tilbury 2008, p. 950. [108] Tilbury 2008, p. 751.

well-trodden but sanctified path of post-Renaissance tradition".[109] He defined social, philosophical and technical 'processes' in experimental music that could be categorised as either *alternative* or *oppositional*, in the sense used by Williams. The American composer John Adams saw a political analogy in Nyman's book: "It's a polemical tract; it reads like a Trotskyite comment on Stalinism. It's definitely an apologia for a particular style of music."[110]

This split between the avant garde and experimentalists remains today, particularly in the reception of experimental music in Britain. After the 1972 Proms concert and Cardew's argument with the BBC, his music was not played in this series until 2010, when *Bun No 1* (1965), a revision of his *Third Orchestral Piece* (1960), was performed. *Bun No. 1*, in Cardew's pre-experimental avant-garde style, was a 'safe', though uninspired, choice, as it is neither alternatively experimental, nor oppositionally political – a curious way to commemorate one of the greatest British exponents of both approaches. Bryars and Skempton, and to a lesser extent, White, Hobbs, Parsons and Smith, are known and played outside of Britain, but they are underrepresented in Britain's academic circles. And this reception points to their difference. White, Hobbs, Bryars, Skempton, Parsons and Smith today do not use such technical features of experimental music as indeterminacy and alternative notation as often as they did before 1972. They still, however, provide a social and musical alternative: an 'experimental' culture opposing the reliance of the avant garde upon tradition, even when its own musical style is now postminimal, and even when the 'avant-garde' culture affects postminimal styles. This experimental opposition to the avant-garde is as strong as it was in the 1960s and early 1970s, when in opposing them they influenced, allied with, and for a short time became a part of the British underground counterculture.

---

[109] Nyman 1999 (1974), p. 1. [110] Adams, appearing as a guest in Amirkhanian 1976.

11 | Anti-authoritarian revolt by musical means on both sides of the Berlin Wall

BEATE KUTSCHKE

Anti-authoritarian agendas in East and West Germany in the 1960s

The consensus among historians is that the period of '1968' lasted approximately two decades from the end of the 1950s until the middle of the 1970s.[1] In this framework, each nation's '1968' revolves around different key events. In West Germany, the student protests, which had been intensifying since the beginning of the 1960s, reached their climax in the summer of 1967 and the spring of 1968. On 2 June 1967, the student Benno Ohnesorg was – accidentally or intentionally – killed by the police during a student demonstration directed against the Iranian Shah who was visiting West Berlin. On 10 April 1968 a mentally disturbed worker shot the charismatic student leader Rudi Dutschke, who only just survived the assassination attempt.[2] In response, Dutschke's combatants and supporters accused the leading right-wing publishing house in West Germany, the Springer Press, of having indirectly caused the attack by stirring up hatred against the student and protest movements. In the view of the students, they did this by depicting Dutschke and the student protesters as dirty, lazy hooligans.

The Springer Press was, no doubt, biased: it spread the image that the New Leftist movement was an anti-social mob. Additionally, they repressed the fact that many of the protesting students, intellectuals and artists, especially their leaders, were driven by serious and justified social critiques that were not just directed at the Springer press. It also included the West German education system, the National Socialist past, the values of the older generation and the passing of the emergency acts by the government. What was the nucleus of these critiques? Although the phenomena that the New Leftist protesters targeted appeared to be rather diverse, they were united by the fact that their agents and institutions were all characterised by authoritarian modes of behaviour. Thus, the New Leftists connected the Third Reich's authoritarian

---

[1] For further detail on the historical debates about '1968' see Rehm 2007.
[2] Dutschke was shot three times and one of the bullets entered his brain and damaged the cerebral speech area. As a result he suffered epilepsy and died in 1979 after a seizure in the bathtub (Dutschke 1996).

regime with the behaviour modes of contemporaries in power: parents, pedagogues and state officials. Lastly, the rhetoric of the Springer Press reflected the authoritarianism of both the past and the present.

While the New Leftists' aversion to the manifestations of authoritarianism in West German society and its link to National Socialism reflected personal experiences, their views were indirectly supported by psychological theories developed since the 1930s. These theories related authoritarian modes of behaviour in social relationships, especially within the family, to the willingness of an individual to submit to fascist ideologies. The former was the cause of the latter. German and American psychologists and philosophers – particularly Wilhelm Reich, Erich Fromm, Max Horkheimer, Theodor W. Adorno and the so-called 'Berkeley group'[3] – maintained that individuals who had been the victims of authoritarian and repressive pedagogy during childhood were most likely to develop an authoritarian personality, i.e. a personality susceptible to serving the needs of an "authoritarian state".[4] In light of such socio-psychological theories, the protesters – students, intellectuals and artists – predicted a dystopian scenario.

They believed that the Federal Republic of (West) Germany (FRG), founded in 1949, was constantly threatened by the reemergence of the Third Reich and by the possibility of a new world war and genocide. The passing of the emergency acts in May 1968, which permitted the government to limit constitutional rights, was considered to be a clear symptom of these tendencies.[5] The students and protesters that Rudi Dutschke baptised as an 'anti-authoritarian movement' felt obliged to oppose these tendencies by fighting everybody and every institution that represented authority: the state, state officials (e.g. police, judges and prosecutors)[6] and academics.[7] Moreover, they encouraged anti-authoritarian modes of social behaviour and teaching methods. Unsurprisingly, the anti-authoritarian impetus also spread to the musical field stimulating composers, performers and music students to contribute to the New Leftist goals by identifying and counteracting authoritarian institutions involved in music production and management.

On the other side of the Iron Curtain, in East Germany, '1968' connotes quite different historical events. Nonetheless, they were also intertwined

---

[3] See Reich 1946 (1933); Fromm 1936, 1980 (1941); Horkheimer 1978 (1940/1942); and Adorno 1950. The Berkeley group comprised the psychologists R. Nevitt Sanford, Daniel J. Levinson and Else Frenkel-Brunswik.
[4] Horkheimer 1978 (1940/1942), p. 102.   [5] See Anonymous 1998 (1962), pp. 158–9.
[6] For example, at their trial in July 1967 in Berlin-Moabit, student rebels Fritz Teufel and Rainer Langhans ridiculed the judges and prosecutors (Langhans and Teufel 1968).
[7] See the students' humiliation of Adorno in 1967 (Müller-Doohm 2003, p. 689).

with authoritarian phenomena. Authoritarianism manifesting itself in the state's control over its citizens was omnipresent. In this light, the (East) German Democratic Republic (GDR), which existed from 1949 to 1990, can be considered as, if not a totalitarian dictatorship, then at least an authoritarian one. This manifested itself most clearly in August 1968 when Warsaw Pact troops (among them soldiers of the East German National People's Army) invaded Czechoslovakia and the East German state robustly repressed its people's protests against the invasion.[8]

Whereas in West Germany authorities only sporadically made rather futile attempts to intimidate the youthful protesters who impertinently confronted society with their dissent, in the authoritarian political climate of the GDR, state officials vigorously repressed protest. Their repression extended to include peaceful independent, self-guided activities such as the East German youth's autonomous emulation of the Western capitalist youth culture and its musical styles. To the authorities, those activities were suspected of hiding anti-authoritarian impulses.[9] And, in fact, the state officials' suspicion was not entirely unjustified. For many young people in East Germany, the performance of Western-capitalist lifestyles served to implicitly articulate their longing for the rights of self-determination and autonomy that the GDR government denied its citizens, including the right to free speech and the freedom of the media, as well as the right to travel and to strike.[10]

Despite the general socio-political climate of authoritarianism in the GDR, the cultural climate in the GDR was relatively liberal and relaxed after the government had stopped the 'brain drain' by building the wall between East and West Germany in 1961. Thus, in the early 1960s, youth culture and individual modes of musical expression were able to emerge in the GDR and in the Eastern bloc as a whole.[11] Once initiated, the further development of youth culture could not be suppressed by official restrictions any more – neither by means of authoritarian interdictions nor by ostensibly liberal offers for alternative cultural modes of expression. The tedious dance 'Lipsi', for instance, that was artificially created in 1959 in order to restrain the propagation of rock music, was without effect.

It is the struggle against authoritarianism in both parts of Germany which distinguishes the German '1968' from the student and protest movements in other countries. How did the different development of youth and protest cultures of '1968' in West and East Germany shape the musicians' response to authorities and matters of authority? To what degree did

---

[8] Mitter and Wolle 1993.   [9] For further information see Brown 2008.
[10] Mitter and Wolle 1993, p. 430.   [11] Brown 2008.

the authoritarian movement affect institutions and music ensembles and manifest itself in musical practices and styles?

Anti-authoritarian revolt by musical means

In both Germanys as elsewhere, rock music epitomised the sound of the revolt of '1968'. The musical event that represented the West German protest song and emerging rock music scene was the first International Essener Songtage (IEST), which was held on 25–9 September 1968. With over 40,000 participants, IEST was the largest popular music festival in the world at the time.[12] The West German bands invited to perform at IEST '68 reflected various types of 'krautrock', by featuring bands such as Amon Düül (I and II), Tangerine Dream, Can and Floh de Cologne. Alongside krautrock, the IEST '68 programme included the singer-songwriters Franz Joseph Degenhardt, Dieter Süverkrüp and Hanns Dieter Hüsch, and international bands such as the Fugs and Frank Zappa and the Mothers of Invention. Because the initiator and organiser of IEST, Rolf-Ulrich Kaiser, dedicated the festival to articulating the politics of the New Left, lectures and panel discussions on political music, especially political song, were also part of the programme.[13]

All the German bands invited to IEST '68 had an anti-authoritarian impetus in one way or another. The bands Amon Düül I and II, emerging from a Munich commune that emulated the Berlin Kommune I, promoted a way of music-making that resembled their lifestyle.[14] Like communal social life that was independent of traditional family hierarchies, Amon Düüls' free improvisation reflected an anti-hierarchical and anti-authoritarian ethos. The bands performed without a conductor and/or a composer, i.e. without figures they considered as authoritarian because they 'told' the other musicians what to do. Promoting free improvisation, Amon Düül I and II had similarities with the international avant-garde ensemble Musica Elettronica Viva (MEV)[15] who had been organising free-improvisation concerts, 'soundpools', in Europe and North America since 1966. Furthermore, like the soundpools, Amon Düül I's events subverted

---

[12] Siegfried 2006, p. 608.
[13] For the complete programme of IEST see Mahnert and Stürmer 2008, pp. 88–92.
[14] Other bands that combined the performance of music with the ethos of the commune were Bröselmaschine (from Duisburg), Lord's Family (from Altmühltal) and the Free Music Group (from Frankfurt) (Siegfried 2006, p. 648; see also Sohar 2003).
[15] Curran 1995.

distinctions between socio-cultural classes by permitting everybody, regardless of their musical knowledge, to contribute to its performances.

Whereas Amon Düül I and II were by-products of an alternative style of living, the Cologne band Can emerged from a kind of artistic patricide. Partially trained as professional classical and avant-garde musicians,[16] Can desired to detach from the highly stylised aesthetics of the Western avant-garde. At the same time, however, they did not eschew them entirely. Like Amon Düül whose members were intimately familiar with the avant-garde art scene, the musicians of Can fused stylistic characteristics of rock and avant-garde music. Rock's beats, grooves, short loop-like harmonic sequences and melodic patterns were combined with what has been called the 'aesthetics of the fragment' in aesthetic discourse.[17] Influences of the latter were evident in Can's use of *objets trouvés* such as recordings of demonstrating French students[18] and distorted chunks of voices speaking and singing.[19] By connecting rock and avant-gardist styles, these bands were unintentionally engaged in a postmodern collapsing of the boundaries between high and low culture.[20]

Krautrock bands emerged not only from communes and the avant-gardist/classical music scene, but also from political cabaret which has per se an anti-authoritarian impetus. Here music was not a purpose in itself, but served as vehicle for satirical critique of politicians and the state. For instance, when Floh de Cologne performed at IEST '68, they presented a spectacle that poked fun at West German prudery. In this comic 'happening', music played only an accompanying role, but it increasingly became an integral aspect of the band's performance style when it transformed into a politrock band in 1969.[21]

In addition to Floh de Cologne, other 'politrock' bands, which were known for their highly politicised and critical lyrics, soon developed. The band Ton Steine Scherben, or Scherben for short, emerged from the musical theatre troupe Hoffmann's Comic Theatre in 1970.[22] In comparison to Amon Düül, Can and Floh de Cologne, Scherben's identity was shaped not so much by the music's primary parameters – melody and rhythm – as

---

[16] Irmin Schmidt, Holger Czukay and David Johnson of Can were all classically trained (Von Zahn 2006, p. 9).

[17] See Adorno 1973 (1969); Dällenbach and Nibbrig 1984; and Kutschke 2007a, ch. "Fragmentarizität".

[18] Von Zahn 2006, p. 22.   [19] See Can's *Monster Movie* (1969).

[20] Fiedler 1969. On the close relationship between the anti-hierarchical, anti-authoritarian spirit of '1968' and postmodern pluralism in music see Luckscheiter 2007; Hentschel 2008; Kutschke 2007a, 2010.

[21] Klemm and Enxing 2010.   [22] Seidel 2005, p. 48.

by performative aspects. For instance, the voice of Ralph Möbius (alias Rio Reiser), the singer and songwriter of the Scherben, varied between actor-like text declamation, on the one hand, and the internally frozen, paralysed yelling of an 'angry young man' on the other.

Scherben's lyrics resonated with changes in the West German anti-authoritarian movements. In the 1970s, New Leftists felt a need to add weight to their socio-political demands by means of violence. The song "Macht kaputt was euch kaputt macht" ("Destroy what destroys you") mirrors the radicalisation that culminated in the left-extremist terrorism of the Red Army Faction (RAF) in the 1970s. It reflects the appetite for violence that the terrorist group justified as a need for self-defence against the oppressive, tyrannical state.[23] The vast majority of people involved in the anti-authoritarian movements, however, did not pursue extreme violence. Rather they shifted focus from the all-embracing goal of abolishing the entire West German 'authoritarian' state and the capitalist system to local and regional struggles and forms of direct action, which included squatting and action against the construction of nuclear plants. The "Rauchhaus Song", for instance, commemorates the 1971 occupation by squatters of a part of the shut-down Bethanien hospital in Berlin-Kreuzberg. The civil disobedience resulted in a positive outcome; it stimulated the Berlin government to lease the building to a youth centre. Three years later, there were further disputes, this time over the main building of Bethanien. The Berlin government's plan to transform the building into an artists' centre, including an urgently needed electronic studio for avant-garde music, provoked protests by New Leftist activists who believed that a children's clinic would serve the inhabitants of Kreuzberg much better. Remarkably, among the activists were also musicians such as the avant-garde composer Erhard Großkopf who would have profited most from the state-subsidised artists' centre. For several years, Großkopf had tried to convince the Berlin cultural administration to finance an electronic studio in Berlin.[24] Now, Großkopf joined the "battle committee" for the clinic and delivered speeches against the artists' centre and the studio.[25] So also did the British experimentalist Cornelius Cardew, who spent the year 1973 in Berlin financed by a fellowship of the German Academic Exchange Service (DAAD). His "Bethanien Song", which was performed during the protests, well exemplifies that the anti-authoritarian struggle did not always inspire new artistic ways of expression. In the "Bethanien Song", socio-political pragmatism clearly ruled out aesthetic considerations (Figure 11.1).

---

[23] Colvin 2009, pp. 31ff.   [24] Großkopf 1974.
[25] The speech of Großkopf has been printed in Großkopf 1974.

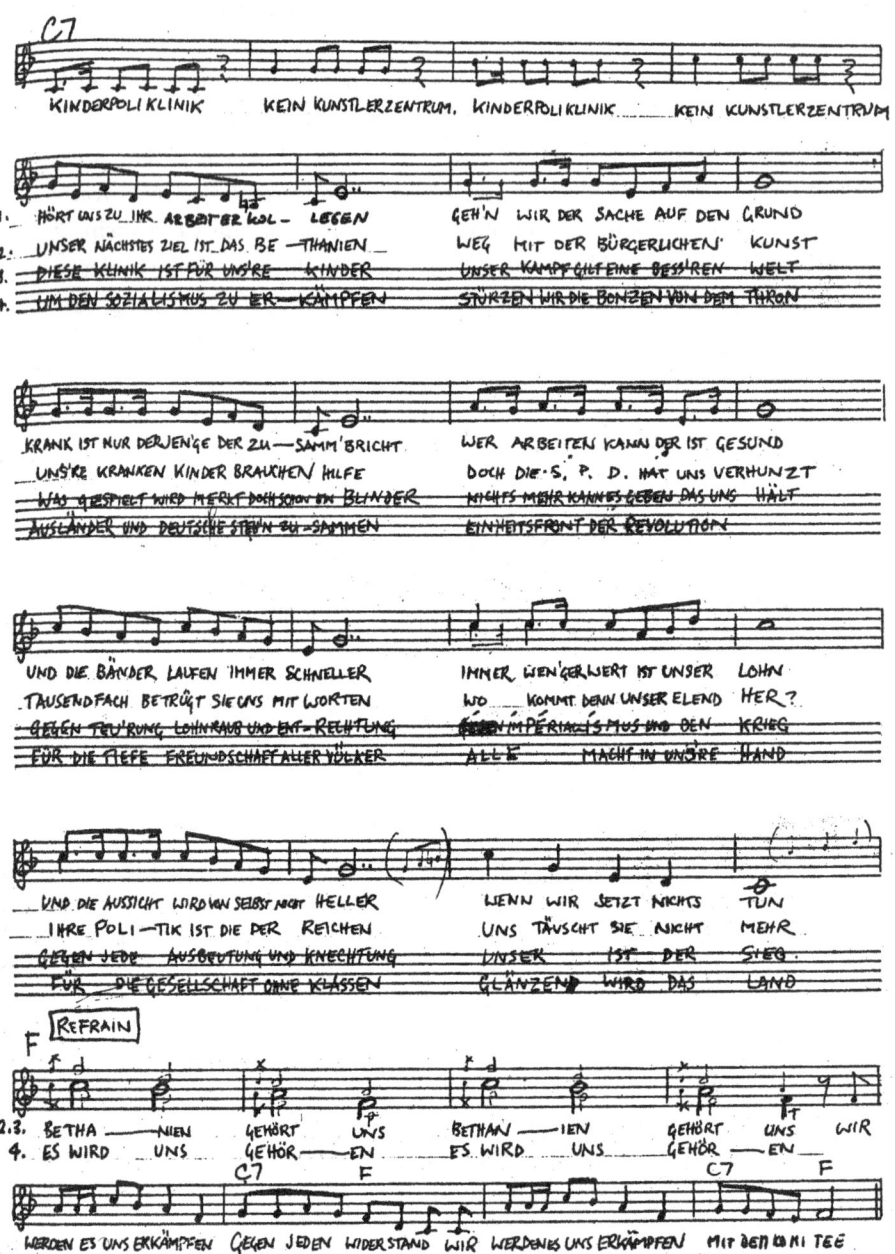

Figure 11.1 Cornelius Cardew, "Bethanien Song" © reproduced by kind permission of Horace Cardew.

Anti-authoritarian music in an authoritarian state

In the GDR, the fans of 'beat music', as rock music was referred to until the mid-1970s, did not initially intend to make a statement that attacked the authorities. However, the intolerant reaction of the state towards rock turned the reception of rock music into an anti-authoritarian act. This was due to the mechanisms that ruled the authoritarian pseudo-socialist system. In light of the goal to implement a true socialist society, the state felt impelled to control the minds and deeds of its citizens. It examined all cultural activities as regards its ideological message and attributed political meanings to them even if they were *not* intended to be political.[26] This politicisation "from above"[27] also embraced rock music. Since rock music was an import from North America and Western Europe, it logically represented the capitalist enemy for East German officials; and the young people who listened to it were considered to be agents of the enemy's value system. Moreover, the autonomous modes of production of rock bands (as well as the rise of the songwriters' scene in the 1960s) subverted the state's cultural and aesthetic monopoly.[28] Not surprisingly, the state made some efforts to assert control over both the beat and songwriters' scene. For instance, the Hootenanny Club – which was founded in East Berlin in 1966 and whose members were influenced by North American singer-songwriters involved in the civil rights movement and the folk music revival[29] – was taken over by the socialist Free German Youth (FDJ) and renamed Oktoberklub in 1967.[30] Under the FDJ, Oktoberklub adopted socialist music aesthetics marked by an optimistic and 'clean' style of collective singing.

In contrast to the more subtle appropriation of the Hootenanny Club, rock musicians became subject to rigid containment. Although the GDR was officially a workers' and farmers' state and the bourgeoisie was the class enemy, petit-bourgeois living styles and aesthetic preferences prevailed. Thus, reports by East German officials often pointed out that the aesthetics of rock – both in terms of its musical style and uninhibited style of performance – expressed an anti-social attitude. According to a Leipzig police department report, "'hot music' provokes youth to commit antisocial acts. Performing

---

[26] Poiger 2000, esp. pp. 107 and 128ff.   [27] Siegfried 1995.
[28] Wicke 1997, pp. 34, 35 and 37.
[29] The Hootenanny Club was founded by the Canadian singer-songwriter Perry Friedman together with Bettina Wegner, Uta Schorn, Reinhold Andert and Jörn Fechner (Böning 2004, p. 201).
[30] Robb 2007, p. 231.

music too loudly creates an atmosphere that inevitably leads to rioting [...] Order and security cannot be assured at any dance party."[31] Evidential support for such assertions by the police was not difficult to find as there were violent incidents in 1964 and 1965. In September 1964, a Soviet soldier was attacked during a concert of the popular band Klaus Renft (until 1965 called The Butlers)[32] and on 15 September 1965 Waldbühne, the West Berlin woodland stage, was demolished after a concert by the Rolling Stones.

In the wake of such violence, the Central Committee (ZK) – the highest administrative body of the Socialist Union Party (SED) that ruled the GDR till the fall of the Berlin Wall – demonstrated their power by banning almost 80 per cent of the fifty-six registered amateur beat bands in the district of Leipzig, including Renft, The Shatters, The Guitarmen and The Towers.[33] This demonstration *of* authority was immediately answered by a demonstration *against* authority: a protest gathering on 31 October 1965 by several hundred young beat fans culminated in a confrontation with the Leipzig police.[34] The interdictions against rock bands as well as various other producers and products of culture were subsequently backed up at the "11th Plenum" organised by the ZK on 16–18 December 1965. This Plenum is now considered as the official end of the thaw, the more liberal cultural climate that prevailed in East German society in the early 1960s. After the Plenum, the state sought to maintain tight control over rock bands through requiring them to attend official auditions, which enabled censorship of their repertory.[35]

In light of the state's authoritarian intrusion, little space was left for the free development of individual or radical styles of rock music – even though the state's grip loosened again in the lead up to the 10th World Festival of Youth and Students in East Berlin in 1973.[36] In contrast to 'ecstatic' British rock bands of the time such as Deep Purple and Led Zeppelin, the songs by bands like Renft (from Leipzig) and The Puhdys (a band from East Berlin) kept 'both feet on the ground': passages of escalation were quickly negated

---

[31] Report of VPKA Leipzig, Abt. K, Kommissariat I/2, 5 March 1965, in: BStU, MfS, Lpz. AOG 1822/68-I, p. 27, quoted in Rauhut 1998, p. 774.

[32] Rauhut 1998, p. 773.

[33] Staatsarchiv Leipzig (StA-L), BDVP Leipzig, 236, pp. 133–5. See also Liebing 2005, pp. 66ff.

[34] This resulted in the arrest of 329 beat fans (Staatsarchiv Leipzig (StA-L), BDVP Leipzig, 236, p. 63).

[35] See Rauhut 1997, p. 579. The auditions basically intensified the execution of a directive of 1958, according to which performers were obliged to play at least 60 per cent GDR-compositions (Rauhut 1997, p. 575).

[36] Through the organisation of this festival the authorities aimed to promote an international image of the GDR as a progressive and liberal state.

by the return of calmer, innocuous refrains or interludes. The general appearance of East German rock was conformist. In Renft's "Wer die Rose ehrt"[37] ("Who Honours the Rose") of 1973, for instance, the diligently performed scales by the flute resonated with the East German music-cultural policy that theoretically required even rock musicians to possess an elementary musical education. The lyrics appeared to be similarly tamed and innocuous, at least on the surface. They touched on sensitive socio-political topics such as the stultifying closeness of East German everyday life,[38] the deceptiveness of the officially propagated climate of love and security,[39] and the state's fear that Anglicisms were incursions by capitalist class enemies.[40] In doing this, they participated in a cat-and-mouse game with the government. Inverting the government's practice to politicise art works that were *not* intended to be political by their creators, musicians presented socio-political critique in the disguise of apolitical fairytale-like narratives. The singer-songwriter Wolf Biermann later described this practice of which he had availed himself in dialectical terms: "what appeared to be really political was the apolitical".[41] In the mid-1970s, however, when the government reasserted tighter control over the public sphere, artistic struggles became more intense and explicit. Starting in 1974, Renft's lyricist Gerulf Pannach increasingly provoked state officials by publicly criticising the GDR in his song lyrics.[42] This led to Pannach and then Renft being officially banned.[43]

The career of Biermann anticipated Renft's fate. Believing to follow the legacy of his Jewish and communist father who had been murdered in Auschwitz, Biermann had voluntarily relocated from Hamburg to East Berlin in 1953. From 1960 onwards his poems pointed out the GDR government's shortcomings. "Soldat, Soldat"[44] ("Soldier, Soldier") (1963) and "Was verboten ist, das macht uns gerade scharf" ("What is forbidden makes us hot") (1964), for instance, criticised East German militarism and authoritarian behaviour. Biermann's fate is particularly tragic because, by criticising the reality of socialism, he was trying to carry out what the state propaganda suggested should

---

[37] Renft 1973.   [38] See the lyrics of Puhdys' "Türen öffnen sich zur Stadt" (Pudhys 1974).

[39] See the lyrics of Renft's "Kinder ich bin nicht der Sandmann" (1972) (Renft 1973).

[40] See the lyrics of Renft's "Baggerführer Willi" by Kurt Demmler (Renft, Panta Rhei, Electra Combo *et al.* 1972).

[41] Biermann 1997, p. 23. Biermann's observation is obviously built on the famous sixties slogan "the private is the political".

[42] The "Rockballade vom kleinen Otto" ("Rock ballad of little Otto"), for instance, revolves around the desire to leave the GDR. In the GDR, leaving the country for a life in West Germany or another capitalist country was criminalised under the label "flight from the republic".

[43] For an account of Pannach's professional and political career see Rauhut 1998.

[44] Anti-militaristic lyrics can also be found in Renft's song "Nach der Schlacht" ("After the Battle") (Puhdys 1974).

be done, that is stimulating the progress and development of the socialist state. Officials of the authoritarian state, however, generally understood idealist, engaged critique as a form of anti-authoritarian revolt. Similarly, the state did not appreciate the engaged criticism of the 1965 film *The rabbit is me* (*Das Kaninchen bin ich*), which revealed the arbitrariness of East German criminal justice especially in regard to suspected dissidents. Not coincidentally, it was a former West German citizen, Reiner Bredemeyer, who composed the music to the film. Like Biermann, he moved to the GDR in the mid-1950s and believed that the film (including his music) would be welcomed by the state. Like many of Biermann's songs, however, the planned premiere screening of *The Rabbit is Me* was not permitted.

A characteristic of the East German government was that it constantly oscillated between 'carrot and stick'. The first performance interdiction for Biermann was instituted in 1963, connected with the rejection of Biermann's application for membership of the SED.[45] A year later, however, his performance ban was annulled and he was even permitted to tour outside the Eastern Bloc. Thus, at the end of 1964, he toured West Germany having been invited by the Socialist Democratic Student Union (SDS) that, from the mid-1960s onwards, was propelling the West German student protests.[46] After the tour, Biermann was banned again, around the 11th Plenum of the ZK, and this ban was only rescinded eleven years later. It was not until September 1976 that Biermann performed publicly, first at a protestant service, then, two months later, he again did a tour of West Germany organised by the workers' union IG Metall. At the end of this tour, however, Biermann was expelled from the GDR because East German government officials judged that the tour programme went against the ideology of the state. Renft's lyricist Pannach and their keyboard player Christian Kunert were also expelled nine months later.[47] In brief, all autonomous engagement, for a musical style such as rock music or a fairer society and state, failed because state authorities classified them as anti-authoritarian revolt.

Class struggle and music for a better world

Although separated by the Berlin Wall after August 1961, young intellectuals and artists in both East and West Germany developed an interest in

---

[45] In the GDR, such a rejection meant that the individual rejected was persona non grata for the East German state officials.
[46] Hippen 1980, p. 173.   [47] Rauhut 1998, p. 781.

music centred on a singer with guitar accompaniment. In West Germany, in connection with the New Leftist climate and anti-authoritarian spirit, this interest grew into a strong fashion for political song.[48] Politicised singer-songwriters expressed the same critical attitude towards the authoritarian National Socialist past and authoritarianism in general as the political movements. The musical aesthetics of singer-songwriters – simple, relaxed, playful, non-kitschy and anti-solemn – were considered to be particularly well suited to the anti-authoritarian impetus. It contrasted with those aesthetics that authoritarian dictatorships, including National Socialism, favoured: (German) folk song and unison singing, on the one hand, and optimistic, cheerful pieces with huge orchestration and choir, on the other.[49]

With the increasing politicisation of the New Leftist music scene in the second half of the 1960s, song aesthetics also changed. The music performed at the annual Waldeck Festivals from 1964 to 1969 is indicative of this transformative process. In the festivals of 1968 and 1969, singer-songwriters like Reinhard Mey, who propagated a rather soft and friendly musical style, were marginalised and heavily criticised by more radical colleagues and listeners[50] who preferred more aggressive performance styles and lyrics that complied with the emotional tension and the subliminal inclination towards violence. As the influential singer-songwriter Degenhardt put it, "nuances only cramp the class struggle",[51] by which he meant that differentiation (for the sake of fairness for instance) was to be neglected because it prevented activists from efficient class struggle. Correspondingly, Degenhardt's vocal style is marked by a rather rough timbre and a slightly aggressive, cynical tone, which is more spoken than sung. This style perfectly suited his lyrics, which attacked petit-bourgeois values and ridiculed the clichés used to demonise the New Left. Other singer-songwriters who performed at the Waldeck festivals, such as Süverkrüp and Walter Mossmann, employed similar musical and verbal means.[52]

Whereas the West German singer-songwriter scene hankered after radically changing the state and society, classical musicians targeted the field of classical music. In doing this, they decisively contributed to its institutional

---

[48] See Holler 2007.
[49] This aesthetic was also propagated in the GDR. See, for instance, the music of the Oktoberklub and Paul Dessau's *Lenin* (1969) respectively. Its Beethovenian from-night-to-light dramaturgy displays the victory and splendid future of the dictatorial system.
[50] Radical leftists like Rolf Schwendter interrupted Mey's performance in 1969 (see Burg Waldeck Festivals 2008 (1964–1969), CD 10, Track 1).
[51] See the refrain of Degenhardt's song with the same title (Degenhardt 1992, Track 6).
[52] See Mossmann's "Lied von den neuen Jakobinern" (1968) and Süverkrüp's "Erschröckliche Moritat vom Kryptokommunisten" (1965).

renewal. Music students became particularly active. In line with the policy of the anti-authoritarian political movement, they publicly unmasked former National Socialist musicians[53] and criticised educational methods, including what they saw as the repressive and profit-oriented aspects of the music education system. Their critique was supported by the composer and writer Konrad Boehmer, who had moved to the Netherlands in 1966. Boehmer described the education of musicians at West German conservatories as "drill and coercion [...] that aims to make musicians ceaselessly reproduce a reactionary ideology and musical values".[54] Seeking support, at the prestigious world premiere of Hans Werner Henze's oratorio *The Raft of the Medusa* in Hamburg in December 1968,[55] music students called on Henze to help them develop "models of music making that cannot be manipulated by state subsidies".[56]

The New Leftist critique of the institutions of classical music and music education was complemented by the development of new art production modes. Like krautrock musicians, music students and avant-garde musicians founded ensembles dedicated to free improvisation[57] which, as mentioned above, favoured anti-authoritarian performance modes that involved neither a conductor nor the use of a score.[58]

The year 1968 resonating in music

Whereas in West Germany the shooting of Rudi Dutschke marked the climax of the protests in 1968, in the GDR the salient event was the invasion of Czechoslovakia by Warsaw Pact troops on 20 August that terminated the Prague Spring and the hope for "socialism with a human face" connected with it. Numerous East German citizens responded with spontaneous, courageous protests.[59] The ensuing repression of these protests in the

---

[53] For instance, during a choir recital dedicated to the composer Philipp Mohler in spring 1969, students at the conservatory in Frankfurt distributed a flyer informing the audience about Mohler's political opportunism during the Nazi era (Sohar 2003).

[54] Boehmer 1970, p. 71.   [55] Kutschke 2007b.

[56] Arbeitskreis Sozialistischer Musikstudenten 1968. For more on avant-garde music and 1968 in West Germany see Kutschke 2007a.

[57] Such ensembles were Hinz und Kunst (from Hamburg) and the Free Music Group (from Frankfurt am Main).

[58] Sohar 2003.

[59] Many GDR citizens courageously protested against the invasion by means of anonymous flyers and political messages on walls, to which the East German authorities responded by severe sanctions such as imprisonment, workplace intimidation and expulsion from the SED (Mitter and Wolle 1993, pp. 430–81).

GDR resulted in a mental attitude marked by a loss of trust in the state, which the historians Armin Mitter and Stefan Wolle have dubbed "graveyard peace" ("Friedhofsruhe").[60] In the long run, this graveyard peace turned out to be the beginning of the decline of the GDR ultimately leading to the fall of the Berlin Wall in 1989.

Not surprisingly, the events of 1968 resonated with songwriters and composers. Biermann, for instance, wrote a utopian song called "Noch" ("Still") that noted the graveyard peace and hinted at open revolt. The vocal melody of the verse is a stagnant Phrygian recitative and the harmonies slowly oscillate between unresolved chords: E minor (with an added ninth or seventh) and F major with a diminished fifth and minor seventh.[61] The song's refrain, however, suggests change and revolt with fast cadential chord progressions that counteract the 'graveyard peace' of the verse. Biermann also commented directly on the events of 1968 in West Germany with his song "Drei Kugeln auf Rudi Dutschke" ("Three Bullets for Rudi Dutschke"). This song accuses the then-incumbent West German chancellor Kurt Georg Kiesinger of being at least partially responsible for the assassination attempt against Dutschke.

Comparison of Biermann's "Noch" with another musical response to the crushing of the Prague Spring, Christfried Schmidt's *Kammermusik I. Von Menschen und Vögeln* (*Chamber Music I. For People and Birds*), reveals the difference between the more or less open critique of Biermann's songs and the subtlety and concealment of 'new music' by East German composers like Schmidt. Schmidt dedicated the third and last movement "Phönix" ("Phoenix") of his *Kammermusik I* to the Czechoslovakian student Jan Palach who immolated himself on 16 January 1969 as a protest against the Warsaw Pact troops' invasion of Prague five months earlier. The sequence of pitches A-A-A-C-B, which is repeated in various forms throughout the movement, is identical with those letters of the student's full name which are also used as pitch names (in German the pitch 'B' is referred to as 'H'): (J) A (N) (P) A (L) A C H.[62] (See, for instance, the beginning of bar 41, performed by the flute, in Figure 11.2.) So, Schmidt was obviously reluctant to unequivocally demonstrate solidarity with the Czechoslovakian people. Instead, he employed subtle, masked and non-verbal musical ways of expressing solidarity.

In contrast to the solitary responses of individual artists to the Czechoslovakian invasion, performances at the Oktoberklub, which were

---

[60] Mitter and Wolle 1993, p. 480.   [61] See the score of "Noch" in Biermann 1968, p. 87.
[62] See Schmidt 1969.

Figure 11.2 Christfried Schmidt, *Kammermusik I. Von Menschen und Vögeln*, score, bars 40 and 41 of "Phönix" © reproduced by kind permission of Christfried Schmidt.

a vehicle for official governmental opinion, encouraged East German citizens to remain on the socialist-communist path. Five days after the invasion, for instance, Oktoberklub performed, for the first time, the song "Sag mir, wo du stehst" ("Tell me what your politics are") at a FDJ concert in Lenz.[63] Clearly drawing on Pete Seeger's protest song "Which side are you on?", the strophes of "Sag mir, wo du stehst" not only commanded its listeners to resolutely devote themselves to the official political purposes (including the support of the invasion of Czechoslovakia), it also urged closet sceptics to denounce themselves; obviously with the goal of indoctrinating them more intensely afterwards.

The fight against musical authorities

The policy of the anti-authoritarian movement manifested itself not only in the fight against living musical authorities, but also dead ones, especially the 'great masters' of the art-music canon. In the context of the anti-authoritarian political climate, the hegemonic discourse about the 'great master' and the 'musical canon' almost inevitably invited critique.

The anti-hagiographical and anti-canonical impetus was especially evident at the Beethoven Bicentennial celebrated in West Germany in 1970.[64] Unlike in the 1950s and 1960s, when West German avant-garde composers had on the whole abhorred references to non-avant-garde styles, the pieces composers wrote for the Bicentennial demonstrated a vital interest in the practice of musical quotation. Whereas, in the classical mainstream, composers had shown respect for the 'great master' Beethoven, the references

[63] Robb 2007, p. 230. [64] See Kutschke 2010.

to his music and person in avant-garde pieces in the 1970 Bicentennial were decidedly irreverent. Mauricio Kagel's *Ludwig van* and Karlheinz Stockhausen's *Shortwaves for Beethoven* presented Beethoven's music in an ironic, fragmented and distorted collage, which seemed to ridicule the 'great master'. In the same vein, Wilhelm Dieter Siebert's piece *Our Ludwig* made fun of the composer's deafness by quoting from the master's conversation books. By doing this, the musicians clearly indicated that they no longer considered Beethoven to be a "sacred cow",[65] as various music journalists put it, who supported the anti-authoritarian revolt against the canon.

In the GDR, quoting the music of the great composers of the past had always played an important role in contemporary composition. According to the official agenda promoted since the GDR's foundation in 1949, artists were expected to support the building of a socialist state by appropriating from the heritage of their predecessors in a progressive and reverential manner.[66] In this light, it is all the more striking that, from the late 1960s till the turn of the 1970s, compositions of a cheeky and rebellious character came to the fore that indicated a sense of liberation from the achievements of the past. For instance, *Battaglia Alla Turca* (1967) by the East German Tilo Medek split Mozart's "*Alla Turca*" into various fragments and rearranged them in a new, anti-logical and anti-organic order. The result was, as with the West German Beethoven Bicentennial pieces, an overall disjointed, fragmentary character. Similarly, *Bagatellen für B* (*Bagatelles for B[eethoven]*, 1970, for orchestra) by Reiner Bredemeyer, the East German by choice, consists of unmediated bits and pieces of Beethoven's *Bagatellen* for piano, op. 119 and 126.[67]

The rebellious, anti-authoritarian attitude, however, was soon replaced by a rather depressive, resigned mindset, which was likewise anti-authoritarian but, at the same time, reflected the dystopian 'graveyard peace' that had spread over the GDR after the crushing of the Prague Spring. Unlike the rock musicians who flourished during the short period of liberalisation between 1971 and 1973, contemporary composers seemed to withdraw from their officially expected role as optimistic promoters of socialist culture. Engagement was replaced by disinterest.[68] This is most apparent in the

---

[65] See Koch 1970, p. 124. For further discussion of the connections between postmodernism in music and irreverent quotation practices by the avant-garde see Kutschke 2010.

[66] One of the models for these sanguine and optimistic pieces is Paul Dessau's *Bach-Variationen* of 1963.

[67] For an in-depth analysis and interpretation of Bredemeyer's *Bagatellen für B* see Noeske 2007, pp. 147–67.

[68] In her monograph, Nina Noeske (2007) has argued that the East German contemporary composers aimed at deconstructing the GDR by musical means.

Sensible Variationen um ein Thema von Schubert (*Sensible Variations on a Theme of Schubert*) (1972) by Medek as the piece is tame and lacks strength and substance. The elaborate orchestral texture of Schubert's popular theme, the entr'acte music from *Rosamunde*,[69] is reduced to a trio for flute, violin or alto flute and violoncello – an orchestration that, especially if performed with an alto flute instead of a violin, makes the composition's Alberti bass resemble the mawkish, mechanistic sound of a street organ. The variations revolve around insipid sequential repetitions and scale-segments, complemented by the allusion to a 7-6-syncopation chain that is based on a sequence of fifths, pop-like off-beat rhythms and etude-like formulas, which make the variations seem trivial.[70] The music does not convey confidence, belief in the future or the sophistication of the source material, as was required by the discourse on respecting musical heritage, neither does it demonstrate anti-authoritarian playful provocation or mockery as the *Battaglia* and *Bagatellen* did before and briefly after the crushing of the Prague Spring. Like Pannach and Kunert discussed above, Medek left the GDR in 1977, a year after Biermann was expelled.

Like the oppositional climate of '1968' in general, anti-authoritarianism was primarily an upheaval *against* the *status quo*, i.e. 'negation' in the jargon of Adorno. In the music scenes of both East and West Germany, however, the anti-authoritarian spirit, despite its negative impetus, also sparked dynamic change and reform. The anti-authoritarian impetus led to the creation and diffusion of new genres and styles such as beat music, krautrock, politrock, the protest songs of the singer-songwriter scene, free improvisation and new styles of contemporary art music based on ironic quotation. Nonetheless, the anti-authoritarian struggles of East and West German musicians and audiences were clearly dissimilar. In East Germany the permanent control of the state over cultural expression generated a continuous tug of war between musicians and state forces, which ultimately resulted in resignation on the two sides. These differences also manifested themselves in the music. In East Germany, potential for creativity was cut off; it only developed in subversive niches, whereas in West Germany, the anti-authoritarian protest succeeded in initiating the transformation of not only the music, but also musical institutions.

---

[69] Franz Schubert, *Zwei Entr'actes zu dem Drama „Rosamunde"*, Nr. 2, B-Dur, Andantino, D 797.
[70] For more details see Kutschke 2012.

12 | '1968' – the emergence of a protest culture in the popular music of the Eastern Bloc?

RÜDIGER RITTER

In 1968, Europe was split into two parts, into the countries of Western Europe and those of the Eastern Bloc. The Cold War was in full bloom and the political battle between the East and West had spread into all aspects of life, including music and culture. Because Europe was divided, it might be assumed that the two sides had nothing to do with one another. Yet, in 1968 there were protests and unrest not only in the West, but also in the East. If the events of 1968 led to the development of a new type of musical protest culture in the West, the question must be asked: did events in the East have similar consequences? This question raises several other fundamental questions. For instance, to what extent were the events of 1968 in the West and East comparable and did the protests have the same or similar origins? Were there mutual influences and points of contact across both sides of the border between the Eastern Bloc and the West?

The complexity of the musical protest culture also prompts further considerations. Too often we conclude without questioning that individual freedom in the socialist systems of Eastern Bloc states was, to varying degrees, strongly curtailed by the state, without properly considering whether or not art and music were understood as forms of social rebellion against repression. The widespread assumption that music was inevitably a medium of protest because of the repressive social situation overlooks the fact that all art created in an authoritarian society does not necessarily have the intention of being an act of social protest. Some music groups in the Eastern Bloc – such as, for instance, the Czech rock band Plastic People of the Universe – asserted that they just wanted to make music and nothing more.

In order to avoid working from a false premise, we must ask whether, how, when, and under what conditions, music was received as 'protest' in the Eastern Bloc and – here we reach the central question of this study – what role did the events of 1968 play in this? One of the most important developments in the Eastern Bloc in 1968 was the Czech reform movement known as the 'Prague Spring'. During the night of 20 August 1968, the Prague Spring was violently ended with a military invasion led by the Soviet Union with troops from neighbouring Eastern Bloc countries. The party and state leader Alexander Dubček had raised the hopes of the Czech people with his policy of "socialism with a human face", but this hope was suffocated after the invasion and his removal from office. The atmosphere of the Prague Spring was optimistic and political protest and engagement appeared to promise success, but the violent repression that followed led to a bleak, pessimistic lethargy. Were these events – in particular the invasion in August 1968 – a decisive turning point in the protest culture of music in the Eastern Bloc?

'1968' in the West and East

For the Eastern Bloc, the year 1968 was defined by the invasion of Prague by Soviet, Polish and Hungarian forces, which violently ended the Prague Spring. This was not only about the abolition of a non-conforming movement, it was also a turning point in the whole socialist system. However monolithic the Eastern Bloc appeared from the outside, it was not homogenous and produced a complicated, interconnected system. Events in one country were followed attentively by opposition movements in other countries, and communication across national borders often took place outside of official channels through a network of personal acquaintances among opposition intellectuals. Upheavals in one country, therefore, often had considerable effects in neighbouring lands.[1] The Czechoslovakian '1968' had great significance for the whole Eastern Bloc, above and beyond the fact that it was troops from the Soviet 'brother lands' that crushed the Prague Spring.

The main difference between the West and East lies in completely different experiences of Marxism–Leninism. While '1968' resonated in the West as an ideological confirmation and remaking of Marxist theses and fundamental ideas (the opinion-leaders themselves had no contact with the implementation of Marxist–Leninist ideals in their daily lives, unlike their colleagues in the state socialist countries), the invasion of Prague destroyed the last remnants of belief in "socialism with a human face" in Central and Eastern Europe.[2] Put simply, in the West, Marxist–Leninist theses were called upon in a revolt against the establishment, while in the East, the rebellion was led against an establishment that officially claimed to pursue Marxist imperatives.

---

[1] The uprisings in Poland and Hungary in 1956 are a prime example of transnational influence as the unrest in each country was closely related. See Tischler 2001.
[2] This is how Dubček and Smrkovský described the goal of their programme at the ZK plenary on 5 April 1968 and the phrase became the buzzword of the Czechoslovakian '1968'. See Hoensch 1978, p. 154.

Further differences become apparent when the student protests in the West and East are compared. In the Eastern Bloc, the students fought to gain the basic civil rights that their colleagues in the West already had. Unlike their Western counterparts, students in the Eastern Bloc could not rely on attention from the press and an open discussion of their demands. Instead, they were acutely aware that they could be dragged off the street by the omnipresent apparatus of the state and be silenced or even murdered.[3] The students in the East began protesting against concrete, material problems (frequent power outages and the like) and only then did the protests change from material to political demands (more freedom – regime change). Often they held demonstrations in the belief that it would be enough if they held on for just a few hours, and then the Americans would come.[4] The difference between the protest culture in the West and East is evident from the diametrically opposed image of the Americans as saviours (in the East) and plunderers (in the West).

These differences continued in music as well. In the Western world the events of '1968' led to a politicisation of music. The genre of political song, which had a new aesthetic, made music into a form of expression for up-to-date political commentary. In the Eastern Bloc, in contrast, social milieus and niches, in which the autonomy of art and artistic freedom was established, had already been developing in the late 1950s. The political unrest during 1968 made these niches even stronger and in Czechoslovakia the opposition culture was known as 'alternative culture'.

The protagonists of the opposition scene had the explicit goal of building a sort of state within a state: through 'underground' activities they wanted to develop what Václav Benda has referred to as a "second polis".[5] In Poland, for instance, the development of 'self publishing' (*samizdat*), which enabled a form of 'second circulation' (*drugi obieg*), was informed by similar goals: authors no longer typed oppositional texts secretly on typewriters and published them privately. Instead, the opposition artistic scenes developed a parallel structure of independent publishing and distribution systems for underground texts and artwork, which were independent of the official cultural structures.

Compared to the West, music developed differently as part of the alternative culture in the Eastern Bloc. While music in the West moved closer to the political debates of the day and increasingly became a medium of social engagement, the music scene in the East, which had already had strong ideas about the social autonomy of art and about musical expression

---

[3] See Eisler 1998, p. 250f.   [4] Tůma 2004, p. 329.   [5] Benda 1978; Veen *et al.* 2007.

being free from social and political control, stressed these ideas even more in the wake of the unrest in 1968.

1956 and the desire for freedom

After Stalin's death in 1953 – at the beginning of the so-called 'thaw' – artists, authors and musicians worked to become free of the rigid system of control. This desire reached all areas of music, not just popular music. In 1956 the first Polish festival for contemporary music, the Warsaw Autumn (*Warszawska Jesień*), was held.[6] In view of the fact that composers in the Eastern Bloc had no way of taking part in current international trends, Polish composers invited their colleagues not only from neighbouring socialist countries, but also from Western countries to Warsaw. In the following years, this festival developed into an internationally recognised form of artistic exchange from both sides and attracted important composers such as Penderecki and Lutosławski. The festival acted as a kind of cultural window into the West, not just for Poland but for the entire Eastern Bloc.

Musical exchange was intended, nothing more. The Warsaw Autumn festival in 1956, however, acquired a political dimension because the regime was confronted with a situation in which it had to deal with a large number of music students not only from Poland but from other socialist lands as guests. Although the festival was harmless – there were no protests or riots of any kind – the regime was concerned that it would not be able to control such a gathering of people in its own country. The state powers would have preferred to forbid the festival, but this was not possible because the regime wanted to project a public image of normality and openness. Forbidding the festival would therefore have been counterproductive.

In the same year there were two festivals in the Polish city of Sopot (near Gdańsk). Under the direction of the well-known publicist and literary figure Leopold Tyrmand, jazz ensembles from Poland and other Eastern Bloc countries convened and performed jazz publicly for the first time since 1949. A high point was the presence of the Joki Freund Ensemble with Albert Mangelsdorff from West Germany, who appeared at the second festival in Sopot in 1957. At least for Poland, these events meant the beginning of an independent musical scene. In short, the year 1956 was a foundational year: the desire for personal and artistic freedom could only begin to be realised after the Stalinist period.

---

[6] See Kalisch 1998; Ritter 2005.

In Hungary, the year 1956 also played a decisive role in the country's musical development. Political developments were a trigger: in 1956 there was an open uprising against the communist government which was crushed by troops loyal to Moscow. This uprising is known as the Hungarian Revolution and it marked a decisive break with repression under Stalin. In the following decades, the Hungarian regime attempted to foster internal stability and peace by granting some small freedoms, which included better travel opportunities and better provision of consumer goods for the general populace. In terms of music, this meant an end to the systematic criminalisation of jazz. In the early years of socialist Hungary, the regime accused jazz fans of being hooligans; they declared that they were not only troublemakers but also enemies of the state. In this way, the regime cleverly used the public's desire for stability in social life after the war for its own purposes.[7] After the Hungarian uprising of 1956 had been suppressed, however, the leadership did not continue its crackdown on jazz. Instead, it implemented a cautious programme of tolerance. In 1962, a milestone in the history of Hungarian jazz was reached when Café Dalia opened and it quickly became one of the most important centres for jazz.[8] Paradoxically the policy of liberalisation towards jazz was bound up with a loss of interest in it. At the end of the 1950s, young people were becoming more and more interested in rock 'n' roll, rather than jazz. The development of Hungarian rock 'n' roll is closely linked with the new social situation after 1956. Rock 'n' roll drew its provocative strength from its critique of the apparent stabilisation in the social sphere.[9]

The post-Stalinist thaw in Poland and Hungary, then, resulted in a fundamental shift in the social situation and the music culture. Taking into account this historical situation, what influence did the events of 1968 have? To answer this question, this chapter concentrates on developments in the popular music of three countries – the Czechoslovak Socialist Republic (CSSR), Poland and Hungary – in which the cultural trends that were characteristic of the whole Eastern Bloc are particularly clear.

'1968' in the CSSR

The chroniclers of Czechoslovakian rock describe the early 1960s as a 'golden period'.[10] At that time there was a lively, decentralised, self-organising rock

---

[7] Havadi 2010.   [8] Simon 1999, p. 155.   [9] Runner and Kosztolányi 2000.
[10] Lindaur and Ondřej 2001, pp. 32–55; Lindaur and Ondřej 1990.

music or 'beat' scene and the culmination of this scene was marked by three Czechoslovakian 'beat' festivals, the first of which was held in 1967 and the last in 1971. The turn of the 1970s, however, was marked by state repression of culture, which affected a generation of intellectuals, artists and musicians. As a result of repressive state policies, the Czechoslovakian rock scene – which was recognised as being the "most modern of all the socialist states [ ] with a high musical level" – went into a phase of "stagnation" and "resignation".[11]

In the spring of 1967, weaknesses began to show in the system of state control. At the fourth conference of the Authors' Union, Pavel Kohout read an open letter in a grand gesture; he read the same letter that was read by Solzhenitsyn in May at the conference of the Authors' Association of the USSR. The letter criticised the practice of censorship in the Soviet Union. With this Kohout demanded – indirectly, but clearly – reform in the press and publishing from the state and party leadership. Attempts by Novotný, the General Secretary of the Communist Party, to regain control of the party through purges, led to student protests and open public uproar.

In January 1968, Novotný was replaced by Alexander Dubček. In contrast to his predecessor, Dubček was sympathetic to the demands of intellectuals and brought in some fundamental changes. In April 1968 he created a programme for 'Socialistic Democracy' in the CSSR and showed his intention to reform the socialist system from the ground up.

In the wake of these reforms, there were some spectacular performances and recordings of Czechoslovakian rock groups which illustrated the strong, Western, orientation of rock in the CSSR. The state-run record company Supraphon produced the album *Želva* by the group Olympia in 1968, which included some tracks that were influenced by Jimi Hendrix,[12] and the band The Primitives also performed covers of Jimi Hendrix and Frank Zappa. Such performances gave a voice to the desire for more freedom: traditionally people in Czechoslovakia did not see themselves as part of Eastern Europe and not as a part of the Eastern Bloc, but rather as a Central European country. The institution of Dubček's reforms appeared to offer the opportunity to make this consciousness a reality. Covers of Western songs were a strong symbol of political will and brought about an optimism in Czechoslovakian society that defined the first half of that year.[13]

Some concerts took the form of spontaneous, even anarchistic, 'happenings'. When The Primitives organised a 'fish fest' in Prague, the musicians and

[11] Lindaur and Ondřej 2001, p. 54.   [12] Lindaur and Ondřej 2001, p. 41.
[13] See Šustrová 2009, p. 156.

audience threw fish at each other.[14] At the fish fest chaos ruled and the 'happening' destroyed the social decorum and standards for interaction, which were highly prized in socialist society. This is an excellent example of the spirit of freedom that was characteristic of '1968'. The fish fest was neither a riot against political repression nor a statement of western political orientation. Rather, it was a 'happening' which saw the younger generation rebelling against the behavioural standards of their parents – something which was also typical of the Western '1968'. As troops from Warsaw Pact countries finally invaded on 20 August 1968, the younger generation saw their newly won freedom threatened, and therefore the front ranks of protesters in Prague, Bratislava and other cities were occupied by long-haired youths and hippies.

The military power of the Warsaw Pact not only suffocated the social resistance of the youth but also did away with the government. Dubček and the entire political leadership had to go to Moscow and swear their allegiance to Moscow. After his return, Dubček announced that the Prague Spring was not over. Indeed, in the autumn of 1968 the first hippie meeting took place in Slovakia. Nevertheless, the mood after the invasion was very depressed and this was demonstrated most clearly by the self-immolation of the 21-year-old philosophy student Jan Palach in Wenceslas Square. In his farewell letter, Palach gave the looming helplessness that he felt after the invasion as the reason for his action.

Drastic changes were made. Dubček was deposed and in 1970 he was thrown out of the Party. Gustáv Husák was his successor as the head of the Central Committee and head of state. The period of restoration that he began was a hard test for Czechoslovakian society: through raids and arrests the state tried to gain control over those sympathetic to the Prague Spring. An entire generation of the country's intellectuals was prohibited from working in their respective fields and were forced into physical labour. The individual freedoms of the Prague Spring were taken back and censorship was increased. The party leadership spoke about this period – in a euphemistic and cynical way – as 'normalisation' (*normalizace*).

Czech musicians and songwriters, who were part of the alternative scene prior to 'normalisation', portrayed the mood in their melodies and lyrics. One of the most popular protest songs after August 1968 was "Modlitba pro Martu" ("Prayer for Marta") by Waldemar Matuška. The song was performed by Marta Kubišová, who became a symbol of '1968'. The song text by Petr Rada cleverly linked the contemporary situation with the past: it

---

[14] How The Primitives performed on stage was unusual for the time in comparison to other bands in the CSSR, see Lindaur and Ondřej 2001, p. 45.

drew on a seventeenth-century text by the Moravian theologian Jan Amos Komenský, which expressed Czech hopes for self-rule and independence. The song proved an outlet for the frustration that people felt about the hopeless political situation and its melody was played as the theme song for Czechoslovakian television until the song was banned in 1969.

In the year 1969, the 21-year-old singer-songwriter Karel Kryl became the musical mouthpiece of disaffected Czech youth. In his song "Bratříčku, Zavírej" ("Little Brother Close the Gate"), which was recorded by Supraphon, Kryl set up an allegory in which the Soviet Union was a horrible older brother to the CSSR. In June of the same year, he also wrote the song "Cancer" in which he musically sketched the climate of suffocation. Kryl went to Munich in September 1969 to perform a large concert and after the concert the CSSR authorities closed the border so he could not return. He was eventually employed by Radio Free Europe in Munich, and hearing his voice from Munich made Czechoslovakian youth even more aware of their powerlessness.[15]

Another important event after the crushed Prague Spring was a concert by the Beach Boys in May 1969 at the Lucerna, the main concert hall in Prague. The group dedicated the song "Breaking Away" to Dubček, who was in the audience.[16] For the rock scene, however, a campaign called 'requalification' (*rekvalifikace*), which was implemented from 1972 onwards, was the decisive turning point. Under the guise of professionalising musical life and increasing quality, the regime's programme of 'requalification' centralised musical life and caused the destruction of the independent musical infrastructure.[17] Nevertheless, in the 1970s, meetings organised by rock, pop and jazz groups continued, and these were of great importance for the national music scene in face of the government's restrictions.[18]

During the 1970s the political climate for rock became increasingly restrictive. Fans were escorted to concerts and in the towns of Rodolfov and Kdyně there were bloody conflicts between police and concert-goers in 1974 and 1977 respectively. But the official Czechoslovakian association of composers did not protest against the state's actions. The leading rock group of the time, the Plastic People of the Universe (or Plastic People for short), provides a good example of how music and politics were linked in the 1970s. The Plastic People was formed by members of The Primitives and they made no explicit political demands, despite their disillusionment after the invasion of 1968.

---

[15] Tůma, 2004, p. 320. [16] Yanosik 1996.
[17] Lindaur 2001, pp. 59–60. For further discussion of Czechoslovakian rock at this time see Chadima 1992.
[18] See Lindaur 2001, pp. 87–8.

As Milan Hlavsa, the bassist and founding member of the group explained in the late 1990s, the members of the band only had the naïve idea of becoming famous and they were strongly influenced by the musical ideas of Western rock musicians and groups, like Jimi Hendrix, the Rolling Stones and Frank Zappa. Frank Zappa was particularly well known and loved in Czechoslovakia.[19] Although the restrictive climate of the *normalizace* led to the Plastic People's public performances often being prohibited, the band nonetheless continued to exist and pursue its artistic goals.

The situation became more difficult, however, when the musicians engaged the dissident author Egon Bondy as a lyricist.[20] From this point onwards, all attempts to gain official permission to perform and to have themselves listed among the country's permitted musical groups failed.[21] Until 1976, they continued to perform at underground concerts, but then the leading members of the band were put on trial and sentenced to several months imprisonment for being 'agitators of the West'.[22] This resulted in a wave of solidarity from the rock scene, as well as from many intellectuals who had been silenced since 1969, because it was believed that "this time it is not a political enemy but another lifestyle that stands before the court".[23] In terms of the change in protest culture after 1968, this quote is important because it points out that both rock musicians and political intellectuals were now being put on trial and this caused a mobilisation of both groups in the following years.

The political function of the music of the Plastic People was not intentional, but came from confrontation with authorities. The demonstration of solidarity from intellectuals with the Plastic People and the symbolism that went with it – especially long hair and the wearing of jeans that were symbols of a Western orientation – gave their music a clear political character. An important consequence of this politicisation was the creation of the Charta '77, at the turn of the year from 1976 to 1977. The Charta '77 was an oppositional organisation which, in a petition with the same name, insisted on the upholding of the human rights conventions of the Helsinki Accords of 1975.[24] Not only civil liberties, but also ideas about freedom and individuality were important to Charta '77, and this can be seen as one of the indirect effects of the ideas of the Prague Spring.

An attempt to work around the oppressive situation of the 1970s can be seen in the activities of the Jazz Section, a subgroup of the Czechoslovakian Musicians' Union, which was the official composers' union of the CSSR.

---

[19] Interview with Milan Hlavsa, in Unterberger 1998, pp. 190–6. [20] Bondy 1980.
[21] Bondy 1980. [22] For details see Anonymous 1976. [23] See Pauer 2000, p. 55.
[24] Pauer 2000, pp. 52–63.

The Jazz Section had begun as an open forum for those interested in jazz, but soon developed into an independent concert agency working outside of state control and later it also organised a publication arm that bypassed the state censorship system. In the 1980s, however, this initiative was crushed by the state.[25]

'1968' in Poland

After the violent end to the Prague Spring in August 1968, the Polish authorities took another route to bring the music scene under control. They developed a strategy of guaranteeing certain freedoms in order to avoid the risk of social and political destabilisation. This approach was a continuation of the strategy that the regime had already used when dealing with the music festivals in 1956. The difference was that in 1956, the establishing of musical freedom seemed to be a victory over the regime while in 1968 the granting of the same musical freedom was regarded as a matter of course.

Due to the strategy adopted by the Polish authorities, the popular music scene in Poland managed to extensively consolidate and stabilise itself in the late 1950s and 1960s. It oscillated between copying rock 'n' roll and American country melodies, adapting Polish folk songs and developing a style of 'romantic' pop, which was called 'bigbit', the Polish version of 'big beat'. The first Polish long-playing (LP) record of the new bigbit style was the eponymously titled album by the band Niebiesko-Czarni (Blue-Blacks), which was released in 1962.[26]

The press agency of Polish Youth, Sztandar Młodych, began reporting extensive on the rock scene in the West in the early 1960s and defended rock against conservative voices.[27] As reported by Sztandar Młodych, the Polish regime considered itself to be progressive. The musical tolerance of the regime was so great that, unlike elsewhere in the Eastern Bloc where the political leadership was the main opponent of rock music, it was the musical conservatives who were the main opposition. In March 1966, for instance, as the British band The Hollies were accompanied to their hotel by enthusiastic fans after a concert in Kraków, the band were faced by a group of students holding banners stating "Long live Chopin! Hollies go home!".[28] Rock groups in Poland were not necessarily on the side of protesters and against the ruling establishment, as was typical during the '1968' in the

---

[25] Srp 1994. [26] Zieliński 2005, p. 19. [27] Ryback 1990, p. 92. [28] Ryback 1990, p. 93.

West. This indicates that rock music in the Polish '1968' had a very different function compared with that of the West.

Because the Polish state wanted to allow freedom, they promoted rather than prohibited concerts by Western rock bands. In 1963 Paul Anka played in Warsaw and in 1967 the Rolling Stones also played. Additionally, various lesser-known rock bands from Great Britain came to Poland in these years like The Hollies (mentioned above), The Animals, The Marmalades and The Tremeloes. After scenes of vandalism, a relocation of future rock concerts was considered, but there was no general ban.[29]

With this strategy, the regime seemed to have found its peace with the music scene. The Polish rock scene was calm, sweet and harmless, and only in some special cases were some deeper messages hidden behind the idyllic façade. The song "Dziwny jest ten Świat" ("Miraculous is this World") by Czesław Niemen, which became a very famous song in Poland, was one of the few examples of music with higher aspirations from that time. In the style of a Western protest song, which was new in the context of the Polish popular scene at that time, Niemen described in simple terms the relations between people and the widespread hatred and social problems in society. Although the lyrics might be understood as being naïve, they stressed the existence of people who had the intention of solving the ills of society. In Poland, this song, which is still well known today, was widely discussed for three reasons: the first was the high artistic quality of Niemen as a rock musician, singer and lyricist; the second was that Niemen introduced the genre of protest song following Western models (e.g. Bob Dylan) into the Polish musical scene; and the third was the fact that social problems were expressed clearly for the first time in Polish popular music.[30]

The seemingly frictionless contact between the music scene and the state was ended by several key events in 1968.[31] In March 1968 the performance of a play by Adam Mickiewicz was forbidden. Mickiewicz was regarded with great respect and esteem as the greatest Polish national poet, and he remains a national icon today. The banning of the play resulted in student protests, which quickly escalated from the specific issue into more fundamental demands about the socio-cultural system. Eventually in October the party newspaper, the *Trybuna Ludu*, opined that it no longer wanted to tolerate the "hooligan-excess of the youth".[32] A great number of students including Adam Michnik and Jan Lityński were arrested, suspended from university and pressed into military service.

---

[29] Ryback 1990, p. 95; Zieliński 2005, p. 86. [30] Zieliński 2005, p. 87. [31] Eisler 1998, p. 168.
[32] Cited in Eisler 1998, p. 168.

This describes the beginning of cultural repression in Poland before the crushing of the Prague Spring. The party leadership reacted to the unrest not with expert composure but with hectic uncertainty. This was in part due to a power struggle within the party for the leadership and in part because of increasing nervousness in the party leadership over developments in the CSSR. It was precisely the guarantee of a degree of tolerance that, for example, let the rock scene remain relatively harmless. But when – as was feared – opposition intellectuals took up social initiatives, the leadership saw its position to be endangered.

The Polish '1968' that followed consisted of three parts: student protests, a power struggle at the top of the Polish United Workers' Party (PZPR),[33] and a massive anti-Semitic campaign.[34] The anti-Semitic campaign in particular was a distinctive feature of the Polish '1968'. In Poland, state-controlled repression took on the quality of a "pogrom against the intelligentsia", and it was the case that many of the persecuted intellectuals were Jewish or had Jewish connections.[35]

When the news about the suppression of the Prague Spring and the active role of the Polish army reached Poland, students in Warsaw reacted strongly. Writers like Jerzy Andrzejewski and Sławomir Mrożek protested; and a former teacher named Roman Siwiec immolated himself in Warsaw on 8 September and died a few days later.

The events of March 1968 in Poland marked a generation. The rejection of the system was more apparent than ever before and interest in counter-cultures among open-minded Polish youth grew considerably. However, initially the protests had little effect because they were limited to student groups and the workers had not yet joined in support. At first the students and workers campaigned separately. Indeed, the students did not join the workers when they took to the streets two years later in protest at poor standards of living. Only in the late 1970s did the two social groups join together when the independent trade union Solidarność was formed, and this led to a new type of resistance.[36]

Despite the traditional Polish pride in their long history of uprisings, the events of 1968 are still regarded in Poland with an odd sort of shyness because the attempted protests were unsuccessful.[37] The regime, which had

---

[33] Polska Zjednoczona Partia Robotnicza.   [34] Genest 2009, p. 91.   [35] Eisler 2009, p. 168.
[36] Ruchniewicz 2004, p. 282.
[37] The national 'master narrative' in Poland constructs a line of continuity from the Kościuszko rebellion of the eighteenth century, to the rebellions of the nineteenth century, to the fight against repression in the first and second world wars, to the foundation of the Union Solidarność, which finally led to independence. See, for example, Paczkowski 2003.

previously managed to stabilise the cultural and political system through a strategy of guaranteeing relative openness, was able – even in the years after 1968 – to regain peace and order. Music was part of this process. The Polish record company, Polskie Nagrania, which had made an effort in the 1960s to accommodate the taste for rock among the young, became an instrument of control for the state. In 1968, the Polish rock ensemble Blackout released a disc which included among others a song entitled "Te Bomby Lecą na nasz Dom" ("These Bombs Fly on our House"), which clearly alluded to the American Vietnam bombings. Like rock groups in the West, Blackout demanded the end of the war through its music and with that, showed a typical element of the Western '1968'. Blackout's position in regard to the Vietnam War was, however, in accordance with the official position of governments in the Eastern Bloc, who also denounced the American involvement in the Vietnam War. A rock group like Blackout that criticised the American action played *nolens volens* into the hands of the state, and from this it can be presumed that the group were officially condoned.[38]

A new generation of Polish bands such as Trubadurzy, Skałdowie and No to Co were also promoted by the state. They produced 'harmless' folk-influenced rock without a political edge. Maryla Rodowicz, who became the leading pop and folk music star of the 1970s, is a famous example of the generation of Polish rock musicians who began to professionalise themselves. Some rock musicians received state support and became emblematic of the Polish state. Czesław Niemen and his band, for instance, opened the 1972 Olympic Games in Munich, despite his surprisingly open critique in the song "Miraculous is this World", mentioned above. Niemen was able to effortlessly adapt himself to new political situations and new groups of listeners, and he became aligned with the state without losing his popularity.[39]

'1968' in Hungary

In Hungary, 1968 was not experienced as a radical breaking point, unlike in the CSSR. There was no uprising like there had been in 1956, even though the critical intelligentsia and opposition artists of the country supported the goals of the Prague Spring. However, there was a break in the development of Hungarian popular music in 1968. This becomes evident when the historical context since 1956 is taken into account. To restore calm in the country after 1956, the leadership began to 'loosen the reins', not simply

[38] Zieliński 2005, p. 87. [39] Gaszyński 2004.

through guarantees for greater freedom, but through establishing a system of censorship based on what might be characterised as 'institutionalised arbitrariness'. The system of censorship was based on the so-called 'three Ts' as each piece of art to be performed or exhibited and each literary work was examined by the censor's office and placed into one of three categories: *'tiltott'* (forbidden), *'támogatott'* (supported) and *'tűrt'* (tolerated). The last of these categories meant permanent legal uncertainty because a work with that stamp drifted between tolerated and forbidden, and the regime could discontinue its 'tolerance' at any time. A consequence of the system of 'three Ts' was that self-censorship (*öncenzura*) became common. Intellectuals, authors and musicians often tried to make sure that their creative work would at least be deemed *tűrt* if not *támogatott*. The relationship with the censors fundamentally affected the thought of the Hungarian opposition.[40]

In the 1960s, the establishment of a 'grey area' – an uncertain space between forbidden and permitted cultural expression – led slowly to the emergence of a decentralised rock scene. Small, local rock bands in schools and youth clubs sprang up and a few groups of national importance like Illés, Metró and Omega were also formed. These groups not only gave official performances but were also able to make music and recordings that provoked Hungarian society. The song "Még Fái Minden Csók" ("Every Kiss Still Hurts") by Illés caused a scandal in 1966 partly because of the singing style of the group: the lead singer Szörenyi sang the melody in chest voice, while the bassist sang along on the refrain in falsetto, and this produced an unconventional and challenging sound. The popularity of the group Illés was only rivalled by Omega, and this delivered a musical competition very similar to that between the Beatles and the Rolling Stones in the UK.

The Hungarian leaders regarded the events of 1968 in the West and East with concern. They were less concerned about Western influence or the adoption of ideas from the Western '1968' – this they could deal with. Indeed, the rise of Hungarian rock had a lot to do with the broadcasts of Radio Luxembourg directed at Hungary from the beginning of the 1960s and those in power wanted to oversee and channel this influence. They worried much more about the repercussions of the Prague Spring and feared another uprising by the people against a Hungarian regime that was obedient to Moscow, as had happened in 1956. It was a concrete goal of this regime to not allow such an event to occur again in Hungary.

---

[40] For further discussion of the censure system see the writings of Miklos Haraszti: *A Cenzura Eszetetikája* [*The Aesthetics of Censure*].

This concern steered the entire official decision-making process in Hungary until the collapse of socialist Hungary in the 1990s.[41]

In 1966 the Hungarian Communist Party had already introduced a new economic programme, the so-called 'new economic mechanism'.[42] Through this mechanism the Party aimed to provide the public with a better choice of consumer goods and with some freedoms, especially better travel opportunities, in order to help ensure public support for the Party. In contrast to Poland, the leadership in Hungary successfully avoided unrest with this strategy.

In 1968, the state still permitted rock concerts as it had done before 1968. However, it was not long before the limits of permitted freedoms were strained: rock musicians could not develop a musical infrastructure that was independent of the state and even officially permitted rock groups got into trouble.[43] For instance, when the group Illés openly criticised the Hungarian government during a stay in London they were met with a year-long performance ban and a fine on their return to Hungary. Illés' song "Sárga Rózsa" – with lyrics by János Bródy and music by Levente Szörényi – was also banned because the lyrics were understood by the censors as a condemnation of the state and an expression of Bródy's sadness about Hungary's participation in the invasion of Czechoslovakia, even though the lyrics used floral metaphors.[44] Illés disbanded in 1973 and events of this kind were the exception because self-censorship was very common. In general, rock musicians sought opportunities for work in the official, commercial sector because the state had effectively blocked the articulation of social and political problems in popular music.

In the 1970s the position of rock musicians and the state took a very different form: the musicians who had established themselves in the 1960s worked with communist cultural officials to help control Hungarian youth and the strategy of 'the three Ts' continued. Rock musicians increasingly conformed to state-supported socialist objectives. For example, the rock opera *Fictitious Report on an American Pop Festival*, which was based on a novel by Tibor Déry and performed in 1972 in Budapest, was a socialist rock opera that damned the capitalist rock scene.[45] Such socialist rock complied with the cultural views of the communist leadership and as a result rock changed from being a 'culture of protest' to a 'culture of acclamation'. By the end of the 1970s an open agreement had been reached between musicians and the state. Rock musicians were even granted great

---

[41] For information on the strategies of the regime and the secret services attitude towards rock, see Szőnyei and Sebes 2005.
[42] For information on Hungarian economics and politics in this period see Tőkés 1996.
[43] Szemere 2001, p. 33.   [44] Szemere 2001, p. 36.   [45] Ryback 1990.

privileges – for example some were given private houses in Rózsadomb, a quarter of Budapest – as an incentive for them to behave in a way that would help maintain the *status quo* of the socialist system.

In the early 1980s, however, the youth rebelled against the official scene in the form of the 'no future' generation, who were known as *csöves* (lit. 'pipes'). These young people distinguished themselves from their predecessors by adopting the ethos and the musical resistance that were evident in British punk rock.[46] Hungarian youth used popular music in the 1980s and 1990s as a means of expressing social resistance, and this is also evident in the Hungarian rap scene that developed during this period.[47] In Hungary, it is this generation of popular musicians that can be regarded as the heirs of the spirit of '1968', rather than rock musicians of the 1960s and 1970s.

Conclusion

The development of popular music in Czechoslovakia, Poland and Hungary was linked to the particular social situation in each country; it did not simply follow the West, even though rock music from Western countries, particularly from the US and the UK, functioned as a stylistic model. In the Eastern Bloc, the year 1968 was a turning point in the political, social and musical spheres as well as in the formation of a protest culture. This becomes evident when the situation in the 1960s is compared with the period after 1956, which marked the end of Stalinism.

The year 1956, which saw Khrushchev end the dispute over succession and begin the process of 'destalinisation', marked the beginning of social and musical change throughout the communist world. For musicians and their fans in the Eastern Bloc, musical activity was less about political engagement than about winning back individual and artistic freedoms and trying to ensure that artistic interests could be pursued without repression. In the following years, national rock scenes were established, but they still had to deal with repression and interference from the state. The socialist leaders in the Eastern Bloc tried various methods to integrate popular music into socialist society. Even in states where some freedom of musical expression was granted, as was the case of Poland, the state still asserted cultural control, not least because the ideological orientation of Western rock music was regarded as irreconcilable with the ideals of

---

[46] Szemere 2001, p. 39.   [47] Miklódy 2004, p. 197.

socialist society. The freedoms that were won back in 1956 could not be taken for granted and were permanently under threat.

The violent pacification of societies after the crushing of the Prague Spring created a 'climate of agony', which was strongest in Czechoslovakia, but which also extended to Poland and Hungary. In this climate, neither musicians nor their fans took the idea that music should be politicised. Rather, they sought refuge from the state's grasp by creating rock music scenes that enabled a degree of artistic autonomy and individual freedom. After 1968, if rock music in Eastern Bloc countries had tried to achieve political ends it would have had to conform to official political discourse. Protests like those seen in the West in the 1960s and early 1970s were not possible in the communist countries because they would have been stopped by the state authorities and the secret police. Due to the lack of opportunities for public activism, artists and musicians in the Eastern Bloc withdrew from participation in official discourse and instead established a parallel culture sphere with an alternative discourse. In this sense, '1968' in the Eastern Bloc was different from the West; Eastern Bloc musicians sought to establish a parallel space that was beyond the grasp of the state, whereas musicians in the West often aimed to protest and change society.

Nonetheless, the spirit of '1968' in the West had repercussions in the Eastern Bloc. Musicians tried to speak out about the protection of artistic freedom and commented ironically on the attempts by regimes to pacify societies. The adoption of the musical style of Western rock by groups in Czechoslovakia, Poland and Hungary was inherently political, because it symbolically demonstrated a move away from a political orientation centred on Moscow. Rock bands such as the Plastic People in Czechoslovakia established an alternative cultural milieu, which led to the development of oppositional structures. These structures had a decided political function and ultimately they contributed to the breakdown of the Eastern Bloc in 1989.

13 | Gendering '1968': womanhood in model works of the People's Republic of China and movie musicals of Hong Kong

HON-LUN YANG

Introduction

'1968', the year that rocked the world,[1] was marked by a profusion of protests and student movements, which led to social, political and cultural change worldwide.[2] Asia was not untouched by the zeitgeist and was 'rocked' by different upheavals. In the People's Republic of China, or PRC, there was a decade-long Cultural Revolution from 1966 to 1976,[3] and even though the Cultural Revolution was not directly related to the protests in the West due to communist China's isolation, there are some striking commonalities between the Cultural Revolution and the phenomenon of '1968'.[4] In the then British colony Hong Kong, there were two unprecedented riots in 1966 and 1967, which some commentators attributed to the supporters of the Cultural Revolution.[5] Whether or not the

---

[1] This phrase appears in the title of Mark Kurlansky's book *1968: The Year that Rocked the World* (2004).

[2] I would like to express my deepest gratitude to the editors of this volume for their detailed comments and suggestions, which have played an important part in the final shape of this chapter. I am also grateful to my colleague John Winzenburg for taking the time to read and comment on the chapter. Naturally, I am responsible for any imperfections in it. All the translations from Chinese to English are mine unless otherwise specified. In rendering the transliteration of Chinese names and titles into English, the Romanised pinyin system is used.

[3] The Cultural Revolution was initiated in August 1966 at Beijing University after a proclamation by Mao and the issuing of "Sixteen Guidelines" by the Chinese Communist Party (CCP). The mobilisation of students, workers and peasants soon escalated to a nationwide revolution, involving mass participation in protests and power struggles, which were played out at different levels of society and in every region of the country. Uncontrollable chaos ensued and continued for a decade. See Cushing and Tompkins 2007 for a summary of the Cultural Revolution.

[4] Dirlik 1998, p. 298.

[5] The first riot started as a series of peaceful demonstrations about the Star Ferry's fare hike, but later turned violent when rioters looted shops and attacked bystanders. The second riot, which escalated to uncontrollable violence that lasted for months, arose from a series of labour disputes over the working conditions of factory workers. The violence included terrorist attacks and bomb raids led by pro-communist rioters who utilised militia support from the PRC. The official death toll was fifty-one, although the actual number of fatalities was probably much higher. See Jones 2007, pp. 375–408, for further detail about the 1966 and 1967 riots, and Bickers and Yep 2009 for in-depth discussion of the 1967 riot.

unrest in the PRC and Hong Kong was directly related to the Western '1968' is perhaps not as important as the fact that it also led to profound social and cultural change.

The events of '1968' led to the development of countercultures and generational clashes, and also had a profound impact on gender relationships, not only in the West but also in the East. New gender-related ideals were captured in political and social movements but they were also evident in cultural forms such as music, films, novels and periodicals. As Frazier and Cohen point out,

> aesthetics and models of countercultural mobilisation and political change not only circulated (albeit unevenly) across continents but [ ] they were themselves gendered and sexualised. Juxtaposing political processes with gender and sexuality [ ] allows us to tease out the ways in which the often contradictory practices of the sixties relied on gender, sex, and sexuality, intertwined with liberatory political projects.[6]

Drawing on Frazier and Cohen's insight, I will suggest that two forms of music drama – the model works and movie musicals of the PRC and Hong Kong respectively – were reflections of the zeitgeist, particularly in their portrayal of womanhood. The model works were intended to be a new cultural form for a new socialist society, whereas movie musicals embodied the sentiments of a new generation. Both of these genres provided not only ideological indoctrination or visual pleasure for their spectators, they also projected aspirations for an alternative reality.[7] Such alternative reality, I argue, offers a unique perspective on the transformative power of '1968' as well as the interconnectivity of cultural forms as they were played out in different locales, here the PRC and Hong Kong. Rather than treating music as an agent in '1968' protests, I examine how the zeitgeist of '1968' was captured in cultural manifestations in the East and how the themes of model works and movie musicals intertwined and interacted with Chinese traditional culture and patriarchy.

Model works as a revolutionary genre

Model works, which were known in Chinese nomenclature as 'revolutionary model operas' (*gemin yangbanxi*), were the musical form that epitomised the Cultural Revolution. They included not just operas but also ballets

[6] Frazier and Cohen 2009, pp. 2–3.   [7] Mulvey 1975, p. 7.

and a symphonic work. Due to the predominance of the radical left and its cultural rhetoric at the time, traditional theatrical forms and Western instrumental works were condemned, and the creation of new forms and models for cultural practice was strongly supported by the Chinese Communist Party (CCP). They are credited as the brainchild of Mao Zedong's wife Jiang Qing, who, seizing the opportunity to be on the political stage, selected a number of pre-existing contemporary works with revolutionary themes and developed them into model works.[8] An official list of model works was released in Beijing in May 1967 to commemorate the twenty-fifth anniversary of Mao's "Talk at the Yan'an Forum".[9] This list included the following eight works: the Beijing operas *Shajiabang* (*Shajia Bang*), *The Red Lantern* (*Hongdeng Ji*), *Taking Tiger Mountain by Strategy* (*Zhiqu Huifushan*), *On the Docks* (*Haigang*) and *Raid on the White Tiger Regiment* (*Qixi Baihu Tuan*); the ballets *The White-haired Girl* (*Baimao Nu*) and *The Red Detachment of Women* (*Hongse Niangzijun*); and the *Revolutionary Symphony Shajiabang* (*Geming Jiaoxiangqu Shajia Bang*). These works received high levels of publicity and were accorded a sanctified status for edifying "Mao's revolutionary line on art and literature, serving workers, peasants, and soldiers, as well as proletarian politics".[10]

The model works were quite distinct from musical forms of the pre-1949, pre-communist period. On a musical level, the operatic model works were expected to introduce changes to local operatic genres and to demonstrate the possibility of synthesising Western and Chinese elements. As local operatic genres were largely based on well-defined and limited role types with musical motifs and styles associated with particular roles, which limited staging variations, they were ripe for modernisation.[11] No longer entirely dependent upon pre-existing tunes for the arias, new melodies were composed to best suit the character and dramatic situation, as in Western operas. The newly created works thus resulted in the mixing of different schools of singing as well as a more integrated art form with plots better supported by set design and drama.[12] While the singing style was largely traditional, the other musical elements drew on the Western operatic tradition: scores were written using

---

[8] The first reference to model works was in a news report on 6 December 1966 in the *People's Daily* titled "Carrying out Chairman Mao's Line on Literature and Art: Brilliant Models". See Hui 2010 for one of the most comprehensive discussions in Chinese language on the model works.

[9] Mao's "Talk at the Yan'an Forum" was delivered to cultural workers in Yan'an, the communist base camp in 1942. The Talk was treated as the primary cultural directive of the PRC until the country's economic reform after the Cultural Revolution. For more information on music as propaganda in the PRC, see Perris 1983 and McDougall 1984.

[10] News release on 16 July 1967 by Xinhua News Agency, mentioned in Bai 2010, p. 188.

[11] Clark 2010, p. 169.   [12] See Wang 1999, pp. 42–103.

Western staff notation, each work opened with an overture, instrumental accompaniments were a hybrid of traditional Beijing operatic and Western symphonic style, and new sonorities were created through a mixture of Western and Chinese instruments.[13] As Mittler notes, these new operas were "manifestations of a hybrid taste which calls for the transformation of Chinese tradition according to foreign standards, a taste which for more than a century has determined compositional practice in China".[14]

On an ideological level, the model works were propaganda: their clear objective was to propagate socialist ideology in order to counteract the themes found in traditional operas, which were criticised by Jiang Qing as being "only about emperors and generals, literati and beauty, and feudalism and capitalism".[15] Nonetheless, the genre's aspiration to place workers and peasants 'centre stage', featuring grass-roots protagonists was revolutionary,[16] which was in tune with the Zeitgeist of 1968. As Clark points out,

> these works were models, not solely for a new Chinese culture, but also for a new Chinese person. Behaviour, attitudes, and beliefs were to be modeled on those of the heroes in the new works. The self-sacrifice, cooperation, determination to succeed, devotion to the Chinese Communist Party and Chairman Mao, stoicism in adversity, and firm belief in the ultimate triumph of the cause were all model qualities of the men and women placed firmly centre stage in the model operas and ballets.[17]

Speaking with historical hindsight, Dirlik regards the Cultural Revolution as "an undertaking where the commitment to the creation of such a new culture was to assume the dimension not just of a moral but also of a religious imperative".[18] What was striking about the Cultural Revolution, as Dirlik suggests, was the moral fervour with which the party leaders addressed the problem of social division and alienation. For supporters of the radical left in the West, the Cultural Revolution provided an alternative revolutionary model for students who propelled the movements in '1968' in the PRC.[19] Others, however, have highlighted how the Cultural Revolution was deeply rooted in socio-political factors including policy disputes, party power struggles and conflicts among different factions of the society, and how culture was merely

---

[13] The East–West hybrid sonority anticipated the innovative work of later generations of renowned Chinese composers such as Tan Dun, Bright Sheng, Chen Qigang and Chen Yi. Mittler (2003) and Rao (2009) have both pointed out the influence of model works on the art music of this recent generation of Chinese composers.
[14] Mittler 2003, p. 53.   [15] Jiang 1967 (1964).
[16] Chinese scholars however tended to discard Jiang Qing's notion of "letting the workers, peasants and soldiers take the centre stage", regarding it as too radical, leftist a view. See Wang 1999, p. 8.
[17] Clark 2010, p. 171.   [18] Dirlik 1998, p. 300.
[19] Ronald Fraser, for instance, held such a view. See Fraser 1988, p. 322.

used as a pretext for political struggle and social change.[20] Radical cultural rhetoric such as "smashing the four olds" – old ideas, old culture, old customs and old habits – led to outlandish behaviour that caused the loss of many lives and the destruction of cultural artefacts, traditions and property. In that regard, the origin and impact of the Cultural Revolution were far more complex than other '1968' movements elsewhere and its product, the model works, were more radically experimental than any previous artistic reforms in China. As will be discussed below, radical experimentation in the model works included the development of new representations of womanhood.

New womanhood in the model works

How come my father and my uncle are not afraid of danger?
It is because they want to save China, save the poor, and defeat invaders.
When I think about it, I know I have to do such things and be like them.

The above lyrics are from the aria "Such is the Way to Lead a Life" ("Zuoren yao zuo Zheyang de Ren") sung by the female protagonist Li Tiemei in the model work *The Red Lantern*.[21] Li's aspiration to be like her uncle and father in order to help save the country bespeaks a new form of Chinese womanhood – the female is no longer a passive victim, but an active fighter, one who is strong, brave and selfless, one who does not shy away from being on equal terms with the other sex, and one who chooses to protect others rather than being protected. The fact that Li is self-conscious of her own role to be on equal terms with her male counterpart renders her different from women of the pre-Communist era. Her courage to continue the revolutionary mission left by her parents who have sacrificed their lives makes her a heroine, a prototype of new socialist woman.

The melody of Tiemei's aria befits her character. It opens with a rather slow and free passage which proceeds to a more determined and faster final part that soars high in the vocal register and makes use of extensive melisma, vividly evoking her determination to share her father's burden (Figure 13.1).

[20] Wang (2003, pp. 58–91) points out the complexity of the sources of the Cultural Revolution.
[21] The model work, *The Red Lantern*, has its origin in a movie as well as a version of a Beijing opera produced by the Harbin Beijing Opera Troupe. The aria "Such is the Way to Lead a Life" is from Scene 5 of the opera. The score entitled *Revolutionary Modern Beijing Opera: The Red Lantern* (*Geming xiandai jingju hongdengji*) was published by Renmin Chubanshe in 1970. The authorship of the score is attributed collectively to the Chinese Beijing Opera Troupe. For more information about the composition history of the work, see Shen 2004.

Figure 13.1 Excerpt of the Beijing opera aria "Such is the Way to Lead a Life" from *The Red Lantern*.

The musical style of this aria helps portray a strong character who is on an equal footing with her male counterparts, not least because this style of aria was traditionally reserved for male characters. In conventional Beijing opera practice, female and male characters had their own, separate melodic formulas. The female arias did not generally go up to a very high register or entail so much vocal melisma. Audiences familiar with the convention of Beijing opera would readily spot the uncommon melodic style of Tiemei. Indeed, Tiemei's arias borrowed features from male arias. A memoir about the history of the work makes clear that the director at the time believed that crossing the gender-based melodic formulas of operatic convention was the best way to musically express the emotion of the character.[22] Tiemei's characterisation and musical style are therefore innovative features that transcend traditional gender boundaries and the gender-based melodic style of Beijing opera.

All the female protagonists from the model works are prototypes of the kind of new womanhood that Li Tiemei embodies. These characters might have been victims of landlords who were often portrayed by the CCP as the embodiment of the patriarchal and enemy class, but they have all chosen the 'correct' communist path. The character Xi-er from the ballet *The White-haired Girl* is a classic example. She is the victim of misfortune and cruelty – her father is beaten to death, her fiancé is driven away and she is raped by her family's vicious landlord – and her character has been interpreted as a representation of the suffering of women in Chinese history.[23] Rather than taking her own life, however, she survives by dwelling in a cave and eating sacrificial food from a temple, and her hair turns white after years of not seeing sunlight. Cast as a proletariat heroine for her perseverance, in the end Xi-er is reunited with her fiancé and joins the Eighth Route Army, which liberates her village. Wu Qinghua from the ballet *The Red Detachment of Women* (*Hongse Niangzijun*) is another example. Persecuted by a wicked landlord, she finds her salvation after running away from forced imprisonment by her landlord and joins the army. During the course of the ballet, she learns from her superior the importance of putting the Party's larger mission, which was to liberate all the sufferers of injustice, above her own impulse to seek immediate revenge.

[22] Shen 2004, p. 78.
[23] Cheung (2010) interprets the suffering of Xi-er as a format of 'sounding bitterness' which is a type of communist political ritual. There are many adaptations of the white-haired girl legend which circulated in the left-wing region of the CCP in the 1930s and 1940s. The Western-style opera *The White-Haired Girl* was made in 1945, the earliest adaptation of the story. A movie adaptation was made in 1950 and a Beijing opera adaptation was made in 1958. The ballet adaptation was made by the Shanghai City Dance School in 1964 and premiered in 1965.

Aside from self-empowerment through joining the communist army as represented by the experiences of Xi-er and Wu Qinghua, female protagonists in model works were generally portrayed as brave, smart and capable. This is evident, for instance, in the following characters: Fang Haizhen from *On the Docks* (*Haigang*), Jiang Shuiying from *Ode to the Dragon River* (*Longjiang Song*) and Ke Xiang from *Azalea Mountain* (*Dujuan Shan*).[24] Fang Haizhen, a party secretary and supervisor of the docks, a job largely held by men, successfully prevents a scam perpetuated by an anti-party subordinate. Jiang Shuiying, also a party secretary, leads the villagers to a fight against drought, despite the interference of the male village leader Li Zhitian. Ke Xiang, likewise, is a ferocious communist warrior who leads her troops to numerous successful battles against enemies during the communist uprising. These protagonists are feminist figures, as Bai discusses: "its [the model works] feminism lies in its systematic construction of the heroic images of women against the background of Communist Party history, and of these women's strategic appropriation of class and political identities in order to escape from subordinate gender roles. Within a discourse of class struggle, model theatre creates a feminist utopia where androgyny, 'the only social form in which we [women] can live freely,' is very much prevalent."[25] Interestingly, a prototype of brave, smart and capable Chinese women is also found in the quite different context of Hong Kong movie musicals.

Movie musicals and new womanhood in Hong Kong

Long live the factory girls, oh, long live the factory girls!
In the factory, many capable women are supporting themselves,
Eager to make money,
Having fun together like sisters, making fun of each other.

The above lyrics from the song "Long Live the Factory Girls" ("Gongchang mei Wansui") from the 1969 movie musical *Her Tender Love* (*Lang ru Chunri Feng*) capture the essence of the new womanhood that was emerging in Hong Kong in the late 1960s. The song's glorification of factory life, while highly romanticised, epitomises a feministic outlook, which celebrated women's economic independence and self-sufficiency. The movie

---

[24] *Ode to the Dragon River* and *Azalea Mountain* were not among the original eight model works but were introduced after 1969. Both were Beijing operas.
[25] Bai, 2010, pp. 190–1.

star Connie Chan (Chen Baozhu), who played the main character in *Her Tender Love*, was one of the two most popular icons in Hong Kong at the time, the other being Josephine Siao (Xiao Fangfang).[26]

Chan and Siao were seen as the embodiment of a new form of female identity in Hong Kong.[27] The roles Chan and Siao played in movie musicals, which were known as 'youth movie musicals' (*qingchun gewupian*), projected a new form of womanhood not found in previous Hong Kong movies.[28] Female characters from the films of the 1950s and early 1960s were often portrayed as victims who typically had to endure either their husband's betrayal or their in-laws' rejection. If happiness finally came, it was because of their virtue, their patience and tolerance of the injustice done to them. It was thus sympathy rather than aspiration that was elicited from the viewer.[29] The characters played by Chan and Siao were different. They were not victims but rather victors in relationships as they were often cast as girl friends of good men rather than wives and mothers, and they generally did not have to make the kind of sacrifices that their on-screen predecessors had to. They won over their audience not because of their suffering but because of their 'modern' attributes. They were not only fashionable, confident and self-assured but also articulate and educated, and their talents at singing and dancing were iconic of the new youth culture.[30]

Hong Kong movie musicals with singing and dancing in Cantonese dialects emerged in 1966, the same year that the Cultural Revolution was initiated.[31] Although movie musicals only flourished for three years from 1966 to 1969, at least a few dozen films of this genre were produced during this short period.[32] Not merely films with inserted songs and/or dances, the movie musical genre is characterised by integrated and non-integrated song-and-dance sequences, which temporarily suspend the story line, allowing viewers to move between diegesis and non-diegesis.[33] The changes

---

[26] See Ku 1997 and Law 1996.   [27] See Anonymous 1996.

[28] Although they are indebted to the influence of Hollywood movie musicals, Cantonese movie musicals of Hong Kong from the late 1960s are quite distinct in that the number of songs in each film is smaller and songs have different origins. For more information on the musical aspects of the genre, see Wu 2006, and Wu and Liu 2007.

[29] Law 1996, p. 88.

[30] For more information on Hong Kong movies of the 1950s and 1960s, see Teo 1996.

[31] The first Cantonese movie musicals were *Movie-Fan Princess* and *Colourful Youth*, both produced in 1966.

[32] The classification of the genre of Cantonese films is not always precise. While Wu, Chen and Lino (2007) suggest that there were a total of forty-six youth movie musicals in her study of Cantonese musical films, some of the works that fit her category are listed as 'melodramas' in the Hong Kong Film Archive's catalogue.

[33] Laing 2000, p. 5.

in the mode of presentation from speaking to singing therefore serve various narrative and expressive purposes. While some of the songs are non-integrated in that they are sung by one of the characters as a performance number, a handful are integrated into the filmic narrative. In such cases, the characters shift to singing as a way of heightening emotional expression.

Just as the format of the model works – especially the genre of the Beijing opera – was not entirely alien to the broad masses of the PRC, Hong Kong movie musicals demonstrated certain parallels to other movie genres that were popular at the time.[34] Unlike the model works, they were not politically or ideologically driven. Instead, their emergence coincided with economic development in the colony thanks to the entrepreneurs who escaped from the mainland after 1949. There was almost a six-fold increase in the number of factories and workers in just one-and-a-half decades from the early 1950s to the mid-1960s. The intense industrialisation provided increased employment opportunities for women, but such economic opportunity was grounded in patriarchy in that most families "responded to the new possibilities of social advancement by placing differential premiums on sons and daughters", as the sociologist Chun-Hung Ng points out.[35] While sons were seen as assets to invest in, daughters were utilised for immediate economic gain. Many young women started work at an early age to support their families so their brothers could go to school, and these women made up the main audience of movie musicals.

The movie musicals were targeted at young women who had gained a certain degree of economic independence as factory workers and who went to the cinema to have a vicarious experience of the lifestyle of their idols.[36] The lives of factory workers were mundane, but in films Chan and Siao played characters such as factory workers, students, clerks, private tutors, movie stars, singers, dancers, flight attendants and reporters, who engaged

---

[34] Such genres included Mandarin movie musicals, Cantonese opera films (adapted from traditional Cantonese operatic repertoire with characters wearing stage attire) and Cantonese singing films (with Cantonese operatic-style songs inserted into an otherwise contemporary setting and story).

[35] Ng 2004, p. 235.

[36] One film critic wrote about his movie-going experience in 1966: "One evening, I went to see a re-run of 'Girls Are Flowers' (*Guniang shiba yiduo hua*). It was a full house. I at last got a ticket. In the movie theatre, I felt that I was too old as I was surrounded by burgeoning teenagers. They were anxious as well as excited, as though expecting something. When Chen Baozhu's name appeared on the screen, they screamed. They must have watched the film many times based on the way they chit-chat non-stop the entire time. I was so moved and wished that I were one of them. To be able to love [one's idol] wholeheartedly is a blessing." Originally published in *Chinese Youth Weekly* (*Zhongguo xuesheng zhoubao*), 16 December 1966, p. 11, reprinted in Law 1996, 88.

in leisure pursuits such as cycling, basketball, bowling, partying and sightseeing. Although many of the working girls had little leisure time in real life, they could aspire to these middle-class activities through watching their cinema idols and their eyes were opened to the spirit of the new era.[37] Many young women saw their aspirations realised in roles played by Chan and Siao, and this confirms Stacey's notion that movie-going is often a form of escapism.[38]

The youth culture of the 1960s is perhaps most strongly evident in the song-and-dance sequences of movie musicals in which the protagonists perform songs that praise the spirit of the youth. For instance, the song "Youth A-go-go" ("Qingchun Agege") from the 1968 movie *A Romantic Thief* (*Duoqing Miaozei*), which is sung by Connie Chan's character at a nightclub, carries the following lyrics: "youthfulness never fades away, so keep practicing a-go-go". Similarly, the song "I Love A-go-go" ("Wo ai Agege"), which is sung by Josephine Siao in the 1967 movie of the same name, has similar lyrics about everyone enthusiastically dancing the a-go-go. Both of these songs were covers of Western pop songs that were extremely popular at the time,[39] and they were seen as the embodiment of the 'swinging 60s' in the West.

New womanhood and patriarchy

The zeitgeist of '1968' was embodied in PRC model works and Hong Kong movie musicals alike, although they were based on entirely different ideologies: radical leftist ideals of class/gender equality and counterculture sentiments respectively. It would be mistaken, however, to presume that Chinese traditional values and patriarchy gave way to the new era overnight. In fact, negotiation between tradition and modernity, between old values and new aspirations, between patriarchy and modern womanhood, was evident in the 1960s and has continued ever since. Although women were given important roles in both model works and movie musicals, a careful study of these characters reveals that the grip of patriarchy is still present.

In Hong Kong movie musicals, the female characters operate in a male-dominated society, no matter how 'chic' and 'modern' they may appear.

---

[37] Such a notion is suggested by Ku 1997 and Law 1996. [38] See Stacey 1994, pp. 80–125.
[39] "Youth A-go-go" is a cover of Harry Belafonte's "Day-O" ("The Banana Boat Song"), though the sequence in the movie suggests that it was influenced by a version of the song by the folk group Tarriers, which was released in 1956. "I Love A-go-go" is a cover of The McCoys's well-known song "Hang on Sloopy", released in 1965.

Their thoughts and actions are ingrained with the value system of patriarchy. For example, Siao's character in the 1966 film *Young Lady's Heart* (*Shaonu Xin*) is a professional reporter. However, her total devotion to a poor student she loves conforms to the gender stereotypical that women should always sacrifice themselves for men. To help her lover, she pretends to be a spoiled teenager who needs tutoring, in order to giver her lover a tutorial job. To secure the means to pay for the tutorial fees, she takes on a singing job at a nightclub. Even though Siao's impersonation of a teenager is exploited for comic effect and provides an opportunity to show off her singing and dancing talents, Siao's character reveals a sense of lack, as though she would be incomplete without her lover. She not only helps him, but hides her good deeds in order to avoid hurting his feelings and pride. Later in the film, when he is forced to become a smuggler because of his dire circumstances, Siao's character forgives him and tries to rescue him from his downfall.

In a similar way, the character played by Chan in *Her Tender Love* takes up a factory job in order to help her lover finish his university education. She is also exploited by her own evil brother: he steals her money, tricks her to take on his debt and encourages a womaniser to take advantage of her in exchange for money. Despite her brother's maltreatment, she still forgives him, which renders her the embodiment of womanly virtues, in a similar way to Siao's character in *Young Lady's Heart*. Even though Chan's character is a modern woman and factory worker who is strong and smart, she is not able to prevent the exploitation of her body and when she has the option of letting her lover support her, she chooses to sacrifice herself in order to ensure his advancement.

The sequence in *Her Tender Love* in which the song "Long Live the Factory Girls" is sung vividly reveals the contradictions and ambiguities in Hong Kong's new womanhood in the 1960s (see Figure 13.2). The song is performed by Chan's roommates after Chan shares with them her worry about not being able to fit in with her fiancé's friends if she attends the Christmas party at his university. The clash of different social and class values is embodied in the arrangement of the song itself. The fact that the song is scored for a combination of Chinese and Western instruments is symbolic, and is intensified by Chan's singing, which sounds very 'Chinese' due to her earlier training in Cantonese opera. The setting of the modern, forward-looking lyrics to a Chinese-style melody in the *sol* mode is a striking juxtaposition. On a different level, there is also a contradiction between women being hailed for their economic independence in the song's lyrics and their subjugation to the ideals of traditional womanly virtue, which includes being submissive and self-sacrificing.

Figure 13.2 "Long Live the Factory Girls" from the movie musical *Her Tender Love*.

In the same vein, the female protagonists of the model works, even though they were devised as a kind of prototype of the new socialist woman, were not free from the grip of state patriarchy. The way in which the plot of *Shajiabang* was revised is a case in point. Originating from a Shanghainese opera, the drama revolved around the underground female worker, Ah Xingshao, who uses her cunning to rescue a troop of communist soldiers.[40] However, changes were made to the story of *Shajiabang* in the making of the model opera because of Jiang Qing's concern that the original work did not have a communist hero as the leading character, which contravened the 'three prominences' (*san tuchu*) principle.[41] In the process of reworking *Shajiabang* as a model work, the dramatic importance of the male protagonist Guo Jianguang was therefore elevated by giving him (as well as his comrades) additional arias to draw attention to his character.

---

[40] Like the other model works, *Shajiabang* has a convoluted history. It originated as a 1957 novel about a group of volunteers' battle against the Japanese at the Shajia village. It was then made into a Shanghai opera with the new title *Ludang Huozhong* in 1959. It was adapted as a Beijing opera in 1964 prior to being sanctified as a model work.

[41] The 'three prominences' was an ideological principle that guided the making of the model works. This principle dictated that characters of the highest political standing, the so-called prominent heroic characters, must be given the most prominent position both visually and musically. The heroic characters of a lesser political standing would be given slightly less visual and musical emphasis than the prominent heroic characters but more emphasis than the normal 'good' characters. The 'three prominences' ensured that the audience could readily distinguish the political as well as ideological hierarchy of the characters. See Hui 2010, pp. 57–8.

Reportedly, this revision was made because Guo Jianguang could not be outshone by a female protagonist who had a lower political status.[42] Even if the revision itself was driven by political rather than gender issues, its consequence was the same: the female protagonist was again subordinated to the male one.

The ideal embodied in the female protagonists of the model works was that women in socialist China were capable of 'holding up half of the sky'. As Yang has argued, however, achieving such a status for women involves gender erasure.[43] The female protagonists in the model works, for instance, were constructed to show little or no femininity: they were invariably portrayed like their male counterparts with their eyes filled with hatred and with 'clenched fists'. Tani Barlow also argues that the state's efforts to promote a new form of socialist womanhood was exclusively due to the need for mass mobilisation, which was required to speed up the process of industrialisation and to rebuild the country after decades of war and unrest.[44] While it is the case that in socialist China after 1949 women were 'liberated' in the sense that they were granted equal rights with men in the political, economic, cultural, educational and social domain, they were nonetheless subjugated to the political ideology of the state. The following reflection by the female film director Shuqin Huang is illuminating about the nature of state patriarchy:

both the Cultural Revolution and the commercialised society [of the post CR era] have been based on male power. In this respect, they are the same. The [only] difference is that during the Cultural Revolution, men wanted women to become masculinised [whereas] in [the] commercial society nowadays, men want women to become feminised.[45]

Indeed, until women are free to make their decisions on what gender image to project, they remain under the shadow of patriarchy. One of the hallmarks of the Cultural Revolution was the unisex blue-and-grey attire for both men and women,[46] and wearing dresses or putting on makeup was branded as petit-bourgeois and prohibited. Female protagonists of the model works were, then, prototypes of new socialist women, but this new representation of womanhood was imposed by the state rather than being initiated by women themselves.

---

[42] Reminiscent of Cengqi Wang mentioned in Fu 2002, p. 130.   [43] Yang, 1999, p. 40.
[44] Barlow 1994, p. 270.   [45] Quoted in Yang, 1999, 35.   [46] See Yang, 1999, p. 40.

Conclusion

China is a country with a long history of patriarchy. Until the New Culture movement in the 1920s, which brought about some changes in gender relations, women's sphere was limited to the home. Even into the 1960s, women's status in society was not on an equal footing with men and they did not engage in the same professions as men. In this context, the degendered portrayal of womanhood in the model works of the Cultural Revolution is very forward looking, even though political motivation and state patriarchy were key factors in the creation of these works. In quite different ways to the model works, the female characters of Hong Kong movie musicals are feminist in that they are resilient and persistent in pursuing their dreams, even though their dreams are often connected to helping the men they love. Despite often being subjugated to the womanly virtues of patriarchy, the female protagonists of the movie musicals radiate a sense of self-esteem and self-reliance, which is a quintessential trait of the new type of womanhood that the post-1968 feminists aspired to.[47] In this respect, the aria "Such is the Way to Lead a Life" from the model work *The Red Lantern* and the movie musical song "Long Live the Factory Girls" are emblematic of the gender aspirations of '1968'. The model works and Hong Kong movie musicals did not directly document the Cultural Revolution in the People's Republic of China or the riots in Hong Kong respectively, and they emerged in contexts that were far removed from the centre of '1968' protests. Nonetheless, the female protagonists in both the model works and movie musical captured different gendered aspects of the zeitgeist of '1968'.

---

[47] It is interesting to note that the representations of women in movies in the West did not necessarily reflect the changes in the status of women during the 1960s and 1970s. Haskell's seminal monograph about women in the movies, for instance, observes that, in contrast to the strong spirit of revolt of the women's movement in the early 1970s, there was not a "corresponding influx of bold and defiantly up-to-date screen women" in the movies of the 1960s or 1970s in the West (Haskell 1987 (1974), p. vii.). Haskell considered the male-dominated movie industry to be the main cause of this. With that in mind, it is not entirely far-fetched to suggest that model works of the PRC and movie musicals of Hong Kong were relatively forward looking in their portrayal of new forms of womanhood.

14 | A revolution in sheep's wool stockings: early music and '1968'

KAILAN R. RUBINOFF

What could '1968' mean to historical performers, who aim to recreate the music of the distant past by reconstructing old playing techniques, reviving period instruments and studying treatises, early manuscripts and printed editions?[1] Could musicians interested in early music – Bach, Corelli, Machaut et al. – be at all relevant to a period marked by the rhetoric of renewal, revolution and progressive change? Accounts of 1960s music typically describe electric guitars and electronics, not crumhorns and harpsichords.[2]

Yet, it is not only producers of *new* music – popular, jazz and contemporary 'art' musicians – who were active circa 1968. The late 1960s also resonate for Early Musicians, or historical performers,[3] who sometimes reflect nostalgically on this era as a Golden Age of the Early Music movement – 'movement' here connoting a social movement, not just a way of making music. HIP, a common acronym for historically informed performance, further highlights Early Music's associations with hipness and hippies, its "'brown rice and sandals' image",[4] and its embracing of an alternative lifestyle. The implication is that HIP musicians, like hippies, advocated simplicity, authenticity and purity – from footwear (Birkenstock sandals and woolly socks), to consumption of whole foods (brown rice and granola), to pursuing pared-down, 'authentic' performances on period instruments strung with natural gut.

The Early Music revival, however, long predates the hippie counterculture. In the early twentieth century, pioneers such as Arnold

---

[1] Earlier versions of this paper were read at the University of North Carolina at Greensboro (UNCG) and the Sixth Biennial International Conference on Music Since 1900 (2009). I gratefully acknowledge support from UNCG New Faculty, Summer Excellence and Kohler Fund grants. I thank also the historical performers who consented to be interviewed and/or corresponded with me via email. The interpretations and opinions expressed in this article, however, represent my own perspective.

[2] E.g. Kurlansky 2004, pp. 181–3; 188–9.

[3] I use the capitalised 'Early Music' (following Dreyfus 1983) throughout to refer to historical performers, i.e. musicians engaged in recreating the music of the past using period instruments. For more on defining this community, see Rubinoff 2006, pp. 4–9.

[4] Perlman 1998, p. 36. Similarly, Cohen and Snitzer (1985, p. 99) refer to HIP's early practitioners as "dulcimer-strumming flower children".

Dolmetsch, Wanda Landowska, Safford Cape and August Wenzinger explored early instruments and repertoire.[5] By the 1920s and 1930s, the Collegium Musicum in German universities and the amateur *hausmusik* movement were increasing public awareness of pre-1800 music and instruments such as harpsichords, viols and recorders. Moreover, numerous recordings on period instruments from the early twentieth century belie the common perception that Early Music developed in the 1960s.[6]

Nevertheless, HIP is often associated with '1968' in popular and scholarly accounts of the Early Music movement, which frequently employ the language of counterculture, protest and rebellion typical of '68ers. As John Butt remarked, "many involved in the movement during the seminal decades of the 1960s and 70s were, in fact, counter-cultural [ ] seeing in HIP a way of redeeming music from its elitist and hierarchical connotations".[7] Thomas Kelly likewise connects HIP to 1960s protest and counter-culture movements and the folk music revival, noting that, "to the extent that early music was seen as non-traditional, and participatory (there were, and are, a great many summer workshops where early music is played), it could be seen as part of a cultural trend toward music of the people, music without pretense, music that expresses a general union of popular and learned".[8] Baroque flutist Barthold Kuijken connected his own involvement with HIP to the 'spirit of 1968' in a recent interview:

at the same time, the early music movement was growing in Europe. My older brothers [Sigiswald and Wieland] were playing early instruments already, and though I did not feel that I should necessarily do the same as they did, I was still very much interested. Also, the time was right: the end of the 1960s just after the famous Paris student revolt of May 1968, when there was a whole new wind blowing – of discovering things, of freshening, of doing things for yourself, not necessarily blindly believing authority. I was sitting in the middle of all that.[9]

To some observers, the generation of performers emerging in the 1960s represented not only an alternative musical culture but also a sort of *avant-garde* whose approach to playing early music was revolutionary. In his 1983 article "Early Music Defended against Its Devotees", Laurence Dreyfus engages with Theodor Adorno's scathing critique of the fledgling historical performance movement of the 1950s,[10] countering that Adorno "did not

---

[5] Haskell 1996 (1988); Brown 1988. Both Cape and Wenzinger continued teaching and performing in the postwar period.
[6] Philip 2004, p. 204.   [7] Butt 2002, p. 9.   [8] Kelly 2011, p. 3.
[9] Quoted in Hook 2004, p. 32.
[10] Adorno 1967. This text first appeared in German in 1951 (reprinted in *Prismen*, 1955).

know Early Music as it blossomed in the late 1960s and 1970s".[11] The latter period, Dreyfus argues, was marked by "The Revolt of the Advance Guard" – Gustav Leonhardt, the Kuijken brothers, Frans Brüggen and Anner Bylsma – who "created an inimitable antistyle" of Baroque performance.[12] Nicholas Kenyon, in discussing this revolutionary 1960s Early Music cohort, includes David Munrow and Nikolaus Harnoncourt, remarking that, "two very different activities can be seen as achieving popular recognition at almost exactly the same time around 1968: first the revival of forgotten repertories played on unfamiliar instruments, and second the performance of familiar repertories from the past in a radically different manner". He cites Harnoncourt's 1968 recording of J. S. Bach's B Minor Mass[13] as especially ground-breaking.[14] Neal Zaslaw concurred, stating that Harnoncourt's "performance sounded light, brilliant, fast – *it rocked*! [ ] Harnoncourt's historicisation or recontextualisation of a recognised masterpiece proved to be a subversive act."[15] Zaslaw compares 'authentic' performances of Baroque music with the genre associated with 1960s rebellion and revolt: rock.

Acknowledgement of the 1960s' importance to HIP is so widespread as to suggest more than mythologising. Yet to what degree could a movement that is essentially retrospective in repertoire also be progressive aesthetically and politically? How do musicians who lived through this period interpret its importance?

To address these questions, I focus on the Netherlands, the UK and the US – Early Music's emergent postwar centres – drawing on programmes, reviews and other documents, and personal interviews I conducted with musicians active during the 1960s. The 'long 1968' (circa 1965 to 1975) was transitional; HIP concerts flourished and period instruments were widely adopted. This critical mass of activity increased HIP's visibility, thus accounting for a lingering popular (mis)perception that historical performance emerged in the 1960s. At the same time, HIP's association with leftist causes, education and concert life reform movements led to its perception as radical or revolutionary, though the actual political beliefs of performers and audience members varied. HIP's growth in the late 1960s was part of a

---

[11] Dreyfus 1983, p. 310. See also "The Avant-garde of the Distant Past" in Cohen and Snitzer 1985, pp. 3–10.
[12] Dreyfus 1983, p. 320. He again references the late 1960s and early 1970s – and this group of Low Countries performers – in Dreyfus *et al.* 1992, p. 115.
[13] Bach 1968.
[14] Kenyon 1988, pp. 2–4. Brown (1988, p. 50) also associates Early Music with radicalism.
[15] Zaslaw 2001, p. 9. Emphasis in original. See also Haynes 2007, p. 45.

broader interest in the music cultures of the past, coupled with a questioning of traditional means of engaging with them – a process of interrogating authoritarian structures historical performers shared with many '68ers, including contemporary composers, students and anti-war demonstrators.

(Period) instruments of change

The Early Music movement in the 1960s was undergoing what can only be termed a paradigm shift. Historical performers increasingly turned their attention from the mere rediscovery and revival of hitherto unknown repertoire towards a new philosophical approach to its performance: they aimed to reconstruct early music 'authentically', as it might have sounded to the composer.

This "authenticity revolution of the 1960s", as Bruce Haynes termed it, was central to HIP's association with rebellion and revolt, and to its success with audiences. "In the 1960s," he remarks, "it is doubtful whether a movement could have had credibility if it did not have an element of protest and revolution about it. A mainspring of HIP in the 1960s was a rejection of the status quo."[16] Thus, to play 'authentically' was to revolt against mainstream classical musicians, who performed all musical works using the same playing techniques regardless of the period in which they were composed.[17]

Leading historical performers of the 1960s demonstrated their allegiance to an authenticity aesthetic by adopting period instruments or more faithful historical copies.[18] Harpsichordist Gustav Leonhardt, who began his career as a recording artist in the mid-1950s,[19] released an influential LP entitled *Harpsichord Music on Original Instruments* in 1967.[20] He allied himself

---

[16] Haynes 2007, pp. 40–1. Bruce Haynes, Baroque oboist, recorder player and scholar, wrote extensively about HIP in his book *The End of Early Music*. In an interview in 2008, Haynes generously shared his recollections about Early Music in the 1960s with me, providing a rich personal history that profoundly shaped this article. His passing in May 2011 was a tremendous loss to the HIP community.

[17] Haynes (2007, pp. 48–64) describes this mainstream style as "strait" or "chronocentric", marked by literal interpretation of scores, continuous vibrato, legato phrasing, rigid tempi and lack of metrical hierarchy.

[18] By the 1980s, the issue of authenticity in performance came to a head, as scholars and performers alike debated its meaning, merits and practicality (e.g. Kenyon 1988 and Taruskin 1995). Some argued that 'authentic performance' was being used as a vapid marketing label by record companies and the press, a practice dating from the late 1960s (Fabian 2001 pp. 159–60). As Haynes (2007, p. 10) remarked, "[t]here was a time when 'authentic' sold records like 'ORGANIC' sells tomatoes".

[19] Leonhardt 1953.   [20] Leonhardt 1967.

with the builder Martin Skowroneck, whose handcrafted instruments had a timbre and mechanism unlike the mass-produced harpsichords available in pre-war Germany, or the cast iron-framed Pleyel harpsichords of Landowska. In 1964, Frans Brüggen likewise began concertising on original recorders and hand-crafted copies at the 'Baroque pitch' of A-415Hz by the Dutch workshop of Hans Coolsma.[21]

String players also began adopting period instruments. In the Low Countries, Sigiswald Kuijken was among the first violinists to play without shoulder and chin rests, beginning in 1965; by 1969 he made his first attempts at chin-off playing.[22] Lucy van Dael also began using a Baroque violin bow and eventually a Baroque violin while a student at the Royal Conservatory in The Hague. In 1968, she became the first Dutch violinist to play her final exam on both Baroque and modern violins, a feat that raised some eyebrows.[23] By the late 1960s, it was possible to marshal an entire orchestra of period-instrument players, as shown in Jean-Marie Straub and Danièle Huillet's 1968 film *Chronicle of Anna Magdalena Bach*.[24] The use of period instruments in this avant-garde art film further contributed to HIP's perceived 'alternative' status.

The adoption of period instruments coincided with increasing musicological performance practice scholarship.[25] Many treatises and primary sources were translated, published and disseminated for the first time in the 1950s and 1960s,[26] and performance practice manuals, comparing and synthesising primary sources, also appeared.[27] The journal *Early Music*, established in 1973, provided a forum for performers and scholars to respond to each other's writings, performances and recordings in ways that were not previously possible. Like the '68ers, HIP challenged 'ivory tower' elitism by making scholarship more accessible through practical applications like performance. Embracing the spirit of experimentation and discovery, musicians felt empowered to 'be their own musicologist',

---

[21] E. H. 1965; Haynes 2007, p. 44; Haynes 2008.
[22] Van der Klis 1991, pp. 158–9. 'Chin-off' players rest the violin on the shoulder instead of holding it under their chin.
[23] Van Dael 2004.
[24] Instead of actors or mainstream musicians, Straub and Huillet engaged historical performers (Leonhardt, Harnoncourt, Concentus Musicus Wien and the Schola Cantorum Basiliensis) to play Bach's music using period instruments and costumes (Rubinoff 2011).
[25] Taruskin (1995, p. 43) dates the origins of what he terms the "performance-practice movement" to the early 1960s, and to a positivist or scientific approach to music studies.
[26] Norrington 2009. English translations of treatises (dates in parentheses) include Leopold Mozart (1948), Quantz (1966), C. P. E. Bach (1949), Bénigne de Bacilly (1968), Jean-Antoine Bérard (1969), Pier Francesco Tosi (1968) and Johann Friedrich Agricola's translation of Tosi (1966).
[27] E.g., Dart 1967; Dolmetsch 1969; Donington 1974 (1963); Neumann 1978.

reading primary sources themselves as guides to interpretive practice. This do-it-yourself ethos even extended to instrument-building. Haynes, having trained as a recorder maker with Friedrich von Huene from 1967 through 1969, was obliged to construct his own Baroque oboe after studying surviving models in museums and private collections. As he remarked, "[t]hat was the only alternative. I couldn't afford to buy an old one, and I couldn't find anybody else who could make one for me."[28]

Old instruments, new technologies

The turn towards period instruments – a deliberately archaic technology – seems incongruous with a decade known for its technological innovations, e.g. space exploration, lasers and colour television. In part, HIP's adoption of period instruments represented a rejection of the modernist narrative of progress, an evolutionary view that imagined music – and instruments – had gradually become perfected over time.[29] Instead of viewing the Steinway piano as a clearly superior descendent of the 'primitive' Ruckers harpsichord, HIP considered the latter instrument as equally sophisticated. Such a critical view of modernity resonates with the broader questioning of science and technology by 1960s protest and counterculture movements, as expressed through anti-war and anti-nuclear demonstrations, environmentalism and interest in natural foods.

Yet HIP's simultaneous embrace of other 1960s technologies, especially recording innovations, suggests a more complex relationship with technology and modernity. Recording companies, including EMI, Decca and Telefunken, burgeoned in the postwar period, benefiting from developments such as stereo LPs, magnetic tape and multitrack recording; they became key promoters of HIP.

Munrow and the Early Music Consort of London (established in 1967), developed an international reputation through recordings, mostly made in EMI's Abbey Road studios (of Beatles fame).[30] Munrow's high technical standards and showmanship qualities made Renaissance and Medieval music entertaining to general audiences; his popular BBC radio programme "Pied Piper" ran daily from 1971 until his death in 1976. Decca also became involved in HIP when Peter Wadland took over their associate label

---

[28] Haynes 2008. [29] Haynes 2007, p. 7.
[30] Bowman 2009. Bowman noted that Angel distributed these recordings in the US, building the ensemble's reputation abroad and serving as publicity for acquiring concert engagements.

L'Oiseau-Lyre in 1968. Under the Florilegium series, Wadland recorded numerous HIP musicians, including James Tyler and Anthony Rooley, the Consort of Musicke (established by Rooley and Tyler in 1969), Emma Kirkby, Christopher Hogwood and the Academy of Ancient Music (established in 1973).[31]

While Decca and EMI producers were recording medieval and Renaissance music, Wolf Erichson of Telefunken focused on later repertoire.[32] He began producing recordings of J. S. Bach and other Baroque composers with Leonhardt in 1962, with Harnoncourt's Concentus Musicus Wien in 1963, and with Bylsma, Brüggen and the Kuijken brothers soon afterwards. Released on Das Alte Werk, these recordings culminated in Leonhardt and Harnoncourt's Bach cantata project (1971–90), the first complete set using period instruments and boys' voices.

Telefunken demonstrated its marketing savvy by promoting Frans Brüggen, the first recorder player to become an international superstar. Between 1966 and 1971, Brüggen recorded the four-volume series *Recorder Music on Original Instruments*, with recorders from museums and his private collection. The first three volumes were reissued with a pin-up publicity poster.[33] As Cohen and Snitzer remark,

> around 1968 Telefunken, which was releasing solo recitals by Brüggen on a regular basis, began packaging a poster-size photograph of their star with some of his albums. The handsome virtuoso, heavy-lidded and weary of this mortal frame, gazed out from the photo, past the solicitations of his adoring fans, toward some profound and mysteriously burdensome Unknown. Large numbers of artistic and sensitive young ladies affixed the poster to their bedroom walls.[34]

Thus, the highlighting of historical recorders and Brüggen's physical attractiveness together formed a significant component of Telefunken's advertising campaign.[35] Such mass marketing increased audiences while also complicating HIP's idealistic associations with authenticity and non-commercially mediated expression.

---

[31] Robins 1996.
[32] For a complete discography of Erichson's Telefunken recordings (1960–72) see Otto and Piendl 2007, pp. 258–60. These were marketed through a joint Telefunken/Decca venture (Teldec). Erichson also recorded medieval music with the Studio der Frühen Musik.
[33] These were released as Vol. 1 (SAWT-9482 A, 1966), Vol. 2 (SAWT-9545 A, 1969), Vol. 3 (SAWT-9582 A, 1969 [1971]) and Vol. 4 (SAWT 9511-B, 1968).
[34] Cohen and Snitzer 1985, p. 61. Tellingly, Cohen associates this album with 1968, although it was actually released in the US four years later (Brüggen 1972). Cohen, a lutenist and conductor, assumed the direction of the Boston Camerata in 1968.
[35] Ehrlich 1993.

Not only were historical performers garnering major recording contracts and impressive sales figures, but by tackling mainstream repertoire, they also moved from the fringes into the forefront of critical and aesthetic debates.[36] For HIP and conventional classical musicians, the music of Bach and the Baroque became a contested territory.

Discussions about HIP appeared in both popular and scholarly presses. In 1968, *Hifi Stereophonie* featured articles on harpsichord reproduction by Skowroneck.[37] This German audiophile magazine, replete with advertisements for the latest stereo equipment, seems a peculiar venue for essays on historical instrument-building. Yet it not only demonstrates increasing public interest in Early Music (HIP recording reviews were common in this periodical): it is also indicative that by 1968 *historical fidelity* in performance practice was strongly correlated with *high fidelity* in sound reproduction. In other words, *Hifi Stereophonie* implies, not only would a good listener want to hear every note in the score – they should also want to hear every note exactly as it might have sounded to the composer. Historical fidelity and high fidelity were thus two sides of the same authenticity coin.

Bridging high and popular culture

For historical performers, the adoption of period instruments was an aesthetic and philosophical choice, but it was also a visible and audible sign of difference separating them from mainstream musicians. At the same time, the use of hand-crafted, more faithful historical copies also distinguished professional players from amateur musicians. If some performers argued for the inclusivity of HIP's amateur component, goals in line with '68ers promoting participatory democracy and grass-roots engagement,[38] others were uncomfortable with such dilettantish associations. As playing standards on early instruments rose (spurred in part by the pursuit of perfection on recordings), the gulf between amateur and professional players widened.

In the Netherlands, Brüggen sought to create a new image of the recorder distinct from its association with children, *huismuziek*,[39] and other professionals like Carl Dolmetsch. Dolmetsch played on a modernised recorder with a fingering system his father Arnold developed. While the Dolmetsch

---

[36] For Das Alte Werk sales figures, see Horowitz 1973. Lee Hofberg, manager of London Imports (distributor of Telefunken, Argo and L'Oiseau-Lyre in the US), reported that more than 30,000 copies of Das Alte Werk Bach cantata albums sold in less than one year.
[37] Skowroneck 1972 (1968).   [38] Horn 2007, pp. 194–8.
[39] The Dutch equivalent of the German *hausmusik* movement.

firm promoted the educational use of plastic recorders with schoolchildren, Brüggen was clearly pursuing another aesthetic ideal and a different target audience.

In the UK, Munrow and his followers likewise sought to distance themselves from the Dolmetsches.[40] The countertenor James Bowman and early brass specialist Michael Laird both noted that Munrow was the first performer of medieval and Renaissance music they encountered who had high technical standards and who had truly mastered early instruments; prior to Munrow, Laird noted, Early Music had been "a sort of a joke".[41] Bowman credited Munrow with awakening his interest in historical performance:

I didn't set out to go into Early Music at all. It wasn't my thing at all. I mean, I couldn't even take it particularly seriously because before David Munrow came along, performances were pretty terrible. He was the first person to be professional about it.[42]

Together, Munrow, Bowman and Laird formed the Early Music Consort with the harpsichordist Hogwood, the viol player Oliver Brookes and lutenist James Tyler, performing their London debut in 1968. Bowman emphasised that the Early Music Consort primarily performed at university campuses when touring, rather than venues associated with amateurs (e.g. Haslemere).

Nevertheless, amateur HIP aficionados provided the market for concerts, recordings, instruments and instructional workshops. Zuckerman harpsichord kits were all the rage in America by 1968. As *House and Garden* magazine reported, harpsichords appealed to men and women, professionals ("doctors and scientists") and housewives, older adults and college students alike. The instrument seemed to offer a respite from the travails of the modern world:

[T]he gentle harpsichord stands for everything that life today is not. In this tense, speed-crazed age of jets and computers and glass-walled architecture, the sedate instrument strikes a quivering chord within all of us who long for a more ordered, more dignified world. Just looking at a harpsichord bemuses us. It conjures up a harmonious, unneurotic time so unlike the twentieth century (or so we fondly believe). And its music embodies no nineteenth-century romantic excesses, no *sturm und drang*. Instead, it includes the precise discipline of Bach, the sparkling

---

[40] Arnold Dolmetsch established the Haslemere Festival in 1925; successively directed by other Dolmetsch family members, it continues to attract devotees of early instruments, dance and amateur music-making.
[41] Bowman 2009; Laird 2009.   [42] Bowman 2009.

sonatas of Scarlatti, the stately ballroom melodies of Versailles when Louis XIV gravely danced the pavane.[43]

If the harpsichord represented nostalgia to adults, early instruments represented novelty to young people. Harpsichord, lute and recorder had their own timbral appeal; their frequent use in popular music typified the experimentation, unconventional materials and blurred boundaries between 'high' and 'low' culture seen in other 1960s art forms. HIP references abound in rock and folk, including Judy Collins' recording of Landini on *Wildflowers* (1967), with instrumental arrangements by Joshua Rifkin;[44] the recorder in the Rolling Stones' "Ruby Tuesday" (1967); and the harpsichord in the Beatles' "Piggies" (1968a). But such crossovers worked both ways: a hi-tech album of the high Baroque became a surprising hit, as Wendy Carlos' *Switched-on Bach* (1968), recorded on a Moog synthesiser, went gold in 1969 and eventually platinum, selling more than a million copies.

Early music and new music: strange bedfellows?

A more important type of crossover – in terms of countercultural cachet – was HIP's connection to contemporary music. It would be an oversimplification to assume that historical performers and audiences turned to the music of the past because they rejected contemporary music's complexity and dissonance. There are numerous examples of interactions between historical performers and composers circa 1968: violinist Catherine Mackintosh credited Sir Harrison Birtwistle with sparking her interest in early music; conductor Andrew Parrott worked with Sir Michael Tippett; countertenor Bowman premiered works by Benjamin Britten, Sir Peter Maxwell Davies, Elisabeth Lutyens and other British composers;[45] and Sir Roger Norrington conducted more than fifty premieres.[46] Likewise, Lucy van Dael, Barthold Kuijken and Stanley Hoogland performed with contemporary music ensembles earlier in their careers before focusing more on HIP in the 1970s.[47]

---

[43] Russcol 1968, p. 74.
[44] Rifkin also worked on Collins' previous album. His own tongue-in-cheek *Baroque Beatles Book* (Rifkin 1965) contained orchestral arrangements of Beatles hits.
[45] Britten and Maxwell Davies also served as honorary presidents of the British Society of Recorder Players.
[46] Mackintosh 2008; Parrott 2008; Bowman 2009; Norrington 2009. Norrington conducted many of these premieres as music director of the Kent Opera (1969–82), and continues to play contemporary music with the Stuttgart Radio Symphony Orchestra.
[47] Van Dael 2004; Kuijken 2008; Hoogland 2008.

Brüggen aggressively commissioned new music for the recorder, deeming contemporary pieces essential to the instrument's survival. Such works include Louis Andriessen's *Sweet for Recorders* and tape (1964), and Luciano Berio's *Gesti* (1970 [1966]), a *Sequenza*-like work that became Brüggen's signature piece. As Haynes remarked, "[e]arly music and new music were like cousins. Or brothers or sisters. They were both protest musics, and probably of about equal impact at that time."[48] Composers and historical performers similarly objected to the staleness of mainstream concert repertoire and to the conventional means of playing it.

Concerts and festivals frequently became sites of interaction between new and early music circa 1968. In the Netherlands, the Holland Festival featured contemporary music under the directorship of Jaap den Daas (1966–76). During his tenure, Andriessen, Reinbert de Leeuw, Misha Mengelberg, Peter Schat and Jan van Vlijmen jointly composed *Reconstructie*, which premiered at the 1969 Festival.[49] This opera, which depicted the life of Che Guevara, included a prominent solo on an amplified contrabass recorder for Frans Brüggen. With its multiphonics, vocalisations, flutter-tonguing, and other special effects, Brüggen's solo sounded a world removed from the recorder's Early Music associations. Yet by the late 1970s, as Frans de Ruiter took over the Festival's direction, HIP was also frequently programmed, suggesting that contemporary and period instrument ensembles attracted similar audiences.[50]

Dutch historical performers and composers sought to restructure public concert life, then dominated by heavily subsidised symphony orchestras. Following the notorious 1969 *Notenkrakersactie*, in which composers (led by Andriessen and Schat) and students disrupted a concert by the Concertgebouw Orchestra, public meetings were held to discuss possibilities for programming and arts funding reform. This resulted in a number of experimental collaborative or *inclusief* concerts, which typically took place in unusual venues outside the concert hall circuit, and combined HIP with jazz and contemporary music.[51]

In the UK, an important forum mixing new and early music was the English Bach Festival, established by harpsichordist Lina Lalandi in 1963. Igor Stravinsky, who appeared at the Festival in 1964, became its honorary president (1966–71). By the late 1960s and early 1970s, the Festival became an intriguing site of intersecting musical 'avant-gardes' in both the early and

---

[48] Haynes 2008.   [49] Andriessen *et al.* 2008 (1969).   [50] De Ruiter 2008.
[51] See Adlington 2007b and Rubinoff 2009.

new music spheres. Bach performances on conventional instruments directed by Adrian Boult, Charles Mackerras and Neville Marriner were gradually supplanted by performances with period instrument specialists, including Paul Badura-Skoda, the Schola Cantorum Basiliensis, Brüggen, Leonhardt, Collegium Aureum, Musica Antiqua Amsterdam (predecessor of the Amsterdam Baroque Orchestra), Roger Norrington and John Eliot Gardiner. Contemporary music was featured prominently in Festival concerts, including significant commissions and premieres; here, too, the music of Stravinsky and Messiaen, representing the 'old guard', was juxtaposed with that of Xenakis, Berio, Stockhausen, Ligeti, Kagel and Maxwell Davies. Lalandi aimed to present not only Bach's music "in as authentic a manner as research and practical reasons will allow", but also that of "20th-century composers whose way of thinking is nearer to [Bach's] than to that of the Romantic age".[52] Lalandi's idealistic vision may have been off-putting to her core audience of Bach enthusiasts.[53] Nevertheless, the Festival was an important British venue for historical and contemporary music that offered concertgoers an alternative to mainstream repertoire.

Education reform

Historical performers and composers were active in music education reform movements. To accommodate the baby-boomers, the Dutch government restructured public school curricula in the 1960s; under new music pedagogy guidelines, the recorder became ubiquitous in Dutch classrooms by 1965.[54] That the antiquated recorder seemed out of place in modern society was not lost on some musicians. Konrad Boehmer, composer and critic for *Vrij Nederland*, argued in a 1968 column entitled "The Recorder Can Not Stand Up to the Beatles" that the instrument was inadequate for educating children about contemporary music, and irrelevant in a world of rapidly developing music technologies such as records, tape and radio.[55] If the recorder was a polarising instrument among critics, its very ubiquity was also a democratising force, increasing public familiarity with HIP.

Music education reforms were especially far-reaching at the post-secondary level, and there musicians' demands for change resemble those of 1960s student protestors. Dutch and British higher education

---

[52] Lalandi 1963. [53] Bowman (2009) recalled that new music concerts were poorly attended.
[54] Rubinoff 2006, pp. 339–43.
[55] Boehmer 1968. Boehmer's column provoked criticism from recorder advocates – and a response from Boehmer – in a subsequent issue of *Vrij Nederland* (29:17).

institutions experienced student unrest during this period, though on the whole these protests were less violent than those in West Germany, France and the US. The Netherlands did not really experience a '1968'; its own rebellious youth movement, Provo, had occurred earlier (1965–7),[56] while student protests in Tilburg and at the University of Amsterdam did not become heated until the spring of 1969.[57] Likewise, in England the student and anti-Vietnam War movements defy easy categorisation.[58] Most English protesters were not radical or violent; they sought not to overthrow institutions but rather to reform them, for example by demanding the relaxing of parochial restrictions or greater student input in university administration.[59] Similarly, historical performers aimed to reform music education institutions from within.

In England, the two most selective and elite universities – Oxford and Cambridge – experienced few demonstrations and disruptions in 1968,[60] yet they were hotbeds of Early Music activity. The list of HIP alumni to emerge from Oxbridge in the 1960s is impressive: Parrott, Kirkby and Bowman studied at Oxford, while Hogwood, Munrow, Gardiner and Simon Standage attended Cambridge. Norrington, also a Cambridge graduate, credited that institution with fostering students' "historical attitude", developed by studying subjects like history, classics and English literature – an attitude he felt was not developed adequately in music colleges.[61] Moreover, Oxbridge presented many opportunities for informal music-making, and the longstanding organ and choral traditions encouraged students' interests in Renaissance and medieval music. Parrott, who became a member and eventually conductor of the Oxford Schola Cantorum, discovered in this chamber choir "lots of bright people who were prepared to tread untrodden paths", including non-mainstream repertoire (both early and modern). Moreover, he remarked,

[f]or me the most important thing about what I got from Oxford was the freedom to put on performances, because it wasn't part of the course at all, no one was saying "You can do one concert a year and we'll examine you on it." If I could get together groups of friends, colleagues and persuade them that something was worth doing, then I learned the whole business, musically and administratively, of putting on concerts. So that was excellent training. But – and this applies even to the very first concert I did, which was of Tudor and Jacobean music – I didn't feel that I could

---

[56] Pas 2008. [57] Righart 1995, pp. 256–62; Kennedy 1995a, pp. 318–30. [58] Nehring 2008.
[59] Thomas 2002.
[60] British institutions most affected by student unrest were the London School of Economics and Birmingham, Manchester, Leeds, Liverpool, Bristol, Keele and Leicester Universities (Thomas 2002).
[61] Norrington 2009.

write the essays that I was expected to write on a weekly basis without some more direct experience of the music, which was not known in performances.[62]

The lack of available recordings of pre-1800 repertoire meant Parrott had to organise and stage his own performances in order "to learn [the music] from inside".

Likewise, Frans de Ruiter, who studied musicology at Utrecht University (1964–72) and harpsichord at the Sweelinck Conservatorium in Amsterdam, recalled an active student performance scene in Utrecht during this period, with Professors Eduard Reeser, Hélène Nolthenius and Kees Vellekoop fostering interest in HIP.[63] Still, De Ruiter recalled that the traditional nature of Utrecht's programme prompted forty first-year musicology students to stage a sit-in around 1968. The students protested that the curriculum should have "more societal responsibility", such as coursework in music journalism, management or programming – an argument that fell on deaf ears. Nevertheless, by the late 1960s, Dutch and English students were establishing that universities – not just conservatories – could also be sites of practical music-making and important centres for HIP.[64] Universities served as Early Music patrons, hosting concert series, educating audiences and fostering an independent, pragmatic attitude among music students, typical of 'the spirit of '68'.

The conservatories, inherently conservative, were slower to respond to growing interest in HIP. Historical performers emerging from these institutions in the 1960s had to adopt a do-it-yourself mentality. Catherine Mackintosh recalled little exposure to Early Music while studying at the Royal College in 1965–8, apart from her lessons on treble viol with Roddy Skeaping; as a Baroque violinist she was largely self-taught.[65] Stephen Preston, who studied modern flute at the Guildhall School, worked independently when he began playing the Baroque flute in the early 1970s.[66]

---

[62] Parrott 2008.
[63] De Ruiter 2008. As coordinator of KOSMU (Koördinerend Orgaan Studenten Muziekgezelschappe Utrecht) circa 1969, De Ruiter produced several early music dramas (Van der Klis 1991, pp. 195–7).
[64] Kelly noted that similar trends were underway at American universities, where HIP similarly blended scholarly enquiry into the music of the past with practical performance. He established the Early Music programmes at Wellesley, where he taught from 1972–9, and at the Five Colleges (MA) in 1979 before moving to Oberlin in 1988 (Kelly 2008).
[65] Mackintosh 2008.
[66] Preston 2008. While on tour with the Galliard Trio, an ensemble he formed with harpsichordist Trevor Pinnock and cellist Anthony Pleeth in 1966, a chance encounter with an eighteenth-century flute stimulated Preston's interest; though he studied performance practice with Wieland Kuijken, he was largely self-taught on the Baroque flute.

Bart Kuijken, who had studied modern flute at the conservatories of Brugge, Brussels and The Hague, was also self-taught on the Baroque flute.[67]

The Royal Conservatory in The Hague, however, stood out as a unique institution in the late 1960s. Upon assuming the directorship in 1970, composer Jan van Vlijmen overhauled the theory and orchestral training curricula, instituted the dance academy, expanded programmes in electronic and contemporary music, and established the Early Music Department, which soon attracted hundreds of students from abroad.[68] Recorder player Kees Boeke, who studied with Brüggen and Bijlsma (1967–9) remembered the Royal Conservatory as,

> an incredible place at that point. It was about as much anarchy as you could possibly hope for in a school. Everything 'went'. We had these, what we called something like sit-ins, or be-ins – *hear*-ins, in the conservatory, where basically the school, including the cafeteria, was open; there were concerts and movies and everything, everywhere in the building – it went on until four in the morning. No limits! And an extremely stimulating place.[69]

In this environment, students could mix contemporary music, improvisation and electronics freely with Early Music. The conservatory circa 1968 had become not just a training institute for professional musicians, but a meeting place and discussion forum that promoted interactions between genres and styles.

Early music and politics in the 1960s: some conclusions

The question remains whether or not HIP truly functioned as a resistant counterculture circa 1968. The generational, geographical, philosophical and class divides among historical performers of this period complicate any attempt to provide a definitive answer.

Anecdotes from musicians about their experiences in 1968 underscore these differences. For some, concordances between 1960s protests, leftist politics and HIP were strong; as Haynes put it, "[i]t seems there's a direct,

---

[67] Kuijken 2008. In Brussels in the 1960s, Kuijken noted that the repertoire taught was limited to the period from Bach to Stravinsky and Prokofiev. During his studies with Frans Vester in The Hague, he focused primarily on contemporary music, while taking recorder lessons with Brüggen.

[68] While studying recorder in The Hague from 1965–7 with Brüggen, Haynes (2008) was one of the few foreigners. Upon returning to teach recorder in 1972 (and eventually Baroque oboe in 1973), he noted that Dutch students were rare.

[69] Boeke 2008.

obvious connection, but it's hard to articulate. Mostly it was a revolutionary feeling – I mean, we used to talk about 'come the revolution'".[70] For others, the timing of political events with musical ones seemed purely coincidental, sometimes comically so. Baroque violinist Simon Standage's recollections of 1968 were shaped by his year studying in New York on a Harkness fellowship with Ivan Galamian, and by the Columbia University protests, which occurred during his stay.[71] To Boeke, who was eighteen in 1968, the year connoted a curious conflation of French Baroque music and French demonstrations. On a research trip to Paris with Quadro Hotteterre (formed that year with Walter van Hauwe, Wouter Möller and Bob van Asperen), he noted,

> I had gotten extremely interested in French music, in Hotteterre, because during my lessons with Frans [Brüggen], we played this duo, and I said, "Wow! This is something that speaks to me". I got so curious that we went to Paris in May '68 and we saw the   [laughs] I was there! We ran, we ran for the police. We were there, right then.[72]

Despite the disruption by protesters, Boeke was able to copy old prints and manuscripts of Marais, Hotteterre and Dornel trio sonatas at the Bibliothèque nationale, music which was little known in the 1960s. For Boeke, the '1968' Zeitgeist represented experimentation and an openness to new things, "a spirit of discovery, whether it was contemporary music or any music whatsoever".

HIP thus had the strongest associations with rebellion for musicians who came of age during the late 1960s. The singer Jill Feldman was involved in anti-Vietnam protests as a student at the University of California, Santa Barbara, in the early 1970s; she later moved to the Bay Area, where she became an avid follower of the Grateful Dead:

> If they were anywhere within reach I would hear them play [   ] So I would do my Baroque concert and then I would go off and listen to them play, either in the form of the Jerry Garcia band or The Grateful Dead themselves. So it's a funny mixture, and it's all very much connected to the rejection of the society – the fact that my generation was being called to the war in Vietnam and drafted [   ] That woke us up, perhaps faster than we would have been awakened, had we not been threatened. And so we – I was part of all those anti-war demonstrations and I was very much connected to the rejection of the classical music scene. And an interest in this early music singing.[73]

For Feldman, HIP singing represented, like rock music, a revolt against opera and classical music.

---

[70] Haynes 2008.   [71] Standage 2008.   [72] Boeke 2008.   [73] Feldman 2008.

In the Netherlands, historical performers active during the 1960s are often associated with progressivism, though they did not necessarily consider themselves part of a left-wing social movement. Here, figures like Ton Koopman and Frans Brüggen were perhaps exceptional cases; they were, as De Ruiter put it, "a bit what we called 'geitenwollen sokken'" (sheep's wool stockings).[74] De Ruiter further noted that the strong amateur *huismuziek* component of the Dutch Early Music scene's core audience was sympathetic to left-wing causes:

They were not so politically active but they were against a lot of things: against nuclear weapons, and against nuclear plants and against experiments with animals   so a bit against a lot of things which were generally done with society. So they were more at the background, not shouting too much but [embracing] alternative living, a bit free sexuality also, but it was a more or less progressive part of society.

Moreover, Brüggen's outspokenness on orchestra reform, his alliances with left-wing composers, and the extensive coverage of HIP in the left-leaning Dutch press (*Groene Amsterdammer, Vrij Nederland, Volkskrant*) further reinforced the association of Early Music with progressivism.

Yet the HIP community was hardly unified in its political and aesthetic beliefs. The recorder trio Sour Cream, formed by Brüggen, Boeke and Van Hauwe in 1972 to react against (in Boeke's words) the "state and formal" aspects of the Early Music world, shocked HIP's conservative contingent with rock arrangements and experimental music. Pianist Stanley Hoogland, who later specialised in fortepiano, participated in the 1968 'politiek-demonstratief experimenteel' concerts,[75] and like Brüggen performed in the infamous *Reconstructie* premiere at the 1969 Holland Festival. He found these experiences exciting, but thought the blunt mixing of left-wing politics and music was one-sided and lacking in subtlety.[76] To Gustav Leonhardt, HIP and the political uprisings of 1968 were not at all connected. As he put it,

[i]t's like when many years ago, a plane crashed on an apartment building in the Bijlmer.[77] Well, anyway, soon afterwards we were phoned by people from England and from Switzerland, [asking] "Are you hurt?" I mean, it's horrible, what happened, but it's so local, and I think the whole '68 thing was – what we still see in

---

[74] De Ruiter 2008, referring to the preferred footwear of many HIP fans. See also footnote 4 above.
[75] 'Political-demonstrative experimental' concerts. See Adlington 2009a.   [76] Hoogland 2008.
[77] Leonhardt is referring to the crash of El Al cargo plane Flight 1862 on 4 October 1992 in the Bijlmermeer neighbourhood of south-west Amsterdam. The crash site is more than 10 km from Leonhardt's home.

photographs, and waving red flags and all that – well, it happened but it was so local, and the impact was I think – well, it had some impact, but much less than they tried to make of it.[78]

For Leonhardt (born in 1928), 1968 was less of a watershed than the Second World War. Likewise, James Bowman also did not feel that the political events of the 1960s and the growth in historical performance were at all related; he bluntly stated that, "[t]here is no connection between music and politics".[79]

An assessment of '1968's impact on HIP is further complicated by discomfort with the dilettantism connoted by hippie associations. If some musicians noted that audiences were made up of a "fair smattering of 'brown rice and sandals'" (Mackintosh) or "open-sandaled, lentil-eating types" (Parrott), they were quick to qualify that HIP's hippie image could be an "unfair stereotype" (Bowman).[80] Bowman, Laird and many others espoused an ethos of professionalism; most musicians were simply interested in performing and supporting themselves rather than becoming involved in a social movement.

The status of HIP as an avant-garde or counterculture is relative, dependent on musicians' own experiences during the 1960s and their perceptions of that tumultuous decade. This labelling is sometimes used as a marketing tactic, and one could argue that the increasing commercialism of HIP in the 1980s failed to produce lasting systemic change to the recording industry and the music education system. As such, one must be wary of the sometimes nostalgic interpretations of Early Music in the 1960s. Yet the one common thread that unites the disparate views expressed by historical performers active in the 'long 1968' is the idea, as Norrington put it, of "questioning": questioning the past traditions of playing (including the then-standard approach to performing early music) and questioning authorities (both scholarly figures and conservatory teachers). It is this process of questioning that has been the driving creative force behind HIP's exploration of the musical past, resulting in the Early Music movement's transformative – and arguably revolutionary – effect on the musical life of the twentieth century.

---

[78] Leonhardt 2008.   [79] Bowman 2009.   [80] Mackintosh 2008; Parrott 2008; Bowman 2009.

15 | Music and May 1968 in France: practices, roles, representations

ERIC DROTT

> *Psychodrama.* Of course this expression needs some qualification. But nevertheless everyone of us indulged in role-playing during this period [May–June 1968]. Take me for a start. I have told you that I played the part of Tocqueville, which is not without a touch of the ridiculous, but others played Saint-Just, Robespierre or Lenin, which all things considered was even more ridiculous.[1]

Of all the interpretations the protests and general strike of May–June 1968 have elicited over the years, few have generated as much controversy as the single word Raymond Aron used to assess the event: psychodrama. First uttered during a radio interview on 1 June 1968, when the wave of demonstrations and factory occupations commenced weeks earlier had not yet run its course, Aron's expression seemed calculated to deprive the May movement of the historical weight it had already begun to accrue. Both halves of the portmanteau term 'psychodrama' contributed to this deflationary effect. At a time when most commentators were busy stressing the singular character of the uprising – the unprecedented degree of solidarity between workers and students; the central place accorded cultural agitation in the movement; the experimentation with direct democracy and other, non-hierarchical forms of political organisation – Aron's depiction of the protest movement as a kind of theatrical performance apparently minimised its innovative aspects. What was emphasised was not the event's break with but its reliance upon existing models of political action. Each role, each gesture within this collective performance had already been played out in advance, inscribed in a historical continuum that subsumed the peculiarities of the present into the familiar patterns of the past. Furthermore, the addition of the prefix 'psycho' to the substantive 'drama' divested the event of its claim to efficacy. Not only did Aron cast May 1968 as an empty spectacle of revolution; he cast it as one that took place on an imaginary plane, a form of make-believe disconnected from social and political realities.

---

[1] Raymond Aron 1969.

Despite Aron's manifest antipathy towards the protest movement – most clearly evinced in the reductive portrait he painted of its participants – his description of May 1968 did not entirely lack merit. In particular, the theatrical metaphor that he deployed, with its emphasis on individuals' adoption of recognised roles and associated forms of conduct, touched upon a key aspect of the uprising. But what Aron posited as a failing peculiar to May 1968 turns out upon closer inspection to be neither a failing nor all that peculiar. Far from delegitimising the May movement, recourse to pre-existing models is a fairly natural, even unremarkable feature of political protest. As Charles Tilly and other social movement theorists have pointed out, the forms that protest assumes within a particular socio-historic context exhibit a high degree of consistency.[2] The collective actions by means of which groups are able to press their claims are typically drawn from a relatively stable repertoire. From the universe of possible forms of political intervention participants in a given collective action only make use of a small subset, their margin of manoeuvre effectively constrained by received tradition. Public protest, it would seem, is hardly spontaneous or unmediated, but involves the performance of learned roles and routines. The same is true of musical practices employed for the purposes of political mobilisation, as we shall see shortly. No less than other types of protest, forms of musical engagement are likewise drawn from a delimited fund of proven practices. So too are the political roles that musicians and other artists assume: these are equally fashioned in accordance with established historical types. And while the repertoires that both musical and political agents avail themselves of are liable to change over time, by and large this change unfolds gradually. From this perspective, the sort of 'role-playing' identified by Aron was not a defect of the May movement, but a necessary condition of political mobilisation. Individuals and groups had little choice but to look to existing practices of public protest to orient their activities.

There is yet another sense in which Aron's account proves instructive – albeit not in substantive terms, but as a symptom of a broader reaction that the May events provoked. Namely, Aron's remarks exemplify the tendency manifest both during and after May 1968 to use discourse (and technologies of representation more broadly) to contain the singular, disruptive and inexplicable aspects of the protests and general strike. His assertion that protesters merely acted out parts scripted in advance participated in what Michel de Certeau characterised as a widespread effort to draw the event back into the very order of representation it had pierced: "Everywhere there

---

[2] Tilly 1986 and 2008.

is an urgent need to understand what happened. It aims at overcoming the irrationality of the event. For some it is a question of defending oneself against it; for others, of defending the event itself; for all it is almost certainly a question of explaining and repairing the tear that has rent the system of social relations".[3] This drive to fit the protests and general strike into some pre-formed interpretive grid may be witnessed across the entire spectrum of ideological positions, from the Trotskyist argument that the uprising represented a "dress rehearsal" for an imminent socialist revolution,[4] to Charles De Gaulle's insinuation that the uprising had been orchestrated from the sidelines by the Parti Communiste Français.[5] The impulse to bring the May events into alignment with some familiar discursive framework may also be witnessed across a range of media. Music was no exception. No less than the countless articles, pamphlets and books to which May 1968 gave rise, songs and compositions written in its aftermath participated in this collective, obsessive effort to attach a determinate meaning to the revolt. But in all of these cases, irrespective of ideology or medium, the attempt to pin down the causes and consequences of May 1968 had the opposite effect. Ironically, the more observers tried to define what May was, the more they tried to fix and thereby contain its significance, the more it eluded such interpretive endeavours.

The present chapter examines the place of music in May 1968, situating it in relation to the two contradictory impulses identified above. On the one hand, precedent clearly informed how music was put to use during May, with a number of recognised practices enlisted to advance the protests and strike movement. The same was true of the different political stances struck by musicians involved in the May events; they too engaged in the kind of "role-playing" described by Aron, looking to existing paradigms of artistic engagement to orient their actions. On the other hand, music (and discourse about music) also participated in the unceasing effort to establish the precise import of what happened during May. But in doing so, songs and compositions only served to further obscure that which they sought to specify, adding to the already heavy significative burden placed upon the event.

The three sections that follow address how each of these impulses played out in the world of music, both during and after May–June 1968. In the first section, I examine the repertoire of musical practices that militants drew upon during the protests and general strike. These include the writing of new, topical texts set to familiar tunes and the performance of classic revolutionary songs – most notably "L'Internationale", which was intoned

---

[3] Certeau 1994 (1968), pp. 78–9. [4] Bensaïd and Weber 1968. [5] Gaulle 1968.

in a wide variety of collective actions during the course of the revolt. The second section addresses a different kind of repertoire mobilised during May, namely the roles that musicians assumed in order to make a meaningful contribution to the protest movement. Here two models proved crucial to musicians' efforts at refashioning themselves as political agents, those of the vanguard artist and the trade unionist. Finally, in the third section I turn to the ramifications that ensued from the struggle to define May's meaning. Of particular importance is how the proliferation of texts seeking to make sense of the uprising (including musical ones) paradoxically contributed to the event's semiotic indeterminacy. Rather than clarifying its meaning, the numerous interpretations that have accumulated around May over the years would appear to have transformed it into an 'empty' or 'floating' signifier. But even if the revolt has eluded subsequent efforts at fixing its social, political and cultural significance, always slipping through the discursive mesh authors weave about it, this has not diminished its relevance or impact. On the contrary: the event's lack of determinate meaning is, in fact, what ensures its continuing use-value, as it is unceasingly invoked to explain any and every significant development in French culture since 1968. Music no less than other media provides a site where this instrumentalisation of May's legacy may be observed, with transformations in a host of genres attributed to the change in sensibility that the uprising is alleged to have wrought.

Practices

One of the first university buildings to be occupied during the May uprising was the Censier annex of the Université de Paris. Students seized control of its premises on 11 May, the day following the famous 'night of the barricades', during which the Latin Quarter had been transformed into the site of violent skirmishes between police and youth. Shortly after the students' take-over of Censier, a leaflet bearing the title "Le chant des barricades" was posted on its walls. Written upon it were six stanzas commemorating the fighting that had taken place the night before. Two stanzas evoked the soundscape of that eventful night:

We sung while building barricades
between Boul'Mich and the rue Gay-Lussac
that the CRS aren't pigs but bastards
BASTARDS! BASTARDS! responded the echo

At the height of the fighting comrades
We were blinded and burned by grenades
Good people threw us some water –
WATER, WATER responded the echo.[6]

At the bottom of the page a short note invited "comrade musicians and singers" to come participate in producing a record of the song, the proceeds of which would be donated to the "wounded of the barricades". So that potential participants might have some idea of the music that would accompany "Le chant des barricades", the note added that the chorus would be sung to the rhythm of "Tayo-ho-tayo".

There is no evidence that "Le chant des barricades" was ever recorded. But this does not detract from the song's significance. For the text posted at Censier was representative of a broader practice revived during the May events: that of composing new, topical lyrics to be sung to existing tunes. The recycling of familiar melodies, or *timbres*, to address contemporary issues has long occupied a distinguished place in French popular culture.[7] But it has long occupied a no less distinguished place in *representations* of French popular culture, shaping the value observers have accorded song as a medium of political expression. Histories of the *chanson* have often treated this practice as exemplary, a testament to the genre's vaunted status as tribune of the people. By this logic, the use of well-known melodies not only had the benefit of lowering barriers to the dissemination and collective performance of songs; it also democratised musical production, ensuring that those lacking the ability to read or write music could nonetheless partake of this particular form of cultural expression.[8] That the writing of texts on existing tunes had dwindled from the late nineteenth century on – a decline typically ascribed to the growth of the music industry and the separation it ostensibly instituted between (active) producers and (passive) consumers – only served to increase the symbolic value accorded to this older practice.[9] For many postwar historians of the *chanson*, the increasingly standardised, professionalised and commercialised forms of contemporary popular music threw into relief how far the *chanson* had strayed from its true vocation, that of providing the masses a means by which

---

[6] A copy of the song is conserved at the Centre d'Histoire Sociale, Archives 1968, Fonds I, Carton 17, Dossier no. 1, "Organisations culturelles".
[7] The term *timbre* refers specifically to the title (or first verse) of an existing tune. In practice, however, it is synonymous with the tune itself.
[8] Calvet 1976, p. 28.
[9] For representative accounts of this narrative of decline, see Coulonges 1969; Dillaz 1973; and Marty 1985.

it could represent itself musically. "The *chanson*", one author noted, "has deserted the people in order to become the business of professionals." This contrasted starkly (and negatively) with the older practice of rewriting existing songs, which had permitted "the non-professional to make a personalised work".[10] Viewed from this perspective, the fact that individuals once again began to write texts to familiar tunes during May 1968 – a trend signalled by "Le chant des barricades", among others – appeared to portend a return to a more active, participatory form of popular expression.

The value attached to this practice also derived from the rich semiotic interplay it afforded, as newly composed lyrics played off a given melody's prior textual and musical associations. If, as Ralph Locke has noted, "considerations of style and previous text were clearly crucial" to nineteenth-century *chansonniers* like Pierre-Jean Béranger, the same was no doubt true for Béranger's twentieth-century successors.[11] A common approach was to update older revolutionary *chansons*. Examples include "La commune n'est pas morte", a revision of Eugène Pottier's paean to the memory of the Paris Commune, or "La Grappignole", an updated version of the revolutionary song "La Carmagnole" (1792), which pilloried Pierre Grappin, dean of the Nanterre campus of the Université de Paris. As was the case with antecedents from previous centuries, adaptations of older revolutionary songs benefited from the familiarity of their originals, abetting their circulation and performance among movement participants. At the same time, they legitimised the May movement, by framing contemporary struggles as part of a longer history of popular protest.

With other songs, the interaction of text and *timbre* was less straightforward. In the case of "Le chant des barricades", the tune that it set was a traditional 'bawdy song' (*chanson paillarde*), "La petite Emilie", from whose refrain the nonsense syllables "Tayo-ho-tayo" were drawn. Here as elsewhere the choice of song is significant. It would seem that, far from being a drawback, the vulgarity of the original was seen as a distinct advantage – vulgarity here understood in its etymological sense, as pertaining to the *vulgus*, or common people. In other instances, the relation that existed between text and tune was one of parodic inversion. A case in point was Dominique Grange's "A bas l'état policier" ("Down with the police state"), set to the Wehrmacht marching song "Heidi Heido". The use of a song indelibly tainted by its association with the memory of the German occupation accomplished a number of related goals. Not only did it produce a somewhat jarring disjunction with Grange's text, throwing

[10] Dillaz 1973, p. 175. [11] Locke 1987, p. 434.

into relief the lyrics' anti-authoritarian sentiment, but at the same time it served to equate De Gaulle's government with a repressive, quasi-fascist force, a key rhetorical frame employed by anti-government protesters during May 1968 (most clearly evinced by the chant "CRS-SS", which protesters used to vilify the Compagnies Républicaines de Sécurité, the French riot police).

Finally, there are those songs whose textual revision simply brought to the surface an allegorical potential latent in the original. Perhaps the most famous example of the latter was Jacques Le Glou's rewriting of Jacques Dutronc's then-recent hit single, "Il est cinq heures, Paris s'éveillent" ("It's five am, Paris awakens"). Notable is that the source music for Le Glou's song was drawn not from the repertoire of traditional *chanson*, but from the ranks of the contemporary hit parade. Notable, too, is how little Le Glou had to change in order to draw out the resonances between Dutronc's musical depiction of Paris at daybreak and the May revolt. Indeed, the chorus of Dutronc's original was so conducive to allegorical (mis)reading – readily interpreted as a prescient description of a city awakening from its political slumber – that many radio stations withdrew it from their playlists during the May uprising, lest they be seen as fomenting anti-government protests.[12]

In addition to writing new, topical texts to songs, movement actors availed themselves of other practices drawn from the established repertoire of musical contention. By far the most widespread of these was the collective singing of revolutionary *chansons*. Old standbys like "La jeune garde", "Le drapeau rouge", and, above all, "L'Internationale" featured prominently in demonstrations, public meetings and rallies during May–June 1968. Among the functions served by such collective performances, one of the most important was to signal participants' political commitment – commitment not just to the particular struggle at hand, but to the broader world-view that lent meaning to this struggle. This signalling was directed both within and without. When sung as part of a demonstration, for instance, "L'Internationale" was addressed not only to outside observers, but to other protesters, a way of reaffirming that all were bound by the same common purpose – hence Louis-Jean Calvet's remark that such performances were "above all signs".[13] But, as he went on to observe, they were signs for which connotation weighed more heavily than denotation:

---

[12] Koechlin 1968, pp. 12–13. [13] Calvet 1976, p. 136.

> Who [ ] would dream of taking the words of "L'Internationale" or "La jeune garde" as a message whose terms one would decode? Nobody, for [ ] these songs function on a second level, that of connotation. What do they connote? Membership in a group, first of all (we're together, we sing the same songs), the desire to claim for oneself a certain past or a certain analysis of the past, a revolutionary experience itself transformed into a sign.[14]

But if such performances were signs, then, like all signs, they were subject to multiple interpretations, their meaning itself an object of contention. Consider the role of "L'Internationale" during the May 1968 protests. Even if it was, as Calvet observes elsewhere, the preferred musical vehicle for student protesters and striking workers during the May events, differences in the song's use and interpretation helped diverse ideological factions to draw lines of demarcation between one another. For anarchists, it was a song that was to be brandished as much against the Communist party as the Gaullist regime, the former seen as no less repressive than the latter. For Trotskyists, "L'Internationale" was above all a means by which a small vanguard group could interpellate the working-class as a historical agent, and thereby incite the masses to political action. Finally, for the Parti Communiste Français, the song occupied a more ambiguous position. On the one hand, it allowed the PCF and its allies to define themselves against their Gaullist adversaries. On the other hand, the PCF distinguished itself from its Anarchist, Trotskyist and Maoist rivals by refusing to set "L'Internationale" in opposition to "La Marseillaise" – a song that by 1968 had come to represent for much of the far left an outmoded expression of bourgeois nationalism. For the PCF, by contrast, the two anthems formed part of the same heritage, a heritage at once French and revolutionary, national and international.[15]

At a broader level, different interpretations of the place of revolutionary *chanson* in the May protests reflected divergent conceptions of music's relation to politics. For some observers – particularly members of the non-communist or extreme left – the spectacle of student militants singing "L'Internationale" was a source of inspiration, bespeaking a rejuvenation of political activism. As one observer remarked, "to hear 20,000 young people singing 'L'Internationale', I've never seen anything so moving". The revivification of left-wing militancy – signalled here by the resurgence of revolutionary song – was particularly gratifying given the sense of alienation that

---

[14] Calvet 1976, pp. 136–8.
[15] For a more extensive discussion of the varying uses to which "L'Internationale" was put in May 1968, see Drott 2011, ch. 1.

years of political demobilisation had engendered: "All of a sudden, I no longer felt alone in a hostile and uncomprehending world. I was with my brothers, my friends, my buddies."[16] For others, however – particularly observers of France's musical life – recourse to revolutionary song was viewed less positively, a symptom of militants' dearth of musical creativity. "Clearly, the movement was a little short on songs", music critic Jacques Vassal noted, adding that "the neo-bureaucratic groupuscules totally lacked imagination on this point".[17] But militants were not the only guilty party; the moribund state of political song in France circa 1968 also bore some responsibility. Here Vassal rehearses a standard (if highly reductive) narrative, according to which political song, after flourishing in the late nineteenth and early twentieth century, had steadily deteriorated in the decades after the First World War. Thus he blames the paucity of songs occasioned by the May revolt as resulting from "the break of close to a century in the tradition of popular singing in France (as opposed to the continuity on this level that for example Ireland, Brittany, the United States, or Greece enjoy)".[18] As with "L'Internationale", the very practice of singing revolutionary song during May 1968 was itself subject to competing interpretations, valorised or denigrated according to the interests of the parties involved. For someone like Siné, for whom questions of originality and musical value were subordinate to the overriding political imperative of expressing solidarity or commitment, the turn to "classic" revolutionary song was a cause for rejoicing, not concern. For Vassal, by contrast, political value was not so easily separated from musical value. Indeed, as his criticism of "neo-bureaucratic groupuscules" implies, Vassal conceived musical imagination as an index of political imagination. The lack of newly composed songs or innovative cultural practices signalled a more troubling lack, an inability on the part of Trotskyist and Maoist militants to conceive of new modes of political action.

Roles

Traditions of popular contention not only shaped the kinds of musical practices militants put to work during May 1968. They also determined what forms of political engagement musicians and other artists were able to avail themselves of in response to the political demands of the moment. These demands were not inconsiderable. On the one hand, the central place

[16] Siné 1968, p. 2.   [17] Vassal 1976, pp. 13–14.   [18] Vassal 1976, p. 14.

that culture occupied within the May movement – viewed as both a valuable resource to be exploited and an ideological apparatus to be criticised (and, in some cases, dismantled) – made the activities of artists at once vital *and* problematic. On the other hand, the spread of the strike movement after mid-May forced musicians to take a stand, either for or against the growing revolt. The music community in France thus found itself grappling with a host of thorny questions: What role, if any, did cultural producers have within the May movement? What concrete contribution could they make to political struggle? How could they justify their artistic pursuits in the face of such radical social upheaval? Or were such justifications impossible when more pressing political tasks were at hand?

To address such questions musicians could look to a handful of established models, roles appropriate to both the exigencies of the political moment and their vocation as artists. The historical avant-garde provided one such model of artistic engagement. The Dadaist and Surrealist movements of the interwar period, as well as more recent vanguard groups (such as the Provos and Situationists) furnished a clear point of reference for radicalised elements within the French cultural sphere. A case in point was the Comité Révolutionnaire d'Agitation Culturelle (CRAC), a heterogeneous group of artists, musicians, students and professors who endeavoured to mobilise various sectors of the art world from their base in the occupied Sorbonne. Another was the Comité d'Action Révolutionnaire (CAR), the entity responsible for the occupation of the Odéon theatre in Paris from mid-May to mid-June 1968. Both CRAC and CAR drew from the organisational template of the small cell of vanguard artists, whose provocative acts of 'cultural agitation' sought to exercise a catalysing effect on the masses (a model based in turn on the Leninist idea of the vanguard party). CAR's takeover of the Odéon theatre was perhaps the most dramatic manifestation of this approach to cultural action. By commandeering a state-run theatre, opening its doors to all comers and inverting the traditional relation between actor and audience – such that speech no longer emanated from the stage but from the auditorium – CAR's intervention aimed at spurring the formation of a more participatory culture.

Ideologically, the historical avant-garde's unfinished project of fusing art and everyday life seems to have informed the activities of CRAC, CAR and other groups devoted to cultural agitation.[19] There was some variability, however, in how these groups interpreted this overarching objective. What, precisely, did it mean to conjoin these separate domains of human

---

[19] Bürger 1984 provides the classic account of the avant-gardist project.

experience? And what was the best means of achieving this admittedly utopian goal? One way of responding to these questions involved a radical democratisation of creative activity. The problem, according to this line of thinking, was not that art constituted a distinct area of human activity per se, but that a small, elite group monopolised its production and consumption. What was necessary was to open up the cloistered sphere where art and music were confined. For the group Art et Révolution, based in the occupied Faculté des Lettres at the Université de Lyon, for instance, it was imperative to recognise "the right of the greatest number to determine themselves the means of their own creation, the forms of their own culture."[20] CRAC expressed a similar sentiment in a number of their communiqués. One published on 11 June 1968 declared: "*We must open up* the streets [ ] to creation and invention. *We must welcome* on the ruins of its Pantheons all who have been excluded, the poor and oppressed of bourgeois culture [ ] We must liberate the creative forces that our society represses, together with all the workers."[21]

Another, more radical approach to the fusion of art and life demanded nothing less than the abolition of art as a specialised sphere of activity altogether. By this logic, the utopian moment embedded in art is precisely what made it so problematic: by offering individuals an imaginary outlet for aspirations frustrated in the existing social world, art channelled and thereby defused grievances that might otherwise serve as a potential source of political mobilisation. This understanding of culture's role in sustaining the modern capitalist system was evident in a pair of objectives CAR outlined in explaining the rationale behind the occupation of the Odéon theatre. First and foremost, the group called for "[t]he scuttling of everything 'cultural'", seeing this as a way of ensuring "the prioritisation of political struggle above all else". Along related lines, they advocated the "systematic sabotage of the culture industry and in particular show business [*industrie du spectacle*]", considering this a necessary precondition for the institution of "veritable collective creation".[22] Here as elsewhere a desire to surpass the limits of art is clearly in play. If art's utopian energies were to be released, it was necessary to eliminate the institutions (the culture industry, show business) that captured these energies and diverted them into politically innocuous activities.

---

[20] Centre d'Histoire Sociale, Archives 1968, Fonds I, Carton 7, Dossier 2 ("CRAC").
[21] CRAC, quoted in Schnapp and Vidal-Naquet 1971, p. 444.
[22] CAR, quoted in Brau 1968, p. 106.

An alternative model of political engagement was provided by trade union culture. Like other roles musicians were able to adopt in their efforts to square political and artistic commitments, that of the culture worker entailed a host of obligations, expectations, and 'scripted' forms of conduct. But it also provided musicians with an extensive repertoire of recognised political actions they could partake of: work stoppages could be organised, petitions drafted, lists of demands drawn up and submitted to governmental agencies and work sites occupied. Instances of these varied forms of collective action may be identified throughout the months of May and June 1968. Opera houses in Paris, Lyon and other cities were occupied by their personnel, along with conservatories and other art music institutions. Venues associated with the performance of popular music, such as the Olympia, Bobino and Pacra concert halls in Paris, were likewise seized. A musicians' strike was called on 21 May, observed by virtually every branch of the profession (composers, singers, instrumentalists). And there was no shortage of demands submitted to state agencies and other holders of political and economic power. A communiqué circulated by students participating in the occupation of the Paris Conservatoire, to take one example, called for a complete restructuring of music education in France. Among other things, the communiqué demanded that the Ministries of Education and Cultural Affairs abolish "the current system of separation and dispersal in music education", and replace it with a system where music and the arts would form part of the general university curriculum. What was vital was "the progressive integration of musical culture into the new society, a musical culture that appears to be an instinctive need of the individual".[23]

More concretely, the institutional infrastructure furnished by musicians' unions facilitated efforts to find a practical outlet for performers' talents. It was through entities like the Syndicat Français des Acteurs (SFA), the main union representing both stage actors and *chanson* artists, that information concerning a variety of actions was disseminated among artists and their participation encouraged.[24] Beyond this, the fact that the SFA and other musicians' unions belonged to larger labour federations – in particular, the communist-aligned Confédération Générale du Travail (CGT) – enabled them to make contact with and, in many cases, perform before workers in

---

[23] A copy of this communiqué is located at the Centre d'Histoire Sociale, Archives 1968, Fonds I, Carton 7, Dossier "CAR-Odéon".

[24] A case in point was a benefit concert organised by variety artists, announced during the general assembly of the SFA on 20 May. See "Assemblée Générale, 20 Mai 1968", in Archives Départementales Seine-Saint Denis, Archives Syndicat Français des Artistes-Interprètes, 175 J 230.

occupied factories. A key intermediary in this regard was the organisation Travail et Culture (TEC), a group affiliated with the CGT. Founded in 1944, the principal mission of TEC was to promote workers' access to culture by bringing art, music and theatre to factories and other places of work. During the general strike of May 1968, TEC served as a conduit by means of which *chanson* artists like Jean Ferrat, Georges Moustaki and Francesca Solleville were enlisted to entertain striking workers. And yet recourse to the organisational resources furnished by trade unions and labour federations also imposed constraints. Such groups could just as easily assume a gatekeeper role, determining who was allowed to appear before striking workers and who was not. A communiqué issued by SFA on 29 May underlined this point: "In the case of solidarity performances, intended to collect funds for workers on strike [ ], only the strike committee for the 'varieties branch' of the SFA is empowered to grant exemptions [from the work stoppage]."[25] Musicians who did not heed such injunctions risked being ejected from factories. This was particularly true for musicians like singer Dominique Grange, whose more extreme ideological stance ran counter to the party line espoused by union officials: "we were thrown out by the CGT. *L'Huma* [*L'Humanité*, organ of the PCF] denounced [us as] leftist singers."[26]

There were other, more significant constraints imposed by the trade union model. Chief among these was a tendency to construe the strike movement as a means of redressing professional grievances rather than effecting sweeping political change. This narrow conception of the strike's significance engendered a good deal of antipathy towards musicians' and other artists' unions during May, especially among more radical segments of the movement. This was particularly so once the leadership of the SFA, along with that of the Syndicat National des Artistes-Musiciens, entered into negotiations with the Ministry of Cultural Affairs late in the month. Among striking musicians a small splinter group going by the name of Action Musique issued a series of tracts that reproached the union leadership for its willingness to "play the game of power" – its willingness, that is, to sell out the strike movement to advance its corporatist agenda.[27] Similar broadsides were launched from outside the ranks of striking musicians, by members of vanguardist groups like CRAC and CAR. CRAC denounced artists' unions for having reached a negotiated settlement with the government in early June. In the eyes of CRAC's members, the unions were guilty

---

[25] See SFA (Branche Variétés), "Communiqué" (29 Mai 1968), in Archives Départmentales Seine-Saint Denis, Archives Syndicat Français des Artistes-Interprètes, 175 J 230.
[26] Grange 2008.   [27] Comité Action Musique 1968, p. 15.

of "sabotaging the workers' strike [ ] by urging the public to return to the fake world of commercialised dreams".[28] Such disputes over the aims of the musicians' strike movement overlaid a more profound dispute regarding how, precisely, the upsurge of social unrest during May was to be interpreted. Was it to be seen as an expression of dissatisfaction with how the fruits of France's recent economic growth had been distributed, or as an expression of a deeper dissatisfaction with the system that had produced this economic growth, the capitalist mode of production itself? Even after the strike movement had ended, political struggle continued, if only at a symbolic level. What was now at stake was the meaning(s) henceforth attached to May 1968. It is to this struggle that I turn in the concluding section.

Representations

At the opening of this chapter I noted how the singular character of the May revolt gave rise to a proliferation of interpretations, as individuals strove to find reason or sense in the sudden outburst of social protest. It was as if the hard kernel of the irrational that lay at the heart of the uprising acted as an irritant, provoking an almost compulsive urge to explain it away. Aron's description of May as a "psychodrama" was a prime example of this tendency, partaking of what Jean-Marie Coudray described as the impulse "to name the event that has shaken French society, [ ] to bring it back to what is known".[29] More generally, the sheer proliferation of texts addressing *les événements* – a proliferation already underway by June 1968 – bespoke a collective drive to deprive the event of its eventfulness, to return it to the stable order of representation. Yet this labour of exegesis (which continues unabated to this day) has not only failed to grasp its object; it has made it all the more elusive. Buried under the accumulated weight of interpretation, the import of May 1968 has become ever more difficult to establish. The result has been its transformation into a "floating signifier". Here it may be useful to recall Claude Lévi-Strauss' discussion of the concept in his *Introduction à l'œuvre de Marcel Mauss*:

> [A]lways and everywhere these types of notions [floating signifiers], somewhat like algebraic symbols, occur to represent an indeterminate value of signification, in itself devoid of meaning and thus susceptible of receiving any meaning at all; their sole function is to fill a gap between the signifier and the signified.[30]

---

[28] CRAC, in Schnapp and Vidal-Naquet 1971, p. 444.   [29] Coudray in Morin *et al.* 1968, p. 37.
[30] Lévi-Strauss 1987 (1950), pp. 55–6.

Floating signifiers, by this reading, have the function of 'soaking up' a surplus of meaning. They maintain the fragile equilibrium that exists between signifier and signified – or, in this case, between an event and the meaning attached to it. How this concept might apply to the May uprising is easy to discern. Faced with a movement whose origins, aims and consequences defied easy, univocal explanation, individuals proposed a range of interpretations to account for the protest and general strike. But every attempt to affix a determinate sense to the May events had – paradoxically – the opposite effect. In this way the accumulation of discourse transformed May 1968 into a receptacle that could receive (as Lévi-Strauss puts it) virtually "any meaning at all".

Music played a part in this accretion of competing interpretations. Songs written and recorded in the wake of the uprising offered listeners a variety of readings of May's significance. But what set musical texts apart from their verbal counterparts was the fact that they operated primarily at an affective rather than conceptual level. This was abetted by generic conventions, which normalised certain modes of musico-poetic representation. Consider Évariste's song "La révolution", recorded in summer 1968. Reinforcing its portrayal of the May events in terms of generational conflict were the conventions of the pop-rock genre to which it belonged. Inasmuch as this genre was widely regarded as a form of 'youth music' (at least compared to 'adult' genres like the *chanson à texte* or classical music), Évariste's musical interpretation of May as an event that set rebellious youth against the adult world appeared altogether natural. Genre acts here not only as a filter, emphasising certain features of the protest movement and de-emphasising others, but as a means of disguising the selective character of the interpretation it presents.[31]

The same interaction of music, genre and representation may be seen elsewhere, in connection to other kinds of music. Works by avant-garde composers, for instance, reflected the concern with timbre, texture and the materiality of sound then prevalent in the world of contemporary music. Viewed in this light, May 1968 offered a rich field of sonic resources for composers to harvest. Hence the use of slogans chanted during May in Maurice Ohana's *Cris* (1969), or François Bayle's incorporation of recordings of street protests and police sirens in the "Aventure du cri" sequence of his cycle *L'Expérience acoustique* (1970–2). As was the case with Évariste's song, the imperatives of genre shaped how May was portrayed in these

---

[31] Drott 2011, ch. 2 examines in greater detail Évariste's song, and genre's role in mediating musical representations of May 1968.

works. The titles of the two pieces give some indication of how this emphasis on the timbral and textural characteristics of May's soundscape resulted in a selective reading of the May events. The invocation of the 'cry' in both suggested that collective action was in some sense inarticulate, a violent, inchoate expression of collective discontent. And once more genre served to normalise this selective representation of the May events, this tendency to privilege the sound of protest over its sense.

It was not just music that contributed to the jumble of interpretation surrounding May 1968. Discourse about music also participated in the struggle to define the protest movement. Perhaps the clearest example of this was to be seen in the writings of sociologist Alfred Willener, whose 1970 book *L'Action-image de la société* argued that the unrest of May 1968 was nothing other than the birth-pangs of a new social order coming into being. Whereas older "established" societies relied on the individual's adaptation to existing norms, the emerging "non-established" society was defined by its repudiation of such normative constraints: "Non-established society [ ] rejects all fixity, believes that society should be adapted to the individual rather than the reverse, and advocates permanent change."[32] One symptom of this social transformation was the development of new forms of cultural expression. Willener singled out free jazz in this regard, which in his eyes offered the perfect analogue to the new forms of political action developed during May 1968: "The revolutionary activities of the students put the emphasis on the individual, who redefines his roles, invents others and rejects the adaptation of a 'play' that he himself did not write. By practising collective improvisation, the students rediscovered procedures that had been practised at earlier times and in other places, and sometimes drew inspiration from those examples."[33] American free jazz offered one such model for collective improvisation: "'Free form jazz' [ ], which many regard as the expression of a revolutionary desire for social emancipation, is also an artistic – or anti-artistic – school that seeks the emancipation of the non-formal."[34] Free jazz and the new forms of politics on display during May mirrored one another, both adumbrating new, "non-established" forms of social interaction.

But if music (and writing on music) participated in the collective effort to make sense of May 1968, the reverse was also true. May, understood as a floating signifier, proved useful insofar as it soon came to function as a stand-in for virtually any force for social change, however un- or under-specified it may have been. It is small wonder, then, that May 1968 has been

---

[32] Willener 1970, p. 189.   [33] Willener 1970, p. 230.   [34] Willener 1970, pp. 230–1.

invoked to explain all sorts of transformations in the world of French music in subsequent years. Mutating public tastes, the changing hierarchy of genres in the French cultural field, the emergence of new musical practices and the disappearance of older ones – such developments have all been attributed to the sea-change in attitudes that May was said to have produced.[35] The first glimmerings of this trope could be seen as early as mid-June 1968, in a notice published in the news weekly *L'Express*: "Strange phenomenon: one of the signs of the effervescence of youth [during May] was the growing surge of interest in engaged songs."[36] French youth's ostensible abandonment of the frivolous pop music of yesteryear, *yéyé*, becomes in this reading an index of its politicisation. A strange, circular logic is at work here: the protest movement is deemed to have altered musical preferences, even as this change in preferences is itself taken as a symptom of the movement's far-reaching impact on social and cultural life.

Similar narratives were woven around other genres in the years following 1968. The emergence of song movements in Occitanie, Brittany and other regions during the late 1960s – all of them defined in opposition to the centralising pressures of jacobin Republicanism – was widely regarded as a response to May 1968 and the "prise de parole" it had encouraged.[37] Likewise, growing public interest in avant-garde music during the same period was more often than not treated as the expression of a new-found openness to 'critical' or 'contestatory' art, an openness presumably imparted by the protest movement. During a round-table discussion on the subject "Art in May–June 1968", one commentator pointed to the high attendance at a recent new music festival as evidence of this profound cultural shift: "Not only the quantitative success, but the attitude of the public in the auditorium [during the festival] showed that something has changed."[38] Even if these and other accounts exaggerated the impact that May 1968 exercised on musical life – after all, not every subsequent development in the world of music can be laid at the event's feet – it is clear that such accounts themselves constitute an important effect of the protest movement. In other words, one of the most significant consequences of May 1968 was the belief that it had in fact produced such significant consequences, a belief that shaped how individuals conceived the musical field and how they acted in accordance with this conception. Here William I. Thomas' famous dictum – that a situation defined as real by its participants is real in its effects – finds

---

[35] For instance, see Castanet 1993 and 1999 (on avant-garde music); Vassal 1976 (on *chanson*); Victor and Regoli 1978; Coulomb and Varrod 1987; and Castanet 1992 (on pop-rock); and Rouquette 1972; and Marti 1975 (on regional song movements).
[36] Kahn 1968, p. 5. [37] See, for instance, Marti 1975, pp. 26–7. [38] Bellour *et al.* 1969, p. 83.

corroboration.[39] And this in turn casts Aron's dismissive assessment of the protests and general strike in an altogether different light. For even if one were to accept his claim that May 1968 was a psychodrama, a form of collective delirium, this does not necessarily diminish its real-world impact. To the extent that May 1968 may be described as an imaginary revolution, it was one whose consequences – whether social, cultural or musical – were anything but.

[39] Thomas and Thomas 1928, pp. 571–2.

Bibliography

Adlington, Robert. 2007a. "'A sort of guerrilla': Che at the opera", in *Cambridge Opera Journal*, 19:2, pp. 167–93.

    2007b. "Organizing labor: composers, performers, and 'the renewal of musical practice' in the Netherlands, 1969–72", in *Musical Quarterly*, 90:3–4, pp. 539–77.

    2008. "1968 and new music in the Netherlands", in Beate Kutschke, ed., *Musikkulturen in der Revolte: Studien zu Rock, Avantgarde und Klassik im Umfeld von '1968'* (Stuttgart: Franz Steiner Verlag), pp. 103–14.

    2009a. "Forms of opposition at the 'politiek-demonstratief experimenteel' concert", in Robert Adlington, ed., *Sound Commitments: Avant-garde Music and the 1960s* (New York: Oxford University Press), pp. 56–77.

    (ed.). 2009b. *Sound Commitments: Avant-garde Music and the Sixties* (New York: Oxford University Press).

Adorno, Theodor W. 1950. *The Authoritarian Personality* (New York, NY: Harper).

    1967. "Bach defended against his devotees", in *Prisms*, trans. by Samuel and Shierry Weber (London: Spearman), pp. 133–46.

    1973 (1948). *Philosophy of Modern Music* (original German title: *Philosophie der Neuen Musik*), trans. by Anne G. Mitchell and Wesley V. Blomster (New York: Seabury).

Ajello, Nello. 1997. *Il lungo addio. Intellettuali e PCI dal 1958 al 1991* (Bari: Laterza).

Alegre, L. and Camacho G. 2006. "'Voto por voto, casilla por casilla': music of the civil resistance movement for the defence of the vote", unpublished paper presented at the International Association for the Study of Popular Music (IASPM) Conference, Mexico.

Allen, Clifford. 2008. "Chris McGregor: eclipse at dawn and very urgent" (www.allaboutjazz.com/php/article.php?id=29595, accessed 30 August 2011).

Allen, Michael. 2005. "'I just want to be a cosmic cowboy': hippies, cowboy code and the culture of a counterculture", in *Western Historical Quarterly*, 36:3, pp. 275–99.

Alquati, Romano. 1975. *Sulla FIAT e altri scritti* (Feltrinelli: Milano).

Alter, Nora M. 1996. *Vietnam Protest Theatre: The Television War on Stage*. (Bloomington and Indianapolis: Indiana University Press).

Amirkhanian, Charles. 1975. "The Politics and Music of Cornelius Cardew", interview, radio programme, KPFA, Berkeley, 21 January.

    1976. "Ode to Gravity: New Music and New Books on Music", review, radio programme, KPFA, Berkeley, 25 February.

Andriessen, Louis. 1964. *Sweet for Recorders* (Amsterdam: Donemus).

Andriessen, Louis, Reinbert de Leeuw, Misja Mengelberg, Jan van Vlijmen and Peter Schat. 1967. *Achter de muziek aan. Het Concertgebouworkest ter discussie* (Amsterdam: De Bezige Bij).

2008 (1969). *Reconstructie: een moraliteit*, libretto by Hugo Claus and Harry Mulisch (Amsterdam: Donemus).

Anonymous. 1965. Without title (inside front cover), in *Provo*, 1.

Anonymous. 1968a. "The constant flux", in *International Times*, 33, p. 2.

Anonymous. 1968b. Advert for Macnaghten concerts (Cardew, Stravinsky, and others, 3 October, Wigmore Hall; Williamson, 18 November, Euston Town Hall; Stockhausen visit, 25 November), in *International Times*, 40 (20 September to 3 October), p. 18.

Anonymous. 1968c. "Phil Ochs' songs to stay around", in *Rolling Stone* Issue 5, February 10, p. 4.

Anonymous. 1970a. "Daniel Viglietti" in *Punto Final* 108 (Santiago de Chile), p. 23.

Anonymous. 1970b. "What is 'appening", events page, in *International Times*, 71, p. 28.

Anonymous. 1971. Scratch calendar, April. Unpublished.

Anonymous. 1976. *ČSSR 1976: Junge Kultur unter Anklage* (Hamburg: Amnesty International).

Anonymous. 1996. "Chan Bochu [Connie Chan]: new image of Cantonese women", in *Cantonese Cinema Retrospective (1960–69)*, catalogue of the Sixth Hong Kong International Film Festival, reprint of 1982 (Hong Kong: The Urban Council of Hong Kong), pp. 88–93.

Anonymous. 1998 (1962). "SDS – der Affe Sultan, Bericht der dem RCDS nahe stehenden Studentenzeitschrift 'Ovis' über die XVII. SDS-Delegiertenkonferenz in Frankfurt, November 1962", in Wolfgang Kraushaar, ed., *Frankfurter Schule und Studentenbewegung: von der Flaschenpost zum Molotowcocktail 1946–1995*, Vol. 2 (Hamburg: Rogner and Bernhard bei Zweitausendeins), pp. 157–9.

Anonymous. 1999. "Jieitai ni Hairô: Takada Wataru" (www1.linkclub.or.jp~kury/ ct/abunaiuta/jieitai.html, accessed August 2011).

Anonymous. 2002. Uncredited review in *Record Collector* (May), p. 43.

Anonymous. 2009. "Apollon, fabbrica occupata" (www.rassegna.it/video/2009/02/ 06/154/apollon-fabbrica-occupata, accessed February 2011).

Anonymous. 2011. "Die Sestigers" (http://diesestigers.wordpress.com/2011/05/12/ hello-world/, accessed 31 August 2011).

Anonymous. 2012a (or earlier). "Zengakuren – the struggle of the Japanese students" (www.media68.net/eng/japan/japan.htm, accessed 18 February 2012).

Anonymous. 2012b (or earlier). "Festival of Political Songs" (de.wikipedia.org/wiki/ Festival_des_politischen_Liedes, accessed 12 March 2012).

Anonymous. 2012c. "Four Jacks and a Jill" (en.wikipedia.org/wiki/Four_Jacks_and_ a_Jill, accessed 20 January 2012).

Arbeitskreis Sozialistischer Musikstudenten. 1968. Arbeitskreis Ssozialistischer Musikstudenten (Hamburg), flyer without title, Staats- und Universitätsbibliothek Hamburg Carl von Ossietzky, heritage of Hedwig Florey.

Aron, Raymond. 1969. *The Elusive Revolution: Anatomy of a Student Revolt*, trans. by Gordon Clough (New York: Praeger).

Arvidsson, Alf. 2008. *Musik och Politik hör Ihop: Diskussioner, Ställningstaganden och Musikskapande 1965-1980* (Möklinta: Gidlunds).

Ascough, Richard. 1999. "The Scratch Orchestra and the counterculture", unpublished article.

Bai, Di. 2010. "Feminism in the revolutionary model ballets *The White-Haired Girl* and *The Red Detachment of Women*", in Richard Kind, ed., *Art in Turmoil: The Chinese Cultural Revolution 1966-76* (Vancouver: UBC Press), pp. 188-202.

Barlow, Tani. 1994. "Theorizing woman: *Funu, Guojia, Jiating*", in Tani Barlow and Angela Zito, eds., *Body, Subject and Power in China* (Chicago: University of Chicago Press), pp. 253-89.

Beckett, Alan. 1966. "Morton Feldman", interview, in *International Times*, 3 (14–27 November), p. 7. Republished in *Tempo*, 60, pp. 15–20.

Bellour, Raymond, Daniel Charles, Mikel Dufrenne, Dominique Jameux, Gilbert Lascault, Jean Laude *et al.* 1969. "L'Art en mai-juin 1968", in *Revue d'esthétique*, 22:1, pp. 75–96.

Benda, Václav. 1978. "Paralelní polis", in *Informace o Chartě 77*, 9, pp. 15–20.

Benedetti, Mario. 1974. *Daniel Viglietti* (Madrid: Edicion Júcar).

Bensaïd, Daniel and Henri Weber. 1968. *Mai 1968: Une Répétition Générale* (Paris: Maspero).

Bensen, Bert, trans. 1968. "Interview with Rudi Dutschke", in *International Times*, 29 (19 April to 2 May), p. 6 (original German interview from *Konkret Magazine*, n.d.).

Berio, Luciano. 1964. "Eugenetica musicale e gastronomia dell'"impegno', in *Il Convegno Musicale*, 1:2, pp. 123–31.

  1967. "Commenti al rock", in *Nuova Rivista Musicale Italiana*, 1:1, pp. 125–35; short version in English: "Comments on Rock", in Elizabeth Thomson and David Gutman, eds., *The Lennon Companion* (New York: Da Capo Press, 1987 and 2004), pp.97–9.

  1970 (1966). *Gesti, for Alto Recorder (1966)* (London: Universal Edition).

Bermani, Cesare. 1997. *Una storia cantata. 1962-1997: Trentacinque anni di attività del Nuovo Canzoniere Italiani/Istituto Ernesto De Martino* (Milano: Jaca Book).

Bernstein, David W. 2008. *The San Francisco Tape Music Center: 1960s Counterculture and the Avant-garde* (Berkeley, CA: University of California Press).

Bickers, Robert and Ray Yep. 2009. *May Days in Hong Kong: Riot and Emergency in 1967* (Hong Kong: Hong Kong University Press).

Biermann, Wolf. 1968. *Mit Marx- und Engelszungen* (Berlin: Wagenbach).

  1997. *Wie man Verse macht und Lieder. Eine Poetik in acht Gängen* (Cologne: Kiepenheuer and Witsch).

Biko, Steven. 2002 (1978). *I Write What I Like* (Chicago: University of Chicago Press).

Bingham, Howard L. 2009. *Howard L. Bingham's Black Panthers 1968* (Pasadena: Ammo Books).

Björnberg, Alf. 1993. "'Teach you to rock'? Popular music in the university music department", in *Popular Music*, 12:1, pp. 69–77.

1998. *Skval och Harmoni: Musik i Radio och TV 1925–1995* (Stockholm: Stiftelsen Etermedierna i Sverige).

Forthcoming. "Invincible heroes: the musical construction of national and European identities in Swedish Eurovision Song Contest entries", in Dafni Tragaki, ed., *Singing Europe: Spectacle and Politics in the Eurovision Song Contest* (Lanham, MD: Scarecrow Press).

Bjurström, Erling. 1983. "Det kommersiella tomrummet", in *Nordisk Forum*, 18:3–4, pp. 111–13.

"Bo". 1971. "Yoko Ono/Plastic Ono Band. *Fly*", review, in *International Times*, 119 (16–30 December), p. 19.

Boehmer, Konrad. 1968. "De crisis van het muziekonderwijs: de blokfluit kan tegen de Beatles niet op", in *Vrij Nederland*, 29: 4, p. 11.

1970. "Musikhochschule und Gesellschaft", summary by the editors, in *Sozialistische Zeitschrift für Kunst und Gesellschaft*, 1:4, pp. 68–72.

Boeke, Kees. 2008. Interview by Kailan Rubinoff, 15 July, Arezzo, Italy.

Boenisch, Hanne. 1971–2. *Journey to the North Pole*. Munich: Bavarian Television.

Boldini, Sergio. 1975. *Il canto popolare, strumento di comunicazione e di lotta* (Rome: Editrice Sindacale Italiana).

Bondy, Egon. 1980. *Básně z Roku 1976* (Popelnice: Samizdat).

Böning, Holger. 2004. *Der Traum einer Sache* (Bremen: edition lumière).

Borio, Gianmario. 2007. "Avantgarde als pluralistisches Konzept: Musik um 1968", in Arnold Jacobshagen and Markus Leniger, eds., *Rebellische Musik* (Cologne: Dohr), pp. 15–34.

Forthcoming. "Key questions of antagonist music-making: a view from Italy", in Robert Adlington, ed., *Red Strains: Music and Communism Outside the Communist Bloc* (British Academy/Oxford University Press, forthcoming 2013).

Bosio, Gianni. 1967. *L'intellettuale rovesciato. Interventi e ricerche sulla emergenza d'interesse verso le forme di espressione e di organizzazione "spontanee" nel mondo popolare e proletario* (Milano: edizioni del Gallo).

Bowman, James. 2009. Interview by Kailan Rubinoff, 1 July, London.

Boyd, Joe. 2008. "Joyful anarchy", in *Prospect*, 146 (May), p. 37.

Brau, Jean-Louis. 1968. *Cours, camarade, le vieux monde est derrière toi! Histoire du mouvement révolutionnaire étudiant en Europe* (Paris: Albin Michel).

Brown, Howard Mayer. 1988. "Pedantry or liberation? A sketch of the historical performance movement", in Nicholas Kenyon, ed., *Authenticity and Early Music: A Symposium* (New York: Oxford University Press), pp. 27–56.

Brown, Timothy. 2009. "'1968' East and West: divided Germany as a case study in transnational history", in *American Historical Review*, 114:1, pp. 69–96.

2008. "East Germany", in Martin Klimke and Joachim Scharloth, eds., *1968 in Europe: A History of Protest and Activism, 1956–1977* (Basingstoke: Palgrave Macmillan), pp. 189–98.

Brown, Timothy and Beate Kutschke. 2008. "Politisierung, Pop und Postmoderne E-Musik", in Tobias Schaffrik, ed., *68er-Spätlese. Was Bleibt von 1968?* (Münster: LIT), pp. 78–97.

Bullivant, Joanna. 2009. "Modernism, politics, and individuality in 1930s Britain: the case of Alan Bush", in *Music and Letters*, 90:3, pp. 432–52.

Bürger, Peter. 1984. *Theory of the Avant-Garde*, trans. by Michael Shaw (Minneapolis: University of Minnesota).

Butt, John. 2002. *Playing with History* (Cambridge: Cambridge University Press).

Bửu Chỉ. 2005 (2001). "Về Trịnh Công Sơn và Những Ca Khúc Phản Chiến Của Anh", in Trịnh Cung and Nguyễn Quốc Thái, eds., *Trịnh Công Sơn: Cuộc Đời, Âm Nhạc, Thơ, Hội Họa, Suy Tưởng* (Ho Chi Minh City: Nhà Xuất Bản Văn Hóa Sài Gòn), pp. 14–26.

Cage, John. 1961. *Silence* (Cambridge, MA: MIT Press).

Calvet, Louis-Jean. 1976. *La production révolutionnaire* (Paris: Payot).

Cardew, Cornelius. 1961. "Stockhausen's *Carré*", in *The Musical Times*, part 1, 102:1,424, pp. 619–22; part 2, 102:1,425, pp. 698–700.

1966. "One sound: la monte young", in *The Musical Times*, 107:1,485, p. 959.

1967. "Stockhausen's Plus-Minus", in *London Magazine*, 7:1 (April), pp. 86–8.

1969a. "A Scratch Orchestra: draft constitution", in *The Musical Times*, 110:1,516, pp. 617 and 619.

(ed.) 1969b. *Nature Study Notes* (London: Experimental Music Catalogue).

(ed.) 1972. *Scratch Music* (London: Latimer Press).

(ed.) 1974. *Stockhausen Serves Imperialism* (London: Latimer Press).

Carocci, Giovanni. 1960 (1958). *Inchiesta alla FIAT. Indagine su taluni aspetti della lotta di classe nel complesso FIAT* (Firenze: Parenti).

Carrasco, Eduardo. 2003, *Quilapayún: La revolución y las estrellas* (Santiago de Chile: RIL).

Casiccia, Alessandro and Michele L. Straniero 1975. "Condizioni e prospettive della 'nuova demologia'", in *La Musica Popolare* 1, pp. 5–11.

Castanet, Pierre-Albert. 1992. "Les années 1968: les mouvances d'une révolution socio-culturelle populaire", in Antoine Hennion, ed., *1789–1989: Musique, histoire, démocratie* (Paris: Editions de la Maison des sciences de l'homme), pp. 145–52.

1993. "1968: a cultural and social survey of its influences on French music", in *Contemporary Music Review*, 8:1, pp. 19–43.

1999. *Tout est bruit pour qui a peur: Pour une histoire sociale du son sale* (Paris: Editions Michel de Maule).

Central Committee of the Youth Song Movement. 1968. "Một Bó Hoa Đẹp Tặng Phong Trào 'Tiếng Hát Át Tiếng Bom'", in *Tiền Phong* (16 May), p. 3.

Certeau, Michel de. 1994 (1968). *La Prise de parole* (Paris: Seuil).

Chadima, Mikoláš. 1992. *Alternativa. Svědectvi o Českém Rock & Rollu Sedmdesátých Let (od Rekvalifikací k "Nové Vlně se Starým Obsahem")* (Brno: Host).

Chambers, Iain. 1985. *Urban Rhythms* (Basingstoke: Macmillan).

Chant, Michael. 2010. Email to Virginia Anderson, 23 October.

Chapman, Rob. 2010. *Syd Barrett: A Very Irregular Head* (London: Faber and Faber).
Cheung, Joys H. Y. 2010. "'The north wind blows': sounding bitterness in *The White-Haired Girl*, a communist political ritual", in *Reading Chinese Music and Beyond* (Hong Kong: Chinese Civilisation Centre, City University of Hong Kong).
Christophoulos, Jim and Phil Smart. 2005. *Van der Graaf Generator: The Book* ("Phil and Jim", www.vandergraafgenerator.co.uk).
Clark, Paul. 2010. "Model theatrical works and the remodelling of the cultural revolution", in Richard Kind, ed., *Art in Turmoil: the Chinese Cultural Revolution 1966–76* (Vancouver: UBC Press), pp. 167–87.
Clarke, Arthur C. 1956. *Childhood's End* (London: Pan).
Cohen, Joel and Herb Snitzer. 1985. *Reprise: The Extraordinary Revival of Early Music* (Boston: Little, Brown and Company).
Cohn-Bendit, Daniel. 2007. "Interview by Jean-Paul Sartre, 20 May 1968", in Jeremi Suri, ed., *The Global Revolutions of 1968* (New York: Norton), pp. 132–40.
Colvin, Sarah. 2009. *Ulrike Meinhof and West German Terrorism: Language, Violence, and Identity* (Rochester, NY: Camden House).
Comité Action Musique. 1968. "Les musiciens et la révolution de mai", in *Jazz-Hot*, 34:242 (August/September), pp. 14–16.
Constandse, Alexander L. and Harry Mulisch. 1966. "Gesprek met Roel van Duyn", in *De Gids*, 129:1, pp. 17–26.
Coulomb, Sylvie and Didier Varrod. 1987. *Histoire de chansons, 1968–1988: de Julien Clerc à Etienne Daho* (Paris: Balland).
Coulonges, Georges. 1969. *La chanson en son temps: de Béranger au jukebox* (Paris: Les Éditeurs Français Réunis).
Cross, Jonathan. 2001. "Manchester school", in *Grove Music Online. Oxford Music Online* (www.oxfordmusiconline.com/subscriber/article/grove/music/49722, accessed July 2010).
Curran, Alvin. 1995. "On spontaneous music", in response to Sabine Feisst, for her Doctoral thesis, 15–17 July 1995, (www.alvincurran.com/writings/spontaneous.html, accessed 17 October 2010).
Cushing, Lincoln and Ann Tompkins. 2007. *Chinese Posters: Art from the Great Proletarian Cultural Revolution* (San Francisco, CA: Chronicle Books).
Dael, Lucy van. 2004. Interview by Kailan Rubinoff, 16 July, Amsterdam.
Dällenbach, Lucien and Christiaan L. Hart Nibbrig (eds.). 1984. *Fragment und Totalität* (Frankfurt am Main: Suhrkamp).
Dane, Barbara and Irwin Silber. 1969. *The Vietnam Songbook* (New York: Guardian Books).
Đặng Tiến. 2005 (2001). "Trịnh Công Sơn Đời và Nhạc", in Trịnh Cung and Nguyễn Quốc Thái, eds., *Trịnh Công Sơn: Cuộc Đời, Âm Nhạc, Thơ, Hội Họa, Suy Tưởng* (Ho Chi Minh City: Nhà Xuất Bản Văn Hóa Sài Gòn), pp. 155–65.
Dart, Thurston. 1967. *The Interpretation of Music*. 4th edn. (London: Hutchinson).

Davis, Belinda. 2010. "A whole world opening up. Transcultural contact, difference, and the politicization of 'New Left' activists", in Belinda Davis, Martin Klimke and Wilfried Mausbach, eds., *Changing the World, Changing Oneself: Political Protest and Collective Identities in West Germany and the US in the 1960s and 1970s* (New York and Oxford: Berghahn Books), pp. 255–76.

Davis, Belinda, Martin Klimke and Wilfried Mausbach (eds.). 2010. *Changing the World, Changing Oneself: Political Protest and Collective Identities in West Germany and the US in the 1960s and 1970s* (New York and Oxford: Berghahn Books).

Davis, Madeleine. 2006. "The Marxism of the British New Left", in *Journal of Political Ideologies*, 11:3, pp. 335–58.

  2008. "The origins of the British New Left", in Martin Klimke and Joachim Scharloth, eds., *1968 in Europe: a History of Protest and Activism, 1956–1977* (New York: Palgrave Macmillan).

Dawbarn, Bob. 1969. "The greatest shake-up pop has known", in *Melody Maker* (16 August), p. 15.

Denisoff, R. Serge. 1973. *Great Day Coming: Folk Music and the American Left* (Baltimore: Penguin Books).

Department of Laws and Institutions (ed.). 2010 (1946). *Genkô Nihon Hôki* (Tôkyô: Gyôsei).

Dessì, Simone and Giaime Pintor (eds.) 1976. *La chitarre e il potere: gli autori della canzone politica contemporanea* (Rome: Savelli).

Díaz, Clara. 1994. *Pablo Milanés: con luz propia* (Tafalla: Txalaparta).

Dillaz, Serge. 1973. *La chanson française de contestation: Des barricades de la Commune à celles de mai 1968* (Paris: Seghers).

Dirlik, Arif. 1998. "The third world in 1968", in Carole Fink, Philipp Gassert and Detlef Junker, eds., *1968: The World Transformed* (Cambridge: Cambridge University Press), pp. 295–317.

Doggett, Peter. 2007. *There's a Riot Going On: Revolutionaries, Rock Stars and the Rise and Fall of '60s Counter-Culture* (Edinburgh: Canongate).

Dolmetsch, Arnold. 1969 (1946). *The Interpretation of the Music of the Seventeenth and Eighteenth Centuries*, revised edn, reprint (Seattle: University of Washington Press).

Domoy, S. 1968. "Avantpop is gevaarlijk, Hitweek is gevaarlijk", in *Hitweek* (20 September), p. 12.

Donington, Robert. 1974 (1963). *The Interpretation of Early Music*, revised edn (London: Faber and Faber).

Dreyfus, Laurence. 1983. "Early music defended against its devotees: a theory of historical performance in the twentieth century", in *Musical Quarterly*, 69:3, pp. 297–322.

Dreyfus, Laurence, Joseph Kerman, Joshua Kosman, John Rockwell, Ellen Rosand, Richard Taruskin and Nicholas McGegan. 1992. "The early music debate: ancients, moderns, postmoderns", in *The Journal of Musicology*, 10:1, pp. 113–30.

Drott, Eric 2008. "Free jazz and the French critic", in *Journal of the American Musicological Society*, 61:3, pp. 541–81.

   2011. *Music and the Elusive Revolution: Cultural Politics and Political Culture in France, 1968–1981* (Berkeley, CA: University of California Press).

Dunn, Christopher. 2001. *Brutality Garden. Tropicália and the Emergence of a Brazilian Counterculture* (Chapel Hill and London: University of North Carolina Press).

Dutschke, Gretchen. 1996. *Wir hatten ein barbarisches, schönes Leben* (Cologne: Kiepenheuer and Witsch).

Duyn, Roel van. 1966. "Eksperimenten!", in *Provo*, 7, pp. 25–6.

   1967. *Het witte gevaar. Een vademekum voor Provos* (Amsterdam: Meulenhoff).

   1985. *Provo. De geschiedenis van de provotarische beweging, 1965–1967* (Amsterdam: Meulenhoff).

Dyer, Geoff. 2010. *Working the Room: Essays and Reviews, 1999–2010* (Edinburgh: Canongate Books).

E. H. 1965. "True Baroque fingering", in *Recorder and Music*, 1:11, p. 346.

Eco, Umberto. 1976 (1962). *Opera aperta. Forma e indeterminazione nelle poetiche contemporanee* (Milano: Bompiani); English translation. *The Open Work* (Cambridge: Harvard University Press, 1989).

   1989. *The Open Work*, trans. Anna Cancogni (Cambridge, MA: Harvard University Press).

Ehrlich, Robert. 1993. "Frans Brüggen, oder: die vermarktung eines star-musikers", in *Tibia*, 18:2, pp. 449–53.

Eisler, Jerzy. 1998. "March 1968 in Poland", in Carole Fink, Philipp Gassert and Detlef Junker, eds., *1968: The World Transformed* (Cambridge: Cambridge University Press), pp. 237–52.

   2009. "Poland: the March events of 1968", in Philipp Gassert and Martin Klimke, eds., *1968. Memories and Legacies of a Global Revolt* (Washington, DC: German Historical Institute), pp. 167–70.

Elteren, Mel van. 1994. *Imagining America: Dutch Youth and its Sense of Place* (Tilburg, Netherlands: Tilburg University Press).

Engelbrecht, Carine. 2009. "Krotoa: aka. Eva of the Cape" (www.suite101.com/content/the-pocahontas-of-southern-africa-a92050, accessed 5 March 2012).

Eriksson, Bengt. 1975. *Från Rock-Ragge till Hoola Bandoola: den Svenska Popens Historia eller Berättelsen om ett Land under Kulturimperialistiskt Förtryck* (Stockholm: Tiden).

Eyerman, Ron and Andrew Jamison. 1998. *Music and Social Movements: Mobilizing Traditions in the Twentieth Century* (Cambridge: Cambridge University Press).

Fabian, Dorottya. 2001. "The meaning of authenticity and the early music movement: a historical review", in *International Review of the Aesthetics and Sociology of Music*, 32:2, pp. 153–67.

Faggiano, Pierpaolo. 2003. *Un cielo di Stelle. Parole e musica di Mario Schiano* (Rome: Manifesto Libri).

Fairley, Jan. 1985. "Annotated bibliography of Latin-American popular music with particular reference to Chile and *nueva canción*", in Richard Middleton and David Horn, eds., *Continuity and Change (=Popular Music 5)* (Cambridge: Cambridge University Press), pp. 305–57.

2002. "Inti illimani: living a life through making music", in Jan Fairley and David Horn, eds., *I Sing The Difference: Identity and Commitment in Latin American Song* (Liverpool: University of Liverpool, Institute of Popular Music), pp. 60–79.

2006. "An accidental hero", in *The Guardian* (15 September), p. 15 (www.guardian.co.uk/music/2006/sep/15/popandrock.worldmusic, accessed January 2012).

2008. "A universal language", in *The Scotsman* (30 January), pp. 34–5.

2009. "Backpage from Havana, Cuba", in *Songlines*, 64 (November/December), p. 120.

Feldman, Jill. 2008. *Interview by Kailan Rubinoff*, 15 July, Arezzo.

Feldstein, Ruth. 2005. "'I don't trust you anymore': Nina Simone, culture, and black activism in the 1960s", in *The Journal of American History*, 91:4, pp. 1,349–79.

Fiedler, Leslie. 1969. "Cross the border – close the gap", in *Playboy*, 16:12 (December 1969), pp. 151, 230, 252–4, 256–8.

Fiori, Umberto. 1984. "Rock and politics in Italy", in *Popular Music* 4, pp. 261–77.

Folk Camp (ed.). 1969. *Folk wa Mirai o Hiraku* (Tôkyô: Shakai-shimpô).

Fornäs, Johan. 1979. *Musikrörelsen: en Motoffentlighet?* (Gothenburg: Röda Bokförlaget).

Fortini, Franco. 1965. *Verifica dei Poteri. Scritti di Critica e di Istituzioni Letterarie* (Milano: Il Saggiatore).

Fountain, Nigel. 1988. *Underground: The London Alternative Press, 1966–74* (London: Routledge).

Fowler, Luke. 2006. *Theatre Poster Collage for the Film Pilgrimage from Scattered Points* (directed by Luke Fowler, UK: Shaddaz).

Francese, Carl and Richard S. Sorrell. 1995. *From Tupelo to Woodstock: Youth, Race and Rock and Roll-and-Roll in America 1954–1969* (Dubuque, Iowa: Kendall/Hunt).

Frank, Thomas. 1997. *The Conquest of Cool: Business Culture, Counterculture, and the Rise of Hop Consumerism* (Chicago: Chicago University Press).

Fraser, Ronald (ed.). 1988. *1968: A Student Generation in Revolt* (London: Chatto and Windus).

Frazier, Lessie J. and Deborah Cohen (eds.). 2009. *Gender and Sexuality in 1968: Transformative Politics in the Cultural Imagination* (New York: Palgrave Macmillan).

Frith, Simon. 1989. Euro pop, in *Cultural Studies*, 3:2, pp. 166–72.

1996. *Performing Rites: On the Value of Popular Music*. Cambridge, MA: Harvard University Press.

Fromm, Erich. 1936. "Sozialpsychologischer teil", in Max Horkheimer, ed., *Studien über Autorität und Familie* (Paris: Alcan), pp. 77–135.

1980 (1941). *Die Furcht vor der Freiheit* (New York: Farrar and Rinehart).

Fu, Ji. 2002. *Xin Zhongguo Xiju Shi* (Hunan: Hunan Meishu Chubanshe).

García, M. I. 2009. "El Nuevo Cancionero. Aproximación a una expresión de modernismo en Mendoza", unpublished paper.

Gaszyński, Marek. 2004. *Niemen. Czas jak Rzeka* (Warszawa: Prószyński i S-ka, 2004).

Gaulle, Charles de. 1968. "La Déclaration du Président", in *Le Monde* (1 June), p. 2.

Gelmetti, Vittorio. 1964. "Venezia ventisette", in *Marcatrè*, 11, pp. 207–9.

Genest, Andrea. 2009. "From oblivion to memory: Poland, the democratic opposition and 1968", in *Cuadernos de Historia Contemporánea*, 31, pp. 89–106.

Gibbs, Jason. 2004. "The West's songs, our songs: the introduction and adaptation of Western popular song in Vietnam before 1940", in *Asian Music*, 34:1, pp. 57–83.

2007. "The music of the state: Vietnam's quest for a national anthem", in *The Journal of Vietnamese Studies*, 2:2, pp. 129–74.

Gilcher-Holthey, Ingrid (ed.). 2008. *Vom Ereignis zum Mythos* (Frankfurt am Main: Suhrkamp).

Ginsborg, Paul. 2003. *A History of Contemporary Italy* (New York: Palgrave Macmillan).

Gleason, Ralph J. 1968. "The politics of rock dissent", in *San Francisco Chronicle*, 27 May.

Grange, Dominique. 2008. "Dominique Grange et Tardi: défendre les valeurs de 68" (http://bdethightech.blogs.lavoixdunord.fr/archive/2008/08/13/dominique-grange-et-tardi.html, accessed 2 October 2010).

Gravem, Dag Falang. 2004. *Revolusjonære Toner? Den Radikale Musikkbevegelsen i Norge ca. 1970–1983*, MA thesis, University of Oslo (www.duo.uio.no/publ/historie/2004/21537/21537.pdf, accessed November 2010).

Green, Jonathon. 1988. *Days in the Life* (London: Heineman).

Green, Richard. 1968a. "Or do we need something new?", in *New Musical Express (NME)*, 1,112 (4 May), p. 16.

1968b: "American violence inspired The Nice", in *Melody Maker* (6 July), p. 14.

Grissim, John. 1968. "Joan Baez, *Baptism*", review, in *Rolling Stone*, 19 (October 12), p. 30.

Gross, Alex. 1968. "The German mind explodes", in *International Times*, 30 (3–16 May), p. 2.

Großkopf, Erhard. 1974. No title, in *Sozialistischer Zeitschrift für Kunst und Gesellschaft*, 23/24, pp. 36–8.

Grossman, Loyd. 1976. *A Social History of Rock Music: From the Greasers to Glitter Rock* (New York: McKay).

Hà Thúc Cần. 1974. *Đất Khổ*, DVD (Westminster, CA: Dzui Entertainment).

Hanley, Bill. 2011. "Ricok against racism" (www.billhanley.org/projects/safrica/, accessed 31 August 2011).

Hanlon, Richard and Mike Waite. 1998. "Notes from the left: communism and British classical music", in Andy Croft, ed., *A Weapon in the Struggle: The Cultural History of the Communist Party in Britain* (London: Pluto Press).

Harman, Chris. 1988. *The Fire Last Time: 1968 and After* (London: Bookmarks).

Harris, Bryn. 1983. Interview by Virginia Anderson, 15 April.

Haskell, Harry. 1996 (1988). *The Early Music Revival: A History*, revised edn. (Mineola, NY: Dover Publications).

Haskell, Molly. 1987 (1974). *From Reverence to Rape: The Treatment of Women in the Movies* (Chicago: University of Chicago Press).

Hata, Masa'aki. 1993. "Hata Masa'aki Interview", in Susumu Kurosawa, ed., *Nippon Folk Ki* (Tôkyô: Shinko Music), pp. 54–70.

Havadi, Gergő. 2010. "Individualista, tradicionalista, forradalmár vagy megalkuvó emberek? A jazz politikai és társadalmi megítélése az ötvenes ás az hatvanas években", in *Korall*, 11:39, pp. 31–57.

Haynes, Bruce. 2007. *The End of Early Music* (New York: Oxford University Press).
2008. *Interview by Kailan Rubinoff*, 13 September, Montreal.

Heerma van Voss, A. J. 1972. "De jeugd-revolutie is weggeëbd. De historie van Hitweek", in *Haagse Post* (6 September), pp. 28–37.

Hellqvist, Per-Anders. 1977. *Ljudspåren Förskräcker: om Grammofonskivor, Grammofonbolag och Musikindustrins Makthavare* (Stockholm: Forum).

Hendler, Herb. 1987. *Year by Year in the Rock Era* (New York: Praeger).

Hentschel, Frank. 2008. "Ein Popkonzert und die ästhetische Entdogmatisierung der 'Neuen Musik' nach 1968", in Beate Kutschke, ed., *Musikkulturen in der Revolte* (Stuttgart: Steiner), pp. 39–54.

Herzfeld, Michael. 1997. *Cultural Intimacy: Social Poetics and the Nation State* (New York and London: Routledge).

Vũ Thư Hiên. 2001. "Trịnh Công Sơn – A Great Poet" ("Trịnh Công Sơn – Một Nhà Thơ Lớn") (available at www.trinh-cong-son.com/vthien.html, accessed December 2011).

Higgins, Hannah. 2002. *Fluxus Experience* (Berkeley, CA: University of California Press).

Hippen, Reinhard. 1980. "Wer kann Wolf Biermann nicht verkraften. Der genosse und die westdeutsche linke", in Heinz Ludwig Arnold, ed., *Wolf Biermann* (Munich: text + kritik), pp. 170–209.

Hirosé, Masaru. 1969. "Aratana chikara to hôkô o: Kansai Folk undô no tenkai", in Kenji Muro, ed., *Jidai wa Kawaru: Folk to Guerilla no Shisô* (Tôkyô: Shakai-shimpô), pp. 207–25.

Hoàng Tá Thích. 2007. *Như Những Dòng Sông: Tản Mạn Về Nhạc Sĩ Trịnh Công Sơn* (Ho Chi Minh City: Nhà Xuất Bản Văn Nghệ).

Hobbs, Christopher. 2010. Email to Virginia Anderson, 19 October.

Hobsbawm, Eric J. 1994. *Ages of Extremes: the Short Twentieth Century, 1914–1991* (London: Michael Joseph).

Hoensch, Jörg K. 1978. *Geschichte der Tschechoslowakischen Republik 1918–1978* (Stuttgart: Kohlhammer).

Holler, Eckard. 2007. "The Burg Waldeck Festivals, 1964–1969", in David Robb, ed., *Protest Song in East and West Germany since the 1960s* (Rochester, NY: Camden), pp. 97–132.

Home, Stewart. 1991. *Assault on Culture: Utopian Currents from Lettrisme to Class War* (London: AK Press).

Hoogland, Stanley. 2008. Interview by Kailan Rubinoff, 2 July, Amsterdam.

Hook, Sara Anne. 2004. "Barthold Kuijken: confessions of an autodidact", in *Early Music America*, 10:1, pp. 31–6, 62.

Hopkins, John. 1968. "An open letter to Mr Tariq Ali", in *International Times*, 29 (19 April–2 May), p. 15.

Horkheimer, Max. 1978 (1940/1942). "The authoritarian state" (1940/1942), in Andrew Arato and Eike Gebhardt, eds., *Essential Frankfurt School Reader* (Oxford: Blackwell), pp. 95–117.

Horn, Gerd-Rainer. 2007. *The Spirit of '68: Rebellion in Western Europe and North America, 1956–1976* (New York: Oxford University Press).

Horowitz, Is. 1973. "Classicomment: London imports: 'Back-to-Bach' hits spur its large growth", in *Billboard*, 79 (14 April), p. 29.

Hui, Yanbing. 2010. *Yangbanxi Yanjiu* (Beijing: Zhongguo Shehui Kexue Chubanshe).

Iddon, Martin. 2008. "Pamphlets and protests: the end of Stockhausen's Darmstadt", in Beate Kutschke, ed., *Musikkulturen in der Revolte* (Stuttgart: Steiner), pp. 55–63.

Issitt, Micah L. 2009. *Hippies: A Guide to an American Subculture* (Santa Barbara, CA: Greenwood Press).

Iwai, Hiroshi. 1992. "Iwai Hiroshi interview", in Susumu Kurosawa, ed., *Nippon Folk Ki* (Tôkyô: Shinko Music), pp. 72–80.

Jacobshagen, Arnold and Markus Leniger (eds.). 2007. *Rebellische Musik* (Cologne: Dohr).

Jaffe, Harry and Tom Sherwood. 1994. *Dream City: Race, Power, and the Decline of Washington* (New York: Simon and Schuster).

James, David. 1989. "The Vietnam War and American music", in *Social Text* 23 (Autumn–Winter), pp. 122–43.

Jiang, Qing. 1967 (1964). "Tan Jiangju geming: 1964 nian 7 yue zai jiangju xiandaixi guanmuo yanchu renyuan zuotanhui shang de jianghua", talk presented at the symposium for performers of contemporary Beijing opera festival held in July 1964, in *Renmin Ribao* (10 May 1967).

Jones, Carol. 2007. *Criminal Justice in Hong Kong* (New York: Routledge-Cavendish).

Kahn, Jean-François. 1968. "Hit-parades", in *L'Express*, special issue (June), p. 5.

Kalisch, Volker. (ed.). 1998. *Warschauer Herbst und Neue Polnische Musik* (Essen: Die Blaue Eule).

Karl, Gregory. 2002. "King Crimson's *Lark's Tongues in Aspic*: a case of convergent evolution", in Kevin Holm-Hudson, ed., *Progressive Rock Reconsidered* (New York: Routledge), pp. 121–42.

Karnow, Stanley. 1984. *Vietnam: A History* (London and New York: Penguin Books).

Keen, N. J. 1961. "Living jazz", letter to the editor, in *New Left Review*, 1:11, p. 52.

Kelly, Thomas Forrest. 2008. Interview by Kailan Rubinoff, 14 July, Uzzano, Italy.
  2011. *Early Music: A Very Short Introduction* (New York: Oxford University Press).

Kennedy, James C. 1995a. "Building New Babylon: Cultural Change in the Netherlands during the 1960s", Ph.D. dissertation, University of Iowa.
  1995b. *Nieuw Babylon in Aanbouw. Nederland in de Jaren Zestig* (Amsterdam: Boom).

Kenyon, Nicholas, ed. 1988. *Authenticity and Early Music: a Symposium* (New York: Oxford University Press).

Kernodle, Tammy L. 2008. "'I Wish I Knew How it would Feel to Be Free': Nina Simone and the redefining of the freedom song of the 1960s", in *Journal of the Society for American Music*, 2:3, pp. 295–317.

Klemm, Dieter and Vridolin Enxing. 2010. Interview by Beate Kutschke with members of Floh de Cologne, Dieter Klemm and Vridolin Enxing, 11 October 2010.

Klimke, Martin. 2010. *The Other Alliance: Student Protest in West Germany and the United States in the Global Sixties* (Princeton, NJ: Princeton University Press).

Klimke, Martin and Joachim Scharloth (eds.). 2008. *1968 in Europe: A History of Protest and Activism, 1956–1977* (New York: Palgrave Macmillan).

Klis, Jolande van der. 1991. *Oude muziek in Nederland: Het verhaal van de pioniers 1900–1975* (Utrecht: STOOM).

Knights, Vanessa. 2007. *Sexo Contra Muerte: AIDS and Popular Music*, unpublished paper read at Society for Latin American Studies Conference Music in Latin America: Memory, Activism and Social Change, Newcastle.

Koch, Gerhard R. 1970. "Beethoven a tempo", in *Musica*, 24:2, pp. 124–5.

Koechlin, Philippe. 1968. "La chanson dynamite", in *Le Métier*, 5, pp. 12–13.

Kokita, Kiyohito. 2002. "Imjin-gawa no sûki-na unmei", in *Aera* (12–19 August), pp. 18–20.

Ku, Ho Kwan. 1997. "Image and identity: a study of Connie Chan Po Chu and Josephine Siao Fong Fong as popular icons for women in the cultural industry of Hong Kong", M.Phil. thesis, The Chinese University of Hong Kong.

Kuijken, Barthold. 2008. *Interview by Kailan Rubinoff*, 30 June, Brussels.

Kuisel, Richard F. 1991. "Coca-Cola and the cold war: the French face Americanization, 1948–1953", in *French Historical Studies*, 17:1, pp. 96–116.

Kurlansky, Mark. 2004. *1968: The Year That Rocked the World* (New York: Ballantine Books).

Kurosawa, Susumu (ed.). 1992. *Nippon Folk Ki*. (Tôkyô: Shinko Music).

Kutschke, Beate. 2007a. *Neue Linke/Neue Musik* (Cologne and Weimar: Böhlau).

Kutschke, Beate. 2007b. "L'esthétique musicale de la nouvelle gauche", in Alessandro Arbo, ed., *Perspectives et méthodes de l'esthétique musicale* (Paris: Harmattan), pp. 339–51.

(ed.). 2008. *Musikkulturen in der Revolte* (Stuttgart: Steiner).

2010. "The celebration of Beethoven's bicentennial in 1970 – the anti-authoritarian movement and its impact on radical avant-garde and postmodern music in West Germany", in *The Musical Quarterly*, 93:3–4, pp. 560–615.

2012. "Collagen, variationensätze und hommagen – zitattechniken in der DDR nach der niederschlagung des prager frühlings", in Amrei Flechsig and Stefan Weiss, eds., *Postmoderne hinter dem Eisernen Vorhang* (Hildesheim: Olms).

Laing, Heather. 2000. "Emotion by numbers: music, song and the musical," in Bill Marshall and Robynn Stilwell eds., *Musicals: Hollywood and Beyond* (Exeter/Portland, OR: Intellect), pp. 5–13.

Laird, Michael. 2009. *Interview by Kailan Rubinoff*, 26 June, London.

Lalandi, Lina. 1963. "The English Bach Festival", in *Musical Times*, 104:1444, p. 413.

Langhans, Rainer and Fritz Teufel. 1968. Rainer Langhans and Fritz Teufel, eds., *Klau mich* (Frankfurt am Main and Berlin: Edition Voltaire).

Langston [sic, Langdon] Jones, Jack H. Moore, Victor Schonfield and others. 1968. "*IT* New Music Supplement", in *International Times*, 25 (2–15 February), pp. 7–10.

Law, Kar. 1996. "Introduction", in *The Restless Breed: Cantonese Stars of the Sixties, catalogue of the twentieth Hong Kong International Film Festival* (Hong Kong: The Urban Council of Hong Kong), p. 10.

Leeuw, Reinbert de. 1973. *Muzikale anarchie* (Amsterdam: De Bezige Bij).

Leonhardt, Gustav. 2008. *Interview by Kailan Rubinoff*, 3 July, Amsterdam.

Leopold, Silke. 1994. "Barock", in Ludwig Finscher, ed., *Die Musik in Geschichte und Gegenwart* (Kassel: Bärenreiter).

Lester, Julius. 1969. *Look Out, Whitey! Black Power's Gon' Get Your Mama!* (New York: The Dial Press).

Lévi-Strauss, Claude. 1987 (1950). *Introduction to the Work of Marcel Mauss*, trans. by Felicity Baker (London: Routledge).

Lewis, George E. 2008. *A Power Stronger than Itself: The AACM and American Experimental Music* (Chicago: University of Chicago Press).

Liebing, Yvonne. 2005. *All you need is beat. Jugendsubkultur in Leipzig 1957–1968* (Leipzig: Forum).

Lindaur, Vojtěch and Konrád Ondřej. 1990. *Život v tahu aneb Třicet roků rocku* (Praha: Tvorba).

 2001. *Bigbít* (Praha: Torst).

Lindblad, Peter. 2008. "Backstage pass: Bill Bruford – always close to the edge", interview, in *Goldmine*, 34 (5 June), no pagination (www.goldminemag.com/article/Backstage_Pass_Bill_Bruford_Always_close_to_the_edge/, accessed September 2009).

Lindelof, Anja Mølle. 2004. *Rockkulturen i Dansk Fjernsyn: 1970'erne in Concert* (rockhistorie.dk/antologi/Lindelof.pdf, accessed November 2010).

 2007. "Rockens Rulletekster: en Undersøgelse af Dansk TVs Formidling af Rock 1951–1988", Ph.D. dissertation (University of Copenhagen, Department of Arts and Cultural Studies).

Litweiler, John. 1984. *The Freedom Principle: Jazz After 1958* (New York: Da Capo Press).

Locke, Ralph. 1987. "The music of the French chanson, 1810–1850", in Peter Bloom, ed., *Music in Paris in the Eighteen-Thirties* (Stuyvesant, NY: Pendragon).

Lovecraft, H. P. 1951. "The call of Cthulhu", in *The Haunter of the Dark* (London: Gollancz).

Loy, Stephen. 2006. "Beethoven and Radicalism: Socio-political Engagement and Awareness of Tradition in New Music, 1968–1977", Ph.D. dissertation, Conservatorium of Music: University of Sydney.

Lucia, Christine. 2002. "Abdullah Ibrahim and the uses of memory", in *British Journal of Ethnomusicology*, 11:2, pp. 125–43.

Luckscheiter, Roman. 2007. "Der postmoderne impuls: '1968' als literaturgeschichtlicher katalysator", in Martin Klimke and Joachim Scharloth, eds., *1968. Handbuch zur Kultur- und Mediengeschichte der Studentenbewegung* (Stuttgart: Metzler).

Lummis, Charles Douglas. 1993. "Japan's radical constitution", in Setsuko Tsunéoka Norimoto and C. Douglas Lummis, eds., *Nihonkoku Kenpô o Yomu* (Tokyo: Kashiwa-shobô), pp. 155–93.

Macan, Edward. 1997. *Rocking the Classics* (New York: Oxford University Press).

2006. *Endless Enigma: A Musical Biography of Emerson, Lake and Palmer* (Peru, IL: Open Court).

Macchiarella, Ignazio. 2005. *Il canto necessario. Giovanna Marini compositrice, didatta e interprete* (Udine: Nota).

MacDonald, Ian. 1995. *Revolution in the Head: The Beatles' Records and the Sixties* (London: Pimlico).

Mackintosh, Catherine. 2008. *Interview by Kailan Rubinoff, 12 June*, London.

Màdera, Romano (ed.). 1978. *Ma non è una malattia. Canzoni e movimento giovanile* (Rome: Savelli).

Maéda, Yoshitaké and Kôji Hirahara, eds. 1993. *60 Nendai: Folk no Jidai* (Tokyo: Shinkô Music).

Mahnert, Detlev and Harry Stürmer. 2008. *Zappa, Zoff und Zwischentöne* (Essen: Klartext).

Mai Văn Bộ. 1993. "Giải Phóng Miền Nam: Một Tác Phẩm Hoàn Chỉnh Tuyệt vời của Cao Trào Đồng Khởi", in Nguyễn Hữu Thọ, ed., *Chung Một Bóng Cờ.* (Hanoi: Nhà Xuất Bản Chính Trị Quốc Gia), pp. 641–7.

Mailer, Norman. 1968. *Miami and the Siege of Chicago: An Informal History of the Republican and Democratic Conventions of 1968* (New York: Primus).

Marcus, Greil. 1969. *Rock and Roll will Stand* (Boston: Beacon Press).

1997. *Invisible Republic: Bob Dylan's Basement Tapes* (New York: Henry Holt).

Marsh, Hazel. 2010. "'Writing our history in songs': Judith Reyes, popular music and the student movement of 1968", in *Bulletin of Latin American Research*, 29:1, pp. 144–59.

Marti, Claude. 1975. "Mai 68: naissance d'une chanson occitane", in *Politique Hebdo* (12 June), pp. 26–7.

Martijn 1965. "Protestbiet", in *Provo*, 5 (1965), pp. 24–7.

Martin, Bill. 1998. *Listening to the Future: the Time of Progressive Rock 1968–1978* (Peru, IL: Open Court).

Marty, Laurent. 1985. *Chanter pour survivre: Culture ouvrière, travail et techniques dans le travail. Roubaix, 1850–1914* (Paris: L'Harmattan).

Marx, Karl. 1973 (1858). "Fragment on machines" in Karl Marx, *Grundrisse: Foundations of the Critique of political Economy* (original German title: *Grundrisse der Kritik der Politischen Ökonomie*), trans. by Martin Nicolaus (Harmondsworth: Penguin), pp. 690–712.

McDougall, Bonnie S. (ed.). 1984. *Popular Chinese Literature and Performing Arts in the People's Republic of China, 1949-1979* (Berkeley: University of California Press).

McGregor, Maxine. 1995. *Chris McGregor and the Brotherhood of Breath* (Flint, MI: Bamberger).

McLuhan, Marshal. 1962. *The Gutenberg Galaxy* (London: Routledge).

Messinis, Mario and Paolo Scarnecchia (eds.). 1977. *Musica e politica. Teoria e Critica della contestualità sociale della musica, voci sull'est, testimonianze e letture di contemporanei* (Venice: Marsilio).

Middleton, Richard. 1990. *Studying Popular Music* (Milton Keynes: Open University Press).

Mihashi, Kazuo. 1975. "Nippon folk nenpyô", in Kôtarô Yamamoto, Kazuo Mihashi, and others., eds., *Waréra Folk Sedai*. (Tokyo: Aréchi Shuppan), pp. 229-43.

1979. *Folkutté Nanda* (Tokyo: Nippon Hôsô Kyôkai).

Miklódy, Éva. 2004. "ART, Klikk, KAOS, and the rest: Hungarian youth rapping", in Heike Raphael-Hernandez, ed., *Blackening Europe. The African American Presence* (New York: Routledge), pp. 187-200.

Miles, Barry. 1967a. "Miles interviews Paul McCartney", in *International Times*, 6 (16-29 January), pp. 8-10.

1967b. "Miles trip", in *International Times*, 16 (30 June-14 July), p. 7.

1968a. "UFO is dead – long live UFO", in *International Times*, 29 (19 April-2 May), p. 3.

1968b. "Multi-purpose Beatle music", in *International Times*, 45 (29 November-12 December), p. 10.

1997. *Paul McCartney: Many Years from Now* (London: Secker and Warburg).

Miller, Lloyd and James K. Skipper, Jr. 1972. "Sounds of black protest in avant-garde jazz", in R. Serge Denisoff and Richard A. Peterson, eds., *The Sounds of Social Change* (Chicago: Rand McNally and Company), pp. 26-37.

Mills, Gordon. 1968. "Bob Dylan, *John Wesley Harding*", review, in *Rolling Stone*, 6 (February 24), p. 21.

Mitsui, Tôru. Forthcoming. "Enka", in John Shepherd and David Horn, eds., *Encyclopedia of Popular Music of the World*, Vol. 10 (London: Continuum).

Mitter, Armin and Stefan Wolle. 1993. *Untergang auf Raten* (Munich: Bertelsmann).

Mittler, Barbara. 2003. "Cultural revolution model works and the politics of modernization in China: an analysis of *Taking Tiger Mountain by Strategy*", in *The World of Music*, 45:2, pp. 53-82.

Mol, Pieter-Jan. 1985. "Paradise lost. Een generatie op drift: *Hitweek* 1965-1969", in *Jeugd en Samenleving*, 15, pp. 612-68.

Molasky, Michael. 2005. *Sengo Nihon no Jazz Bunka* (Tokyo: Seidosha).

Moller, Karen. 2006. *Technicolour Dreamin': The 1960s Rainbow and Beyond* (Victoria, BC: Trafford Publishing).

Moore, Allan F. 1996. "Signifying the spiritual in the music of Yes", in *Contemporary Music Review*, 14:3-4, pp. 25-33.

2002. "Authenticity as authentication", in *Popular Music*, 21:2, pp. 209–23.

2004. "The contradictory aesthetics of Woodstock", in Andy Bennett, ed., *Remembering Woodstock* (Aldershot: Ashgate), pp. 75–89.

Moore, Robin D. 2006. *Music and Revolution: Cultural Change in Socialist Cuba* (Berkeley: University of California Press).

Mori, Tatsuya. 2003. *Hôsô Kinshi Uta* (Tokyo: Kôbunsha).

Morin, Edgar, Claude Lefort and Jean-Marc Coudray. 1968. *Mai 1968: La Brèche* (Paris: Fayard).

Morita, Minoru. 1984. "International", in Kunihiko Shimanaka, ed., *Heibonsha Daihyakka Jiten*, Vol. 2 (Tokyo: Heibonsha).

Muller, Carol and Sathima Bea Benjamin. 2011. *Musical Echoes: South African Women Thinking in Jazz* (Durham: Duke University Press).

Müller-Doohm, Stefan. 2003. *Adorno. Eine Biographie* (Frankfurt am Main: Suhrkamp).

Mulvey, Laura. 1975. "Visual pleasure and narrative cinema", in *Screen*, 6:3, pp. 6–18.

Münkler, Herfried. 2005 (2002). *New Wars (original German title*: Die Neuen Kriege*)*, trans. by Patrick Camillier (Cambridge: Polity).

Muro, Kenji. 1969. "Document: Tôkyô Folk Guerilla" in Kenji Muro, ed., *Jidai wa Kawaru: Folk to Guerilla no Shisô* (Tokyo: Shakai-shimpô), pp. 7–61.

Nagira, Ken'ichi. 1995. *Nippon Folk Shitéki Taizen* (Tokyo: Chikuma-shobô).

Nakagawa, Gorô. 1969. "Boku ni totté uta-towa nanika", in Folk Camp, ed., *Folk wa Mirai o Hiraku* (Tokyo: Shakai-shimpô), pp. 184–99.

Nasson, Bill. 2008. "Apartheid South Africa in 1968: not quite business as usual", in Nora Farik, ed., *1968 Revisited: 40 Years of Protest Movements* (Brussels: Heinrich Böll Foundation), pp. 43–8.

Negri, Antonio. 1991. *Marx beyond Marx: Lessons on the Grundrisse* (Brooklyn: Autonomedia).

Nehring, Holger. 2008. "Great Britain", in Martin Klimke and Joachim Scharloth, eds., *1968 in Europe: A History of Protest and Activism, 1956–1977* (New York: Palgrave Macmillan), pp. 125–36.

Neumann, Frederick. 1978. *Ornamentation in Baroque and Post-Baroque Music: With Special Emphasis on J. S. Bach* (Princeton, NJ: Princeton University Press).

Ng, Chun-Hung. 2004. "Bringing women back in: family change in Hong Kong", in Anita Kit-wa Chan and Wong Wai-ling, eds., *Gendering Hong Kong* (Hong Kong: Oxford University Press), pp. 196–218.

Nguyen, Phong T. 2007. "'Our Songs can Drown Out the Bomb!': musical change in Vietnam since the war", in *Senri Ethnological Reports*, 65, pp. 147–65.

Nguyễn Trọng Tạo and Nguyễn Thụy Kha (eds.). 2001. *Trịnh Công Sơn: Một Người Thơ Ca, Một Cõi Đi Về* (Hanoi: Nhà Xuất Bản Âm Nhạc).

Nihon Kokugo Dai-jiten Henshû Iinkai (ed.). 2000. *Nihon Kokugo Dai-jiten*, Vol. 1 (Tokyo: Shôgakkan).

Nihon Sengo Ongaku-shi Kenkyû-kai (Group for the Study of Post-war Music in Japan) (ed.). 2007. *Nihon Sengo Ongaku-shi*, Vol. 1 (Tokyo: Heibonsha).

Noeske, Nina. 2007. *Musikalische Dekonstruktion: Neue Instrumentalmusik in der DDR* (Cologne and Weimar: Böhlau).
Nono, Luigi. 1960. "The historical reality of music today", in *The Score*, 27, pp. 41–5.
    2001. Angela Ida De Benedictis and Veniero Rizzardi (eds.), *Scritti e colloqui*, 2 vols. (Lucca/Milano: LIM/Ricordi).
Nono, Luigi, Giovanni Pirelli and Two Workers from Turin. 1975 (1971). "Uso del suono nella lotta proletaria. Conversazione tra Luigi Nono, Giovanni Pirelli e due operai torinesi" (Turin, 7 May 1971), in *Cultura di base in fabbrica* (= *Il Nuovo Canzioniere Italiano*, third series, n. 2) (December), pp. 47–59.
Nordström, Sixten, Lars Westin and Hans Åstrand. 1975. *Vi Tycker om Musik: en Debattbok Kring Musiken i Sverige* (Stockholm: Liber).
Norrington, Sir Roger. 2009. Interview by Kailan Rubinoff, 30 June, Newbury, UK.
Norse, Harold, Alexander Trocchi and Robert Tasher. 1968. "Three views on the Anti-University", in *International Times*, 26 (16–29 February), p. 6.
Norton, Barley. Forthcoming. "Music and censorship in Vietnam since 1954", in Patricia Hall, ed., *The Oxford Handbook of Music Censorship* (New York: Oxford University Press).
Nuttall, Jeff. 1968. *Bomb Culture* (London: MacGibbon and Kee).
Nylöf, Göran. 1967. *Musikvanor i Sverige* (Stockholm: Esselte).
Nyman, Michael. 1999 (1974). *Experimental Music: Cage and Beyond* (Cambridge: Cambridge University Press).
Ochoa, Amparo. 2012. "La maldición de la Malinche", in *Lyrics Time* (www.lyricstime.com/amparo-ochoa-la-maldici-n-de-la-malinche-lyrics.html, accessed 27 January 2012).
O'Connell, John Morgan and Salwa El-Shawan Castelo-Branco (eds.). 2010. *Music and Conflict* (Urbana and Chicago: University of Illinois Press).
Okabayashi, Nobuyasu. 1969. "Oré to folksong no Ayashii Kankei ni Kansuru Hôkoku", in Folk Camp, ed., *Folk wa Mirai o Hiraku* (Tokyo: Shakaishimpô), pp. 109–60.
Original Confidence (ed.). 1997. *Oricon Chart Book* (Tokyo: Oricon).
Ossorio, José M. 1967, "Encuentro de la canción protesta: cronica", in *Revista Casa de las Americas* 7:45, pp. 138–56.
Otto, Thomas, and Stefan Piendl. 2007. *Erst mal Schön ins Horn tuten* (Regensburg: ConBrio).
Owen, Gorwel. 2009. Email to Virginia Anderson, 15 December.
Paczkowski, Andrzej. 2003. *Strajki, Bunty, Manifestacje Jako "Polska Droga" Przez Socjalizm* (Poznań: Poznańskie Towarzystwo Przyjaciół Nauk).
Palisca, Claude V. 2002. "Baroque", in Stanley Sadie, ed., *The New Grove* (London: Macmillan).
Parrott, Andrew. 2008. Interview by Kailan Rubinoff, 8 June, Oxford.
Parsons, Michael. 1964. "John Cage", in *New Left Review*, 1:23, pp. 83–6.
Pas, Niek. 2002. "Political art als provotarisch wapen. De expressieve politiek van Provo (1965–1967)", in *Spiegel Historiael*, 37:11–12, pp. 482–7.

2003. *Imaazje! De verbeelding van Provo, 1967–1967* (Amsterdam: Wereldbibliotheek).

2008. "Subcultural movements: the provos", in Martin Klimke and Joachim Scharloth, eds., *1968 in Europe: A History of Protest and Activism, 1956–1977* (New York: Palgrave Macmillan, 2008), pp. 13–22.

2009. "De problematische internationalisering van de Nederlandse jaren zestig", in *Bijdragen en Mededelingen betreffende de Geschiedenis der Nederlanden*, 124:4, pp. 618–32.

Pasolini, Pier Paolo. 1999. *Saggi sulla letteratura e sull'arte*, 2 vols., Walter Siti and Silvia De Laude (eds.) (Milano: Mondadori).

Pauer, Jan. 2000. "Charta 77. Moralische opposition unter den bedingungen der diktatur", in Wolfgang Eichwede, ed., *Samizdat. Alternative Kultur in Zentral- und Osteuropa: die 60er bis 80er Jahre* (Bremen: Edition Temmen), pp. 52–63.

Peace for Vietnam Committee (ed.). 1974. *Shiryô: "Beheiren" Undô*, Vol. 1 (Tokyo: Kawadé-shobô Shinsha).

Peel, John. 1968. Untitled piece in *New Musical Express* (27 July), p. 24.

People's Army Publishing House. 1968. *Tiếng Hát Át Tiếng Bom* (Hanoi: Nhà Xuất Bản Quân Đội Nhân Dân).

Perlman, Marc. 1998. "Early-music talk begins to heat up again", in *New York Times* (Sunday, 14 June), pp. 29, 36.

Perone, James E. 2004. *Music of the Counterculture Era* (Westport, CT and London: Greenwood).

Perris, Arnold. 1983. "Music as propaganda: art at the command of doctrine in the People's Republic of China", in *Ethnomusicology: Journal of Society for Ethnomusicology*, 27:1, pp. 1–28.

Pettan, Svanibor. 1998. "Music, politics, and war in Croatia in the 1990s: an introduction", in Svanibor Pettan, ed., *Music, Politics, and War: Views from Croatia* (Zagreb: Institute of Ethnology and Folkore Research), pp. 9–29.

Phạm Duy. 2001. "Đẹp Như Tranh Trừu Tượng", in Nguyễn Trọng Tạo and Nguyễn Thụy Kha, eds., *Trịnh Công Sơn: Một Người Thơ Ca, Một Cõi Đi Về.* (Hanoi: Nhà Xuất Bản Âm Nhạc.), pp. 59–63.

Philip, Robert. 2004. *Performing Music in the Age of Recording* (New Haven: Yale University Press).

Piil, Beate S. 1981. *Beat på Dansk* (Aarhus: PubliMus).

Pintor, Giaime. 1974. "Sulla musica pop", in *Ombre rosse* 8, pp. 46–56.

Pitt, Arthur A. 1970. "Stop the music", review, in *International Times*, 73, p. 11.

Platoff, John. 2005. "John Lennon, 'Revolution' and the politics of musical reception", in *Journal of Musicology*, 22:2, pp. 241–67.

Plaut, Martin. 2010. *History Workshop Journal*, 69:1, pp. 195–205.

Plummer, Mark. 1970. "Classical heads" in *Melody Maker* (19 December), p. 7.

Poiger, Uta. 2000. *Jazz Rock and Rebels: Cold War Politics and American Culture in Divided Germany* (Berkeley: University of California Press).

Pols, Bram. 1991. "Juni '66 – wim bieler (Q'65)", in *NRC Handelsblad* (28 June), p. 2 (also online at www.q65.org, accessed 27 April 2011).

Poniatowska, Elena. 1971. *La Noche de Tlatelolco* (Mexico: ERA).

1992 (1975). *Massacre in Mexico* (New York: Viking).

Potter, Keith. 1995. "Cornelius Cardew: some (postmodern?) reflections on experimental music and political music", in Mark Delaere, ed., *New Music, Aesthetics and Ideology* (Wilhelmshaven, Germany: Noetzel), pp. 152–69.

Povey, Glenn. 2007. *Echoes: The Complete History of Pink Floyd* (Chesham: Mindhead Publishing).

Preston, Stephen. 2008. *Interview by Kailan Rubinoff*, 10 June, London.

Rao, Y. H. 2009. "The power of hybrid musical gesture: Chinese opera percussions from model opera to Tan Dun", paper presented at the International Conference *East Meets West: Sino-Western Musical Relations/Intersections/Receptions/Representations*, held on 16–19 April at Hong Kong Baptist University (see conference website: http://musconf.hkbu.edu.hk/call_for_paper.htm).

Rauhut, Michael. 1997. "'Wir müssen etwas besseres bieten'. Rockmusik und Politik in der DDR", in *Deutschlandarchiv*, 30:4, pp. 572–87.

1998. "Blues in rot", in *Deutschlandarchiv*, 31:5, pp. 773–82.

Regtien, Ton. 1988. *Springtij: Herinneringen aan de Jaren Zestig* (Houten: Wereldvenster).

Rehm, Clemens. 2007. "1968 – was bleibt von einer Generation?", in *H-Soz-u-Kult* (http://hsozkult.geschichte.hu-berlin.de/tagungsberichte/id=1573, accessed 22 February 2011).

Reich, Wilhelm. 1946 (1933). *Mass Psychology of Fascism*, trans. by Theodore P. Wolfe (New York: Orgone Institute).

Righart, Hans. 1995. *De eindeloze jaren zestig: Geschiedenis van een generatieconflict* (University of Amsterdam Press).

2004. *De wereldwijde jaren zestig: Groot-Britannië, Nederland, de Verenigde Staten* (Utrecht: Uitgeverij Verloren).

2006. *De eindeloze jaren zestig: Geschiedenis van een generatieconflict*, second edition (Amsterdam University Press).

Ritter, Rüdiger. 2005. *Music as Vehicle for Politics. "Warsaw Autumn" between Socialist Power and Opposition in Poland, GDR and Hungary*, paper delivered at the conference of the British Association for Slavonic and Eastern European Studies (BASEES) in Cambridge, 4 April 2005.

Robb, David. 2007. "The cat-and-mouse game with censorship and institutions", in David Robb, ed., *Protest Song in East and West Germany since the 1960s* (Rochester, NY: Camden), pp. 227–54.

Robins, Brian. 1996. "An interview with Anthony Rooley of musica oscura", in *Fanfare*, 20:1, pp. 102, 104, 106, 108, 110.

Rodríguez, Silvio. 1996. *Canciones del Mar* (Havana, Cuba: Ediciones Ojalá en colaboración con Casa de las Americas).

Roessner, Jeffrey. 2006. "We all want to change the world: postmodern politics and the Beatles' *White Album*", in Kenneth Womack and Todd F. Davis, eds., *Reading the Beatles: Cultural Studies, Literary Criticism, and the Fab Four* (Albany, NY: State University of New York Press), pp. 147–58.

Rouquette, Yves. 1972. *La nouvelle chanson occitane* (Toulouse: Privat).

Rubin, Jerry. 1970. *Do It!* (New York: Simon and Schuster).

Rubinoff, Kailan R. 2006. "The Early Music Movement in the Netherlands: History, Pedagogy and Ethnography". Ph.D. dissertation, University of Alberta.

— 2009. "Cracking the Dutch early music movement: the repercussions of the 1969 *Notenkrakersactie*", in *Twentieth-century music*, 6:1, pp. 3–22.

— 2011. "Authenticity as a political act: Straub-Huillet's *Chronicle of Anna Magdalena Bauch* and the post-war Bach revival", in *Music and Politics*, 5: 1.

Ruchniewicz, Krzysztof. 2004. "Antistalinisten und Chartisten, Reformer und politische Aussteiger. Die verschiedenen Oppositionsgenerationen im real existierenden Sozialismus", in Hendrik Bispinck, Jürgen Danyel, Hans-Hermann Hertle and Hermann Wentker., eds., *Aufstände im Ostblock. Zur Krisengeschichte des Realen Sozialismus* (Berlin: Christoph Links), pp. 275–86.

Ruiter, Frans de. 2008. Interview by Kailan Rubinoff, 29 November, Boston.

Runner, Blade and Gusztáv Kosztolányi. 2000. "From Beats to Bass: a brief history of beat and rock music in Hungary", in *Central Europe Review* 2:12 (www.ce-review.org/00/12/bladerunner12.html, accessed 2 July 2011).

Russcol, Herbert. 1968. "Looking and listening: boom goes the harpsichord", in *House and Garden*, 134:4, pp. 74, 76, 78.

Ryback, Timothy. 1990. *Rock around the Bloc. A History of Rock Music in Eastern Europe and the Soviet Union* (New York: Oxford University Press).

Sanguineti, Edoardo. 2001. *Ideologia e linguaggio* (Milan: Feltrinelli).

Sanz, Joseba. 1994. *Silvio Memoria Trovada de una Revolución* (Tafalla: Txalaparta).

Savage, John. 2002 (1991). *England's Dreaming: Anarchy, Sex Pistols, Punk Rock and Beyond* (New York: St Martins Griffin).

Schafer, John C. 2007a. "The Trịnh Công Sơn phenomenon", in *The Journal of Asian Studies*, 66:3, pp. 597–643.

— 2007b. "Death, Buddhism, and Existentialism in the songs of Trịnh Công Sơn", in *The Journal of Vietnamese Studies*, 2:1, pp. 144–86.

Schafer, R. Murray. 1963. *British Composers in Interview* (London: Faber and Faber).

Scharloth, Joachim. 2010. *1968. Eine Kommunikationsgeschichte* (Paderborn: Fink).

Schat, Peter. 1966. "Tooi die danseres na de idioot", in *De Gids*, 129:1, pp. 44–50.

— 1968. "Inleiding", in *Muzikale en politieke commentaren en analyses bij een programma van een politiek-demonstratief experimenteel concert* (Amsterdam: Polak and Van Gennep), pp. 5–6.

Schmidt, Christfried. 1969. "Kammermusik I", unpublished.

Schnapp, Alain and Pierre Vidal-Naquet. 1971. *The French Student Uprising, November 1967–June 1968: An Analytical Record*, trans. by Maria Jolas (Boston: Beacon Press).

Schneemann, Carolee. 1997 (1979). *More than Meat Joy: Performance Works and Selected Writings* (Kingston, NY: McPherson and Co.).

Schonfield, Victor. 1968. "Musical compliment", letter, in *International Times*, 26 (16–29 February), p. 2.

Scratch Orchestra. 1971. Concert flyer, 5 March.

Seidel, Wolfgang. 2005. "Berlin und die Linke in den 1960ern. Die Entstehung der Ton Steine Scherben", in Wolfgang Seidel, ed., *Scherben. Musik, Politik und Wirkung der Ton Steine Scherben* (Mainz: Ventil), pp. 25–50.

Shen, Fan. 2004. *Gang of One: Memoirs of a Red Guard* (Lincoln: University of Nebraska Press).

Shrapnel, Hugh. 2010. Email to Virginia Anderson, 26 October.

Siegfried, Detlef. 1995. "Unsere Woodstocks: Jugendkultur, Rockmusik und gesellschaftlicher Wandel um 1968", in Stiftung Haus der Geschichte der Bundesrepublik Deutschland, ed., *Rock! Jugend und Musik in Deutschland. Begleitbuch zur Ausstellung* (Berlin: Christoph Links), pp. 52–61.

2006. *Time is on my Side* (Göttingen: Wallstein).

2008. "Music and protest in 1960s Europe", in Martin Klimke and Joachim Scharloth, eds., *1968 in Europe: A History of Protest and Activism, 1956–77* (New York: Palgrave Macmillan), pp. 57–70.

Sievers, Rudolf (ed.). 2004. *1968: Eine Enzyklopädie* (Frankfurt am Main: Suhrkamp).

Simon, Géza Gábor. 1999. *Magyar Jazztörténet* (Budapest: Magyar Jazzkutatási Társaság).

Simonetti, Gianni Emilio. 1973a. "Probapossible prolegomena to idealreal history of pop", in Riccardo Bertoncelli, ed., *Pop Story: suite per consumismo, pazzia e contraddizioni* (Rome: Arcana), pp. 5–17.

1973b. *Dalla causa alla cosa delle rivoluzione. Soggettività della Cultura alternativa giovanile e movimento reale del proletario* (Rome: Arcana).

1975. *Critica dell'orecchio. Osservazioni sull'ideologia della Controcultura e della Musica in Particolare* (Milan: Multhipla).

Sinclair, John. 1968. "White Panther Statement", in *Berkeley Barb* (29 November to 5 December), p. 13.

Siné. 1968. "Lettre de Siné à la redaction du Point", in *Le Point* 16, p. 2.

Skowroneck, Martin. 1972 (1968). "Probleme des Cembalobaus aus historischer Sicht", in *Hifi Stereophonie* 5, pp. 700, 781, 875. Eng. trans. by Philip Howard and Max Horton in *The Diapason*, 62:12 (1971), pp. 16–17; 63:1 (1972), pp. 14–15; 63:2 (1972), pp. 10–11.

Smith, Dave. 2010. Email to Virginia Anderson, 27 July.

Smith-Sivertsen, Henrik. 2007. "Kylling med Soft Ice og Pølser: Populærmusikalske Versioneringspraksisser i Forbindelse med Danske Versioner af Udenlandske Sange i Perioden 1945–2007", Ph.D. dissertation (University of Copenhagen, Department of Arts and Cultural Studies).

Soéda, Azenbô. 1963. *Enka no Meiji-Taishô-shi* (Tokyo: Iwanami Shoten).

Soéjima, Teruhito. 2002. *Nihon Free Jazz-shi* (Tokyo: Seidosha).
Sohar, Miriam. 2003. Interview by Beate Kutschke with the former member of Free Music Group, Miriam Sohar, Berlin, 12 March 2003.
Sontag, Susan. 1979. *On Photography* (London: Penguin Books).
Srp, Karel. 1994. *Výjimečné Stavy. Povolání Jazzová Sekce* (Prague: Pragma).
Stacey, Jackie. 1994. "Hollywood cinema and the great escape", in *Star-Gazing: Hollywood Cinema and Female Spectatorship* (London: Routledge), pp. 80–125.
Stafford, Andy. 2012 (or earlier). "Senegal: May 1968, Africa's revolt" (www.ghi-dc. org/files/publications/bu_supp/supp006/bus6_129.pdf, accessed 18 February 2012).
Standage, Simon. 2008. Interview by Kailan Rubinoff, 11 June, London.
Stephan, Cora. 1993. *Der Betroffenheitskult: eine Politische Sittengeschichte* (Berlin: Rowohlt).
Stokes, Martin. 2010. *The Republic of Love: Cultural Intimacy in Turkish Popular Music* (Chicago and London: University of Chicago Press).
Šustrová. P. 2009. "Czechoslovakia: lines of tanks in Prague", in Philipp Gassert and Martin Klimke, eds., *1968. Memories and Legacies of a Global Revolt* (Washington, DC: German Historical Institute), pp. 155–8.
Sveriges Riksdag. 1974. *Kungl. Maj:ts Proposition Angående den Statliga Kulturpolitiken* (Proposition 1974:28) (www.riksdagen.se/Webbnav/index. aspx?nid=37&dok_id=FX0328, accessed November 2010).
Szemere, Anna. 2001. *Up from the Underground: The Culture of Rock Music in Postsocialist Hungary* (University Park, Penn.: Pennsylvania State University Press).
Szőnyei, Tamás and Katalin Sebes. 2005. *Nyilván Tartottak. Titkos Szolgák a Magyar Rock Körül 1960–1990* (Budapest: Magyar Narancs).
Taka'ishi, Tomoya. 1969. "Uta to minshû", in Folk Camp, ed., *Folk wa Mirai o Hiraku* (Tokyo: Shakai-shimpô), pp. 19–108.
Taruskin, Richard. 1995. *Text and Act* (New York: Oxford University Press).
  2009. "Internalized conflict", in *Music in The Late Twentieth Century. The Oxford History of Western Music* (www.oxfordwesternmusic.com/view/Volume5/ actrade-9780195384857-div1-002007.xml, accessed 30 October 2010).
Taylor, Philip. 2001. *Fragments of the Present: Searching for Modernity in Vietnam's South* (Honolulu: University of Hawai'i Press).
Teo, Stephen. 1996. "The decade with two faces: Cantonese cinema and the paranoid sixties", in *The Restless Breed: Cantonese Stars of the Sixties,* catalogue of the Twentieth Hong Kong International Film Festival (Hong Kong: The Urban Council of Hong Kong), pp. 18–25.
Thomas, Nick. 2002. "Challenging myths of the 1960s: the case of student protest in Britain", in *Twentieth Century British History*, 13:3, pp. 277–97.
Thomas, William I. and Dorothy Swaine Thomas. 1928. *The Child in America: Behavior Problems and Programs* (New York: Knopf).
Thyrén, David. 2009. "Musikhus i Centrum: två Lokala Praktiker inom den Svenska Progressiva Musikrörelsen: Uppsala Musikforum och Sprängkullen i Göteborg",

Ph.D. dissertation (Stockholm University, Department of Musicology and Performance Studies).

Tijen, Tjebbe van. 1999. "Je bevrijden van de drukpres. Jongeren en hun eigen pers in Nederland, 1945–1990" (www.iisg.nl/tvt/tijen06.html, accessed 27 April 2011).

Tilbury, John. 2008. *Cornelius Cardew: a Life Unfinished* (Matching Tye, Essex: Copula).

Tillekens, Ger. 2008. "Plezier en protest. Popmuziek, maatschappijkritiek en de vrolijke jaren zestig", in *Soundscapes: Journal on Media Culture*, 11 (www.icce.rug.nl/~soundscapes, accessed 27 April 2011).

Tilly, Charles. 1986. *The Contentious French* (Cambridge, MA: Harvard University Press).

  2008. *Contentious Performances* (Cambridge: Cambridge University Press).

Tischler, János. 2001. *"I do Szabli   " Polska i Węgry. Punkty Zwrotne w Dziejach obu Narodów w Latach 1956 oraz 1980–1981* (Warsaw: Ludowa Spółdzielnia Wydawnicza).

Tőkés, Rudolf L. 1996. *Hungary's Negotiated Revolution: Economic Reform, Social Change, and Political Succession, 1957–1990* (Cambridge: Cambridge University Press).

Torres Alvarado, Rodrigo. 2002. "Singing the difference: Violeta Parra and Chilean song", in Jan Fairley and David Horn, eds., *I Sing The Difference: Identity and Commitment in Latin American Song* (University of Liverpool, Institute of Popular Music), pp. 39–60.

Trịnh Công Sơn. 1989. "Phác Thảo Chân Dung Tôi", in Lê Giang and Lư Nhất Vũ, eds., *Đời và Nhạc* (Ho Chi Minh City: Nhà Xuất Bản Tổng Hợp Hậu Giang), pp. 455–82.

  2005 (1996). "Tình Yêu và Tiếng Hát", in Nguyễn Trọng Tạo and Nguyễn Thụy Kha, eds., *Trịnh Công Sơn: Một Người Thơ Ca, Một Cõi Đi Về* (Hanoi: Nhà Xuất Bản Âm Nhạc), pp. 170–1.

Trịnh Cung and Nguyễn Quốc Thái (eds.). 2005 (2001). *Trịnh Công Sơn: Cuộc Đời, Âm Nhạc, Thơ, Hội Họa, Suy Tưởng* (Ho Chi Minh City: Nhà Xuất Bản Văn Hóa Sài Gòn).

Tronti, Mario. 1962. "La fabbrica e la società", in *Quaderni rossi* 2, pp. 2–31.

Trudu, Antonio (ed.). 2008. *Luigi Nono. Carteggi concernenti politica, cultura e Partito Comunista Italiano* (Florence: Leo S. Olschki).

Tsurumi, Yoshiyuki. 2002. *Beheiren* (Tokyo: Misuzu-shobô).

Tú Ngọc, Nguyễn Thị Nhung, Vũ Tự Lân, Nguyễn Ngọc Oánh and Thái Phiên (eds.). 2000. *Âm Nhạc Mới Việt Nam: Tiến Trình và Thành Tựu* (Hanoi: Viện Âm Nhạc).

Tůma, Oldřich. 2004. "Das kommunistische Regime in der Tschechoslowakei und seine Gegner. Phasen, Zäsuren und Generationen der Opposition 1948–1989", in Hendrik Bispinck, ed., *Aufstände im Ostblock. Zur Krisengeschichte des realen Sozialismus* (Berlin: Christoph Links), pp. 309–34.

Turino, Thomas. 2008. *Music as Social Life: The Politics of Participation* (Chicago: University of Chicago Press).

Turner, Rick. 1978 (1972). *The Eye of the Needle: Toward Participatory Democracy in South Africa* (New York: Orbis Books).
Unterberger, Richie. 1998. *Unknown Legends of Rock'n'Roll. Psychedelic Unknowns, Mad Geniuses, Punk Pioneers, Lo-fi Mavericks and More* (San Francisco: Miller Freeman Books).
Valcarenghi, Andrea. 2007 (1973). *Underground: a pugno chiuso!* (Rimini: NdA Press/Rome: Arcana).
Văn Cao. 2001 (1995). "Trịnh Công Sơn Người Thơ Ca", in Nguyễn Trọng Tạo and Nguyễn Thụy Kha, eds., *Trịnh Công Sơn: Một Người Thơ Ca, Một Cõi Đi Về* (Hanoi: Nhà Xuất Bản Âm Nhạc), pp. 9–10.
Vassal, Jacques. 1976. *Français, si vous chantiez* (Paris: Albin Michel).
Veen, Hans Joachim, Ulrich Mählert and Peter März (eds.). 2007. *Wechselwirkungen Ost-West. Dissidenz, Opposition und Zivilgesellschaft 1975–1989* (Cologne: Böhlau).
Verbij, Antoine. 2005. *Tien rode jaren. Links radicalisme in Nederland, 1970–1980* (Amsterdam: Ambo).
Vermeulen, Ernst. 1968. "In gesprek met Louis Andriessen", in *Ouverture*, 2:5 (January), pp. 5–7.
   1969. "Overheid en avantgarde: *AKT* in gesprek met minister Klompé", in *Algemeen Kunsttijdschrift* (June), pp. 121–4.
Vestey, Michael. 1967. "Raving London", in *London Look* (11 February), pp. 10–16.
Victor, Christian and Julian Regoli. 1978. *Vingt ans de rock français* (Paris: Albin Michel).
Vila, Pablo. 1987. "Rock *nacional* and dictatorship in Argentina", in *Popular Music*, 6:2, pp. 129–48.
Vogelaar, Jacq. 1993. "Correspondentie", in Frits van der Waa, ed., *De slag van Andriessen* (Amsterdam: De Bezige Bij), pp. 111–30.
Wallerstein, Immanuel. 1989. "1968. Revolution in the world-system" in *Theory and Society*, 18:4, pp. 431–49.
Wallis, Roger and Krister Malm. 1984. *Big Sounds from Small Peoples: The Music Industry in Small Countries* (London: Constable).
Wang, Renyuan. 1999. *Jingju 'Yangbanxi' Yinyue Lungang* (Beijing: Renmin Yinyue Chubanshe).
Wang, Shaoguang. 2003. "The structural sources of the cultural revolution", in Kam-yee Law, ed., *The Chinese Cultural Revolution Reconsidered* (New York: Palgrave Macmillan), pp. 58–91.
Ward, Brian. 1998. *Just My Soul Responding: Rhythm and Blues, Black Consciousness, and Race Relations* (Berkeley: University of California Press).
Welch, Chris. 1968. "Is the day of the thinking man's pop group upon us?", in *Melody Maker* (3 August), pp. 12–13.
Westhues, Kenneth. 1972. "Hippiedom 1970: some tentative hypotheses", in *The Sociological Quarterly*, 13:1, pp. 81–9.

Whahnel, Paddy, and Alan Lovell. 1961. "Living jazz", interview with Bruce Turner, in *New Left Review*, 1:10, pp. 41–50.

Whitehead, Kevin. 1999. *New Dutch Swing* (New York: Billboard Books).

Wicke, Peter. 1997. "'Wenn die Musik sich ändert, zittern die Mauern der Städte'. Rockmusik als Medium des politischen Diskurses im DDR-Kulturbetrieb", in Bernhard Frevel, ed., *Musik und Politik* (Regensburg: ConBrio), pp. 33–44.

Willener, Alfred. 1970. *The Action-Image of Society: On Cultural Politicization*, trans. by A. M. Sheridan Smith (New York: Pantheon).

Williams, Raymond. 2005 (1980). "Base and superstructure in Marxist cultural theory", in *Culture and Materialism* (London: Verso), pp. 31–49.

  1970. "If Wagner were alive he'd work with King Crimson", in *Melody Maker* (1 May), p. 10.

Wilmer, Valerie. 1992. *As Serious As Your Life: John Coltrane and Beyond* (London: Serpent's Tail).

Wilson, Tony. 1968. "Roy Harper – folk's one-man mother", in *New Musical Express* (20 July), p. 14.

Winter, Eric. 1968. "A kind of polite riot at the festival", in *Melody Maker* (6 July), p. 19.

Witcover, Jules. 1997. *The Year the Dream Died: Revisiting 1968 in America* (New York: Warner Books).

Wolfe, Tom. 1968. *The Electric Kool-Aid Acid Test* (New York: Farrar).

Wolff, Christian. 1998. *Cues/Hinweise* (Cologne: Edition MusikTexte).

Wright, Steve. 2002. *Storming Heaven: Class Composition and Struggle in Italian Autonomist Marxism* (London: Pluto Press).

Wu, Yuehua. 2006. "Geying Paihe: yueyu Qingchun Gewupian yu Dianying de Guanxi (1966–1969)", M. Phil. thesis, Hong Kong Baptist University.

Wu, Yuehua, Jiale Chen and Zhiqiang Liao. 2007. *Tongchang Guangying* (Hong Kong: International Association of Theatre Critics).

Xuân Hồng. 1989. "Từ Tiếng Độc Huyền", in Lê Giang and Lư Nhất Vũ, eds., *Nhạc và Đời* (Ho Chi Minh City: Nhà Xuất Bản Tổng Hợp Hậu Giang), pp. 191–254.

  1993. "Hoạt Động Ca Nhạc ở Miền Nam Việt Nam", in Nguyễn Hữu Thọ, ed., *Chung Một Bóng Cờ* (Hanoi: Nhà Xuất Bản Chính Trị Quốc Gia), pp. 648–54.

Yang, Mayfair Mei-hui. 1999. "From gender erasure to gender difference: state feminism, consumer sexuality, and women's public sphere in China", in Mayfair Yang Mei-hui, ed., *Spaces of Their Own: Women's Public Sphere in Transnational China* (Minneapolis, MN: University of Minnesota Press), pp. 35–67.

Yanosik, Joseph. 1996. *The Plastic People of the Universe*, March 1996 (www.furious.com/perfect/pulnoc.html, accessed 7 May 2011).

Zahn, Robert von. 2006. *Czukay, Liebezeit, Schmidt: CAN* (Cologne: DuMont).

Zaslaw, Neal. 2001. "Reflections on 50 years of early music", in *Early Music*, 29:1, pp. 5–14.

Zieliński, Przemysław. 2005. *Scena Rockowa w PRL. Historia, Organizacja, Znaczenie* (Warsaw: Trio).

Zimmerman, Nadya. 2008. *Counterculture Kaleidoscope* (Ann Arbor, MI: University of Michigan Press).

Zolov, Eric. 1999. *Refried Elvis: The Rise of the Mexican Counterculture* (Berkeley, CA: University of California Press).

Discography

AMM. 1966. *AMMMUSIC*. LP, Elektra UK 256. Re-released as a CD with additional material: ReRMegacorp AMMCD, 1989.
Bach, Johann Sebastian. 1968. *Mass in B Minor, BWV 232* (Concentus Musicus Wien, ensemble; Harnoncourt, Nikolaus, cond.), LP, Telefunken SKH-20.
Baez, Joan. 1968a. *Baptism: A Journey through our Time*. LP, Vanguard, VSD 79275.
1968b. *Any Day Now*, LP, Vanguard, VSD 79306.
Band, The. 1968. *Music from Big Pink*. LP, Capitol Records, SKAO 2955.
Beatles, The. 1967. *Magical Mystery Tour*, LP, Parlophone PCTC 255.
1968a. *The Beatles* (aka *The White Album*), LP, Apple PCS70678.
1968b. *Revolution*, Single, Apple R 5722.
Benjamin, Sathima Bea. 1997. *A Morning in Paris*, CD, Enja Records ENJ 9309 2.
Blue Notes. 2008 (1968). *Very Urgent*, CD, Fledgling, B00.1A9TBPU.
Brand, Dollar. 1973. *African Sketchbook*, CD, Enja Record LP ENJA 2026.
1992a. *Reflections*, CD, Black Lion BLCD 760110.
1992b. *Anatomy of a South African Village*, CD, Black Lion, BLCD 260172.
1992c. *Round Midnight at the Café Montmartre*, CD, Black Lion, BLCD 760111.
1997 (1964). *Duke Ellington Presents the Dollar Brand Trio*, CD, Reprise, 2–6111.
Brand, Dollar and Gato Barbieri, 1974. *Confluences*, LP, Arista, AL 1003.
Brown, James. 1968. *Say it Loud – I'm Black and I'm Proud*, Single, King Records 45–6187.
Brüggen, Frans. 1972. *Frans Brüggen spielt 17 Blockflöten*, LP, Telefunken SMA 25 073-T/1–3.
Burg Waldeck Festivals. 2008 (1964–9). *Die Burg Waldeck Festivals, 1964–1969*, CD, BCD 16017.
Camel. 1976. *Moonmadness*, LP, Decca 6376118.
Caravan. 1971. *In the Land of Grey and Pink*, LP, London PS593.
Carlos, Wendy. 1968. *Switched-on Bach*, LP, Columbia.
Chambers Brothers, The. 1967. *The Time Has Come*, LP, Columbia, CS 9522.
Collins, Judy. 1967. *Wildflowers*, LP, Elektra.
Country Joe and the Fish. 1967. *I-Feel-Like-I'm-Fixin'-to-Die*, LP, Vanguard, VRS 9266.
Creedence Clearwater Revival. 1969. *Willy and the Poor Boys*, LP, Fantasy, 4C06290988.
Degenhardt, Franz Joseph. 1992. *Degenhardt Live*, CD, POL 115012.
Doors, The. 1968. *Waiting for the Sun*. LP, Elektra, EKS-74042.

Dylan, Bob. 1963. *The Freewheelin' Bob Dylan*, LP, Columbia CL 1986.

    1968. *John Wesley Harding*, LP, Columbia, KCS 9604.

Dylan, Bob and The Band. 1975. *The Basement Tapes*, LP, Columbia, C2 33682.

Emerson, Lake and Palmer. 1971. *Tarkus*, LP, Island ILPS 9155.

    1972. *Pictures at an Exhibition*, LP, Island HELP 1.

    1973. *Brain Salad Surgery*, LP, Manticore K 53501.

Genesis. 1972. *Foxtrot*, LP, Charisma CAS 1058.

Gentle Giant. 1972. *Octopus*, LP, Vertigo 6360 080.

    1973. *In a Glass House*, LP, WWA 002.

Gnidrolog. 1972. *In Spite of Harry's Toe-Nail*, LP, RCA Victor SF 8261.

Gracious. 1970. *Gracious!*, LP, Vertigo 6360 002.

Greenslade. 1973. *Greenslade*, LP, Warner Bros, K 46207.

Grupo de Experimentación del ICAIC. 1973. *Grupo de Experimentación del ICAIC*, LP, Areito EGREM, LDA 3401.

    1974. *Grupo de Experimentación del ICAIC*, LP, Areito EGREM, LDA 3460.

    1975. *Grupo de Experimentación del ICAIC*, LP, Areito EGREM, LDA 3456.

    1976. *Grupo de Experimentación del ICAIC*, LP, Areito EGREM, LDA 3482.

Grupo de Experimentación Sonora. 1984. *25 años Cine Cubano Revolución*, Vol. 1, LP, EGREM Areito, LD4175.

Gryphon. 1977. *Treason*, LP, Harvest SHSP 4063.

Havens, Richie. 1968. *Mixed Bag*, LP, Verve Forecast, FTS3006.

Impressions, The. 1968. *This Is My Country*, LP, Curtom, CRS 8001.

Jazz Epistles. 1958. *Verse One*, LP, Gallo, unknown.

    1992 (1959). *Jazz in Africa, Volume One*, CD, Kaz Records CD 24.

Jethro Tull. 1973. *A Passion Play*, LP, Chrysalis CHR 1040.

John Coltrane Quartet, The. 1961. *Africa/Brass*, LP, Impulse!, AS-6.

King Crimson. 1969. *The Court of the Crimson King*, LP, Island ILSP 9111.

    1970. *In the Wake of Poseidon*, LP, Island ILPS 9127.

    1973. *Larks' Tongues in Aspic*, LP, Island ILPS 9230.

    1974a. *Starless and Bible Black*, LP, Island ILPS 9275.

    1974b. *Red*, LP, Island ILPS 9308.

    1981. *Discipline*, LP, E.G. EGLP 49.

    1995. *Thrak*, CD, Discipline Global Mobile KCCDY 1.

    1996. *THRaKKaTaK*, CD, Discipline Global Mobile DGM9604.

    2000. *The ConstruKction of Light*, CD, Virgin 7243 8 49261 2 0.

    2003. *The Power to Believe*, CD, Sanctuary SANCD-155.

Last Poets, The. 1970. *The Last Poets*, LP, Douglas, Z 30811.

Leonhardt, Gustav. 1953. *Goldberg Variations, BWV 988*, LP, Vanguard SRV175SD.

    1967. *Cembalomusik auf Originalinstrumenten aus den Niederlanden, Italien, Deutschland und England um 1650–1750*, LP, Telefunken Das Alte Werk SAWT 9512.

Los Folkloristas. 1975. *El Cancionero Popular*, LP, DP1006.

MC5, The. 1969. *Kick Out the Jams*, LP, Elektra, EKS 74072.

Moody Blues, The. 1969. *To our Children's Children's Children*, LP, Threshold THS 1.
Nice, The. 1968. *America*, Single, Immediate IM 068.
Ochs, Phil. 1968. *Tape from California*, LP, A&M Records, SP-4148.
Pink Floyd. 1967. *The Piper at the Gates of Dawn*, LP, EMI SCX 6157.
　1968. *A Saucerful of Secrets*, LP, EMI SCX 6258.
Procol Harum. 1967. *A Whiter Shade of Pale*, Single, Deram DM 126.
Puebla, Carlos. 1972. *Carlos Puebla*, LP, Areito, EGREM LD-3305.
　1976. *Y en eso llego Fidel*, LP, Areito/Movieplay Gong, 17.0874/9.
Puhdys, The. 1974. *Die Puhdys*, LP, Amiga 855 348.
Quilapayún. 1973. *Por Vietnam*, LP, EMI/ DICAP 2C 062-94-151.
Renft. 1973. *Klaus Renft Combo*, LP, Amiga 855 326.
　1974. *Rock aus Leipzig. Renft-Combo live*, LP, Teldec-Sonderauflage 66.22093.
Reyes, Judith. n.d. (early 1970s). *Cronica Mexicana*, LP, Le Chant du Monde France LDX 74421.
　n.d. (early n.d. *Judith Reyes*, LP, Vendemiaire VDES 021.
Rifkin, Joshua. 1965. *Baroque Beatles Book*, LP, Elektra EKL-306.
Rodríguez, Silvio. 1991. *Silvio Rodríguez en Chile with Chucho Valdés, Irakere, Isabel Parra y su Grupo*, CD, Fonomusic Spain 1109–1110.
Rodríguez, Silvio and Milanés Pablo. 1984. *En Vivo en Argentina*, CD, EMI Alfiz 5304182.
Rolling Stones, The. 1967. *Flowers*, LP, London ABKCO PS 509.
　1968. *Beggars Banquet*, LP, London PS 539.
Seeger, Pete. 1967. *Waist Deep In the Big Muddy and Other Love Songs*, LP, Columbia, CS 9505.
Simon & Garfunkel. 1965. *The Sound of Silence*, Single, CBS 201977.
Simone, Nina. 1968. *'Nuff Said*, LP, RCA Victor, LSP-4065.
Smith, Harry. 1952. *Anthology of American Folk Music*, LP, Folkways, SFW 40090.
Strawbs. 1971. *From the Witchwood*, LP, A&M AMLH 64304.
　1972. *Grave New World*, LP, A&M AMLH 68078.
String Driven Thing. 1973. *It's a Game*, Single, Charisma CB.215.
Surfaris. 1964. *Hit City 64*, LP, Decca 4487.
Thunderclap Newman. 1969. *Accidents*, Single, Track 2094 001.
Van der Graaf Generator. 1970. *The Least We Can Do Is Wave to Each Other*, LP, Charisma CAS 1007.
　1971. *Pawn Hearts*, LP, Charisma CAS 1051.
　1976. *Still Life*, LP, Charisma CAS 1116.
Various artists. 1974. *La Cancion, un Arma de la Revolución*, LP, Areito EGREM LDA-3464.
Various artists. 1975. *Chacabuco*, LP, Expresión Spontanée ES 36, Paris, France.
Various artists. 1984. *April in Managua Central American Peace Concert*, LP, Netherlands, Varagram TNF 160.
Viglietti, Daniel. 1973. *Daniel Viglietti y el Grupo de Experimentación Sonora del ICAIC*, LP, Areito, EGREM LDA-3395.

Wonder, Stevie. 1972. *Talking Book*, LP, Tamla, T 319L.
    1973. *Innervisions*, LP, Tamla, T326L.
    1974. *Fulfillingness' First Finale*, LP, Tamla, T6-332S1.
Yes. 1970. *Time and a Word*, LP, Polydor 2400 006.
    1972. *Close to the Edge*, LP, Atlantic K 50012.
    1977. *Going for the One*, LP, Atlantic K 50379.
    1979. *Tormato*, LP, Atlantic K 50518.

Index

1968
  'long 1968s', 5, 46, 97–8, 99, 117, 154–70, 239, 254
  'short 1968s', 154–70
  'small 1968s', 9, 11
  spirit of '1968', 3–7, 9
  'spirit of the sixties', 3
"A bas l'état policier" ("Down with the Police State") (Grange, lyrics), 260
A floresta é jovem e cheja de vida (The Forest is Young and Full of Life) (Nono), 40
Abba, 146
Abbey Road studios, 242
Academy of Ancient Music, 243
"Accidents" (Thunderclap Newman), 165
Action Musique, 267
L'Action-image de la société (Willener), 115
Adams, Eddie, 48
Adams, John, 187
Adlington, Robert, 3
Adorno, Theodor W., 1, 43, 175, 189, 204, 238
aesthetics of the fragment, 192
Africa/Brass (Coltrane), 60
African National Congress (ANC), 64, 67
African Sanctus (Fanshawe), 175
African Sketchbook (Dollar Brand), 74, 76–7
Afrikaans, 68
"Ain't Got No – I Got Life" (Simone), 56–7
"Akiramé-bushi" ("Resignation Song") (Azenbô), 91–2
"Al Vent" (Raímon), 126
Albergoni, Sergio, 42
Alegre, Lizette, 123
Ali, Tariq, 171, 180
Alice in Wonderland, 183
"Alla Turca" (Mozart), 203
Allen, Clifford, 78
Allen, Michael, 183
Allende, Salvador, 130, 131
alternative culture/lifestyle
  British music, 156, 168, 171–2, 174–5, 178, 179, 181, 187
  China and Hong Kong, 223
  early music movement, 237, 238, 241, 248, 253–41
  Eastern Bloc, 207, 211, 221
  Germany, 190, 192
  Latin America, 131
  Netherlands, 13, 23
  Scandinavia, 144, 145, 146–7
  South Africa, 79
Alternativfestivalen (Alternative Festival), Sweden, 146–7
Altra Italia (concert series), 40
Alvarado, Rodrigo Torres, 131
The Ambassadors, 23
America
  black pride, 54–60
  'old, weird America', 51–4
  overview, 10, 46–51
  political engagement, 46–63
  rock music, 60–3
Americana, 53, 54
AMM, 8, 179, 180, 185
AMMMusic (AMM), 179
Amodei, Fausto, 37
Amon Düül (I and II), 191–2
Amsberg, Claus von, 15
Amsterdam, 12, 23–28, 248
An Chung, 106
Anachronie I (Andriessen), 24
Analisi del lavoro (concert series), 35
Anatomy of a South African Village (Dollar Brand), 74, 76
ANC. *see* African National Congress
Anderson, Jon, 154, 167, 167
Anderson, Perry, 173
Anderson, Stig 'Stikkan', 146
"Andorra" (Seeger), 89
Andriessen, Louis, 24
  early music movement, 247
  Netherlands avant-garde, 24, 25, 26, 27
Andrzejewski, Jerzy, 216
Anglican hymnody, 164, 165
The Animals, 70
Anka, Paul, 215

Anthology of American Folk Music (Smith), 53, 54
anti-authoritarianism
  British underground, 180
  early music movement, 240
  France, 261
  Netherlands, 14, 21
  Scandinavia, 144, 153
  spirit of '1968', 8
  Vietnam, 117
anti-authoritarianism in Germany
  anti-authoritarian music in an authoritarian state, 195–8
  anti-authoritarian revolt by musical means, 191–3
  class struggle and music, 199
  fight against musical authorities, 202–4
  overview, 11, 188–91
Antibes Festival, 65, 71
anti-commercialism, 144–7
anti-diatonic progressions, 160, 162–4
anti-Semitism, 216
Anti-University, 180
anti-war music, 51, 98–9
anti-war songs, 82–3, 87, 93, 95, 110, 111, 117
Antonioni, Michelangelo, 34, 35
Any Day Now (Baez), 51
apartheid, 65
  and British rock, 156
  and South Africa, 64–5, 66, 68, 80
Apollon: una fabbrica occupata (Gregoretti), 36
Appunti per l'auto di domani (Mida), 35
April in Managua Central American Peace Concert, 135
Arab Spring, 1
Arabic Numeral (Any Integer) for HF (Young), 176
Arbeit macht frei (Area), 43
Area, 41, 42, 43–4, 45
Argentina, 120, 133, 134, 135
arias, 226–8
Aron, Raymond, 255–6, 268, 272
Arpino, Giovanni, 34
"Arriving UFO" (Yes), 168
art, 265, 271
Art et Révolution, 265
art music, 139, 148–9, 202
Art Spectrum Exhibition, 183
Arti e Mestieri, 41, 42
Arts Lab Festival of New Music, 180
Arvidsson, Alf, 142, 144, 148
Ashley, Robert, 43

Asmussen, Svend, 73
Association for the Advancement of Creative Musicians, 60
"Astral Traveller" (Yes), 168
atonality, 60
Auger, Brian, 53
Aute, Luís Eduardo, 136
'authenticity revolution', 240
authoritarian personality, 189
authoritarianism in Germany
  anti-authoritarian agendas, 188–91
  class struggle and music, 199
  fight against musical authorities, 202–4
avant garde
  American popular music, 59–60
  British experimental alternative tradition, 176
  British music, 158, 174, 175, 181, 187
  early music movement, 238, 247, 254
  France, 264, 269, 271
  Germany, 191, 192, 193, 202
  Italy, 36, 40, 42, 43
  Japan, 81
  May 1968 protests, 264, 269, 271
  Netherlands, 13–14, 17, 18, 24
  Scandinavia, 139, 148
  spirit of '1968', 3, 8, 9
"Awaken" (Yes), 167–168
Ayler, Albert, 77
Azenbô Soéda, 91, 92

Bach, J. S., 162, 164, 237, 239, 243, 244, 247
Badura-Skoda, Paul, 248
Baez, Joan, 49
  American popular music, 49, 51
  Cuban *nueva trova*, 127
  Japan, 83, 87
Bagatellen für B (*Bagatelles for B[eethoven]*) (Bredemeyer), 203, 204
"Bài Ca May Áo" ("Song for Sewing Clothes") (Xuân Hồng), 107
Bai, Di, 229
Baimao nu (*The White-Haired Girl*) (ballet), 78, 81, 82
Baker, Laurie, 186
Balestrini, Nanni, 30
ballad tradition, 141–2
ballet, 223, 224, 228–9
Banco del Mutuo Soccorso, 41
The Band, 16, 17
Banks, Tony, 165
Bantustans, 66, 67
Baptism: A Journey through our Time (Baez), 15

Barbieri, Gato, 74, 76, 77
Barlow, Tani, 234–5
Baroque music
    early music movement, 238, 239, 241, 242, 243, 244, 250
    nature of music, 4
The Basement Tapes (Dylan), 16
Battaglia alla turca (Medek), 203, 204
Bay of Pigs, 125, 127–8
Bayle, François, 269
BBC, 186, 187
The Beach Boys, 69
Beat culture, 171, 172, 174, 177, 178, 179
'beat' music, 16
    Czechoslovakia, 210
    Germany, 195–7, 204
    Netherlands, 16, 17–18, 19, 20
    Scandinavia, 139
The Beatles
    British music, 155, 165, 179
    collage form, 43
    Japan, 81
    Netherlands, 19, 20
    period instruments, 8, 246
    rivalry, 218
Beatrix, Princess, 15, 17
bebop, 65
Beckett, Alan, 173
Beckett, Samuel, 183
Bedford, David, 174, 180
Beefeaters, 142
Beer, Ronnie, 78
Beethoven Bicentennial, 202–3
Beethoven, Ludwig van, 202–3
Beheiren. *see* Peace for Vietnam Committee
Beijing operas, 225, 228
Belafonte, Harry, 64
Benda, Václav, 207
Benjamin, (Sathima) Bea, 64, 65, 66, 70, 72, 79, 80
Bennett, Richard Rodney, 174, 176
Bennink, Han, 24
Béranger, Pierre-Jean, 260
Berberian, Cathy, 44
Berio, Luciano, 34, 40, 43, 180, 247, 248
Berkeley group, 189
Berlin, 5, 191, 193
Berlin Wall, 1, 198, 201
Bernstein, David, 3
Bertelli, Guartiero, 41
Bethanien hospital, Berlin, 193
"Bethanien Song" (Cardew), 193

Beweging voor de vernieuwing van de muziekpraktijk (Movement for the Renewal of Musical Practice), 25
Bieler, Wim, 19
Biermann, Wolf, 197–8, 201, 204
bigbit, 214
Biko, Steve, 65, 68, 80
Birtwistle, Harrison, 174, 246
Black Artists Group, 60
Black Consciousness Movement, 65, 68, 80
Black Dwarf, 155, 178
Black Mountain College, 177
"Black Mountain Rag" (trad.), 91
'black' music, 51, 54–60
Black Panthers, 56, 57, 59, 62
Black Power, 46, 57, 59
Black September, 43
Blackout, 217
Bloemendaal, Wim, 21, 22, 23
Blonde on Blonde (Dylan), 52
"Blowin' in the Wind" (Dylan, lyrics), 51, 88
Blue Cheer, 62
The Blue Notes, 20, 21, 23, 24, 25, 26
blues, 54
Boehmer, Konrad, 200, 248
Boeke, Kees, 251, 252, 253
Boenisch, Hanne, 183, 185
Bolan, Marc, 157
'Bomb Culture' generation, 173, 174
Bond films, 175
Bondy, Egon, 213
Bongaarts, Henk, 21
Borio, Gianmario, 3
Bosio, Gianni, 37
Boulez, Pierre, 176, 180
Boult, Adrian, 248
bourgeois, 15, 36, 41, 148, 149, 195, 265
Bowie, David, 166
Bowman, James, 245, 246, 249, 254
Boyd, Joe, 157
Branca, Antonello, 35
Brand, Dollar (Abdullah Ibrahim), 64, 65, 66, 68, 70, 74, 79, 80
"Bratříčku, zavírej" ("Little Brother Close the Gate") (Kryl), 212
Brazil, 5
"Breaking Away" (The Beach Boys), 212
Bredemeyer, Reiner, 198, 203
Breuker, Willem, 17, 24, 26
Breytenbach, Breyten, 68
bridging high and popular culture, 149, 192, 244–6
Brink, Andre, 68

British music
  alternative British experimental culture, 181–4
  British music in the Old and New Left, 172–4
  early music movement, 247–8, 249–50
  experimental alternative tradition, 174–6
  experimental legacy and counterculture, 186–7
  experimental music in the underground, 178–81
  experimental revolution, 158, 171–87
  Scratch Orchestra opposition and Maoism, 184–6
British music. *see also* British rock
British Musicians' Union, 156
British rock
  aiming for bigger things, 157–60
  anti-diatonic progressions, 162–4
  experimentalism, Beat culture, and the Underground, 177–8
  immediate impact of the events of 1968, 154–7
  overview, 154
  parallel tenth progressions, 164–7
  possible utopias, 167–70
  short '1968' and the long, 154–70
  variety of visions, 160–1
Britten, Benjamin, 172, 246
Bródy, János, 219
Brookes, Oliver, 245
Brotherhood of Breath, 70, 72, 78
Brown, Earle, 171
Brown, James, 55–6, 57, 58
Brown, Timothy, 9
Bruford, Bill, 160, 169–70
Brüggen, Frans
  bridging high and popular culture, 244–5
  early music and new music, 9, 247, 248
  early music and politics, 252, 253
  early music movement, 239
  education reform, 251
  old instruments, new technologies, 243
  period instruments of change, 241
Bryars, Gavin, 185, 187
Buddhist activism, Vietnam, 99–100, 108
Bun No.1 (Cardew), 187
Burckhardt, Birgit, 182
Burdocks (Wolff), 185–6
Burg Waldeck International Festival of Folksong and Chansonniers, 6, 157, 199
Burnin' Red Ivanhoe, 143
Burroughs, William, 177

'bush universities', 67
Bush, Alan, 172, 173, 186
The Butlers, 64
Butt, John, 238
Bylsma, Anner, 239, 243
The Byrds, 44

ca khúc (Vietnamese popular song), 97–9, 107, 109, 111, 117
Ca Khúc Da Vàng (*Songs of Golden Skin*) (songbook), 110
Cacciari, Massimo, 32
Café Dalia, 209
Café Montmartre, 66, 75
Cage, John
  British experimental alternative tradition, 175
  British music in the Old and New Left, 173–4
  experimental revolution in Britain, 171, 172, 177, 179
  Italy, 43, 44
  Scratch Orchestra opposition and Maoism, 185, 186
Calvet, Louis-Jean, 261, 262
Calvino, Italo, 34, 37
Camacho, Gonzalo, 123
Camel, 169
Camerini, Alberto, 43
Can, 191, 192
"Cancer" (Kryl), 212
"Canción con todos" ("Song For All") (Isella, music), 134
El Cancionero Popular (*The Popular Songbook*), 36
Cantacronache, 37, 40
Cantonese opera, 230, 233
Canzoniere del Lazio, 39, 40, 43
Caos (Area), 45
Cape, Safford, 238
capitalism, 3, 15, 17, 23, 28, 190, 195
Captain Beefheart, 23
Caravan, 169
Cardew, Cornelius
  alternative British experimental culture, 174, 175, 176, 181, 182, 183
  British experimental legacy, 187
  British music in the Old and New Left, 174
  Cramps Records, 43
  experimental music in the British underground, 179, 180
  experimental revolution in Britain, 43, 172
  German anti-authoritarianism, 193

Cardew, Cornelius (cont.)
  Scratch Orchestra opposition and Maoism, 184–5, 186
Carlos, John, 46, 59
Carlos, Wendy, 9, 246
"La Carmagnole" (trad.), 260
Carmichael, Stokeley, 57, 62
Carocci, Giovanni, 33
Carpitella, Diego, 38
Carré (Stockhausen), 175
Cartridge Music (Cage), 175
Casa de las Americas, Cuba, 128–9
Castaldi, Paolo, 43
Castro, Fidel, 22, 128, 129, 131, 132
Censier annex, Université de Paris, 258–9
censorship, 67, 210, 211, 218, 219
Cesaire, Aime, 68
The Chambers Brothers, 17
Chambers, Iain, 159
Chan, Connie (Chen Baozhu), 230, 231–2, 233
Chandler, Raymond, 54
chanson paillarde (bawdy song), 260
chansons, 259–60, 261, 262
"Le chant des barricades", 258–9, 260
Chant, Michael, 178, 184
Charta '77, 213
Chen Baozhu. *see* Chan, Connie
Cherry, Don, 77
Chicago blues, 173
"Childlike Faith in Childhood's End" (Van der Graaf Generator), 166
Chile
  Chilean and Cuban musical exchange, 130–2
  dictatorship and solidarity years, 133
  nueva canción (new song) movement, 119, 120
  peace concerts, 135
China. *see* People's Republic of China
Chinese Communist Party (CCP), 224
Christiania, Copenhagen, 144
Chronicle of Anna Magdalena Bach (Straub and Huillat), 241–2
Chun-Hung Ng, 231
Ciao 2001, 42
civil disobedience, 30, 193
Civil Rights Act (1964), 51
civil rights movement, 7, 10, 21, 57, 125, 126
Clark, Paul, 225
Clarke, Arthur C., 166
class, 198–200
La classe operaia va in paradiso (Petri, music by Morricone), 36
classical music

British rock, 158
early music movement, 240, 244, 252
France, 269
Germany, 192, 199–200, 202
Scandinavia, 148
South Africa, 70, 76
spirit of '1968', 3, 4
Club Africana, 71, 72
"Có Chúng Tôi Trên Mặt Đường" ("We are on the Road") (Phạm Tuyên), 101
Coca-Cola, 18
Cohen, Deborah, 223
Cohen, Joel, 243
Cohn-Bendit, Daniel, 79
Coleman, Ornette, 59
collage form, 35, 43, 76, 149, 182, 203
Collegium Aureum, 248
Collegium Musicum, 238
Collins, Judy, 8, 246
Coltrane, John, 60, 77
Columbia University, 5, 47, 252
Comet, 184
Comité d'Action Révolutionnaire (CAR), 264, 265, 267
Comité Révolutionnaire d'Agitation Culturelle (CRAC), 264, 265, 267–8
commercialism, 144–7, 151–2
"La commune n'est pas morte", 260
communism, 22, 25
Communist Party, 172–3, 174, 186, 210, 219, 262
Compagnies Républicaines de Sécurité, 261
Composizione per orchestra n. 2 – Diario polacco '58 (Nono), 33
Concentus Musicus Wien, 243
concernment, 7, 8
Concert Agency Committee, 140
Concertgebouw Orchestra, 17, 24, 25, 247
Confédération Générale du Travail (CGT), 266–7
Confucianism, 172, 182, 186
conquistadores, 121
con-ricerca (collaborative research), 33
conscientious protesters, 2
conservatories, 6, 250–1
Consort of Musicke, 243
consumerism, 17, 23
Contropiano, 32
Coolsma, Hans, 241
Corner, Philip, 171
"Corporal Clegg" (Pink Floyd), 156
corrido, 120–1, 122
Coudray, Jean-Marie, 268

counterculture, 3, 5, 30, 171–2, 186–7, 254
"Court of the Crimson King" (King Crimson), 165
Cousins, Dave, 169
Cox, Tony, 180
Cramps Records, 42–3, 44
Cream, 154
creativity
　France, 263
　Germany, 11, 204
　Italy, 38
　Japan, 95
　Latin America, 123, 125, 127, 131
　Netherlands, 12, 13, 16, 17, 18
　South Africa, 79
Creedence Clearwater Revival, 50
Creeley, Robert, 177
Cris (Ohana), 269
critical masses, 2
Cronkite, Walter, 48
cross-genre activities, 8–9
csőves, 220
Cuba
　and the Netherlands, 22, 25
　Chilean and Cuban musical exchange, 130–2
　Cuban *nueva trova* emerges, 126–30
　Encuentro de Canción Protesta, 6, 124–6
　Latin American 'new song', 134
　nueva canción (new song) movement, 119, 120
　peace concerts, 135
　quinquemio gris ('grey five-year period'), 127
Cuban Cinematographic Institute (ICAIC), 129
Cuban Revolution, 119
cultural expression, 117, 204, 218, 259, 270
cultural imperialism, 123, 150
cultural intimacy, 115–16
Cultural Revolution, 7, 222, 223, 225, 230
culture
　Beat culture, 171, 172, 174, 177, 178, 179
　bourgeois culture, 36, 41, 149, 265
　bridging high and popular culture, 149, 192, 244–6
　counterculture, 3, 5, 12–13, 30, 171–2, 186–7, 254
　democratisation of music culture, 139, 140, 144–5, 148
　role in capitalism, 265
　youth culture, 19–24, 27, 190, 232
Los Curacas, 39
Czechoslovakia
　1968 in the West and East, 206, 207
　and Germany, 190, 200, 201
　and Netherlands, 22
　British rock, 156
　Czechoslovakia in 1968, 209–14
　overview, 6, 11, 205–6, 220
Czechoslovakian Musicians' Union, 213

Dà Xué, 182
Dadaism, 16, 43, 44, 264
"Đại Bác Ru Đêm" ("A Lullaby of Canons for the Night") (Trịnh Công Sơn), 112
Daley, Richard J., 61
Dane, Barbara, 98, 107, 126
Danish Music Bill, 146
Danmarks Radio (DR), 140
Dansktoppen, 141, 152
Darmstadt, 8, 175
Das Alte Werk, 243
Đất Khổ (*The Land of Sorrow*) (Hà Thúc Cần), 34
Davies, Hugh, 180
de André, Fabrizio, 39
de Certeau, Michel, 256–7
De Gaulle, Charles, 257, 261
De Gregori, Francesco, 39
de Groot, Boudewijn, 18
de Leeuw, Reinbert, 24, 247
de Ruiter, Frans, 247, 250, 253
De Simone, Roberto, 39
De Volharding (music ensemble), 26
De Volharding (Andriessen), 26
Debray, Regis, 35
Debussy, Claude, 156, 162
Decca, 242–3
Dedalus, 41
Deep Purple, 196
Degenhardt, Franz Joseph, 191, 199
Democratic National Convention, 60
Democratic Republic of Vietnam (DRV), 97, 98, 100, 106, 117
democratisation of music culture, 139, 140, 144–5, 148
Democrazia Cristiana (DC), 30
den Daas, Jaap, 247
Denmark
　anti-commercialism, 145
　broadcasting media, 140, 141
　development of '1968', 142, 143, 144
　end of '1968', 152
　overview, 10
　politically or aesthetically progressive, 149, 150
　Scandinavia, 139

Déry, Tibor, 219
Il deserto rosso (*Red Desert*) (film), 9
Destruction in Art Symposium (DIAS), 178
"The Devil's Triangle" (King Crimson), 158
Dien Bien Phu, 99, 104
diminished triad, 162
Dirlik, Arif, 225
Dischi del Sole, 37
"Discipline" (King Crimson), 163
Discos Puebla, 122
Dissing, Povl, 142
Dollar Brand Trio, 65, 71, 72, 74
Dolmetsch, Arnold, 237, 244
Dolmetsch, Carl, 244–5
Donaueschingen, 8
The Doors, 15
"Le drapeau rouge" ("The Red Flag"), 261
"Drei Kugeln auf Rudi Dutschke" ("Three Bullets for Rudi Dutschke") (Biermann), 201
Dreyfus, Laurence, 238–9
"Drifter's Escape" (Dylan), 53
Driscoll, Julie, 53
drones, 8
Drott, Eric, 3
"Drowning Man" (Greenslade), 165–6
drugs, 23, 182
"Drunkard Returned from Heaven" (Folk Crusaders), 82, 83, 84, 85, 86, 88
DRV. *see* Democratic Republic of Vietnam
Dubček, Alexander, 205–6, 210, 211, 212
Duerden, Dennis, 76
Dujuan shan (*Azalea Mountain*) (Wang Shu-yuan, author), 229
"Dựng Lại Người Dựng Lại Nhà" ("Rebuild People, Rebuild Homes") (Trịnh Công Sơn), 108–9, 115
Dunn, Christopher, 5
Duoqing miaozei (*A Romantic Thief*) (film), 87, 91
Dutronc, Jacques, 261
Dutschke, Rudi, 5, 180, 188, 189, 200, 201
Dvorak, Antonín, 155
Dylan, Bob
  American popular music, 51, 52, 53–4
  British music, 123, 161, 178
  Cuban *nueva trova*, 127
  Japan, 86, 88, 95–6
  Netherlands, 17, 18, 20
  Poland, 215
dystopian visions, 159–61, 166–7, 169
"Dziwny jest ten świat" ("Miraculous is this World") (Niemen), 215

Early Music Consort, 242, 245
Early Music journal, 241–2
early music movement
  bridging high and popular culture, 244–6
  early music and '1968', 237–54
  early music and new music, 246–8
  early music and politics, 251–4
  education reform, 248–51
  old instruments, new technologies, 242–4
  overview, 3, 11, 237–40
  period instruments of change, 240–2
East Germany
  1968 resonating in music, 200–2
  anti-authoritarian agendas, 189–90
  anti-authoritarian music in an authoritarian state, 195–8
  class struggle and music, 198–200
  fight against musical authorities, 202–4
  overview, 11
Eastern Bloc
  1956 and the desire for freedom, 208–9
  '1968' in Czechoslovakia, 209–14
  '1968' in Hungary, 217–20
  '1968' in Poland, 214–17
  '1968' in the West and East, 206–8
  overview, 6, 11, 205–6, 220
  protest culture, 205–21
  student protests, 207
"Easy Money" (King Crimson), 165
L'eclisse (Antonioni), 9
Eco, Umberto, 30, 34–37
Edizioni del Gallo, 37, 40
education, 10, 121, 131, 145, 188, 200, 248–51, 266
Eight Songs for a Mad King (Maxwell-Davies), 175
Eisler, Hanns, 8, 37
electro-acoustic music, 36, 43, 148
electronic music, 9, 33, 42, 118, 251
Ellington, Duke, 65, 66, 71, 72, 75
Ellison, Psi (Peter), 183
ELP. *see* Emerson, Lake and Palmer
Emerson, Keith, 155–6
Emerson, Lake and Palmer (ELP), 154, 161, 168
EMI, 157, 242
"En Vivo en Argentina" ("Live in Argentina") concert, 134
Encuentro de Canción Protesta (Protest Song Meeting), 6, 124–6
Endrigo, Sergio, 39
England. *see* British music
English Bach Festival, 247–8

enka songs, 83, 91
"Epitaph" (King Crimson), 160–1
Erichson, Wolf, 243
ethnomusicology, 38
Euren, Judith, 182
European Economic Community (EEC), 144, 150
Eurovision Song Contest (ESC), 146, 151
Évariste, 269
"Examination-Hell Blues" (Tomoya Taka'ishi), 82, 86, 88, 95
L'Expérience acoustique (Bayle), 269
experimental art, 16
experimental music, 3
experimental revolution in Britain
    '1968' and the experimental revolution, 171–87
    alternative British experimental culture, 181–4
    British music in the Old and New Left, 172–4
    experimental alternative tradition, 174–6
    experimental legacy and counterculture, 186–7
    experimental music in the underground, 178–81
    experimentalism, Beat culture, and the Underground, 177–8
    Scratch Orchestra opposition and Maoism, 184–6
Experimental Sound Group (GESI), 129
L'Express, 115
Eye of the Needle (Turner), 68
La fabbrica illuminata (*The Enlightened Factory*) (Nono), 8

factory novels, 34
factory workers, 31–6, 231
Falklands/Malvinas War, 134
Family, 154
Fanon, Frantz, 68
Fanshawe, David, 175
Fantasio, 23
Fascism, 29
Federal Republic of (West) Germany, 189 *see also* West Germany
Federation of Italian Communist Youth (FGCI), 31
Feldman, Jill, 252
Feldman, Morton, 171, 175–6, 186
feminism, 5, 11, 229, 236
Ferrat, Jean, 267
Festa del proletariato giovanile, 42

Festival de la Canción Comprometida (Festival of Committed Song), 8
Festival dell'Avanguardia della Musica e Nuove Tendenze, 42
Festival dell'Unità, Italy, 8, 31, 37, 38, 42
Festival des politischen Liedes (Political Song Festival), East Berlin, 8
Festival of Life, 61
Festival of Sanremo, 37, 39
Fête de la Humanité (Humanity Festival), Paris, 8
FIAT, 33
Fictitious Report on an American Pop Festival, 219
Finardi, Eugenio, 43
Finer, Carole, 186
First Festival of Chilean New Song, 130–1
"Flaming Dart" campaign, 103
flash mobs, 1, 2
floating signifiers, 268–9, 270
Floh de Cologne, 191, 192
Florilegium series, 243
Das Floß der Medusa (*The Raft of the Medusa*) (Henze), 68
Fluff, 157
Fluxus, 43, 171, 172, 177
Fly (The Plastic Ono Band), 181
Fo, Dario, 30
"Folk Caravan", 93
Folk Crusaders, 83, 84, 85, 86, 89
Folk Guerilla, 83, 93
folk music
    American popular music, 49–50, 51, 53, 62–71
    Italy, 36–41
    Japan, 81–96
    overview, 2, 3, 8
    Scandinavia, 139, 141–2, 150–1
Folk School concerts, 88
Los Folkloristas, 36, 37
Folk-songs (Berio), 40
Fortini, Franco, 34, 37
"Fortunate Son" (Creedence Clearwater Revival), 50
"Fracture" (King Crimson), 163, 164
"FraKctured" (King Crimson), 164
France
    British rock, 156
    May 1968 as representation, 268–72
    music and May 1968, 255–72
    music as protest practice, 258–63
    overview, 6, 11, 255–8
    role of musicians, 263–8

Franco-Vietnamese War, 99
Frankfurt School, 30
Frazier, Lessie J., 223
Freak Out (Zappa), 23
Free German Youth (FDJ), 195
free jazz
   American, 10, 59, 66, 148
   British music, 173
   European, 66
   France, 270
   Italy, 42
   Japan, 81
   overview, 3, 10
   South Africa, 10, 66, 72, 78
Free Jazz (Coleman), 59
Free Peoples' Concerts, 69
freedom, 78–80
Friendz/Friends, 178
Fripp, Robert, 158, 162
Frith, Simon, 111
Fromm, Erich, 189
The Fugs, 62

G8 summits, 1
Gabriel, Peter, 165, 168
"Gaikotsu no Uta" ("Song by a Skelton") (Okabayashi), 92
Galamian, Ivan, 252
Garay, Sindo, 127
García, Ricardo, 130
Gardiner, John Eliot, 248, 249
Gare, Lou, 179
Garrone, Margherita Galante, 37
Gaslini, Giorgio, 31, 40
"La gatta Cenerentola", 40
"Gẩy Đàn Lên Hỡi Người Bạn Mỹ" ("Play Music for Our Dear American Friends") (Phạm Tuyên), 105–6
GDR. *see* East Germany
Gelmetti, Vittorio, 35
gemin yangbanxi ('revolutionary model operas'), 223 *see also* model works
gender relations, 11, 223, 226, 229, 236
Genesis, 154, 161, 165, 166, 168
Genoa, 29
Gentle Giant, 154, 160, 161, 165
German Academic Exchange Services (DAAD), 193
German Democratic Republic (GDR), 190 *see also* East Germany
Germany
   1968 resonating in music, 200–2
   anti-authoritarian agendas, 188–91
   anti-authoritarian music in East Germany, 195–8
   anti-authoritarian music in West Germany, 191–4
   anti-authoritarian revolt, 188–204
   anti-authoritarian revolt by musical means, 191–3
   class struggle and music, 198–200
   fight against musical authorities, 202–4
   overview, 11
   student protests, 188
Gertze, Johnny, 65, 75
GESI. *see* Experimental Sound Group
Gesti (Berio), 247
"Get 'em Out by Friday" (Genesis), 168
"Gia Tài Của Mẹ" ("A Mother's Legacy") (Trịnh Công Sơn), 115–16
"Giải Phóng Miền Nam" ("Liberate the South") (Huỳnh Minh Siêng), 107
Giannarelli, Ansano, 35
Gillespie, Dizzie, 65
Ginsberg, Allen, 171
"Give Peace a Chance" (Lennon), 105
Gleason, Ralph J., 52, 59
Gli anni del giudizio (Arpino), 34
Gnidrolog, 165
Goehr, Alexander, 174, 175
The Golden City Dixies, 64
The Golden Earrings, 6
Gong, 42
"Gongchang mei wansui" ("Long Live the Factory Girls"), 82, 85, 233
González, Sara, 129
Gracious, 162
Gramsci, Antonio, 30, 35, 38, 38
Granada Television, 179
Grange, Dominique, 260, 267
"La Grappignole", 260
Grappin, Pierre, 260
The Grateful Dead, 11, 99
Gravem, Dag Falang, 147, 150
Great Britain
   aiming for bigger things, 157–60
   alternative British experimental culture, 181–4
   anti-diatonic progressions, 162–4
   British music in the Old and New Left, 172–4
   early music movement, 247–8, 249–50
   experimental alternative tradition, 174–6
   experimental legacy and counterculture, 186–7
   experimental music in the underground, 178–81

experimental revolution, 158, 171–87
experimentalism, Beat culture, and the Underground, 177–8
immediate impact of the events of 1968, 154–7
overview, 154
parallel tenth progressions, 164–7
possible utopias, 167–70
Scratch Orchestra opposition and Maoism, 184–6
short '1968' and the long, 154–70
variety of visions, 160–1
"The Great Digest" (*The Great Learning*) (Cardew), 180, 182, 183, 185, 186
Green, Richard, 154, 155, 156
Greenslade, 165
Gregoretti, Ugo, 35
Grootveld, Robert Jasper, 15
Großkopf, Erhard, 193
The Group Image, 55
"Group Sounds", 81
Gryphon, 161
guajira (country music), 128
Guccini, Francesco, 39
Guest, Roy, 157
Guevara, Alfredo, 128–9
Guevara, Che, 25, 128, 247
Guildhall School, 250
The Guitarmen, 64
Guthrie, Woody, 92, 96

"Hà Nội Điên Biên Phủ" ("Hanoi Dien Bien Phu") (Phạm Tuyên), 103, 104–5
"Hà Nội Những Đêm Không Ngủ" ("Sleepless Nights in Hanoi") (Phạm Tuyên), 103
Hà Thúc Cần, 108
The Hague Royal Conservatory, 251
Haigang (*On the Docks*), 224, 229
Hair, 56, 181
Hamill, Peter, 161
"Handsome Johnny" (Havens), 49–50
Hanoi, 103–4
'happenings', 15, 16–17, 18, 171, 177, 178, 192, 210–11
Harnoncourt, Nikolaus, 239, 243
Harper, Roy, 157–8
Harpsichord Music on Original Instruments (Leonhardt), 240
harpsichords, 238, 241, 242, 244, 245
Harris, Bryn, 183
Hart, Shirley, 157
Harvest label, 157
"Hát Trên Những Xác Người" ("Singing on the Corpses") (Trịnh Công Sơn), 112–13, 115

hausmusik movement, 238
Havens, Richie, 47, 49
Haynes, Bruce, 240, 242, 247, 251–2
Haynes, Jim, 178
"Heidi Heido", 260
"Hell" (Gracious), 162
Hellqvist, Per-Anders, 147
Helsinki Accords, 213
Hendrix, Jimi, 20, 47, 210, 213
Henry Cow, 41, 159
Henze, Hans Werner, 200
The Herd, 43
Herzfeld, Michael, 115
Het Leven, 26
heteronomy, 3
Hifi Stereophonie, 244
high art, 171, 175, 181
high culture, 149, 192, 244–6
Highway 61 (Dylan), 53
Highway 61 Revisited (Dylan), 52
HIP. *see* historically informed performance
hippie culture
 American popular music, 56–7, 61–2
 British music, 158, 181, 183
 Czechoslovakia, 211
 early music movement, 237, 254
 Netherlands, 21, 23
Hirayama, Michiko, 44
Hiroshima bomb, 173
historical fidelity, 244
historical performers, 237
historically informed performance (HIP)
 bridging high and popular culture, 244, 246
 early music and politics, 251–4
 early music movement, 237, 238, 239–40
 education reform, 250
 old instruments, new technologies, 242, 243–4
 overview, 3
 period instruments of change, 240, 241
Hitweek, 14, 17, 20
Hlavsa, Milan, 213
Hồ Chí Minh, 99
Hobbs, Christopher, 181, 182, 185, 187
Hoffmann's Comic Theatre, 192
Hogwood, Christopher, 243, 245, 249
Holiday, Billie, 70
Holland Festival, 247, 253
The Hollies, 214, 215
Holst, Gustav, 158
Hong Kong
 gender relations, 223

Hong Kong (cont.)
    movie musicals and new womanhood, 229–32
    new womanhood and patriarchy, 232–5
    overview, 236
    riots, 222–3
Hongdeng ji (*The Red Lantern*) (model work), 224, 228, 236
Hongse niangzijun (*The Red Detachment of Women*) (ballet), 224, 229
Hoogland, Stanley, 246, 253
Hootenanny Club, 195
Hoover, J. Edgar, 57
Hopkins, John 'Hoppy', 178, 179, 180
Horkheimer, Max, 189
Horowitz, Michael, 171, 176
"Huế Sài Gòn Hà Nội" ("Hue Saigon Hanoi") (Trịnh Công Sơn), 115
Hue, 100, 108, 112
Huillet, Danièle, 241
huismuziek, 244, 253
L'Humanité, 110
Humphrey, Hubert, 56
Hungarian Revolution, 209
Hungary, 11, 209, 217–21
Husák, Gustáv, 211
Hüsch, Hanns Dieter, 191

I Ching, 182
"I Get Up I Get Down", 167
"I Got It Bad and That Ain't Good" (Ellington), 73
"I Got Life", 56–7
Ibrahim, Abdullah. *see* Brand, Dollar
ICAIC. *see* Cuban Cinematographic Institute
Ideological Study (Id) Group, 185, 186
IEST. *see* International Essener Songtage
"I-Feel-Like-I'm-Fixin'-To-Die Rag" (McDonald), 50
Iggy and the Stooges, 62
"Il est cinq heures, Paris s'éveillent" ("Its Five a.m., Paris Awakens") (Dulronc), 261
Illés, 218, 219
"Imjin Gawa" ("Imjin River") (Folk Crusaders), 85, 95
The Impressions, 58, 59, 63
improvisation, 8
    British music, 176, 178, 179, 181
    collective improvisation, 24, 270
    early music movement, 251
    free improvisation, 8, 26, 42, 176, 179, 181, 191, 200, 204
    Italy, 36, 42

Scandinavia, 145, 148, 149
South Africa, 66, 72, 75, 76, 78, 79
In the Court of the Crimson King (King Crimson), 159, 160–1
"In the Land of Grey and Pink" (Caravan), 169
In the Wake of Poseidon (King Crimson), 158
Indeterminacy (Cage), 179
indeterminacy/indeterminism, 174, 176, 186, 187
Indian music, 8, 60
'indie labels', 152
industrial triangle, 30, 32
The Insect Trust, 54
instrument building, 242
intellectuals, 30
International Carnival of Experimental Sound (ICES '72), 185
International Essener Songtage (IEST), 6, 191, 192
International Poetry Incarnation, 178
The International Times (*IT*), 52, 53, 54, 55, 56
"L'Internationale"
    Japan, 82, 95
    May 1968 protests, 258, 261, 262
    Scratch Orchestra, 185
"Interstellar Overdrive" (Pink Floyd), 168
Inti Illimani, 31, 132, 133
irony, 45, 86–7, 115, 161, 203, 204
Istituto Ernesto De Martino, 37, 41
IT. *see The International Times*
Italy
    factory workers, 31–6
    folk music as antagonistic culture, 36–41
    overview, 10, 29–31
    progressive rock and liberation, 41–5
    protest movements, 29–45
"It's a Game" (String Driven Thing), 161
Ives, Charles, 24
Iwai, Hiroshi, 92

Jagger, Mick, 155, 171
Japan
    college-folk music, 82
    enka songs, 91–2
    Folk Guerilla, 93–5
    Kansai folk song movement, 83–7
    overview, 10, 81–3, 95
    rise of underground folk song, 81–96
    Self-Defence Forces, 90
    student protests, 6
Jara, Victor, 131, 132, 133
jazz
    American popular music, 52, 55, 59–60

Eastern Bloc protest culture, 208, 209
Netherlands, 26
overview, 3
Scandinavia, 139, 145, 148
South Africa, 65–6, 67, 69, 79
Jazz Epistles, 74
Jazz Section, 213–14
Jethro Tull, 161
"La jeune garde", 261, 262
Jiang Qing, 224, 225, 234
John Wesley Harding (Dylan), 52–3, 54
Johnson, Lyndon, 47, 48, 54, 125, 126
Joki Freund Ensemble, 208
Jona, Emilio, 37
Jones, Elvin, 77
Jong-Hwan Ko, 85
Jonker, Ingrid, 68
Joplin, Janis, 20
Journey to the North Pole (Boenisch), 183
"Journey's End" (The Strawbs), 169
Juanes, 135

Kagel, Mauricio, 203, 248
Kaiser, Rolf-Ulrich, 191
Kammermusik I. Von Menschen und Vögeln (Chamber Music I. For People and Birds) (Schmidt), 201
Das Kaninchen bin ich (The Rabbit is Me) (Bredemeyer, music), 64
Kansai folk song movement, 82, 83, 88, 94, 95
Karl, Gregory, 161
"Karn Evil 9" (Emerson, Lake and Palmer), 161, 169
Katagiri, Yuzuru, 86
Katô, Kazuhiko, 85
Kawaraban, 86, 89
Kelly, Thomas, 238
Kennedy, John F., 48, 99
Kennedy, Robert F., 46, 47, 48, 55, 63
Kenyon, Nicholas, 239
Khánh Ly, 110, 113, 115
Khrushchev, Nikita, 220
Kick Out the Jams (MC5), 62, 63
Kiesinger, Kurt Georg, 201
King Crimson, 154, 158, 160, 160, 162, 165, 169
King Kong: An African Jazz Opera, 64
King Mob, 184
King, Jr., Martin Luther
  American political engagement, 10, 46, 47, 63
  black pride, 55, 56, 57, 58
  British rock, 155, 164
Kinh Việt Nam (Prayer for Vietnam) (songbook), 110

Kinki Hôsô (Kinki Broadcasting), 85
The Kinks, 6
Kirkby, Emma, 243, 249
Kjelsberg, Sverre, 151
Klaus Renft Combo. *see* Renft
Klavierstück IX (Stockhausen), 176
Klompé, Marga, 28
The Knack, 6
Knights, Vanessa, 122
"Knots" (Gentle Giant), 161
Kobe, 6
Kohout, Pavel, 210
Komenský, Jan Amos, 212
Kontaktnätet (Contact Network), 143
Koopman, Ton, 253
Körsam, 146
Krautrock, 191, 192, 200, 204
Kryl, Karel, 212
Kubišová, Marta, 211
Kuijken brothers, 238, 239, 243
Kuijken, Barthold, 238, 246, 250
Kuijken, Sigiswald, 238, 241
Kunert, Christian, 198
Kurzwellen für Beethoven (Shortwaves for Beethoven) (Stockhausen), 203
"Kuso Kuraé Bushi", ("Go-to-hell song") (Okabayashi), 88, 92
Kyôto, 6

Labyrint (Schat), 17, 24
Lacy, Steve, 43, 45
Laird, Michael, 245, 254
Lake, Greg, 160, 168–9
Lalandi, Lina, 247–8
Lancaster, Byard, 77
Landowska, Wanda, 237–8, 241
Lang ru Chunri Feng (Her Tender Love), 229–30, 233
Latin America
  Chilean and Cuban musical exchange, 130–2
  Cuban *nueva trova*, 126–30
  dictatorship and solidarity years, 132–5
  Mexico, 120–4
  'new song' movement, 119–36
  overview, 7, 10, 25, 119–20
  peace concerts, 135–6
Le Glou, Jacques, 261
Led Zeppelin, 196
Lehner, Gerhard, 73
"Lemmebesomethin" (Silverstein), 41
"Lemmings" (Van der Graaf Generator), 161, 162

"Lên Đàng" ("On the Road") (Lưu Hữu Phước), 107
Leninism, 206, 264
Lennon, John, 155
Leonhardt, Gustav, 239, 240, 243, 248, 253
Leopold, Silke, 4
LeRoux, Etienne, 68
Lesser, Mike, 177, 182
"Let's Join the Riot Police", 95
"Let's Join the Self Defence Forces" (Takada, lyrics), 82–3, 89, 91, 95
Lévi-Strauss, Claude, 268, 269
Leydi, Roberto, 37, 38, 40
Liberation Music Groups (Đoàn Văn Công Giải Phóng), 106
Liberovici, Sergio, 37
'Lipsi' dance, 190
Litany for the 14th of June (Breuker), 17
literature, 34
Lityński, Jan, 215
Live New Departures festival, 176
Locke, Ralph, 260
Lockwood, Annea, 178, 180
"La locomotiva" (Guccini), 39
London Free School, 178
long ballad, 53
"Long Live Man Dead" (Gnidrolog), 165
Longjiang song (*Ode to the Dragon River*), 229
Lotta Continua, 30
Lucier, Alvin, 43
Ludwig van (Kagel), 203
"Luglio, agosto, settembre (nero)" (Area), 43
Luns, Joseph, 28
Lutyens, Elisabeth, 172, 174–5, 246
Lưu Hữu Phước, 106–7
Lytton, Paul, 45
Macan, Edward, 158–9, 160, 164
La macchina del tempo (Branca), 9
"Macht kaputt, was euch kaputt macht" ("Destroy What Destroys You") (Scherben), 193
Mackerras, Charles, 248
Mackintosh, Catherine, 246, 250, 254
Macnaghten Concert series, 180
Mafeje, Archie, 68–9
Mai (record company), 143, 151
Mailer, Norman, 61–2
"Major Disaster" (Gryphon), 161
Makeba, Miriam, 64
"La Maldición de Malinche" ("Malinche's Curse") (Palomares), 121–2
Malvinas/Falklands War, 134

Manchester Group, 174, 175
Mandela, Nelson, 67
Manfred Mann, 53
Mangelsdorff, Albert, 208
Manguaré, 132
Manns, Patricio, 133
Mantovani, Sandra, 40
Mao Zedong, 185, 224
Maoism, 172, 184, 185, 186, 262, 263
Maraini, Dacia, 30
Marcangelo, John, 186
Marcatrè, 38
Marchetti, Walter, 43
Marcus, Greil, 50, 53–4
Marini, Giovanna, 31, 37, 41
Marks, Dave, 65, 69
Marmalade, 155
The Marmalades, 70
Marriner, Neville, 248
"Mars" (Holst), 158
"La Marseillaise", 262
Martin, Bill, 158, 159–60
Marx, Karl, 27, 32
Marxism, 42, 185, 206
Masekela, Hugh, 64
"Master Jack" (Marks), 69
"Masters of War" (Dylan), 88, 161
Matching Mole, 41
Matsuyama, Takéshi, 85
Matuška, Waldemar, 211
Matusow, Harvey, 180, 185
Maxwell Davies, Peter, 174, 175, 246, 248
May 1968 protests
  music and May 1968 in France, 255–72
  musical practices, 258–63
  musical representations, 268–72
  overview, 255–8
  role of music, 263–8
Mayfield, Curtis, 58–9, 63
Mbeki, Govan, 67
MC5, 61, 62
McCarthy, Eugene, 48
McCartney, Paul, 165, 179
McDonald, Country Joe, 49, 50
McGregor, Chris, 65–6, 68, 70, 71, 72, 78, 80
McGregor, Maxine, 71
Mea, Ivan Della, 31, 37
Medek, Tilo, 203, 204
medieval music, 242, 245, 249
"Még fái minden csók" ("Every Kiss Still Hurts") (Illés), 218
Mehegan, John, 74
Melody Maker (*MM*), 154–5, 156, 157, 158

Memoriale (Volponi), 34
Menabò, 34
Mendelssohn, Felix, 164
Mengelberg, Misha, 24, 247
Messiaen, Olivier, 180, 248
Metró, 218
Metrodora (Stratos), 44
Mexico, 5, 6, 46, 59, 63, 120–4
Mey, Reinhard, 199
Meyer, Paul, 70
Michnik, Adam, 215
Mickiewicz, Adam, 215
Mida, Massimo, 35
"The Mighty Quinn" (Dylan), 53
Mihashi, Kazuo, 92
Milan, 29
Milanés, Pablo, 126–9, 132, 134–5
Miles, Barry, 178, 179
militarism and its critique, 14, 108, 197
"Miraculous is this World" (Nieman), 217
"Mississippi Goddam" (Simone), 56
Mitchell, Tim, 183
Mitter, Armin, 201
Mittler, Barbara, 225
MNW (record company), 143, 151
Möbius, Ralph (Rio Reiser), 193
model works
    as revolutionary genre, 223–6
    gender relations, 223
    movie musicals, 231
    new womanhood, 226–9, 234, 236
    overview, 11
modernism, 173
"Modlitba pro Martu" ("Prayer for Marta") (Matuška), 211–12
Moeketsi, Kippie, 75
Moholo, Louis, 78, 80
Mol, Hans, 21
Mol, Pieter Jan, 22, 23
Möller, Wouter, 252
Moncada, 129
Monk, Thelonius, 75
Monterey Festival, 18
The Moody Blues, 169
Moorman, Charlotte, 185
Moravia, Alberto, 30
Morgenrood Rotterdam, 27
Morricone, Ennio, 36
Morris, William, 173
Morrison, Jim, 20
Morrison, Norman, 100, 106
Mossmann, Walter, 199
Mothers of Invention, 43, 191

Motown, 58
Moustaki, Georges, 267
The Move, 43
'movement-oriented turn', 2
movie musicals, 223, 229, 232, 236
Mozambique, 71
Mozart, Wolfgang Amadeus, 203
"Mr Media Man" (PLM), 186
Mrożek, Sławomir, 216
Munich Olympics, 217
Munrow, David, 239, 242, 245, 249
music education, 145, 248–51, 266
music festivals, 8
Music from Big Pink (The Band), 54
music historiography, 3–4
Music Now, 180
Musica Antiqua Amsterdam, 248
Musica Elettronica Viva (MEV), 180, 191
La musica popolare, 10
musical autonomy, 25
musical canon, revolt against, 202–3
Musica-Manifesto n. 1 (Nono), 40
musicians' strike, 266
musicians' unions, 266–8
musicology, 2
Die Musik der Geschichte und Gegenwart, 3
Musikens Makt (*The Power of Music*), 41, 42
Mussorgsky, Modest, 168
Muzak, 42
Muziek Expres, 20
Muziek Parade, 20

Nacksving, 143
Nakagawa, Gorô, 86
Napoli Centrale, 41
National Liberation Front (NLF), 97, 98, 100, 106, 117
National Socialism, 189, 199, 200
NATO, 28
Negri, Antonio, 32
Neruda, Pablo, 131
The Netherlands
    1968 and music, 12–28
    cultural change, 12–13
    "Day of Anarchy", 6, 17
    early music movement, 247, 248–9, 250, 253
    overview, 10, 12–14
    politicisation of avant-garde musicians, 24–8
    popular music and youth culture, 19–24
    Provo and music, 14–19

The Netherlands (cont.)
  Rikskonserter (National Concert Agency), 140, 146, 147, 148
  student protests, 12, 13
New Culture movement, 236
New Departures, 176, 177, 178
new jazz, 59–60
New Left
  British music, 172, 173
  Germany, 6, 188–9, 193, 199, 200
  Japan, 82
  Nieuw Links, 21
  overview, 2, 7, 9
  Vietnam War, 7
New Left Review (*NLR*), 173
New Musical Express (*NME*), 154
New Reasoner, 173
new womanhood. *see* womanhood
"New World" (The Strawbs), 161
New World symphony (Dvorak), 155
New York, 5, 175–6
Newport Folk Festival, 51
Ngô Đình Diệm, 99
"Ngọc Đuốc Mo-ri-xơn" ("Morrison, the Human Torch") (An Chung), 106
"Người Con Gái Việt Nam" ("Vietnamese Girl") (Trịnh Công Sơn), 115
Nguyen Ngoc Loan, 48
Nicaragua, 119, 120, 135
The Nice, 43
Nicola, Noel, 129
Niebiesko-Czarni (Blue-Blacks), 214
Niemen, Czesław, 215, 217
Nietzsche, Friedrich, 166
Nieuw Links, 21
Nieuwenhuys, Constant, 16
Night Rite (MPNR21), 183
Nixon, Richard M., 49, 100
NLF. *see* National Liberation Front
NME. see New Musical Express
'no future' generation, 220
No to Co, 217
"Noch", ("Still") (Biermann), 201
"Nối Vòng Tay Lớn" ("Circle of Unity") (Trịnh Công Sơn), 116
Nolthenius, Hélène, 250
Nono, Luigi
  British music, 174
  Italian music, 31, 32, 33, 36, 40
Nordic Association of Non-Commercial Phonogram Producers (NIFF), 151
Norrington, Roger, 246, 248, 249, 254
Norsk Rikskringkastning (NRK), 140

Norsktoppen, 141
"North Country Blues" (Dylan), 86
North Korea, 85
Norway
  anti-commercialism, 145
  development of '1968', 142, 143–4
  end of '1968', 151
  music in the broadcasting media, 140, 141
  overview, 10, 139
  transnational music, 150
Notenkrakersactie (Andriessen, Schat *et al.*), 247
Novotný, Antonin, 210
Ntshoko, Makhaya, 65, 75
nueva canción (new song) movement, 10
  '1968' in Mexico, 120–4
  Chilean and Cuban musical exchange, 130–2
  dictatorship and solidarity years, 132–5
  overview, 10, 119–20
  peace concerts, 135–6
nueva trova (new song), 10, 120, 126
nuevo cancionero (new song book), 120, 133
'Nuff Said (Simone), 55, 56
Nuova Compagnia di Canto Popolare, 39–40
Nuovo Canzoniere Italiano, 37–40, 41
Nuovo Consonanza, 42–3
Nuttall, Jeff, 171, 173, 178, 179, 181
Nylöf, Göran, 140
Nyman, Michael, 186–7

objets trouvés, 41, 192
Occupy Wall Street, 1, 5
Ochoa, Amparo, 121
Ochs, Phil, 49, 51, 52
octatonic scale, 162
"Ode to Joy" (Beethoven), 133
Odéon theatre, Paris, 264
Ohana, Maurice, 269
Ohnesorg, Benno, 188
Okabayashi, Nobuyasu, 88, 92
Okinawa, 87
Oktoberklub, 195, 201–2
OLAS (Organisation of Latin American Solidarity), 124
Old Left, 2, 172–3, 174
Olson, Charles, 177
Olympia, 210
Olympic Games, 46, 59, 63, 217
Ombre rosse, 30
Omega, 218
OMUS (Organisation of Higher Music Education), 147
"One More Red Nightmare" (King Crimson), 163

Ono, Yoko, 179, 180
opera houses, 6, 266
operaismo, 32
operas, 223, 224–5, 226–8
oral traditions, 39
organic intellectual, 30
Original Confidence, 83
Orme, 41
Ortega, Sergio, 133
Ortiz, Ralph, 178
Ossorio, José, 124–5
the 'Other', 3
Ottieri, Ottiero, 34
Oxbridge universities, 249–50
Oxford Schola Cantorum, 249
Oz, 178

Page, Robin, 177
Palach, Jan, 201, 211
Palisca, Claude V., 4
Palmer, Carl, 168
Palomares, Gabino, 121
Pan Africanist Congress (PAC), 64, 67
Pannach, Gerulf, 197, 198
Panzieri, Raniero, 32
paradigm shifts, 1, 2, 4, 5
Paradiso, 23
parallel tenth progressions, 160, 164–7
Paris, 5, 6, 181, 258–9, 266, *see also* May 1968 protests
Parker, Charlie, 65
Parra, Angel, 129, 131, 132, 133
Parra, Isabel, 129, 131, 132, 133
Parra, Violeta, 131
Parrott, Andrew, 246, 249–50, 254
Parsons, Gram, 156
Parsons, Michael, 173–4, 175, 181, 183, 187
Parti communiste français (PCF), 257, 262, 267–2
Partito Comunista Italiano (PCI), 30–1, 32, 35–6
Partito Socialista Italiano (PSI), 30
Pas, Niek, 12, 13, 16
Pasolini, Pier Paolo, 30
A Passion Play (Jethro Tull), 46
patriarchy, 231, 232–5, 236
Pavese, Cesare, 33
Paz Sin Fronteras (Peace Without Borders) concerts, 135–6
PCI. *see* Partito Comunista Italiano
Peace for Vietnam Committee, 83, 87, 93
Peel, John, 156, 158
peña night clubs, 131

"Penny Lane" (The Beatles), 165
People's Liberation Music (PLM), 186
'the people's music', 43
People's Republic of China (PRC), 7
  model works and movie musicals, 222–36
  model works as revolutionary genre, 223–6
  movie musicals, 229–32
  new womanhood and patriarchy, 232–5
  new womanhood in the model works, 226–9
  overview, 7, 11, 222–3, 236
Peppin, Biddy, 177
Per voi giovani, 42
performance practice scholarship, 241
period instruments, 8, 9, 39, 237, 240, 242, 244, 245, 246
Peru, 120
"La petite Emilie" (trad.), 260
Petri, Elio, 36
Phạm Duy, 112
Phạm Tuyên, 101, 103–6
photographs, 46
Piano Burning (Lockwood), 178
pianos, 178, 242
Pictures at an Exhibition (Mussorgsky), 168–9
"Pictures of a City" (King Crimson), 165
"Pied Piper" (radio programme), 242
Pierrot, Paul, 178
Pietrangeli, Paolo, 31, 37
"Piggies" (The Beatles), 246
Piil, Beate S., 144, 150
"Pilgrims" (Van der Graaf Generator), 166
Pink Floyd
  British rock, 20, 156, 157, 160, 168
  experimental music in Britain, 8, 177, 179
pirate radio, 140–1
Pirelli, Giovanni, 40, 41
Pitt, Arthur A., 184
The Plastic Ono Band, 56
Plastic People of the Universe, 205, 212, 221
"Playa Girón" (Rodríguez), 127–8
Playboy Club, 175
"Playboys and Playgirls" (Dylan), 88
"Plegaría a un Labrador" ("Prayer to a Labourer") (Jara), 131
Plummer, Mark, 158
Plus-Minus (Stockhausen), 176
"Pobre del Cantor" (Pity The Singer), 128
poetry, 171, 174, 178
Poland
  desire for freedom, 208, 209
  effect of '1968', 207, 214–17

Poland (cont.)
  overview, 11, 220–1
  samizdat (self publishing), 207
Polish United Workers' Party (PZPR), 216
political song
  Eastern Bloc, 207
  France, 263
  Germany, 199
  Italy, 36–7
  Netherlands, 22–3, 24–8
Politiek-Demonstratief Experimenteel Concert, 6, 253
politrock, 192, 204
Polskie Nagrania, 217
pop-folk music, 82
popular culture, 244–6
popular music
  America, 46–63
  Britain, 171–2
  Italy, 38
  Japan, 81
  Netherlands, 13–14, 19
  overview, 2
  Scandinavia, 138–9, 141, 142–3, 152
  Vietnam, 118
Portelli, Alessandro, 40
Portsmouth Sinfonia, 185
postmodern plurality, 9, 192
Prague Spring, effects on
  Czechoslovakia, 211, 213
  Germany, 200, 201, 203, 204
  Hungary, 218
  overview, 6, 7, 205–6, 221
  Poland, 216
PRC. *see* People's Republic of China
Premiata Forneria Marconi, 41
Presley, Elvis, 167, 179
Preston, Stephen, 250
Prévost, Eddie, 179
The Primitives, 68, 69
Private Company (band), 184
Procol Harum, 165
progressive music movement, 143–4, 147–9
progressive rock
  British rock, 11, 154, 158
  Italy, 41–5
  Netherlands, 20, 26
Promenade Theatre Orchestra, 179, 184, 185
Proms, 186, 187
protest culture
  American popular music, 46–63
  British rock, 154–70

China and Hong Kong, 222–36
early music movement, 237–54
Eastern Bloc, 205–21
experimental revolution in Britain, 171–87
France, 255–72
Germany, 188–204
Italy, 29–45
Japan, 81–96
Latin America, 119–36
Netherlands, 12–28
overview, 1–3, 5–6
Scandinavia, 137–53
South Africa, 64–80
Vietnam, 97–118
protest songs
  American popular music, 49–51
  Cuba, 125–6
  Italy, 37
  Japan, 82, 95
  Netherlands, 18, 19
  Poland, 215
  Scandinavia, 142
  Vietnam, 107–8
Provo
  "Day of Anarchy", 6
  early music movement, 249
  May 1968 protests, 264
  Netherlands unrest, 10, 12, 13–14, 21
  politicisation of avant-garde musicians, 24, 25, 26–7, 28
  popular music and youth culture, 14–19, 22, 24
provotariaat (vs. klootjesvolk), 15
"ProzaKc Blues" (King Crimson), 164
psychedelia, 8, 20, 23, 54, 170
psychodrama, 255–6, 268, 272
psychological theories, 189
public service broadcasting, 140, 152–3
Puebla, Carlos, 128
The Puhdys, 64
Pulitzer Prize, 48
punk rock, 62, 152, 220
Puxley, Simon, 78

Q'65, 19
"Qingchun agege" ("Youth A-go-go"), 232
Qixi baihu tuan (*Raid on the White Tiger Regiment*), 224
Quaderni piacentini, 30
Quaderni rossi, 30, 32
Quadro Hotteterre, 252

Quảng Đức, 99
Quesada, Armando, 127
Questo vuol dire che… (Berio), 40
Quilapayún, 131–2, 133
Quimantú, 133
Quindici, 30
quotation (musical), 202–3, 204
"Quyết Thắng" ("Determined to Win"), 109
R&B, 55
Rabie, Jan, 68
racism, 67, 173
Rada, Petr, 211
radio, 140–1
Radio Free Europe, 212
Radio Luxembourg, 218
Radio One, 157
Raímon, 125–6
rap music, 59, 220
Rashed, Rafia, 44
"Rauchhaus Song" (Scherben), 193
Re nudo, 30, 42
Reconstructie (Andriessen, de Leeuw, Mengelberg, Schat, van Vlijmen), 25, 26, 28, 247
Record Collector, 159–60
recorder music
    bridging high and popular culture, 244–5, 246
    early music and new music, 247, 253
    early music movement, 9, 238
    education reform, 248
    old instruments, new technologies, 243
    period instruments of change, 241, 242
Recorder Music on Original Instruments, 243
recording innovations, 242
Red Army Faction (RAF), 193
red music (nhạc đỏ), 118
Reeser, Eduard, 250
"Refugees" (Van der Graaf Generator), 166
Reich, Wilhelm, 189
Reiser, Rio (Ralph Möbius), 193
Renaissance, 159
Renaissance music, 242, 245, 249
Renft, 196, 197
Republic of Vietnam (RVN), 97, 98, 100, 117
"La révolution" (Évariste), 269
Revolution (Q'65), 19
"Revolution" (The Beatles), 19, 155
"Revolution No. 9" (The Beatles), 179
Revolutionary Communist Party of Britain (Marxist-Leninist), 186
revolutionary model operas (*gemin yangbanxi*), 223. *see also* model works

revolutionary music
    France, 261, 262–3
    Vietnamese popular song, 109, 118
Revolutionary Symphony Shajiabang (*Geming jiaoxiangqu Shajia bang*), 224
Reyes, Judith, 120, 121, 122–3
Reynolds, Malvina, 89
Rifkin, Joshua, 246
Righart, Hans, 12, 28
"Riot Police Blues", 95
Robben Island prison, South Africa, 67
rock and roll, 18, 209
rock music
    American popular music, 49, 50, 52, 60
    British rock music, 154–70, 177–8
    Czechoslovakia, 209–10
    early music movement, 239, 252
    Eastern Bloc protest culture, 220–1
    Germany, 191, 195–7, 198
    Hungary, 218, 219–20
    Italy, 41–5
    Netherlands, 16, 20, 22, 26
    overview, 2, 3
    Poland, 214–15, 217
    Scandinavia, 138, 142–3, 149, 152
rock nacional (national rock), 134
Rodari, Gianni, 37
Rodowicz, Maryla, 217
Rodríguez, Silvio
    Chilean and Cuban musical exchange, 132
    Cuban *nueva trova*, 126, 127–8, 129
    Latin American 'new song', 123, 134–6
Rojas, Ricardo, 131
The Rolling Stones, 3, 6, 43, 64, 69, 70, 74, 191
"Rolling Thunder" campaign, 33
Romero, Juan, 46
Rooley, Anthony, 243
Rosa, Alberto Asor, 32
Rosamunde, entr'acte music of (Schubert), 204
Rowe, Keith, 179, 185
Royal College, 250
Royal Conservatory, The Hague, 251
Rubinoff, Kailan, 3
rural life, 183
RVN. *see* Republic of Vietnam
Rzewski, Frederic, 176
"Sag mir, wo Du stehst" ("Tell Me What Your Politics Are"), 202
Samspill (musicians' organisation), 143
San Francisco Chronicle, 52
"Sẵn Sàng Bắn!" ("Ready, Fire!") (Tô Hải), 103
Sandinista rebels, 119

Sanguineti, Edoardo, 30
Santamaría, Haydée, 128–9
"San'ya Blues" ("Doss-house Blues")
   (Okabayashi), 89
Sarduy, Pedro, 130
"Sárga Rózsa" (Illés), 219
Sartre, Jean-Paul, 133
Sassi, Gianni, 42, 43
A Saucerful of Secrets (Pink Floyd), 44
Savage Rose, 143
"Say It Loud – I'm Black and I'm Proud"
   (Brown), 56, 57
Scabia, Giuliano, 33
Scandinavia
   anti-authoritarian music movements,
      137–53
   anti-commercialism, 144–7
   culture and politics in 1960s, 138–40
   development of '1968', 141–4
   end of '1968', 151–3
   music in the broadcasting media, 140–1
   overview, 137–8
   politically or aesthetically progressive,
      147–149
   socio-musicological surveys, 139–40
   transnational music and the people's music,
      149–51
"Scatter Shield" (The Surfaris), 162
Schafer, John, 110, 111
Schat, Peter, 247
   early music movement, 247
   politicisation of avant-garde musicians, 17,
      24, 25, 26
Scherben (Ton Steine Scherben), 192–3
Schiano, Mario, 31, 36
Schmidt, Christfried, 201
Schoenberg Ensemble, 26
Schola Cantorum Basiliensis, 248
Schonfield, Victor, 180
'School Raids', 184
Schubert, Franz, 204
Sciascia, Leonardo, 30
Scratch Orchestra, 172
   alternative British experimental culture,
      181–4
   experimental music in the underground, 180
   experimental revolution in Britain, 172
   opposition and Maoism, 184–6
   organisation and ideology, 181–2
   politics, 184
   sex, drugs, travel, community, 182–3
Scratch Orchestra Improvisation Rite MC 10
   (Chant), 178

Searle, Humphrey, 172
second feminist movement, 11
second New Left, 173
Second Viennese School (*Zweite Wiener
   Schule*), 175, 176
Seeger, Pete
   American popular music, 49, 50, 51
   Germany, 202
   Italy, 37
   Japan, 83, 87, 89, 95
   Vietnam, 98, 105, 107
self-organisation, 2, 6–7
Senegal, 5–6
*Sensible Variationen um ein Thema von
   Schubert* (*Sensible Variations on a Theme
   of Schubert*) (Medek), 203–4
sentimental songs, 108–16, 118
Serguera, Jorge, 127
serialism, 60
Die Sestigers, 21, 22
Els Setze Jutges (The Seven Judges), 37
sexual liberation, 3, 21
sexuality, 223
SGS Thomson, 35
Shajia bang (*Shajia bang*), 224, 234
Shaonu xin (*Young Lady's Heart*)
   (film), 233
Sharpeville massacre, 64, 66
The Shatters, 64
Sheaff, Lawrence, 179
"Sheep" (The Strawbs), 162
Shinjuku Station, 93, 94
"Shô Gekijô" ("Little Theatre") movement,
   81
Shrapnel, Hugh, 184
Shuqin Huang, 235
Siao, Josephine (Xiao Fangfang), 230,
   231–2, 233
Siebert, Wilhelm Dieter, 203
Siegfried, Detlef, 16
Sierra maestra (Branca; Gelmetti, music), 35
signifiers, 268–9, 270
Silber, Irwin, 107, 126
Silence (record company), 143, 151
Silva, Vicky, 186
Silverstein, Shel, 142
Simon, Paul, 161
Simone, Nina, 55, 56–7, 58, 59
Simonetti, Gianni Emilio, 42, 43
Sinclair, John, 62
Siné, 263
Sinfield, Peter, 154
Sing Out!, 126

singer-songwriters, 6
   America, 51, 127, 195
   Eastern Bloc, 212
   Germany, 6, 191, 195, 197, 199, 204
   Italy, 39
   Japan, 81, 88, 92, 95, 96
   Latin America, 123, 127, 130, 133
   music festivals, 8
   Vietnam, 99, 108
Sisulu, Walter, 67
Situationism, 16, 43, 264
Situationist International, 16
Sivertsen, Smith, 142
Siwiec, Roman, 216
Sixty-Two Mesostics Re Merce Cunningham (Cage), 44
Skałdowie, 217
Skeaping, Roddy, 250
Skempton, Howard, 181, 187
Skowroneck, Martin, 241, 244
Sladen, David, 176
"The Slaughter of the Innocents" (King Crimson), 164
The Slippery Merchants, 58
Sly and the Family Stone, 47, 58
Smith, Dave, 174–5
Smith, Harry, 53, 54
Smith, Tommie, 46, 59, 187
Smith-Sivertsen, Henrik, 152
Snitzer, Herb, 243
socialist aesthetics/realism, 11, 110, 127, 172, 195, 219–20
'socialist humanism', 173
Soft Machine, 8, 179
"Soldat, Soldat" ("Soldier, Soldier") (Biermann), 197
solidarity, 39, 93, 122–3, 133, 135, 201, 263, 267
Solidarity Committee with the Struggle of the Mexican People (CSLRPM), 122
Solidarność, 216
Solleville, Francesca, 267
Solo with Accompaniment (Cardew), 176
Solzhenitsyn, Aleksandr, 210
"Song Drowns Out the Sound of Bombs" movement, 32, 33
song movements
   Brittany song movement, 271
   Kansai folk song movement, 82, 83, 88, 94, 95
   nueva canción, 10, 119–20, 130, 132, 135
   nueva trova, 10, 120, 126
   nuevo cancionero, 120, 133
   Occitanie song movement, 271
   "Youth Song Movement", 100–3, 109
"Song Within a Song" (Camel), 169
song-and-dance sequences, 230, 232
Songs For My America (Viglietti), 133
Sopot festivals, Poland, 208
Sorbonne, 264
Sosa, Mercedes, 133–4
Soul Folk in Action (The Staple Singers), 58
"The Sound of Silence" (Simon), 161
Sour Cream, 253
South Africa, 10
   Benjamin's aesthetic of spontaneity, 72–4
   British rock, 156
   case studies, 71–8
   Chris McGregor and the Blue Notes, 78
   discourses of freedom, 78–80
   Dollar Brand's kind of freedom, 74–7
   Entertainment and Censorship law, 67
   implementing apartheid, 66–7
   jazz at home and abroad, 69–71
   overview, 10, 64–6
   Publications and Censorship bill, 67
   spontaneity and Black Consciousness, 64–80
   'terrorism' laws, 67
   white rebellion, 67–9
South African Communist Party (SACP), 64, 67
Souvenirs d'enfance (Andriessen), 24
Soviet Union, 210
Soweto uprising, 64
Spoleto festival, 40
spontaneity, 16, 66, 71, 72, 73, 78, 79, 79
Springer Press, 5, 188–9
staatsgevaarlijk anarchisten, 14, 19
Stacey, Jackie, 232
Stalin, Joseph, 208, 209
Stalinism, 172, 173, 208, 220
Standage, Simon, 249, 252
The Staple Singers, 17
Stax Records, 58
Stevens, Bernard, 172, 173
Stockhausen, Karlheinz, 175, 176, 180, 182, 203, 248
Stockholm Conservatory of Music, 148
Stolk, Rob, 14, 16
Stormy Six, 41
Straniero, Michele Luciano, 37
Stratos, Demetrio, 44
Straub, Jean-Marie, 241
Stravinsky, Igor, 162, 247, 248
The Strawbs, 46, 47, 50
Strayhorn, Billy, 71–2, 73

"Street Fighting Man" (The Rolling Stones), 19, 155
strike movement, 264, 266–8, 269
String Driven Thing, 161
string instruments, 241
student protests
  American popular music, 47
  British music, 158
  early music movement, 249–50
  Eastern Bloc, 207, 216
  Germany, 188
  Italy, 32
  Japan, 82
  Netherlands, 12, 13, 22, 25
  overview, 2, 3, 4, 5–6, 11
  South Africa, 67
style(s). *see under* individual styles
subalternity, 38
"Such is the Way to Lead a Life", 226, 236
"Supper's Ready" (Genesis), 168
Supraphon, 210
The Surfaris, 47
Surrealism, 180, 264
Süverkrüp, Dieter, 191, 199
svensktopp, 141
Svensktoppen (The Swedish Top), 141
Sveriges Radio (SR), 140, 141, 146, 148, 149
Sweden
  anti-commercialism, 144–7
  development of '1968', 142–3, 144
  end of '1968', 152
  music in the broadcasting media, 140, 141
  overview, 10, 138–9
  politically or aesthetically progressive, 147–9
  progressive musical movements, 137
  socio-musicological surveys, 139–40
  transnational music, 150, 151
Sweet (Andriessen), 247
"Swinging" London, 51, 53
Switched-on Bach (Carlos), 246
Syndicat Français des Acteurs (SFA), 266, 267
Syndicat National des Artistes-Musiciens, 267
Szczelkun, Stefan, 183
Szörényi, Levente, 219
Szörenyi, Szabolcs, 218
Sztandar Młodych, 214

Takada, Wataru, 89–90, 91–2
Taka'ishi Office, 88, 92
Taka'ishi, Tomoya, 86, 87, 88, 92
Tamayo, Luis Pavón, 126–7
Tân Huyền, 106

Tangerine Dream, 191
Tape from California (Ochs), 52
"Tarkus" (Emerson, Lake and Palmer), 161, 169
Taylor, Philip, 117
Telefunken, 242, 243
Telegraaf, 17
Telephone Request, 84
television, 7, 47–8
Tempi stretti (Ottieri), 34
Tenco, Luigi, 39
terrorism, 38, 43–4, 67, 193
Tet Offensive, 7, 48, 97, 100, 108, 112, 113
'text-sound composition', 148–9
Thälmann Variations (Cardew), 186
Thema (Schat), 26
"Think of Me with Kindness" (Gentle Giant), 165
Third Reich, 188–9
This Is My Country (Curtis Mayfield and the Impressions), 58–9, 63
"This Wheel's On Fire" (Dylan), 53
Thomas, William I., 271–2
Thompson, Edward Palmer, 173
"Thừa Thắng Ta Đi" ("We Go For Victory") (Trương Tuyết Mai), 101, 102, 109
Thunderclap Newman, 165
Tilbury, John, 175, 180, 185, 186
Tillekens, Ger, 19, 20
Tilly, Charles, 256
timbre, 259, 260
"Time Has Come Today" (Chambers Brothers), 58
Time Out, 178
"The Times They Are A-Changin'" (Dylan), 53, 88
"Tình Ca Của Người Mất Trí" ("Love Song of a Mad Person") (Trịnh Công Sơn), 115
Tio i Topp (The Top Ten), Sweden, 141
Tippett, Michael, 172, 246
Tlatelolco massacre, 6
Tô Hải, 103
To our Children's Children's Children (The Moody Blues), 169
To You (Schat), 26
Togliatti, Palmiro, 30
"Tôi Sẽ Đi Thăm" ("I Shall Revisit") (Trịnh Công Sơn), 115
"Tomo-yo" ("My Friends") (Okabayashi), 89, 94, 95
Ton Steine Scherben (Scherben), 192–3
Tôshiba Record Industry, 85
The Towers, 64

trade union culture, 258, 266
Traffic, 154
"La Tragedía de la Plaza de las Tres Culturas" ("The Tragedy of the Plaza of the Three Cultures") (Reyes), 120, 121
transnationality, 5–6, 7–8, 149–51
Travail et Culture (TEC), 267
travel, 7–8
Treason Trials, 67
Treatise (Cardew), 176
The Tremeloes, 70
Trịnh Công Sơn, 10, 92, 99, 108, 117, 118
Tronti, Mario, 32
Trotskyism, 172, 173, 257, 262, 263
Trubadurzy, 217
Trương Tuyết Mai, 101, 109
Trybuna Ludu, 215
Tsurumi, Yoshiyuki, 93
Tube Train Rite (TMTTR38), 183
Tudor, David, 175, 177, 186
Turin, 29
Turner, Bruce, 173
Turner, Rick, 65, 68, 80
Tyler, James, 243, 245
Tyrannosaurus Rex, 157
Tyrmand, Leopold, 208

UFO Club, London, 178, 179
UK (United Kingdom). *see* Great Britain
Umkhonto we Sizwe, 67
Uncommon Market, London, 177, 182
underground
  British rock, 156, 187
  experimental music, 171–2, 177, 180–1
underground folk songs in Japan
  enka songs, 91–2
  Folk Guerilla, 93–5
  Kansai folk song movement, 83–7
  music and protest, 81–96
  overview, 10, 81–3, 95
  rise of underground folk song, 81–96
  student protests, 6
Underground Record Club (URC), 92
Underground: Scene Special, 55
un-gra (underground) songs, 83, 88
union culture, 258, 266
United Kingdom. *see* Great Britain
United States of America
  black pride, 54–60
  National Endowment of the Arts, 60
  'old, weird America', 51–4
  overview, 10, 46–51
  political engagement, 46–63
  rock music, 60–3
Unitelefilm, 35
Universities & Left Review, 173
University of Amsterdam, 12
University of Cape Town, 65, 68, 69
University of the Witwatersrand, 69
"The Unknown Soldier" (The Doors), 50
Unser Ludwig (*Our Ludwig*) (Siebert), 203
Uruguay, 133
USA. *see* United States of America
utopian visions, 158–60, 167–70
Utrecht University, 250

Valcarenghi, Andrea, 42
van Asperen, Bob, 252
van Bergeijk, Gilius, 27
van Dael, Lucy, 241, 246
Van der Graaf Generator, 154, 159, 160, 161, 162, 166
van der Louw, André, 21, 23, 24
van Duyn, Roel, 14, 16, 17, 18, 22
van Hauwe, Walter, 252, 253
van Vlijmen, Jan, 24, 247, 251
vanguard groups, 258, 262, 264, 267
Vår Musikk (*Our Music*), 143–4
VARA (Dutch broadcasting organisation), 21
Vassal, Jacques, 263
Vellekoop, Kees, 250
Venezuela in questo momento di guerriglia (Nono), 40
Very Urgent (Chris McGregor and the Blue Notes), 78, 80
Vestey, Michael, 177
The Vietnam Songbook, 34
Vietnam War
  American popular music, 46–7, 49, 50, 53, 63
  British rock, 155, 156
  early music movement, 252
  Eastern Bloc, 217
  Italy, 30
  Japan, 81, 87, 88
  Netherlands, 21, 22
  overview, 6, 7, 10
  Scandinavia, 149–50
  Vietnamese popular song, 97–8, 99, 117
Vietnam, popular song in
  musical legacy, 117
  overview, 97–9

Vietnam, popular song in (cont.)
    sentimental songs, 108–16
    songs of war and protest, 100–8
    war in Vietnam, 99–100
    war, protest and sentimentalism, 97–118
Vietnamese Communist Party, 100
Viglietti, Daniel, 125, 129, 133
Vinkenoog, Simon, 21
violins, 241
viols, 238
visa/vise (Scandinavian national ballads), 142
visionary music, 158–60
Vitti, Monica, 35
Vittorini, Elio, 34
Vogelaar, Jacq Firmin, 27
volcanto (volcanic song), 120
Volonté, Gian Maria, 36
Volponi, Paolo, 34
von Huene, Friedrich, 242
Vondelpark, 23
Vreeswijk, Cornelis, 142

Wadland, Peter, 242–3
"Waist Deep in the Big Muddy" (Seeger), 49
Waldbühne, 196
Waldeck Festivals, 6, 157, 199
Walker, Scott, 156
Ward, Brian, 60
Warsaw Autumn festival (*Warszawska jesień*), 208
Warsaw Pact, 6, 190, 200, 211
"Was verboten ist, das macht uns gerade scharf" ("What is Forbidden Makes Us Hot") (Biermann), 197
"Watcher of the Skies" (Genesis), 161, 165, 166, 168
"Waterloo" (Abba), 146
Watt (Beckett), 183
"Way of Life" (Gentle Giant), 165
"We Need You, Dany Cohn-Bendit" (manifesto), 180
"We Shall Overcome"
    American popular music, 59–60
    Japan, 86, 88, 95–6
    Latin American 'new song', 134
Webster, Ben, 75
Welch, Chris, 154, 155, 156
Wentink, Victor, 27
Wenzinger, August, 238
"Wer die Rose ehrt" ("Who Honours the Rose") (Renft), 197
West Germany
    anti-authoritarian agendas, 188–9
    anti-authoritarian revolt by musical means, 191–3
    class struggle and music, 198–200
    fight against musical authorities, 202–3
    overview, 6, 11
Westbury Music Fair, New York City, 55
Westhues, Kenneth, 181, 182, 183, 184
Wetton, John, 165
"What Did You Learn in School Today" (Paxton), 88
"Where Have All the Flowers Gone" (Seeger), 87
"Which Side are You On" (Seeger), 202
"White Plans", 15
White, John, 174, 175, 179, 185, 187
"A Whiter Shade of Pale" (Procol Harum), 431
The Who, 6
whole-tone scale, 162–4
"Why? (The King of Love is Dead)" (Simone), 56, 63
Wildflowers (Collins), 246
Wilkie, Colin, 157
Willener, Alfred, 270
Williams, Raymond, 171, 187
Williams, Richard, 158
Wittgenstein, Ludwig, 176
WMA. *see* Worker's Music Association
"Wo ai agege" ("I Love A-go-go"), 232
Wolff, Christian, 171, 175, 180, 185–6
Wolle, Stefan, 201
womanhood
    gender relations, 223, 236
    model works, 226–9
    movie musicals, 229–32
    patriarchy, 232–5
Woodstock Festival, 2, 6, 46–7, 49–50, 65, 69
workerism, 10, 26, 33
workers' movements, 2, 27, 31–6, 216
Worker's Music Association (WMA), 172–3
workers' songs, 26
World Festival of Youth and Students, 196

Xiao Fangfang. *see* Siao, Josephine
Xuân Hồng, 106, 107

Yang, Mayfair Mei-hui, 234
yellow music (nhạc vàng), 117, 118
Yes, 154, 159, 160, 167 169
yéyé, 271

Yippies (Youth International Party), 61, 62, 184
"Yo Canto la Diferencia" ("I Sing The Difference") (Parro), 131
Young Communist (JJCC) movement in Chile, 129–30
Young Flowers, 143
Young, La Monte, 171, 176
Young-Saeng Pak, 85
youth culture, 19–24, 27, 190, 232
'youth movie musicals' (qingchun gewupian), 230. see also movie musicals
youth proletariat, Italy, 42
"Youth Song Movement" (Phong Trào Thanh Niên Ca Hát), 100–3, 109

Zappa, Frank, 20, 23, 191, 210, 213
Zaslaw, Neal, 239
Zavattini, Cesare, 36
Želva (Olympia), 210
Zhiqu huifushan (Taking Tiger Mountain by Strategy), 224
Zolov, Eric, 5

CPSIA information can be obtained at www.ICGtesting.com
Printed in the USA
LVOW03*0022160714

394533LV00004B/51/P